METAPHYSI

Metaphysical Essays

JOHN HAWTHORNE

CLARENDON PRESS · OXFORD

*This book has been printed digitally and produced in a standard specification
in order to ensure its continuing availability*

Great Clarendon Street, Oxford OX2 6DP

Oxford University Press is a department of the University of Oxford.
It furthers the University's objective of excellence in research, scholarship,
and education by publishing worldwide in

Oxford New York

Auckland Cape Town Dar es Salaam Hong Kong Karachi
Kuala Lumpur Madrid Melbourne Mexico City Nairobi
New Delhi Shanghai Taipei Toronto
With offices in
Argentina Austria Brazil Chile Czech Republic France Greece
Guatemala Hungary Italy Japan South Korea Poland Portugal
Singapore Switzerland Thailand Turkey Ukraine Vietnam

Oxford is a registered trade mark of Oxford University Press
in the UK and in certain other countries

Published in the United States
by Oxford University Press Inc., New York

ISBN 978-0-19-929124-3

Contents

Introduction and Acknowledgements

The papers in this volume detail my struggle with a range of topics that lie at the heart of metaphysics. The results are not especially opinionated: metaphysics is a speculative endeavour where firm opinions are hard to come by (or, rather, they ought to be). Nor is there any grand underlying vision: a comprehensive metaphysical system would be nice, but I don't have one to offer. In some areas of debate—absolute versus relative identity (see essay 1), conventionalism about ontology (see essay 3), and the 'bundle' theory of substance (see essay 2)—there is little departure from current orthodoxy. In those cases, my efforts have been directed primarily towards clarifying some radical views and providing a compelling case for the standard ones. In other areas I have merely tried to sharpen the debate by sifting out the best version of one or more of the competing pictures, without attempting to adjudicate among the resulting alternatives. This is so, for example, in the work on properties and causal role (see essays 10 and 11), on teleology (see essay 15), and on vagueness (see essays 8 and 9).

In certain cases, though, I have tried to advance the cause of certain more tendentious metaphysical pictures, and have challenged certain prevalent ones. Let me briefly highlight three themes.

(1) **Plenitude.** Consider all the regions of space-time that are filled with matter. Which of them correspond to the boundaries of an object? The plenitude lover says that all of them do. This view strikes me as correct:[1] as others have rightly noted, other views risk anthropocentrism. This is not to deny that we might *initially* be sceptical of the existence of objects like the outcars and incars entertained by Eli Hirsch,[2] objects that grow and shrink as a car leaves its garage. But we don't think it ridiculous that there are objects that grow and shrink as large rocks move underwater, where the size of the object corresponds to the portion of the rock above the surface of the water: we call such objects 'islands'. It seems clear that none but the most insular metaphysician should countenance islands while repudiating incars; none but the most radical should renounce both. Instead, we should supplement the ontology of common sense with a range of additional objects whose existence we recognize on grounds of parity. This expansion brings with it the added benefit of explaining how it is possible for members of our community to refer successfully so much of the time without having to be lucky. (For relevant discussion, see essays 3, 5, 6, 9, and 12.)

---

[1] That is not to say that the arguments standardly given for plenitude are uniformly convincing. Two such arguments—one that relies on vagueness, the other on recombination—are criticized in essays 4 and 5.

[2] 'The term "incar" applies to any segment of a car that is inside a garage; "outcar" applies to any segment of a car that is outside a garage.' Eli Hirsch, *The Concept of Identity* (Oxford University Press, 1982), p. 32.

Two further considerations might lead us in yet more plenitudinous directions. First, our discussion thus far has left it open whether objects ever share the same spatiotemporal boundary. Even setting aside possible cases where objects spatiotemporally coincide without mereologically coinciding, we must still decide whether pairs of distinct objects ever mereologically coincide for the entirety of their careers. Following the example set by David Lewis, most contemporary plenitude lovers deny the existence of such pluralities of mereologically coinciding objects, and, relatedly, tend to opt for a treatment of essential properties that, in effect, relativizes questions of essence to a mode of classification. I explore a more unbridled plenitude that recognizes a multitude of coinciding objects for any given filled region, and which in turn has no need to invoke Lewis' well-known strategies for making sense of the modal profiles of particular objects.[3] Having allowed for multiple coinciding objects with matching spatiotemporal boundaries, one is naturally led to wonder just how many objects inhabit a given boundary. Here again, it seems arbitrary to suggest anything but the modally plenitudinous answer: for any function from possible worlds to filled regions, there is an object whose modal profile is given by that function.

A second way that a plenitude doctrine might be given extra latitude concerns regions not filled by matter. Suppose we have gone so far as to distinguish the statue from the lump, even in cases where both have the same spatiotemporal profile—the one has a certain form essentially, the other accidentally. With a bit of imagination, we can see how to replicate such contrasts within materially empty regions. Suppose a region of unfilled space-time has a certain curvature profile, induced by a particular distribution of matter in the neighbourhood. We might, by analogy with the statue-lump pair, posit a pair of regions with the same boundaries, one of which has a curvature profile accidentally, the other of which has that profile essentially. Similar pluralities can be recognized by attending to electromagnetic field values at regions, and so on. We should at least take seriously a hypothesis of perfect plenitude according to which *every* space-time region has multiple occupancy.

(2) **Natural properties and microphysics.** We should all recognize, with David Lewis, that properties can be ranked according to how well they carve nature at their joints: some are more gerrymandered, less natural, than others. Natural properties provide the needed veins in the marble of reality. This picture leaves many questions unsettled concerning the role of ideal microphysics in determining the naturalness ranking. Lewis proposed giving microphysics a canonical role: the 'maximally' or 'perfectly' natural properties correspond to the primitive predicates of an ideal microphysics, and the naturalness of other properties is, roughly, a matter of their ease of definability in that microphysical language. We can thus distinguish *microphysicalism*, which is a supervenience thesis that says all of being supervenes on microphysical being, from *micronaturalism*, which is a (far less discussed) thesis about natural joints that says nature's joints are best calibrated by an ideal microphysical language. The pages that

---

[3] Cf. Ernest Sosa, 'Persons and Other Beings', *Philosophical Perspectives* 1 (1987), 155–187, and Stephen Yablo, 'Identity, Essence, and Indiscernibility', *The Journal of Philosophy* 84 (1987), 293–314.

follow are directed in part towards challenging certain formulations of the supervenience thesis (essays 4, 12, 13, and 14 are relevant here), and in part towards putting pressure on micronaturalism from several directions.

Let me quickly mention two developments of the latter theme. First, micronaturalism encourages us to think that the semantic predicates so foundational to our self-understanding pick out hopelessly gerrymandered properties. If naturalness is given a crucial role in providing the metaphysical foundations of semantics, there is good reason to think that such a position is unstable (see essay 9). Second, even leaving aside psychological and semantic joints, we should not be seduced by a simple picture according to which the joint-like properties are those that provide a mimimal supervenience base for the world (a picture that in turn privileges the determinate magnitudes of some ideal microphysics). This supervenience-driven picture overlooks many candidate joints: the determinables of the determinates, fundamental relations between properties, logical joints that correspond to fundamental logical vocabulary, and so on. Thinking carefully about the variety of roles that metaphysically natural kinds are supposed to serve will lead us to a more nuanced picture than the brutish version of micronaturalism just adverted to (see essay 11).

(3) **Stage primacy**. Let us turn from properties to objects. Just as we may be attracted to an inegalitarianism about properties (borrowing a phrase from David Lewis), so might we opt for an inegalitarianism about the denizens of space and time: some of them are, in some good sense, more fundamental than others. Having embraced plenitude, it is tempting to think of the maximally small as being most fundamental: space-time points are the fundamental objects of space-time; and instantaneous, point-sized temporal parts—'stages' of point particles—are the fundamental material beings. One way to put pressure on this picture is by opting for a 'gunky' rather than 'pointillist' picture of matter and space-time, one according to which there are no building blocks of zero measure (see essay 7). But even if we discount gunk, we should hesitate to endorse a picture that reckons instantaneous point-particles as fundamental. Two of the essays in this volume (5 and 6) explore some alternatives, paying special attention to the question of whether pointy beings are the bearers of the fundamental magnitudes.

Six of the essays in this volume appear here for the first time; the remaining ten have been (or are about to be) published elsewhere. I am grateful to the various publishers of these papers for their permission to reprint them here.

A number of these essays have been coauthored by philosophical friends. And even where there is no coauthor, many of the ideas can be traced to discussions with and comments from other people. I was fortunate to have been trained by two brilliant metaphysicians—José Benardete and Peter van Inwagen. Since entering the profession, I have been fortunate again in having spent much of my career with two other brilliant metaphysicians—Ted Sider and Dean Zimmerman. Most of what I do in metaphysics that is any good bears the imprint of one or more of these people. Considerable thanks are also due to David Armstrong, Stuart Brock, Jeremy Butterfield, John Carroll, David Chalmers, Jan Cover, Troy Cross, Sam Cumming, Cian Dorr, Maya Eddon, Adam Elga, Hartry Field, Kit Fine, Delia Graff,

Hilary Greaves, Gilbert Harman, Eli Hirsch, Dave Horacek, Hud Hudson, Mark Johnston, David Manley, Tim Maudlin, Jeffrey McDonough, Brian McLaughlin, Chris Meacham, Trenton Merricks, Angel Pinillos, Oliver Pooley, Stephen Schiffer, Adam Sennet, Ernest Sosa, Jason Stanley, Brian Weatherson, and especially Frank Arntzenius, Daniel Nolan, Mark Scala, Ryan Wasserman, and Timothy Williamson. These people helped considerably with one or more of these papers, and in some cases, helped write them. Special thanks are due to Tamar Gendler, who provided me with very extensive and insightful commentary on most of the new material (and some of the old). I would also like to thank my research assistant, Jason Turner, who helped a good deal both with production issues and with the philosophy, the excellent copy editor at Oxford, Alyson Lacewing, and my editor, Peter Momtchilloff, who has provided me with terrific support and encouragement in recent years. Finally, I would like to thank Diane O'Leary, who provided encouragement and metaphysical direction at times in my career when it was most needed.

My cursory overview has left one important theme unmentioned, one that will no doubt strike anyone who reads these essays. A good proportion of them involve a direct engagement with some segment or other of David Lewis's formidable metaphysical corpus. In this way, I am in the position of most of my friends in metaphysics. We grew up on Lewis. His work was the benchmark of quality, his approval the surest sign of having done a good thing. Doing metaphysics in his absence is quite an adjustment.

1

Identity[1]

1 INTRODUCTION

The topic of identity seems to many of us to be philosophically unproblematic. Identity, we will say, is the relation that each thing has to itself and to nothing else. Of course, there are many disputable claims that one can make using a predicate that expresses the identity relation. For example: there is something that was a man and is identical to God; there is something that might have been a poached egg that is identical to some philosopher. But puzzling as these claims may be, it is not the identity relation that is causing the trouble. The lesson appears to be a general one. Puzzles that are articulated using the word 'identity' are not puzzles about the identity relation itself.

One may have noticed that our gloss on identity as 'the relation that each thing has to itself and to nothing else' was not really an analysis of the concept of identity in any reasonable sense of 'analysis', since an understanding of 'itself' and 'to nothing else' already requires a mastery of what identity amounts to. But the appropriate response, it would seem, is not to search for a 'real analysis' of identity; rather, it is to admit that the concept of identity is so basic to our conceptual scheme that it is hopeless to attempt to analyse it in terms of more basic concepts.

Why is the concept of identity so basic? The point is not that we have inevitable need for an 'is' of identity in our language. Our need for the concept of identity far outstrips our need to make explicit claims of identity and difference. Consider, for example the following two simple sentences of first-order predicate logic:

$\exists x \, \exists y (Fx \text{ and } Gy)$
$\exists x (Fx \text{ and } Gx).$

Both require that there be at least one thing in the domain of the existential quantifier that is F and that there be at least one thing in the domain of the existential quantifier that is G. But the second sentence makes an additional requirement: that one of the things in the domain that is F be identical to one of the things in the domain that is G. Without mastery of the concept of identity it is not clear how we would understand the significance of the recurrence of a variable within the scope of a quantifier.

First published in the *Oxford Companion to Metaphysics* (2004), pp. 99–130. I am grateful for permission to reprint it here.

[1] Thanks to Kit Fine, Daniel Nolan, Brian Weatherson, Timothy Williamson, Dean Zimmerman, an audience at the 2001 Mighty Metaphysical Mayhem conference at Syracuse, and especially Tamar Gendler and Ted Sider for helpful comments and discussion.

In this vein, Quine observes that 'Quantification depends upon there being values of variables, same or different absolutely. . .'[2] Similar remarks apply to sentences of natural language. By way of bringing out the ubiquity of the notion of identity in our language, Peter Geach notes of the pair of sentences 'Jim wounded a lion and Bill shot it' and 'Jim wounded a lion and Bill shot another (lion) dead' that the first expresses identity and the second diversity.[3]

2 CHARACTERIZING IDENTITY

Even if the concept of identity is basic for us, that does not mean that we can say nothing by way of characterizing identity. In what follows, I shall begin with some relatively informal remarks about identity as it relates to logic, some understanding of which is crucial to any metaphysical inquiry into the identity relation. I shall then go on to discuss various ideas associated with Leibniz's law and the principle of the identity of indiscernibles. These preliminaries will leave us well placed to usefully examine some unorthodox views concerning identity.

2.1 *I*-Predicates and Identity

It will help us to begin by imagining a tribe that speaks a language, *L*, that takes the form exemplified by first-order predicate logic. So let us suppose that *L* contains individual constants, quantifiers, variables, truth-functional connectives, together with a stock of one-place predicates, two-place predicates, and so on. The individual constants in the tribe's language (which serve as the names in that language) each have a particular referent, the predicates particular extensions, and so on. Let us thus assume that there is a particular interpretation function, *INT*, from individual constants to bearers (selected from a universe of discourse that comprises the domain of objects that fall within the range of the quantifiers of *L*) and from predicates to extensions (a set of objects from the universe of discourse for a one-place predicate, a set of ordered pairs for a two-place predicate, and so on[4]) that correctly characterizes the extensions of the individual constants and predicates that are deployed in *L*. Assume there is a binary predicate '*I*' in *L* for which the following generalizations hold:

(1) $\ulcorner \alpha I \alpha \urcorner$ is true for any interpretation *INT** of *L* that differs from *INT* at most in respect of how the individual constants of *L* are interpreted.[5]

---

[2] W. V. O. Quine, 'Review of P. T. Geach, *Reference and Generality*', *Philosophical Review* 73 (1964), 100–4, p. 101.

[3] P. T. Geach, 'Replies', in H. A. Leiws, *Philosophical Encounters* (Dordrecht: Kluwer, 1991), p. 285.

[4] I shall not here try to deal with difficult questions that arise from the possibility that the universe of discourse, and, indeed, the range of application of certain predicates, are too big to form a set (and hence for which talk of a predicate's extension is problematic). I do not thereby pretend that these issues are irrelevant to philosophical discussions of identity, as shall be clear from the discussion of Geach.

[5] α, β are metalinguistic variables ranging over individual constants; *F*, *G* metalinguistic variables ranging over predicates. I am using standard corner quote conventions.

(2) $\ulcorner (F\alpha \text{ and } \alpha I\beta) \supset F\beta \urcorner$ is true for any interpretation INT^* of L that differs from INT at most in respect of how the individual constants are interpreted. (F may be a simple or a complex predicate.)

(1) guarantees that 'I' expresses a reflexive relation:[6] (1) and (2) guarantee that 'I' is transitive and symmetric. Postponing the question of whether 'I' expresses the identity relation, we can say that, given its behaviour in L, 'I' behaves just as one would expect of a predicate that did express the identity relation. Let us say that a binary predicate of a language that obeys requirements (1) and (2) is an I-predicate for that language.

Quine has pointed out that, so long as a first-order language has a finite stock of predicates, one can stipulatively introduce a binary predicate that will be an I-predicate for that language:

The method of definition is evident from the following example. Consider a standard language whose lexicon of predicates consists of a one-place predicate 'A', two-place predicate 'B' and 'C' and a three-place predicate 'D'. We then define '$x = y$' as short for:

(A) $Ax \equiv Ay \cdot \forall z (Bzx \equiv Bzy \cdot Bxz \equiv Byz \cdot Czx \equiv Czy \cdot Cxz \equiv Cyz \cdot \forall z' (Dzz'x \equiv Dzz'y \cdot Dzxz' \equiv Dzyz' \cdot Dxzz' \equiv Dyzz'))$

Note the plan: the exhaustion of combinations. What '$x = y$' tells us, according to this definition, is that the objects x and y are indistinguishable by the four predicates; that they are indistinguishable from each other even in their relations to any other objects z and z' insofar as these relations are expressed in simple sentences. Now it can be shown that, when [A] holds, the objects x and y will be indistinguishable by any sentences whether simple or not, that can be phrased in the language.[7]

Of course, if there is not a finite stock of basic predicates in the first-order language L, then an I-predicate for L cannot be mechanically introduced by stipulation in the manner prescribed. But assuming a finite stock, it is coherent to suppose that our tribe had introduced their binary predicate 'I' in this manner. That is not, obviously, to say that where there is an infinite stock, there will be no I-predicate: it is just that its method of introduction could not be the brute-force method that Quine describes.[8]

It is worth noting the way in which the use of variables in the stipulation imposes considerable discriminatory power upon I-predicates that are introduced by Quine's method. Suppose we have two predicates 'is 2 miles from' and 'is a sphere'. Consider a world of two spheres, call them 'sphere 1' and 'sphere 2', that are 5 feet from each other.[9] An I-predicate introduced by Quine's technique will not be satisfied by an

---

It might be that some particular object x has no name in L. (1) requires that $\ulcorner \alpha R\alpha \urcorner$ be true on the deviant interpretation that assigns the same extension to 'I' as INT but that assigns x as the referent of α.

[6] Though of course it is silent on whether it is a necessary truth that everything is I to itself.

[7] *Philosophy of Logic* (Cambridge, Mass.: Harvard University Press, 1970), p. 63.

[8] I leave aside Zeno-style thought experiments in which a tribe makes infinitely many stipulations in a finite space of time by taking increasingly less time to make each stipulation.

[9] I have Max Black, 'The Identity of Indiscernibles', in J. Kim and E. Sosa (eds.), *Metaphysics: An Anthology* (Oxford: Basil Blackwell, 1999) (first pub. in *Mind*, 51 (1952), 153–64) in mind here.

ordered pair consisting of distinct spheres. One of the clauses in the definition of 'xIy' will be '$\forall z(z$ is 2 miles from $x \equiv z$ is 2 miles from $y)$. But this is not satisfied by the ordered pair ⟨sphere 1, sphere 2⟩. (This can be seen, for example, by letting z be sphere 1.) So, given the stipulative definition, it follows that '$\exists x \exists y$ (x is a sphere and y is a sphere and $\sim xIy)$' is true. (Similarly, if there are two angels that don't love themselves but do love each other and for which the tribe has no name, an I-predicate introduced using, *inter alia*, the predicate 'loves' will not be satisfied by an ordered pair of distinct angels.)

Isn't there some robust sense—and one that is not merely epistemic—in which the spheres are indiscernible with respect to that tribe's language? Quine acknowledges a notion of 'absolute discernibility' with respect to a language which holds of two objects just in case some open sentence in that language with one free variable is satisfied by only one of those two objects. Two objects are, meanwhile, 'relatively discernible' just in case there is some open sentence with two free variables that is not satisfied when one of the pair is assigned as the value of each variable but can be satisfied when distinct members of the pair are assigned as the respective values of the two free variables.[10] The two spheres are absolutely indiscernible relative to the simple language just envisaged: any open sentence with just one free variable will be satisfied by both or neither of the spheres. But they are relatively discernible: consider the open sentence 'x is 2 miles from y'.

As Quine himself is well aware, that a predicate is an I-predicate for some language L provides no logical guarantee that it expresses the identity relation itself, nor even that the extension of the I-predicate, relative to the domain of discourse of L, be all and only those ordered pairs from the domain whose first and second members are identical. Suppose L is so impoverished as to have only two predicates, 'F' and 'G', that somehow manage to express the properties of being a dog and being happy respectively.[11] If speakers of L introduce an I-predicate by Quine's technique, then it will hold for all things that are alike with respect to whether they are dogs and whether they are happy. Of course, if a binary predicate expressing the identity relation already existed in the object language, then an I-predicate so introduced would be guaranteed to express[12] the identity relation too. More generally, we can say that if an I-predicate satisfies the following additional condition (3), then it will be guaranteed to hold of all and only those pairs in the domain of discourse that are identical.

---

[10] See Quine, *Word and Object* (Cambridge, Mass.: MIT University Press, 1960), p. 230.

[11] Of course Quine himself will only tolerate properties when they are treated as sets. Most of the points made in the text do not turn on this. Note, though, that if one gives an extensional construal of relations, then any difference in quantificational domains will make for a difference in the relation picked out by an I-predicate. Note also that an extensional conception of the identity relation does not sit well with views that preclude certain entities—say, proper classes—from being members of sets, but which claim of those entities that they are self-identical. Note, finally, that an extensional account of the identity relation will preclude us from certain natural modal claims about the identity relation (assuming the world could have contained different objects).

[12] Or at least extensionally coincide with.

(3) $\ulcorner (F\alpha$ and $\alpha I \beta) \supset F\beta \urcorner$ is true for any interpretation INT^* of L that differs from INT only in respect of how the individual constants and predicates other than 'I' are interpreted.[13]

But the point remains that it is not a logically sufficient condition for a binary predicate in some language L to express the identity relation that it be an I-predicate in L: when an I-predicate is introduced by Quine's machinery, there will be a way of interpreting the non-logical vocabulary[14] in such a way that the definition for the I-predicate is validated (and, correlatively, (1) and (2) hold relative to that interpretation) but where 'I' is not satisfied by all and only those ordered pairs of objects (drawn from the domain of discourse) whose first and second members are identical.

Let us now imagine our tribe to have the machinery to speak about properties. One can imagine this feat to be accomplished in two ways: they might have the apparatus of second-order quantification, whence the tribe has the capacity to quantify into the predicate position. Alternatively, they might have properties within the domain of their first-order variables, and such predicates as 'is a property' and 'instantiates' in their stock, as well as some principles about properties that belong to some segment of their conception of the world that encodes their theory of properties. Either way, the tribe will now have extra expressive resources.[15] First, even given an infinite stock of basic predicates, they could stipulatively introduce a predicate R that will be an 'I'-predicate for their language L. Supposing we opt for second-order machinery, and that the language contains only unary, binary, and ternary basic predicates, we can stipulatively introduce R after the manner Quine suggested. Thus we define '$x = y$' as short for:

$$\forall F \forall R2 \forall R3(Fx \leftrightarrow Fy) \cdot \forall z(R2zx \leftrightarrow R2zy) \cdot (R2zy \leftrightarrow R2zy).$$
$$\forall z'(R3zz'x \leftrightarrow R3zz'y) \cdot (R3zxz' \leftrightarrow R3zyz' \cdot R3xzz' \leftrightarrow R3yzz'),$$

where the properties expressed by the basic monadic predicates are the domain of 'F', the properties expressed by the basic binary predicates are the domain of '$R2$', and so on. The point would still remain that a predicate so introduced is not logically guaranteed to express the identity relation: the second-order machinery guarantees that the predicate so introduced will behave like an I-predicate with respect to the infinite stock of predicates in the language, but if there are plenty of properties and relations unexpressed by the infinite stock (and thus outside the domain of the second-order quantifiers characterized above), that is consistent with the I-predicate's failing to express the identity relation.

But what if we allow the tribe not merely to have the resources to speak about the properties and relations expressible in their current ideology, but to be enlightened

---

[13] Assuming L has at least one basic predicate other than 'I'.

[14] In this context, the predicate 'is identical to', if it exists in the language, counts as non-logical vocabulary.

[15] I shall not pursue here the question of whether the need for second-order variables is a deep one.

enough to speak in a general way about all properties and relations whatsoever? Let us suppose that they are liberal about what counts as a property and what counts as a relation. (This is not a conception of properties and relations according to which only a small subset of one's predicates—the elite vocabulary—gets to express properties and relations.) This would give them yet more expressive power, indeed enough expressive power to stipulatively introduce a predicate that holds of all and only identical pairs (in the domain of discourse). The following definition would do:

(D1) $xIy \leftrightarrow \forall R \forall z(xRz \leftrightarrow yRz)$,

as would

(D2) $xIy \leftrightarrow \forall F(Fx \supset Fy)$,

where D2 corresponds to the standard definition of identity within second-order logic. Assuming, then, that the tribe has the appropriate second-order machinery available, it can stipulatively introduce a predicate that is logically guaranteed to hold of all and only identical pairs (drawn from their domain of discourse).

With suitably enriched expressive resources, the tribe might, relatedly, make some stipulations about how their I-predicate is to behave with respect to extensions of their language, L, or else interpretations of their language other than INT.[16] For example, the tribe might stipulate of 'I' that $\ulcorner(F\alpha$ and $\alpha I \beta) \supset F\beta\urcorner$ is true for any interpretation of L that agrees with INT with regard to the extension of 'I' and with regard to the logical vocabulary and the universe of discourse (but which may differ in any other respect).[17] Alternatively, the tribe might stipulate that $\ulcorner(F\alpha$ and $\alpha I \beta) \supset F\beta\urcorner$ is true for any extension $L+$ of their language that contains additional constants and/or predicates (whose interpretation agrees with that of L for those constants and predicates common to L and $L+$). Both of these stipulations require that the extension of 'I' be the class of identical pairs.[18] Any interpretation of L that assigned 'I' an extension other than the class of identical pairs would be one for which $\ulcorner(F\alpha$ and $\alpha I \beta) \supset F\beta\urcorner$ would be false under some interpretation of the relevant non-logical vocabulary. (If 'I' is true of some distinct x and y, then let the

---

[16] There is, of course, a complex web of issues connected with the threat of paradox generated by semantic machinery, including the question of which expressive resources force a sharp distinction between object and meta-language. Such issues are not irrelevant, as we shall see, to certain deviant approaches to identity: but they cannot be engaged with here.

[17] I assume once again that 'I' is not the only basic predicate in L.

[18] Cf. Timothy Williamson, 'Equivocation and Existence' in *Proceedings of the Aristotelian Society*, 88, (1987/88), 109–27. It is perhaps worth emphasizing the following point: if the domain of the tribe's quantifiers is, say, smaller than ours, then we could not, strictly, say that the extension of 'I' was the class of identical pairs—since the extension of 'is identical to' in our language would include ordered pairs of objects that fell outside the tribe's universe of discourse. Our sense of a single identity relation that can serve as the target of philosophical discourse is tied to our sense of being able to deploy utterly unrestricted quantification. And, as Jose Benardete remarked to me, it seems that our visceral sense that we understand exactly what we mean by 'identity' seems, on the face of it, to be jeopardized somewhat by those philosophical positions that deny the possibility of utterly unrestricted quantification. The issues raised here are beyond the scope of the current chapter.

interpretation assign x and y to the respective individual constants and let it assign the singleton set containing x to the predicate.) Thus any interpretation of L that assigned a relation extensionally different from identity to 'I' would be one to which one could add predicates which under some interpretation would generate a language $L+$ for which the schema did not hold. Hence the tribe's stipulations could only be respected by interpreting 'I' to hold between any x and any y iff x is identical to y. As with second-order machinery, the capacity to talk about extensions of the language brings with it the capacity to place stipulative constraints upon an I-predicate that can only be satisfied if the predicate holds of all and only identical pairs (in the domain of discourse).

Does this discussion conflict with the idea that identity is a basic concept and cannot be analysed? No. That a predicate expressing identity *could be* explicitly introduced by one of the mechanisms stated does not imply that the concept of identity is dispensable or parasitic: the point remains that mastery of the apparatus of quantification would appear to require an implicit grasp of identity and difference (even where there is no machinery available by means of which to effect some explicit characterization of identity). Someone who used second-order machinery to introduce an identity predicate would, by this reckoning, already have some tacit mastery of what the identity relation came to (whether or not a predicate expressing identity was already present in the language). Nor is there any presumption above that in order to grasp the concept of identity, one *must* be in a position to provide some sort of explicit characterization of the identity relation in terms of extensions of one's language, or second-order machinery, or property theory, or whatever.

2.2 The Identity of Indiscernibles

Philosophers often give the name 'Leibniz's law' to the first of the following principles, and 'the identity of indiscernibles' to the second:

(LL) For all x and y, if $x = y$, then x and y have the same properties,
 (II) For all x and y, if x and y have the same properties, then $x = y$.

It is sometimes said, furthermore, that while the first principle is uncontroversial, the second principle is very controversial. Such claims are often driven by a certain picture of what a property is. Consider, for example, the set-theoretic gloss on properties that is standardly used for the purposes of formal semantics. On this rather deflationary conception of properties, the property expressed by a predicate is the set of things of which that predicate is true (the 'extension' of that predicate). (Philosophers who baulk at an ontology of properties—construed as entities that can be distinct even though their instances are the same—frequently have less trouble with the purely extensional notion of a set.) On this conception, the principles can be given a set-theoretic gloss, namely:

(LL) $\forall x \forall y (x = y \supset \forall z (x$ is a member of $z \supset y$ is a member of $z))$.
 (II) $\forall x \forall y ((\forall z (x$ is a member of z iff y is a member of $z)) \supset x = y)$.

Assuming our set theory takes it as axiomatic that everything has a unit set,[19] then, quite obviously, we will be committed to regarding the identity of indiscernibles as a fairly trivial truth. This is because it is crucial to the very conception of a set that x and y are the same set if and only if they have the same members.[20] We may note, relatedly, that in second-order logic, the identity of indiscernibles is normally conceived of in a way that reckons it no more controversial that the set-theoretic gloss.[21] Indeed, any conception of properties according to which it is axiomatic that there is, for each thing, at least one property instantiated by it and it alone (the property of being identical to that thing, for example), will be a conception on which LL and II are equally unproblematic.

To make a controversial metaphysical thesis out of II, one has to provide some appropriate restriction on what can be considered as a property. For example, some philosophers employ a 'sparse' conception of properties according to which only a few privileged predicates get to express properties. (If identity isn't in the elite group, then it may, strictly speaking, be illegitimate even to speak of 'the identity relation', since there is no such relation even though 'is identical to' is a meaningful predicate.[22]) With a sparse conception in place, one might reasonably wonder whether, if x and y have the same sparse properties, then x and y are identical. Another example: one might wonder whether if x and y share every 'non-haecceitistic property', then x and y are identical (where haecceitistic properties—such as *being identical to John* or *being the daughter of Jim*—are those which, in some intuitive way, make direct reference to a particular individual(s)). One may be so interested because one thinks that there are not, strictly speaking, haecceitistic properties in reality[23]; but even if one tolerates haecceitistic properties, one might think it an interesting metaphysical question whether the restricted thesis is true.

For any restricted class of properties, we can usefully imagine a target language in which there are only predicates for the restricted class of properties under consideration, plus quantifiers, an identity predicate, variables, and truth-functional connectives. We can now ask two questions. First, for any pair of objects x and y, will there be some predicate in the language that is true of one of them but not the other? This, in effect, is a test for the relevant restricted identity of indiscernibles thesis. Secondly, we

---

[19] The issue of 'proper classes' complicates matters here. On some versions of set theory, there exist entities that are not members of any set, this being one device to help steer set theory clear of paradox.

[20] Once again there is no point in complaining that, so construed, the identity of indiscernibles cannot now be an 'analysis' of identity, since that ought never to have been the project in any case.

[21] Thus Stewart Shapiro *Foundations without Foundationalism*. (Oxford: Oxford University Press, 1991) writes of the 'identity of indiscernibles' principle '$t = u : \forall X(Xt$ iff $Xu)$' that it is not intended as 'a deep philosophical thesis about identity ... As will be seen, on the standard semantics, for each object m in the range of the first-order variables, there is a property which applies to m, and m alone. It can be taken as the singleton set $\{m\}$' (p. 63).

[22] Of course, the nominalist goes further and says that all ontologically serious talk of properties is illegitimate. Such a nominalist will owe us a nominalistically acceptable version of Leibniz's law. If that version is to apply to natural languages, the context-dependence of certain predicates should not be ignored.

[23] Cf. Black, 'The identity of Indiscernibles', discussed below.

can ask whether an *I*-predicate introduced by Quine's brute force method, using the vocabulary of that language (minus the identity predicate), would have as its extension all and only identical pairs. We need only recall Quine's distinction between things that are 'absolutely discernible' and things that are 'relatively discernible' to realize that the questions are distinct. To illustrate, suppose there are two angels, Jack and Jill. Each is holy. Each loves him- or herself and the other angel. Consider a first-order language *L* containing the monadic predicates 'is an angel', 'is holy', and the diadic predicate 'loves'. Consider also a first-order language *L*+ that contains the predicates of *L* and, in addition, the predicate 'is a member of'. Neither *L* nor *L*+ contains individual constants. Nor do they contain an identity predicate. The angels are not absolutely discernible relative to *L*. That is, there is no open sentence with one free variable constructible in *L* such that Jack satisfies it but Jill doesn't. Nor are the angels relatively discernible in *L*. There is no relational truth of the form '$\exists x \, \exists y$ (*x* is an angel and *y* is an angel and $\exists z$ (*xRz* and ~*yRz*))' that is constructible in *L*. How about *L*+? Relative to *L*+, the angels are not absolutely discernible. But they are relatively discernible. After all, *L*+ has the resources to express the truth: '$\exists x \exists y$ (*x* is an angel and *y* is an angel and $\exists z$ (*x* is a member of *z* and ~*y* is a member of *z*))'.

When we are in a position only to discern relatively but not to discern absolutely a certain pair of objects, that should not makes us queasy about our commitment to the existence of the pair. In his famous 'The Identity of Indiscernibles' Max Black seems on occasion to think otherwise. At a crucial juncture he has one of his interlocutors question whether it makes sense to speak of the haecceitistic properties of unnamed things. One of his interlocutors suggests of two duplicate spheres that are 2 miles from each other that they have the properties *being at a distance of 2 miles from Castor* and *being at a distance of 2 miles from Pollux*. Black's other interlocutor responds: 'What can this mean? The traveller has not visited the spheres, and the spheres have no names—neither 'Castor', nor 'Pollux', nor '*a*', nor '*b*', nor any others. Yet you still want to say they have certain properties which cannot be referred to without using names for the spheres'.[24] Black makes a fair point—which in Quine's lingo is the observation that the properties cannot be absolutely discerned using the resources of our language. That is not to say that they cannot be relatively discerned. To deny the existence of the pair of properties in such a world on the basis of our inability to discern them absolutely is no better, it would seem, than to deny the existence of the pair of spheres in the world on the basis of the fact that we cannot absolutely discern them. Analogously,[25] the singleton sets of spheres cannot be absolutely discerned, but that is not to say that they cannot be relatively discerned; and it would be utterly misguided to reject the claim that each thing has a singleton set on the basis of the fact that, for some pairs, we cannot absolutely discern the sets using our language (or any readily available extension of it).[26] The thought experiment of two lonely duplicate spheres works well to illustrate the thesis that it is possible that there be two things that cannot be absolutely discerned using a language with a rich

[24] Op cit. 69.
[25] And on the set-theoretic gloss of properties, it is more than an analogy.
[26] I leave it open whether some other argument against haecceitistic properties might work.

range of qualitative, non-haecceitistic predicates. But it is not an effective way to make trouble for a liberal view of properties, one that allows the properties instantiated by each sphere to differ.

2.3 Substitutivity, Identity, Leibniz's Law

When we imagined a tribe that used a first-order language, we imagined that single predicates of their language were not such as to enjoy different extensions on different occasions of use. If some predicate F of their language expresses the property of being tall on its first occasion of use in a sentence and of being not tall on its second occasion of use, then 'Either *a* is *F* or it is not the case that *a* is *F*' could hardly be validated by first-order logic. Any language to which the schemas of first-order logic can be mechanically applied will not be a language with predicates whose extension is context-dependent in this way.

When it comes to natural languages with which we are familiar, matters are thus more complicated. We are forced to dismiss the metalinguistic principle that if an English sentence of the form '*a* is identical to *b*' is true, then '*a*' can be substituted *salva veritate* for '*b*' in any sentence of English. This substitutivity principle, as a thesis about English, is false. The pair of sentences 'Giorgione was so called because of his size' and 'Barbarelli was so called because of his size' are counter-examples to the principle as it stands.[27] Here the predicate 'is so called because of his size' expresses different properties in different contexts, the key contextual parameter being the proper name that it attaches to.[28]

It was natural to envisage our earlier tribe as operating with the following inference rule:

(LL*) $\ulcorner \alpha I \beta \urcorner \vdash \ulcorner P \supset Q \urcorner$ (where P and Q are formulae that differ at most in that one or more occurrences of α in P are replaced by β in Q).

As we have just seen, this principle, with 'is identical to' substituted for '*I*', cannot govern natural languages. So it seems very unlikely that our grip on the concept of identity is underwritten by that principle. In the context of discussing first-order languages, logicians often refer to LL* as Leibniz's law. One feels that *something like* that axiom governs our own understanding. But it can't be that axiom itself. So what is the correct understanding of Leibniz's law?

We have, in effect, touched on two alternative approaches. First, we have a property-theoretic conception of Leibniz's law:

(LL1) If $x = y$, then every property possessed by x is a property possessed by y.

---

[27] As Richard Cartwright, ('Identity and Substitutivity', in his *Philosophical Essays* (Cambridge, Mass.: MIT Press), 1987, pp. 135–48) points out, the observation that 'the occurrence of 'Giorgione' ... is not purely referential ... far from saving the Principle of Substitutivity ... only acknowledges that the pair ... is indeed a counterexample to it' (p. 138). As he goes on to point out, the example makes no trouble for a property-theoretic version of Leibniz's law. Also relevant here is Williamson's version of Leibniz's law, discussed below.

[28] Hence it is plausible to maintain that 'is so called because of his size' expresses the property 'is called 'Giorgione' because of his size' when combined with the name 'Giorgione' and the property 'is called 'Barbarelli' because of his size' when combined with the name 'Barbarelli'.

A closely related approach is set-theoretic:

(LL2) If $x = y$, then every set that x belongs to is a set that y belongs to.

Both approaches have their limitations. If one has nominalist scruples against abstract objects, one will dislike both.[29] More importantly, the principles will have no direct bite in certain cases: if the semantic value of a predicate is context-dependent, then we cannot use these principles to test straightforwardly for non-identity. 'Is so called because of his size' is one such predicate: one cannot say which property or set it expresses independently of the proper name it is combined with (unlike 'is called 'Giorgione' because of his size'). This in turn makes for a possible strategy of response when confronted with an argument for non-identity using Leibniz's law: one might try claiming that the predicate in question expresses different properties (or has different extensions) depending on the proper name it is combined with (claiming that either the morphological features of the name or else the mode of presentation attaching to the name or some other crucial contextual parameter is relevant to the extension of the predicate).

Timothy Williamson has offered a third conception of Leibniz's law, which is avowedly metalinguistic, and which will be helpful to our later discussions:

(LL3) Let an assignment A assign an object o to a variable v, an assignment A^* assign an object o^* to v, and A^* be exactly like A in every other way. Suppose that a sentence s is true relative to A and not true relative to A^*. Then o and o^* are not identical.[30]

This principle can obviously be extended to cover individual constants:

Let an interpretation A assign an object o to a constant α, an interpretation A^* assign an object o^* to α, and A^* be exactly like A in every other way. Suppose that a sentence s is true relative to A and not true relative to A^*. Then o and o^* are not identical.

Return to 'Giorgione was so called because of his size'. An interpretation of this sentence that assigned Giorgione as the referent of 'Giorgione' will agree in truth-value with an interpretation of this sentence that assigned Barbarelli as the referent of 'Giorgione' and which in every other respect agreed with the first interpretation. This brings out an intended virtue of the metalinguistic conception: its application need not be restricted to a purely extensional language. And, as Williamson is aware, it promises to be especially useful as a test where the defensive strategy just gestured at is deployed. Suppose one defends the identity of x and y, pleading context-dependence in the face of a pair of true sentences 'Fa' and '$\sim Fb$', where 'a' refers to x and 'b' refers to y. The cogency of the plea can be tested by considering whether 'Fa' gets the same

---

[29] And even if one believes in abstract objects, they may not be the ones required by the relevant principle (for example, we may not believe in sets).

[30] Williamson, 'Vagueness, Identity, and Leibniz's Law' in Giaretta, Bottani, and Carrera (eds.), *Individuals, Essence, and Identity: Themes of Analytic Metaphysics* (Dordrecht: Kluwer, 2001).

truth-value relative to a pair of assignments A and A^* such that A assigns x to 'a', A^* assigns y to 'a', A being exactly like A^* in every other way.[31]

3 DEVIANT VIEWS: RELATIVE, TIME-INDEXED, AND CONTINGENT IDENTITY

3.1 Relative Identity

Famously, Peter Geach argued that the notion of absolute identity should be abandoned.[32] Suppose a lump that is also a statue exists at $t1$. Call it George. The lump gets squashed. A new statue (made by a new craftsman) is fashioned out of the squashed lump at $t2$. Call it Harry. Is George Harry? Geach's framework provides an answer with some intuitive appeal:

(A) George is the same lump as Harry.
(B) George is a different statue from Harry.

Statements of the form 'a is the same F as b' cannot, on this view, be analysed as 'a is an F, b is an F, and a is identical to b'. If such statements as 'Harry is the same lump as George' and 'Harry is the same statue as George' could be so analysed, then A and B, in conjunction with fact that George and Harry are both statues, would yield contradiction.[33] Relative identity predicates of the form 'is the same F as' are thus taken as semantically basic.

What then of the question 'Is George the very same thing as Harry?' On Geach's view, this question makes no sense. We can and must make sense of the world without the notion of absolute identity. Instead, we slice up reality with the aid of various basic sortal-relative identity predicates which, when 'derelativized', yield basic count nouns: 'is a statue', 'is a lump', and so on. On Geach's view, we can only grasp the meaning of a count noun when we associate with it a criterion of identity—expressed by particular relative identity sortal. The predicate 'is a thing' is not admitted as a sortal, and thus does not provide a basis for asking and answering questions of identity.

The 'count' in 'count noun' deserves particular attention. Geach notes the intimate tie between the concept of identity and the concept of number: non-identity between x and y makes for at least two; non-identity between x and y, y and z, and x and z makes for at least three; and so on. If judgements of identity are sortal-relative, so for judgements of number. Just as the question 'Is George identical to Harry?' lacks sense, so does the question 'How many statue-shaped things were there present during the

---

[31] As for its ontological commitments: that depends, of course, on how the notion of 'assignment' is cashed out. The standard model-theoretic approach will of course require sets.

[32] For valuable discussions of Geach's views, see Michael Dummett 'Does Quantification Involve Identity?', in his *The Seas of Language* (Oxford: Oxford University Press 1993), 308–27 and Harold Noonan 'Relative Identity' in Bob Hale and Crispin Wright (eds.), *Companion to the Philosophy of Language* (Oxford: Basil Blackwell, 1997) 634–52.

[33] This point occasionally gets clouded by a use of the term 'diachronic identity' as if it were the name for a relation that is very intimate but not quite the same as identity. Any such use is likely to generate confusion.

process?' (even if we strip the predicate 'statue-shaped' of all vagueness[34]). Relative identity predicates are the basis for any given count. If asked to count statues, I will gather things together under the relation 'is the same statue as'. If asked to count lumps, I will gather things together under the relation 'is the same lump as'. (It is, then, obviously crucial to Geach's approach that relative identity predicates be symmetric and transitive.[35,36])

In this connection, it should be noted that Geach's approach throws set theory into jeopardy. Our conceptual grip on the notion of a set is founded on the axiom of extensionality: a set x is the same as a set y iff x and y have the same members. But this axiom deploys the notion of absolute identity ('same members'). Eschew that notion and the notion of a set has to be rethought. In so far as the notion of a set is to be preserved at all, then identity and difference between sets has to be relativized: the question whether the set containing George is the same set as the set containing Harry cannot be answered in a straightforward fashion. Other concepts central to logic and semantics will also have to be significantly rethought. What, for example, is to count

---

[34] The predicate 'statue-shaped' does not have a criterion of identity associated with it and thus is not, by Geach's lights, a sortal.

[35] A relative identity relation R—say, being the same lump—is not reflexive, since it is not true that everything has R to itself (after all, some things aren't lumps), though any such relation will be such that if $x R$ some y then xRx.

[36] Geach often invokes Frege *The Foundations of Arithmetic* (1884), trans. J. L. Austin, 2nd edn. (Oxford: Basil Blackwell, 1953) in support of his relative identity approach. As far as I can see, Frege's thesis that number concepts are second-order offers little support for Geach's approach. Frege's idea was that such concepts as 'at least two in number' are second-order concepts of first-level concepts, not first-level concepts that apply to objects. The most straightforward argument offered by Frege for this thesis is that it allows us to make excellent sense of claims of the form 'The *F*s are zero in number', a claim that would be unintelligible if 'are zero' had to be a predicate of the things that satisfy '*F*'. No Geachian conclusions should be drawn from Frege's remarks. In particular, Frege had no trouble with a simple binary relation of absolute identity. And his doctrines are perfectly consistent with the thesis that some number attaches to the concept 'x is identical to x' and that there is thus an absolute count on the number of objects in the world. Frege does say of the concept red, 'To a concept of this kind no finite number will belong', on account of the fact that 'We can ... divide up something falling under the concept 'red' into parts in a variety of ways, without the parts thereby ceasing to fall under the same concept 'red'' (see Section 53).' But this is a long way from Geach's thesis that 'the trouble about counting the red things in a room is not that you cannot make an end of counting them, but that you cannot make a beginning; you never know whether you have counted one already, because 'the same red thing' supplies no criterion of identity' (*Reference and Generality*, 3rd edn. Ithaca, NY: Cornell University Press, 1980: 63). Frege's point seems to precisely be that you cannot make an end of counting them, and this for a boring reason: every red thing has red proper parts, this ensuring that 'no *finite* number' will belong to the number of red things. Frege does say that 'if I place a pile of playing cards in [someone's] hands with the words: Find the Number of these, this does not tell him whether I wish to know the number of cards, or of complete packs of cards, or even say of points in the game of skat. To have given him the pile in his hands is not yet to have given him completely the object he is to investigate (see Section 22).' Once again, this does not demonstrate a commitment to a radical view. After all, the proponent of absolute identity and difference would hardly be disposed to read an instruction of the form 'Find the number of these' as 'Find the number of objects in my hand'. As Frege reminds us, such instructions as the former are typically elliptical for an instruction far more mundane than the latter.

as an 'extensional context'? What is it to mean to say that two terms 'corefer'? All of these notions are built upon the notions of simple identity and difference. Abandon those notions and the intelligibility of a large range of logico-semantic concepts is cast into doubt.

Current wisdom about proper names would also need rethinking were Geach's approach to be accepted. According to Geach, in order for a proper name to have a legitimate place in the language, it must have a criterion of identity associated with it—given by a relative identity predicate. The popular view[37] that a name can be cogently introduced by either demonstration—'Let 'Bill' name that thing (pointing)'—or else by a reference-fixing description (that need not encode a sortal in Geach's sense)—'Let 'Bill' name the largest red thing in Alaska'—is thus anathema to Geach. Notice that, strictly speaking, the story with which I began this section did not, by Geach's standards, deploy legitimate proper names. I introduced 'George' as a name of the thing at $t1$ which is both a lump and a statue. But I didn't specify a relative identity predicate that is to govern the use of 'George'. Thus my mode of introduction left it undetermined whether the thing at $t2$ is to count as 'George', and thus how such sentences as 'George is statue-shaped at $t2$' are to be evaluated. Relative to the statue criterion, the latter sentence will be reckoned false—for nothing at $t2$ is the same statue as the statue at $t1$. Relative to the lump criterion, the sentence will be reckoned true—for the lump at $t1$ is the same lump as something that is statue-shaped at $t2$. Geach does not want sentences embedding a proper name that attribute a property to a thing at a time to be invariably indeterminate in truth-value: hence the insistence on an associated criterion of identity. Return to the original case. We can introduce 'George' as the name for the lump at $t1$. Since the lump at $t1$ is also a statue, it is also true that 'George' is the name of a statue. But since 'George' has entered the language as a name for a lump, the rule for 'George' is that everything (at whatever time) that is the same lump as the lump at $t1$ shall count as deserving the name 'George'. Hence, it is the name *of* a statue, but not *for* a statue. (What if we instead insisted that George is not a statue at all? According to this suggestion, George is a lump but is not the same statue as any statue, being not a statue at all. This undercuts the motivation of the approach, one which is supposed to provide an alternative to a metaphysics that postulates distinct but wholly coincident objects. A standard metaphysics of coincident objects can allow that some statue-shaped lump can be the same lump as some statue-shaped lump at a later time without being the same statue as that lump: but it will explain this fact not by invoking a deviant view of identity but by simply pointing out that some statue-shaped lump can fail to be the same statue as anything whatsoever on account of the fact that statue-shaped lumps are not identical to the statues that they constitute.)

Notice that, on Geach's view, one does not come to understand a count noun merely by acquiring the ability to recognize, in any given case, whether or not the count noun applies.[38] Let us suppose that 'is a living thing' is true of a quantity of

---

[37] Saul Kripke, *Naming and Necessity* (Cambridge, Mass.: Harvard University Press, 1972).

[38] Of course, it is not strictly true that mastery requires such recognitional capacities either. We should learn to live without verificationism. We may note that Geach's discussions of criteria of

matter iff it has organic-biological characteristics F, G, and H. This may enable one to say of any quantity of matter whether or not it is a living thing. But this criterion of application would not enable one to discern of any pair of quantities of matter whether or not they counted as the same living thing. If the meaning of 'is the same living thing' is to fix the meaning of 'is a living thing', then a criterion of application will not in general provide the basis for understanding a count noun.[39]

Geach's approach is not merely designed (as the lump and statue example brings out) to give a distinctive treatment of diachronic questions about identity. He has also deployed it to give a distinctive treatment of certain synchronic questions. Consider his treatment of the so-called 'problem of the many': when we truly say 'There is a cat on the mat', there are a plentitude of overlapping cat-shaped quantities of 'feline tissue' that differ ever so slightly with respect to their boundaries. Which of them is the cat? Are we forced to the absurd conclusion that, contrary to common sense, there are many cats on the mat? Geach answers:

Everything falls into place if we realize that the number of cats on the mat is the number of different cats on the mat and c13, c279, and c [where c13, c 279, and c are three cat-shaped quantities of feline tissue] are not three different cats, they are one and the same cat. Though none of these 1,001 lumps of feline tissue is the same lump of feline tissue as another, each is the same cat as any other: each of them, then, is a cat, but there is only one cat on the mat, and our original story stands.[40]

It is easy enough to see a key drawback of Geach's approach here. Let 'Tabby' name c13, and 'Samantha' c279, and suppose that Samantha but not Tabby has some white bit of feline tissue, call it 'Freddy'. Suppose every other bit of Samantha is black (at least near the surface) and that every bit of Tabby is black. By hypothesis, Tabby is the same cat as Samantha and yet, at the time we are considering, the following truths hold:

> Samantha has Freddy as a part
> Tabby does not have Freddy as a part
> Tabby is black all over
> Samantha is not black all over

If I tell you that a certain cat is black all over and that Samantha is the very same cat as the aforementioned cat, wouldn't the inference to 'Samantha is black all over' be utterly compelling? Within the current framework, though, the inference schema

> α is black all over at t
> α is the same cat as β

identity suggests that, on the matter of diachronic identity, he is rather too much in the grip of a verificationist picture.

[39] Crispin Wright *Frege's Conception of Numbers as Objects* (New York: Humanities Press, 1983) was helpful to me here.

[40] *Reference and Generality*, p. 216. This style of treatment, as a number of authors have noticed, offers one gloss on the mystery of the Trinity: there are three persons: Christ is not the same person as God the Father (and so on). There is one divinity: Christ is the same God as the Father.

Therefore, β is black all over at t

is invalid.

A vital feature of the notion of identity is its amenability to Leibniz's law. Within an extensional language, inferences of the form

α is F
α is identical to β
Therefore, β is F

are valid. But inferences of that form are not in general valid within the current framework, even when the predicates are paradigmatically extensional from the standpoint of orthodoxy. (Consider instead Williamson's version of Leibniz's law, ready-made even for languages with intensional predicates. Given Geach's conception, the analogous version for 'is the same cat as', is wrong. 'Tabby is black all over' is true on the intended interpretation. Tabby is the same cat as Samantha. But if we were to assign Samantha as the referent of 'Tabby', keeping the interpretation otherwise unchanged, then on that assignment 'Tabby is black all over' would have to be reckoned false.)

Geach's relative identity predicates do not behave in the way Leibniz's law requires. We shouldn't, however, conclude that *all* inferences of the form

α is F
α is the same G as β
Therefore, β is F

are invalid. After all, there may be particular pairs of predicates for which this inference *is* always truth-preserving. For example, instances of the schema

α is not a duck
α is the same cat as β
Therefore, β is not a duck

are always truth-preserving. Following Peter van Inwagen, let us say that a particular relative identity predicate R 'dominates' a particular predicate F if and only if it is a necessary truth that $\ulcorner \forall x \forall y ((xRy \text{ and } x \text{ is } F) \supset y \text{ is } G) \urcorner$.[41] Van Inwagen notes that, within this kind of framework, there will be plenty of substantive, non-trivial questions concerning which predicates are dominated by which relative identity predicates. We have just noted, for example, that predicates of the form 'being black all over at t' may well not be dominated by 'is the same cat as'. And we noted earlier, in effect, that predicates of the form 'being a statue at t', while dominated by the predicate 'is the same statue as', are not dominated by predicates of the form 'is the same lump as'.

Consider now one of Geach's examples of a relative identity predicate, 'is a surman'. The idea is this: x is to count as the same surman as y iff x is a man, y is a man, and x and y have the same surname. My father, Patrick Hawthorne, is thus the same surman as me. Clearly 'is the same surman as' does not dominate 'was born in 1964', since that is true of me and not of my father. On the other hand, one would

---

[41] Peter van Inwagen, 'And yet they are not Three Gods but One God' in his *God Knowledge, and Mystery* (Ithaca, NY: Cornell University Press, 1995), 222–59.

suppose that it does dominate 'is a man'. Relative identity predicates are supposed to be legitimate bases for the introduction of a proper name. Thus let us introduce 'Bob' as the name for (and not merely of) the surman that is the same surman as me. Thus anything that is the same surman as me will merit that name. Assuming 'is the same surman as' dominates both 'is a man' and 'has the surname 'Hawthorne' '', Bob's surname is 'Hawthorne' and Bob is a man.

But if my hair is brown and my father's black, which colour is Bob's hair?[42] Are we to say that there is a man—Bob—with no hair?[43] The criterion of identity does not seem to be an adequate basis upon which to discern which predicates are applicable to Bob.

There are two reactions here. One is the tack of Geach's later self, namely, to renounce 'is the same surman as' as a legitimate basis for the introduction of a proper name:

> The question is whether I could go on to construct propositions of the forms 'F(some surman)' and 'F(every surman)'. By my account of the quantifying words 'every' and 'some', this would be legitimate only if there could also be propositions of the form '$F(a)$', where 'a' is a proper name for a surman, a name with its built-in criterion of identity given by 'is the same surman as'. But without the unrestricted assumption that any old non-empty equivalence relation founds a class of proper names, there is not the faintest reason to believe such proper names could be given. Dummett and others have hotly attacked the poor surmen; I must abandon them to their doom.[44]

One might instead try to show that, with suitable inventiveness, a proper name for a surman can be given some discipline. We are familiar with the tactic of time-indexing predicates. The lump is spherical at $t1$, flat at $t2$, and so on. This handles predication for things that are present at different times. Bob would appear to be present at different places. So perhaps predications need to be place-indexed. Bob, like myself, is brown-haired at p at t (the place where I am at t), and is black-haired at $p2$ at t (the place where my father is at t). This approach runs into trouble with various platitudes. We want to say that no man could be in two places at the same time. Bob is, by hypothesis, a man, and yet Bob is at $p1$ and at $p2$. Even more awkward is the question of how many men there are.[45] We know that Bob is a man and that Bob is the same surman as John and the same surman as Patrick. But given that 'same man is' is transitive, we cannot say that Bob is the same man as John and the same man as Patrick. So are Bob, Patrick, and John to count as three different men? That will make a hash of our ordinary methods for counting men.

So perhaps we would do better to follow the original tack of jettisoning the idea that 'surman' is a suitable basis for a proper name. But doesn't the problem generalize?

---

[42] This problem is raised in Michael Dummett, 'Does Quantification Involve Identity,' in his *The Seas of Language* (Oxford: Oxford University Press, 1995), 308–27, p. 321.

[43] Granted, it is far from absurd to suppose that there is a hairless man. But this seems like a very dubious basis for thinking that a hairless man exists.

[44] Geach, 'Replies', p. 295.

[45] Similarly, suppose I have changed my name from 'Hawthorne' to 'O'Leary-Hawthorne' and then back again. There are two surman. Which of them am I the same surman as?

Suppose a clay statue is at $t1$ made of a lump, call it 'Lump1,' and at $t2$ made of a slightly different lump (through erosion or small replacements), call it 'Lump2.' Let 'Jerry' name the clay statue that endures throughout the period from $t1$ to $t2$. (I didn't use a particular time, you will note, when introducing 'Jerry' as the name for a clay statue.) Is Jerry the same lump of clay as Lump1? Is Jerry the same lump of clay as Lump2? We don't want to say that Jerry is not a lump of clay at all, since it would be strange to allow that some clay statues are lumps of clay, others not. And since 'is the same lump as' is transitive, we cannot give an affirmative answer to both of the questions just raised. Given the symmetry, we had better give a negative answer to both. So is it, then, the case that at $t1$ there exists a statue that is the same lump of clay as Lump1 and a statue—Jerry—which is not the same lump of clay as Lump1? The original intuitiveness of the approach has evaporated. The problem is structurally analogous to the concern just raised about surmen. But one has no temptation in this case to respond by admitting that the sortal 'is a statue' is an unacceptable foundation for a proper name.

The most promising approach here, I suggest, is to make use of the notion of semantic indeterminacy: it is determinate that Jerry is a statue and determinate that Jerry is either the same lump as Lump1 or the same lump as Lump2, but it is indeterminate whether Jerry is the same lump as Lump1 and indeterminate whether Jerry is the same lump as Lump2.[46] Rampant indeterminacy of this sort will have to be tolerated by the proponent of the approach. But perhaps it is not so damaging.

I shall not inquire further into the depth of this problem as there are even more pressing concerns about Geach's approach. I express four such concerns below.

1. There is something altogether absurd, it would seem, with the following pair of claims:

Jim is black all over at t.
It is not the case that Jim is black all over at t.

How is Geach to explain the patent absurdity? It is natural to appeal to the relative identity sortal that governs the proper name 'Jim'. Perhaps that relative identity sortal dominates the predicate 'black all over', and this fact explains why we cannot endorse both claims. But suppose 'Jim' is the name for a cat and that, for reasons we have just seen, 'is the same cat as' does not dominate 'black all over'. Then we cannot offer that style of explanation. Meanwhile, the style of explanation that is most natural is forbidden, namely: that the reason that the pair of claims cannot be true is that one and the same object cannot be such that it is both black all over and not black all over at the same time. That style of explanation makes use of the rejected notion of identity. Even if we could begin to bring ourselves to live with the idea that Jim is the same cat as Jack and that Jim but not Jack is black all over, it is much harder to live with the cogency of the above pair of claims. Are we to learn to live with that pair too? And if not, what is the mechanism for ruling them out? There would appear to be an especially intimate relationship between Jim and Jim that precludes Jim being black all over and Jim not being black all over that fails between,

---

[46] Cf. standard supervaluationist treatments of vagueness.

say, Tabby and Samantha in our earlier example. Geach seems to lack the resources to explain this.

What, then, if Geach simply claims that the pair are logically contradictory, refusing to explain matters further? Note, though, that the two sentences are not contradictory if the first occurrence of 'Jim' names a cat in Blackpool and the second a quite different cat in Coventry. Some condition has to be satisfied in order for there to be a genuine contradiction here. Orthodoxy has a very easy time saying what the condition is, namely, that the two name tokens are names for the very same thing. The problem is that this story is not available to Geach; and it is utterly unclear what story is to take its place.

2. The proposals concerning the use of a proper name, as I have understood them, are not in fact coherent. Return to the Tabby and Samantha example. Suppose we agree that there is a cat composed of certain parts that exclude Freddy (which you may recall, is a particular candidate cat part). I stipulate that 'Samantha' is the name for that cat, and not merely of that cat. That is to say, I insist on associating the criterion of identity of cathood (as opposed, say, to feline tissue) with 'Samantha'. Having so associated that criterion, one would presume that, suitably informed, I would be able to evaluate claims using 'Samantha'. But how would I do it? Suppose I find that some cat is F. How do I then determine whether that fact is sufficient for the truth of 'Samantha is F'? Well, it would appear that by associating the cat criterion with 'Samantha' I have thereby given myself a procedure: what I do in the case at hand is to determine whether the thing in question is the same cat as Samantha. If it turns out that it is, then I will come to accept the claim that Samantha is F. (Of course, if I had associated a feline tissue criterion with 'Samantha', then the discovery that the F thing was the same cat as Samantha wouldn't have sufficed.) The trouble is that this cannot be the procedure that Geach has in mind. For recall that (*a*) Samantha has Freddy as a part, (*b*) Tabby lacks Freddy as a part, and (*c*) Samantha is the same cat as Freddy. By the proposed procedure, we will now be committed to claiming that Samantha lacks Freddy as a part (since 'Samantha' has the cat criterion associated with it and 'Samantha' picks out a cat that is the same cat as a cat that lacks Freddy as a part). That is intolerable, given (*a*). So how exactly does a criterion of identity ground our competence in a proper name? I remain uncertain.[47]

3. I earlier noted the apparent need for the concept of absolute identity to understand the significance of recurring variables in first-order predicate logic. Consider, for example, the claim '$\exists x(x$ is perfectly round and x is red all over)'. How, if we are Geach, are we to understand the truth-conditions for a claim like this? We can make the worry a little more precise.[48] Suppose a tribe comes along and uses what appears

---

[47] These are also puzzles concerning how to evaluate definite descriptions. Suppose an artefact is composed of Lump1 and is the same artefact as one composed of Lump2. How do we evaluate 'The artefact is composed of Lump1'? Do we reckon it false because even though there is an artefact that is composed of Lump1 and every artefact (in the relevant domain) is the same artefact as it, there is some artefact that is the same artefact as it that is not composed of Lump1? Such questions point to further difficulties for a Geachian semantics.

[48] I am grateful to Kit Fine here.

to be a first-order language without the identity symbol. We can imagine, then, that the tribe writes down sentences like

(S1) $\exists x(x$ is red and x is round).

This tribe then declares that they have read Geach and have been convinced that there is no such thing as absolute identity. The tribe notices our inclination to take S1 in their mouths as expressing the claim that there is a red thing that is identical to some round thing. The tribe insists that this would be to misconstrue the content of what they were saying. They insist that S1 encodes no claim about identity. We have misunderstood. We ask them to explain to us the semantics of S1. We notice that the tribe is careful to use a meta-language without an identity predicate. Our failure to get the hang of what the tribe is supposed to be saying by S then simply recurs when we encounter such semantic claims as

(S2) '$\exists x(x$ is red and x is round)' is true iff $\exists x(x$ satisfies 'is red' and x satisfies 'is round').

The tribe will claim that we have misunderstood when we take S2 to be equivalent to the claim that S1 is true iff something that satisfies 'is red' is identical to something that satisfies 'is round'. It is not that we can show such a tribe that their own rules of inference lead to what is, by their standards, absurdity. In that sense, there is no incoherence charge that we can level against them. But we may justly complain that such a tribe is unintelligible to us. We are simply at a loss to make sense of the variables at work in the tribe's language. In that sense, we may justly worry that a proponent of Geach's views is ultimately unintelligible in just the same way.

Perhaps the proponent of Geach's framework would respond to all this by claiming that S1 is somehow incomplete, and that a relative identity predicate appropriate to the variable needs to be supplied to complete it.[49] First-order predicate logic, even without identity, would then need rewriting. The relevant work remains to be done.

4. A pressing issue for the defender of Geach is to explain *why* the concept of absolute identity is incoherent. Suppose we begin with a language L devoid of a sign of absolute identity, containing only relative identity predicates, proper names, variables, predicates, and so on. What would be wrong with adding a predicate 'I' that is governed by a reflexivity axiom and by Leibniz's law (recall generalizations (i) and (ii) earlier)?[50] Apply it to the problem of the many: we would now be able to extract the conclusion that while Tabby I Tabby (by reflexivity) and Samantha I Samantha (by reflexivity), it is not the case that Tabby I Samantha (by Leibniz's

---

[49] Further radicalizations are possible: perhaps it is a sortal relative matter whether any two given predicate tokens express the same property or not. (It would, after all, be unfortunate if it turned out that Geach was tacitly using a semantics in which the identity and difference of properties is absolute.) This in turn will complicate the matter of assessing various property-theoretic versions of Leibniz's law, as applied to various identity sortals.

[50] One method of introduction would be to apply Quine's method, described earlier, to L, assuming its basic stock of predicates is finite and that it is extensional. If L merely has an extensional fragment, one could apply Quine's method to that fragment.

law).[51] Suppose we continue to maintain that 'Tabby is the same cat as Samantha' is true. We shall then wish to observe that, as the predicate 'is the same cat as' is being used, it does not require that the relation expressed by '*I*' obtains between Tabby and Samantha. It seems that '*I*' will now express genuine identity and that 'is the same cat as' is being used to express a relation that can hold between non-identical pairs. Apply this perspective to the problem of the Trinity: suppose that 'Christ is the same divinity as the Father' and 'Christ is a different person from the Father' both express truths. The natural diagnosis is that since 'Christ is a different person from the Father' becomes false when 'Christ' is reinterpreted as referring to the Father, then, by Leibniz's law,[52] Christ is not identical with the Father. If the relevant sentences are both true, 'is the same divinity as' will have to be treated as expressing a transitive and symmetric relation that can hold between non-identical pairs.

Geach has recognized the possibility of introducing an *I*-predicate into a language that lacked an identity predicate. But he claims that one is never thereby in a position to claim of one's *I*-predicate that it expresses absolute identity:

No criterion has been given, or, I think, could be given for a predicable's being used in a language *L* to express absolute identity. The familiar axiom schemata for identity could at most guarantee, if satisfied, that the relative term under investigation will be true in *L* only of pairs that are indiscernible by descriptions framed in terms of the other predicables of *L*. This cannot guarantee that there is no proper extension of *L*, with extra predicables, that makes possible the discrimination of things which were indiscernible by the resources of *L*.[53]

What Geach is trading on, then, is a point already noted: the mere fact that a predicate is an *I*-predicate for a language is of itself no guarantee that the predicate expresses the identity relation.

What of the attempt to define identity outright using the resources of second-order logic? Here is Geach again:

Sometimes we are told identity is definable in second-order logic: for any F, $F(x)$ iff $F(y)$. But it is gravely doubtful whether such quantification is admissible if quite unrestricted: can a quantification cover *all* properties or concepts, including such as would be expressed by this very style of quantification?[54]

and elsewhere:

'For real identity', we may wish to say, 'we need not bring in the ideology of a definite theory T. For real identity, *whatever* is true of something identical with a is true of a and conversely, regardless of which theory this can be expressed in; and a two-place predicable signifying real identity must be an I-predicable no matter what other predicables occur along with it in the theory.' But if we wish to talk this way, we shall soon fall into contradictions; such unrestrained language about 'whatever is true of a', not made relative to the definite ideology of a theory T, will land us in such notorious paradoxes as Grelling's and Richard's. If, however, we

---

[51] Assuming suitable expressive resources for *L*.

[52] I am using Williamson's version here.

[53] 'Replies,' p. 297.

[54] ibid., p. 297.

restrict ourselves to the ideology of a theory T, then, as I said, an I-predicable need not express strict identity, but only indiscernibility within the ideology of T.[55]

If we assume (*per impossibile* for Geach) that there is such a relation as strict identity, the worry isn't that our imagined I-predicate is false of pairs that are strictly identical. We can all agree that if x and y are identical, then the relation expressed by an I-predicate will hold between x and y. The worry is that the converse does not hold and that, moreover, there is no device available by means of which we can stipulatively ensure that it does hold. We cannot, says Geach, legitimately quantify over all extensions of our language or over all properties and relations. But without the ability to do that, it is not clear how we can ensure that some binary predicate will express strict identity.

I have a number of concerns about this line of resistance.[56]

First, once one realizes that there is at least an I-predicate of English[57]—call it 'English-identity'—that is available, much of the intuitive interest of the original approach disappears. We agree that if there is such a thing as strict identity, then English non-identity guarantees strict non-identity (whether or not English-identity is or isn't the same relation as strict identity). Consider, for example, the treatment of the Trinity: it is certain that Christ is not English-identical to the Father and thus certain that if there *is* strict identity, it fails to obtain between the Father and Christ. The requirements of 'English-identity' *are no more* demanding than strict identity. Christ and the Father fail even to pass those standards.

Secondly, one presumes that Geach will offer an argument to the effect that the concept of absolute identity is incoherent. But what we really find instead is an argument to the effect that there is no straightforward mechanism for defining absolute identity that is provided by the resources of logic (without an identity predicate) alone, nor even by a second-order logic that provides the means for quantifying over a (restricted) domain of properties. But since the concept of identity is plausibly a basic one, it is not clear how to move from these remarks about definition to a conclusion that asserts the incoherence of the concept of absolute identity.

Thirdly, Geach would appear to be trying to have it both ways. Suppose we allow ourselves the English predicate 'is identical to'. We announce the reflexivity of the property it expresses by claiming: 'Everything is identical to itself.' And we announce commitment to Leibniz's law: if x is identical to y, then the truth-value of any English sentence with a name that refers to x will be unaltered on an otherwise similar interpretation that interprets that name as referring to y. If we hadn't read Geach, we would go on and deploy 'is identical to' in mandatory ways: Tabby is not identical to Samantha. Christ is not identical to the Father. But now we are supposed to worry

---

[55] *Logic Matters* (Berkeley, Calif.: University of California Press, 1972), p. 240.

[56] Much of what follows reiterates points made in Dummett, 'Does Quantification involve Identity?'

[57] Of course, since English is not an extensional language, we should strictly say that 'English-identity' is merely an I-predicate with respect to some extensional fragment of English, perhaps idealized to remove elements of context-dependence. Geach, wisely, does not fuss over such issues; neither shall we.

that just maybe 'is identical to' fails to express 'strict identity'. How were we supposed to be convinced that there is a worry here? Geach points out that, just perhaps, there are extensions of English such that predicates of that extended language will distribute differently with regard to some pair that satisfies the ordinary English 'is identical to'. Now it seems we have a ready answer: let us stipulate that 'is identical to' will satisfy Leibniz's law not merely when it comes to English but, moreover, for any extension of English. But in response Geach argues that it is incoherent to quantify over any extension of English in this way. But didn't Geach have to quantify over extensions of English in order to raise the worry in the first place? Either talk of extensions of English is incoherent, in which case a worry that 'is identical to' doesn't express absolute identity cannot be raised, or else we can raise quantify over a domain of extensions of English, relative to which we can point out that perhaps an I-predicate of English will not express identity proper. But in so far as one can coherently quantify over a domain of extensions, one can stipulatively introduce a predicate that will be immune to the relevant worry: with such quantificational apparatus in place, one can introduce a predicate 'is identical to' stipulating that it is an I-predicate relative to any extension. The apparatus required for raising the worry is the very apparatus needed for solving it. It is as if Geach allows himself unrestricted quantification over extensions of our language in order to get the worry going on and subsequently points out that only restricted quantification over extensions of the language is coherent.[58]

Fourthly,[59] even granting for the moment that quantification over absolutely all properties makes no sense,[60] there remains the possibility that it is perfectly coherent to quantify over all relative identity relations (of which the relations expressed by, say, 'is the same cat as' is an example). The threat of paradox raised by quantification over absolutely all properties does not so clearly arise when one's domain is restricted in this way. At the same time, this domain can form the basis, even by Geach's lights, it would seem, of a perfectly serviceable notion of 'absolute identity': x is identical to y iff for all relative identity relations R, xRy.

In sum: it is no mere artefact of philosophical fashion that Geach's relative identity approach has few adherents.

---

[58] There is certainly more to say here on this particular point. The most promising version of Geach's objection will allow that there are larger and larger domains of properties available for properties variables, but no maximal domain (or at least so to speak—it is not clear that such a metasemantic claim as the one just made will be strictly allowable). For any I-predicate introduced by appeal to one domain of properties $D1$, one would then always be able to cite a larger domain $D2$ relative to which it is intelligible that a pair of objects satisfy the original I-predicate but nevertheless differ with respect to certain properties in $D2$. It is beyond the scope of this chapter to evaluate this particular semantic perspective. We should be clear, though, that the mere impossibility of utterly unrestricted quantification hardly serves to vindicate Geach. Even if some ordinary English claims of the form 'Some F is identical to some G' involve restricted quantification, that does not at all by itself imply that, from a perspective in which a more inclusive domain is in view, we can make a speech like '$o1$ (which is F) and $o2$ (which is G) make true the ordinary English sentence 'Some F is identical to some G' even though they are not really identical.' (Thanks to Ted Sider here.)

[59] I am grateful to Kit Fine here.

[60] Whether unrestricted quantification of this sort is possible is not an issue I can pursue here.

3.2 Time-Indexed Identity

A lump of clay (call the lump 'Clay') is fashioned into a statue (call it 'Statue') at
$t1$. At $t2$ it is refashioned into a jug (call it 'Jug'). What is the relationship between
Clay, Statue, and Jug? One feels intuitive pressure towards admitting that Statue no
longer exists at $t2$. One feels intuitive pressure against thinking there are two things in
the same place at the same time at $t1$. And one feels intuitive pressure towards allowing that Clay exists at $t1$ and $t2$. Many standard accounts simply resist along one or
more dimensions of intuitive pressure. Geach's relative identity approach attempts to
accommodate all these intuitions. Another approach similarly designed is that which
insists that identity is time-indexed. Begin by noting that ordinary predications intuitively need a time index. If Clay changes colour from red to blue, we would appear
to need a time index to capture the relevant truths: Clay is red with respect to such-
and-such a time, and blue with respect to a later time. If the truths about colour
need time-indexing, then why not the truths about identity? Why not say that Clay is
identical to Statue with respect to such-and-such a time and that Clay is not identical
to Statue but instead to Jug at a later time? Following some ideas of Paul Grice, this
view was developed by George Myro:

> I think that we should not regard this as a 'new' notion of identity, relativized, identity-at-a-
> time—any more than we should in dealing with an object changing from being red to being
> green, regard ourselves as needing a 'new' notion of being red, relativized, being-red-at-a-time.
> The idea is simply that we should regard statements—*not excluding statements of identity*—as
> subject to temporal qualifications in a systematic and uniform way. Thus, we are to envisage
> having in a 'regimented' sort of way:
>
> > at t, A is red
> > at t', A is green (not red)
>
> and:
>
> > at t, $A = B$
> > at t', $A \neq B$
>
> such that in suitable circumstances, *both* members of each pair are true.[61]

Note that there are certain puzzle cases for which this approach will yield distinctive results where Geach has nothing to offer. Suppose I exist at $t1$ and at $t2$ undergo
fission into two individuals, John1 and John2. Geach cannot say that I am the same
person as John1 and am the same person as John2, since relative identity predicates
are suppose to be symmetric and transitive.[62] Nor can the intuitive difficulties of the
case be traced to my vacillating between a pair of relative identity predicates. Geach's

---

[61] 'Identity and Time' in Michael Rea (ed.), *Material Constitution* (Lanham, Md.: Rowman and
Littlefield, 1997), 148–72, pp. 155–6.

[62] See also Arthur Prior, 'Opposite Number', *Review of Metaphysics* 11 (1957): 196–201.), which
treats fission in a way that adapts the time-relative identity approach to a presentist perspective
(where a presentist is one who thinks that only presently existing individuals exist, so that facts
about the future and past expressed by primitive tense operators no more require the existence of
merely past and future beings than modal operators require the existence of merely possible beings).

account has no new ideas to offer on fission cases. By contrast, Myro's approach is ready-made for this case:

At $t1$ John1 = John2.

At $t2$ it is not the case that John1 = John2.

By contrast, those cases where Geach's approach offers distinctive approaches to synchronic questions about identity (the problem of the many, the Trinity, and so on) are cases where Myro's approach has nothing distinctive to offer.

Myro is well aware of the pressure from Leibniz's law. Consider first the property-theoretic version. Return to the fission case. Let us suppose that at $t2$ John2 is in Paris and John1 is in Rome. It then seems that at $t1$ John1 has the property of being such that he will be in Rome at $t2$, and that at $t1$ John2 lacks that property. But can't we then fairly conclude that at $t1$ John1 is not John2?

Myro himself focuses on the property-theoretic version of Leibniz's law. He insists that all statements must, like colour attributions, be temporally qualified. He thus insists that Leibniz's law first be temporally qualified thus:

At all times, if $A = B$ then A is F if and only if B is F

(where 'F' expresses a property). Aware that this does not, by itself, solve the problem with which we are currently concerned, he goes on to add the following suggested qualification to the law:

So the general way of dealing with the complication is to divide properties into those which are '*time-free*'—like being on the mantelpiece—which are represented by open sentences *not* containing temporal qualifications, and those which are '*time-bound*'—like being on the mantelpiece on Tuesday—which are represented by open sentences which do contain temporal qualifications. And what must be done is that 'Leibniz's Law subject (like other statements) to temporal qualification' is to be, in addition, *restricted* to properties which are '*time-free*'—properly represented by open sentences (or 'predicates') which do not (relevantly) contain temporal qualifications.[63]

There is a natural worry. Suppose we concede to Myro his predicate 'is identical to'. We then introduce our own predicate 'is really identical to', which is governed by Leibniz's law in its unrestricted version.[64] Perhaps Myro will complain: 'But then you will count John1 and John2 as two at $t1$ when they are really one at $t1$.' Given the intimate connection between the identity predicate and counting, it is easy to see through the complaint. Myro is using the relation he expresses by 'is identical to' as a basis for a count at $t1$. But we intend to count by the relation expressed by 'is really identical to'. From the perspective of the latter, Myro will be reckoned to be counting certain equivalence classes of really distinct objects that are bundled together under an equivalence relation of 'have the same time-free properties'.

But perhaps the proponent of time-indexed identity can resist. Let us begin by noting that, following Williamson, we can avoid the detour through properties. Suppose it is now $t1$. By hypothesis, now, John1 = John2. Further now, John1 will be

---

[63] op cit., p. 157.

[64] Note that this move parallels one made earlier in connection with Geach.

in Rome at *t2*. But if John1 is identical to John2, then an interpretation of 'John1 will be in Rome at *t2*' which assigned John2 as the reference of 'John1' but which was in other respects the same as the original ought to preserve truth-value (recall the applicability of Williamson's test to intensional contexts). Myro's best tack would be to allow that such an interpretation *would* preserve truth-value, just as an interpretation of 'Giorgione is so-called because of his size' is true on an interpretation that assigns Barbarelli as the referent of 'Giorgione'. ('Is so called because of his size' generates an intensional context, with the result that substituting the name 'Giorgione' for the name 'Barbarelli' will not preserve truth-value. However, that by itself is no threat to the metalinguistic version of Leibniz's law.) Myro's approach stands or falls at this point, I suspect. Concede that interpreting 'John1' as referring to John2 makes the sentence 'John1 will be in Rome' false, and one is left with no alternative but to suppose that there are two objects in play and that Myro is appropriating 'is identical to' in order to express a relation other than identity.

Let us persist with the Giorgione–Barbarelli analogy.

(1) Giorgione is so called because of his size

is perfectly acceptable. But the existence of an intensional context renders dubious the use of existential instantiation to deliver

(2) There is someone who is so called because of his size.

The inference is unacceptable, since the content of 'is so called because of his size' is context-dependent. In particular, its content depends upon the particular lexical items that precede it.[65] The premiss says that Giorgione was called 'Giorgione' because of his size. The conclusion says, in effect, that someone is called 'someone' because of his size, a claim that hardly follows from the premiss.

The approach we are considering on behalf of Myro allows that

(3) It is now the case that John1 will be in Rome

and

(4) It is now not the case that John2 will be in Rome

are both true, even though the truth-value of (3) is the same on any pair of assignments that assign John1 and John2 respectively to 'John1' (where those assignments are otherwise exactly the same). This can only be so if the content of 'will be in Rome' is context-dependent, so that it has a different meaning (and a different extension) according to the subject term it is combined with. Since, by hypothesis, the referent of 'John1' and 'John2' are the same, and since their superficial orthographic features seem irrelevant in this case, it seems likely that the proponent of the view we are exploring will think that 'John1' and 'John2' have different *meanings*—call them with Frege 'modes of presentation'—which determine a different meaning (and thus extension) for 'will be in Rome' as it occurs in (3) and (4). Thus even though 'John1'

---

[65] As Brian Weatherson pointed out to me, the relevant piece of semantics would have to be complicated further to handle such sentences as 'Giorgione is so called because of his size and so is Tiny Tim'.

and 'John2' now refer to the very same object, 'John1 will be in Rome' is true and 'John2 will be in Rome' is false, since the pair of tokenings of 'will be in Rome' in (3) and (4) are not true of the same objects. Let us imagine, then, that the extension of a given token of 'will be in Rome' depends upon a contextual parameter that is fixed either by the mode of presentation of the subject term or by context. In effect, 'John1' and 'John2', while agreeing in referent, fix the relevant contextual parameter in different ways, owing to the different modes of presentation associated with them.[66]

If the modes of presentation associated with 'John 1' and John 2' are crucial to the meaning of 'will be in Rome' m (3) and (4), then we should expect to be more than a little troubled by the use of existential instantiation on (3) and (4) to deliver:

(5) It is now the case that $\exists x(x$ will be in Rome).
(6) It is now that case that $\exists x(\sim x$ will be in Rome).

On the approach we are considering, (5) and (6) will be incomplete as they stand. We shall only be able to make sense of (5) and (6) by treating them as elliptical for some such claims as the following:

(7) It is now the case that $\exists x(x$ *qua* such and such (for example, *qua* John1) will be in Rome).[67]

and

(8) It is now the case that $\exists x(x$ *qua* so and so (for example, *qua* John2) will not be in Rome).

That the unqualified (5) and (6) should be reckoned incomplete is a claim that seems hard to defend, to say the least.[68] Note in any case that we are now, in effect, exploring an approach to 'time-indexed identity' that is not so far from orthodoxy about *identity* as may first be imagined.[69] After all, on the approach currently being considered, 'will be in Rome' does not have a property associated with it *simpliciter*, since it is

[66] The analogy with the 'Giorgione' case is not perfect, of course. In the latter case, what matters to the content of 'is so called because of his size' is the lexical make-up of the noun phrase or determiner phrase that precedes the predicate. In the current case what plausibly matters (for one who adopts Myro's perspective) is the sense or mode of presentation of the lexical item that precedes the predicate. (I do not by any means intend myself to be *endorsing* the idea that proper names have modes of presentation associated with them.)

[67] I do not pretend that the '*qua F*' construction has been suitably explained. Indeed, I leave it to proponents of the view to make it maximally intelligible. As a first pass, though, we should think of 'will be' as expressing a three-place relation between an object, a mode of presentation, and a property. If the relevant mode of presentation is not explicitly supplied, it will have to be supplied by the context of conversation. Otherwise, a 'will be' utterance will not determinately express a proposition.

[68] Similarly, the view would have it that 'He will be in Rome' (pointing) is incomplete unless some parameter-fixing mode of presentation is supplied.

[69] It should be noted that there is a very different way of handling the issue, suggested by André Gallois *Occasions of Identity* (Oxford: Clarendon Press, 1998). The worry about John1 and John2 proceeded via a very natural assumption: some x is at $t1$ such that it will be F at $t2$ iff at $t2$ x is F. Gallois rejects that assumption. We are thus denied the licence to use the fact that at $t2$ John1 is in Rome and at $t2$ John2 isn't in Rome as a basis for inferring that at $t1$ John1 will be in Rome at $t2$

incomplete. The real future-describing properties, on the view now being explored, are properties like *being such that qua John1 one will be in Rome*. Adopt that perspective on the nature of temporal properties and the restriction of Leibniz's law to 'time-free properties' can, after all, be lifted.[70]

Let me finally remark on Myro's first qualification of Leibniz's law. Instead of

For all x and y: if $x = y$, x has some property F if and only if y has some property F,

he opts for the temporally qualified

At all times, if $x = y$ then Fx iff Fy.

One would think that we can assimilate the second version to the first. What is it for a claim of the form ⌜At t α is red⌝ to be true? A natural suggestion is that to be red is to stand in a certain relation to a time.[71] Orthodoxy tells us, indeed, that the truths about the world can thus be expressed with a timeless quantifier and no temporal prefix. From this perspective 'At t something is red' has the following logical form:

$\exists x(xRt)$

(where 't' picks out a time and 'R' expresses a relation that can hold between objects and times).[72] From this perspective, the time-indexed approach to identity becomes particularly strained. No one can reasonably suppose that 'a is red at $t1$' is an intensional context, forbidding existential instantiation. Suppose John1 is red at $t1$ and is red at $t2$, and that John2 is red at $t1$ and not red at $t2$.

The following claims are now unproblematically licensed:

$\exists x(x$ is red at $t1$ and x is red at $t2)$.
$\exists x(x$ is red at $t1$ and is not red at $t2)$.

But now the inference to

$\exists x(x$ is red at $t1$ and $\exists y(y$ is red at $t1$ and x is not $y))$

is irresistible. The cogency of Myro's approach depends, it would seem, on the unavailability of a description of the world that deploys timeless quantifiers and various relations of objects to times.

---

and at $t1$ it is not the case that John2 will be in Rome at $t2$. The approach is offered as a way of combining temporary identity with Leibniz's law (at least in the 'temporally qualified' form). The intuitive oddity of the view should, however, be evident. Though I shall not pursue the point here, it also seems that the cogency of this approach requires the unavailability of a description of the world that deploys timeless quantifiers and various relations of objects to times.

[70] Another deviant approach to tensed claims that leaves orthodoxy about identity undisturbed is provided by Theodore Sider ('All the World's a Stage', *Australasian Journal of Philosophy*, 74 (1996): 433–53), who adapts counterpart theory to diachronic issues.

[71] Perhaps primitive, perhaps reducible to having a temporal part that is red *simpliciter* that exists at that time.

[72] An alternative view holds that the copula expresses a three-place relation between a thing, a property, and a time. The point that follows could be easily adapted to fit that view.

3.3 Contingent Identity

In *Naming and Necessity* Saul Kripke wrote:

Waiving fussy considerations deriving from the fact that x need not have necessary existence, it was clear from $(x)\Box(x = x)$ and Leibniz's Law that identity is an 'internal' relation: $(x)(y)(x = y \supset \Box x = y)$.[73]

Some have argued, by contrast, that identity is contingent. But coherent versions of the contingent identity view do not present us with a novel conception of identity, and in particular, do not invoke some alternative to Leibniz's law (in either its property-theoretic or else metalinguistic versions). Rather, they attempt to reconcile the contingent identity thesis with an utterly orthodox conception of the identity relation itself. An excellent case in point is provided by David Lewis's defence of the contingent identity view.[74] Lewis defends a counterpart-theoretic approach to modality according to which ⌜α is possibly F⌝ is true just in case there is some appropriately similar entity to the thing designated by α—a 'counterpart' in another possible world—that satisfies F, and ⌜α is necessarily F⌝ is true just in case every appropriately similar entity in modal space satisfies F. He explicitly allows that a thing may have more than one counterpart in another world. A rigorous presentation of this view requires a translation scheme that translates the sentences of quantified modal logic into counterpart-theoretic language. Lewis's suggested translation scheme recommends that we treat the claims that $(x)\Box(x = x)$ as the claim that everything is such that every counterpart of it is self-identical. So translated, the claim comes out as true. Meanwhile, it recommends that we treat '$(x)(y)(x = y \supset \Box x = y)$' as the claim that if x is identical to y, then for all worlds w, if some z is the counterpart of x in w and some v is the counterpart of y in w, then z is identical to v. The full quantificational structure of the latter claim is disguised by the 'perversely abbreviated language of quantified modal logic'[75]. Given that, on Lewis's view, a thing may have a pair of counterparts in another world, this claim comes out false. One may quibble with the translation. But grant the translation and

---

[73] Kripke, op cit., p. 3.

[74] See David Lewis, 'Counterpart Theory and Quantified Modal Logic', in *Philosophical papers vol. i* (Oxford: Oxford University Press, 1983) 39–46. Another excellent case in point is Allan Gibbard 'Contingent Identity', *Journal of Philosophical Logic* 4 (1975): 187–221. The key idea there is one borrowed from Carnap, namely that while in non-modal contexts proper names denote objects and variables range over objects, in modal contexts proper names denote individual concepts and variables range over individual concepts. Suppose (i) $A = B$. Still it may be (ii) Possibly A is not identical to B and it is not the case that possibly A is not identical to A. This will be because in (ii) 'A' and 'B' refer to distinct individual concepts. We are in no way forced to concede that there is a pair of assignments which yield differing truth-values for (ii) differing only in that one assigns A to 'A', and that the other assigns B to 'A'.

[75] Lewis, 'Counterpart Theory and Quantified Modal Logic', p. 46.

that the counterpart relation is sometimes one-many, and one can scarcely think that a suitable version of Leibniz's law will vindicate the truth of the necessity of identity thesis.[76]

This is how it should be. Interesting philosophical doctrines would do well, it seems, to exploit and not challenge our mastery of the concept of identity. It remains unlikely that there really are any serious philosophical puzzles about identity as such. And here we return to the theme with which we began. Puzzles that are articulated using the word 'identity' are almost certainly puzzles about something else.

[76] For more on this, see Lewis, ibid., postscript.

2

Locations

with *Theodore Sider*

Think of 'locations' very abstractly, as positions in a space, any space. Temporal loc-ations are positions in time; spatial locations are positions in (physical) space; partic-ulars are locations in quality space.

Should we reify locations? Are locations entities? Spatiotemporal *relationalists* say there are no such things as spatiotemporal locations; the fundamental spatial and tem-poral facts involve no locations as objects, only the instantiation of spatial and tem-poral relations. The denial of locations in quality space is the *bundle theory*, according to which particulars do not exist; facts apparently about particulars really concern relations between universals.

A 'space', in our abstract sense, consists of a set of objects, together with properties and relations defined on those objects. The objects are the locations of the space, and the distribution of the properties and relations over the locations defines the space's structure. All spaces are thus quality spaces; when the relations are thought of as spa-tiotemporal then the space is also a spatiotemporal space. By not reifying locations one denies that these abstract spaces isomorphically represent the real world. The real world *does* in some sense have a structure that can be non-isomorphically represented by a space (or, more likely, a class of spaces), but the locations in those spaces do not correspond to anything real.

We will examine modal considerations on reifying locations. Denying the existence of spatiotemporal locations excludes certain possibilities for spatiotemporal reality. Denying the existence of qualitative locations excludes certain possibilities for qualit-ative reality. In each case the excluded possibilities are pre-analytically possible. Some of the possibilities can be reinstated by modifying the locationless theories, but at the cost of an unattractive holism.

Do these modal considerations mandate postulating locations? That depends on whether modal intuition can teach us about the actual world. That deep question in the epistemology of modality will not be explored; we merely point out the modal consequences of repudiating locations.

First published in *Philosophical Topics* (2003), 53–76. I am grateful for permission to reprint it here.

1 THE BUNDLE THEORY[1]

The traditional formulation of the bundle theory is that particulars are bundles of universals.[2] We will understand the bundle theory more neutrally, as saying that the fundamental facts about qualities involve only universals, and make no reference to particulars. This leaves open whether particulars are to be eliminated from ontology or constructed out of universals, perhaps as sets or fusions of properties and relations. 'Bundle theory' is therefore a somewhat misleading name for the position we will be exploring, as our bundle theorist need not put forth bundles as entities.

Our bundle theorist's universals are 'sparse', in the sense of not being closed under such operations as negation or disjunction.[3] This is a natural, popular picture, especially if universals are *sui generis* entities, in the ground floor of ontology.

These fundamental facts involving only universals: exactly what form do they take? A careful answer to this question is required before the modal consequences of the bundle theory can be assessed.

Our bundle theorist's ontology contains only universals: properties and relations (each with a fixed, finite-adicy). The theory is *pure* in admitting nothing whatsoever that would play the role of locations in quality space. Thus in addition to lacking particulars, its ontology contains no property instances, tropes, particular events, or any such things.

Its ideology has *compresence* of universals in place of instantiation of universals by particulars.[4] Where we would ordinarily say that a certain particular instantiates properties F, G, and H, the bundle theorist says instead that properties F, G, and H are compresent (with one another). In the limiting case of a thing having a single property F, the bundle theorist will say simply that F is compresent.

Compresence is *irreducibly plural* and *multigrade*.[5] Irreducibly plural: to say that F, G, and H are compresent is not just to say that any two of F, G, and H are pairwise compresent. For suppose, as we would ordinarily say, that some particular is F and G, some other particular is G and H, and a third particular is F and H; but no fourth particular has all three properties. The bundle theorist must say that any two of F, G, and H are compresent; if that were all that 'F, G, and H are compresent' amounted to then it would follow on the bundle theory that the situation is one ordinarily

---

[1] Our discussion of the bundle theory and spacetime relationalism take as their starting points J. A. Cover and John O'Leary-Hawthorne, 'A World of Universals', *Philosophical Studies* 91 (1998): 205–219 and Theodore Sider, *Four-Dimensionalism: An Ontology of Persistence and Time*, (Oxford: Clarendon Press, (2001)), chapter 4, section 8, respectively.

[2] See Bertrand Russell, *Our Knowledge of the External World*, (Chicago, IL: Open Court, 1940), chapter VI.

[3] See David Lewis, *On the Plurality of Worlds*, (Oxford: Basil Blackwell, 1986), pp. 59–69.

[4] Russell (*op. cit.*, part four, chapter VIII) coined the term 'compresence', but gave it a spatiotemporal interpretation and tied it to a phenomenalistic bundle theory. We use 'compresence' rather than 'instantiation' since the latter is usually used in connection with a thing ontology. Whether anything else turns on this traditional distinction is not something we investigate here.

[5] See Cover and O'Leary-Hawthorne, *op. cit.*, section 3.5.

describable as containing a fourth particular with all three properties. Multigrade: it makes sense to say that $F_1, \ldots, F_n$ are compresent, for any finite n.

The account becomes more complicated when relations are introduced. Bundle theorists tend to ignore relations, at best allowing relational properties. But relational properties are complex properties involving the instantiation of relations, and hence rely on a prior account of relations. Our bundle theorist incorporates relations by taking compresence to be multiply plural, in the following sense. For any n-place R, one can say

R is compresent with $(\ldots F_i{}^1 \ldots; \ldots F_i{}^2 \ldots; \ldots; \ldots F_i{}^n \ldots)$.

While this locution is primitive for the bundle theorist, the believer in particulars would regard it as meaning that there exist n particulars, $x_1, \ldots, x_n$, such that $R(x_1, \ldots, x_n)$, and such that x_1 has the properties $F_i{}^1$ (i.e., $F_1{}^1$, $F_2{}^1$, ...), x_2 has the properties $F_i{}^2$, and so on. The order of the strings '$\ldots F_i{}^1 \ldots$'; '$\ldots F_i{}^2 \ldots$'; $\ldots$ is significant, since this order corresponds to the order in which R holds over $x_1, \ldots, x_n$, as we would ordinarily say. However, the order in which the properties are mentioned within each string is insignificant. The $F_i{}^1$'s could equivalently appear as 'F, G, and H', or 'F, H, and G', or 'G, H, and F', and so on.

Suppose some F bears R to some G, as we would usually say. Thus we have:

F — R — G

The bundle theorist would describe this as a case in which R is compresent with (F; G). A case in which some G bears R to some F would be described as a case in which R is compresent with (G; F). As a final example, consider a situation that, as we would usually say, involves three particulars standing in a three-place relation B; the first particular is F and G, the second is H and I, and the third is J, K, and L:

FG - B - HI
|
JKL

This would be described by the bundle theorist as a case in which

B is compresent with (F and G; H and I; J, K, and L).
↑   ↑   ↑   ↑
3-place   3 plural, multigrade slots in which to mention properties

The relation in this case is three-place, so there are three slots in the predication of compresence in which to mention properties. Each of the three slots is plural and multigrade, since in each slot the properties mentioned are said to be collectively compresent, and in each slot any number of monadic properties may be mentioned.

Some will object that understanding the bundle theorist's locutions of compresence requires a prior understanding of the notion of a particular. F and G are said to be compresent in just those cases in which, *as we would normally say*, there exists a particular that has both F and G. If there is no other way to teach the notion of compresence, it will be said, compresence 'presupposes' particulars. This objection is misguided. At best it establishes a *conceptual* priority of thing-talk, whereas the issue is ontological. Even if thought is, in the first instance, of things, the world may yet at bottom contain nothing but universals.

Thus, the bundle theorist aims to describe the world speaking only of the compresence of universals. She may later introduce fusions of properties and relations ('bundles'), but predications of compresence may not mention these bundles. The fundamental facts are all and only those expressible with predications of compresence mentioning only universals.

2 THE BUNDLE THEORY AND POSSIBILITY

The bundle theory, we take it, is put forward as a necessary truth.[6] Therefore, a possibility for the world may be specified by specifying which predications of compresence are true at it. It follows that there cannot exist distinct possibilities in which all the same predications of compresence are true.[7] This, we will see, imposes a severe restriction on what is possible.

The classic bundle theory is generally thought to preclude the possibility of distinct indiscernible particulars, which would be identified with the same bundle of universals and so with each other.[8] While our bundle theory does not reify bundles, it nevertheless implies a corresponding restriction on possibilities involving what we would normally describe as qualitatively indiscernible particulars. Consider two possible worlds, one containing just a single thing with property F, the other containing two things with property F. In neither world is any relation instantiated. The bundle theorist's description of each world will be the same: F is compresent. Therefore the bundle theorist cannot admit that these possibilities are genuinely distinct.

Consider two other possible worlds, like those just considered except that a certain binary relation, R, is instantiated in each world. In the first world the sole particular bears R to itself, whereas in the second world the two particulars bear R to each other:

$$w_1 : \quad \overset{\text{R}}{\underset{\text{F}}{\curvearrowleft \bullet}} \qquad\qquad w_2 : \quad \underset{\text{F}}{\bullet} \leftarrow \text{R} \rightarrow \underset{\text{F}}{\bullet}$$

---

[6] This could be denied—see Cover and O'Leary-Hawthorne, *op. cit.*, section 4.

[7] This is not to assume any strong combinatorial principle of possibility. Combinatorialism claims that all combinations of 'metaphysical elements' are possible, whereas we assume only that all possibilities are combinations of metaphysical elements. This also does not assume the existence of 'negative' facts: a predication of compresence failing to hold does not require the existence of a 'truth-maker' for that failure.

[8] See Russell, *op. cit.*, p. 120, 127; Max Black, 'The Identity of Indiscernibles', *Mind* 61 (1952): 153–164 (who does not consider the bundle theory explicitly, only the identity of indiscernibles); D. M. Armstrong, *Universals and Scientific Realism, volume 1: Nominalism and Realism*, (Cambridge: Cambridge University Press (1978)), chapter 9, section 1; James Van Cleve, 'Three Versions of the Bundle Theory', *Philosophical Studies* 47 (1985): 95–107.

Again, the bundle theorist cannot distinguish the worlds, for in each case the description will be the same: R is compresent with (F; F). Similarly, neither world can be distinguished from any world with any number of F-things, each bearing R to all the rest.

The traditional objection is often put this way: 'the bundle theory cannot allow a world with nothing but two distinct indiscernible particulars'. Strictly speaking, our bundle theorist does not allow worlds with *any* particulars; but consider the objection that the bundle theorist cannot allow worlds we would normally describe as having two distinct indiscernible particulars. This objection is not quite right, for the bundle theorist's description 'R is compresent with (F; F)' is in a sense the bundle theorist's substitute for indiscernible particulars. The real objection is that this description does not distinguish indiscernible particulars standing in R from a single particular bearing R to itself—it does not distinguish world w_1 from world w_2.

The bundle theorist might stick to her guns and argue that w_1 and w_2 are not genuinely distinct. Let R be the relation *being five feet from*. In an earlier publication,[9] one of us suggested the reply that the possibility one would ordinarily call two distinct F-things standing in R is in fact the possibility of F being five feet from itself. The sentence 'there are two F-things five feet apart' is made true, on this view, by facts about universals—by F's being five feet from itself.[10] This reply only addresses the objection that the bundle theory precludes the possibility of indiscernible particulars, whereas the present objection is that worlds w_1 and w_2 cannot be distinguished by the bundle theorist. But the reply could be extended: we are mistaken in thinking that possibilities w_1 and w_2 are distinct; modal intuition is sufficiently satisfied by admitting just the single possibility of R being compresent with (F; F). Against this reply the determined objector must continue to insist that her modal intuitions clearly specify that w_1 and w_2 are distinct possibilities, that there is a difference between a single particular being five feet from itself and distinct particulars being separated by five feet.

That the bundle theory runs into trouble with indiscernible particulars is well known. But in fact, many other pre-analytically distinct possibilities are identified by the bundle theorist. Consider:

$$w_3 : \text{F-R-G-R-H} \qquad \text{vs.} \qquad w_4 : \text{F-R-G} \quad \text{G-R-H}$$

In w_3, an F bears R to a G, which in turn bears R to an H. In w_4, an F bears R to a G, and a distinct G bears R to an H. These possibilities are identified by the bundle theorist, for the same predications of compresence hold in each case: 'R is compresent with (F; G)', and 'R is compresent with (G; H)'.

Or consider two apparently distinct cases involving two particulars each of which has the property F. In the first, binary relations R and S hold between the

---

[9] John O'Leary-Hawthorne, "The Bundle Theory of Substance and the Identity of Indiscernibles," *Analysis* 55 (1995): 205–26.

[10] Compare also Van Cleve, *op. cit.*, p. 104. But his version of the response presupposes substantivalism about places (see his note 30).

particulars in the same direction, whereas in the second case they hold in opposite directions:

$$
\begin{array}{ccc}
\text{R} & & \text{R} \\
\text{F} \overset{\rightarrow}{\underset{\rightarrow}{}} \text{F} & \quad \text{vs.} \quad & \text{F} \overset{\leftarrow}{\underset{\rightarrow}{}} \text{F} \\
\text{S} & & \text{S}
\end{array}
$$

In each case the bundle theorist has the same two predications of compresence: 'R is compresent with (F; F)', and 'S is compresent with (F; F)'.

Neither case involves indiscernible particulars; the problem is different from the traditional one. The bundle theorist could dig in her heels yet again. But identifying these possibilities would involve a massive departure from ordinary modal belief.

How might the bundle theorist respond to this problem? Each case involves a failure of 'linkage' between distinct facts of compresence. In describing w_3 the bundle theorist says that R is compresent with (F; G), and then goes on to say that R is compresent with (G; H); but this leaves out that it is the very same G-thing mentioned in the first statement that bears R to the H-thing mentioned in the second statement. Of course, the bundle theorist cannot say precisely this, since she does not believe in G-*things*. The question is whether predications of compresence can be linked in some legitimate way.

The bundle theorist might further complicate the notion of compresence. In describing w_3, rather than making two separate statements:

R is compresent with (F; G). R is compresent with (G; H).

she might substitute a single statement:

(*) R is compresent with (F; G), the latter of which is such that R is compresent with (it; H).

(*) is *not* a mere abbreviation for the first statement, which is true in both w_3 and w_4; (*) is to be true only in w_3.

In (*), the phrase 'the latter of which' does not merely refer to G; its function is to associate two positions within a single complex sentence form, namely the position occupied by 'G' and the position occupied by 'it'. One could further emphasize this by dropping the second occurrence of 'is compresent with', as this suggests that a second separable attribution of compresence is being made; the form of (*) could then be thought of as the following:

compresence(R_1, F_1, F_2, R_2, F_3)

In sentence (*), R_1 was R, F_1 was F, F_2 was G, R_2 was R, and F_3 was H; thus (*) is 'compresence(R, F, G, R, H)'. The fact that the two places in (*) concerning G are associated is emphasized here by the existence of only a single slot that G occupies (slot F_2)—there are no two slots that could potentially be filled by distinct property names. And though it may appear that (*) speaks of *cases* of G, which could only be particulars (or tropes, or property-instances, or something else playing the role of locations in quality space), in fact (*) is a complex statement about only R, F, G, and H, true in exactly those cases in which we would ordinarily say that an F-thing bears R to a G-thing, which in turn bears R to an H-thing.

As for the pair of cases involving R and S holding between two F-things, in the same direction in one case but opposite directions in the other, in the first the bundle theorist would say:

R is comprent with (F; F), the latter of which is such that S is comprent with (it; F)

whereas in the second she would say:

R is comprent with (F; F), the latter of which is such that S is comprent with (F; it)

Each of these statements is an instance of a different irreducible form of attribution of comprence, for different 'positions' are associated in the two cases. Moreover, each has a form quite different from (*).

Let us explore the bundle theorist's introduction of linkage more carefully. The initial bundle theory invoked the comprence locution:

R is comprent with $(\ldots F^1{}_i \ldots; \ldots F^2{}_i \ldots; \ldots; \ldots F^n{}_i \ldots)$

which was to be true in cases in which, as we would ordinarily say:

there exist n particulars, $x_1, \ldots, x_n$, such that $R(x_1, \ldots, x_n)$, and such that x_1 has the F^1s, x_2 has the F^2s, $\ldots$, x_n has the F^ns

But mere conjunctions (or lists) of such attributions do not allow the expression of linkage. The conjunctive sentence:

R is comprent with $(\ldots F^1{}_i \ldots; \ldots F^2{}_i \ldots; \ldots; \ldots F^n{}_i \ldots)$ & R' is comprent with $(\ldots G^1{}_i \ldots; \ldots G^2{}_i \ldots; \ldots; \ldots G^m{}_i \ldots)$

will be true in just those cases in which, as we would ordinarily say:

there exist n particulars, $x_1, \ldots, x_n$, such that $R(x_1, \ldots, x_n)$, and such that x_1 has the F^1s, x_2 has the F^2s, $\ldots$, x_n has the F^ns
&
there exist m particulars, $y_1, \ldots, y_m$, such that $R'(y_1, \ldots, y_m)$, and such that y_1 has the G^1s, y_2 has the G^2s, $\ldots$, y_m has the G^ms

The existentially quantified variables x_i associated with the first comprence conjunct are different from those variables y_j associated with the second; that is what disallows the expression of linkage. Linkage would be expressed if, in place of some of the variables y_j we could instead write one of the variables x_i. One might, for example, want to link the position occupied by x_1 in the first conjunct with the position occupied by y_1 in the second:

there exist n particulars, $x_1, \ldots, x_n$, such that $R(x_1, \ldots, x_n)$, and such that x_1 has the F^1s, x_2 has the F^2s, $\ldots$, x_n has the F^ns
&
there exist $m-1$ particulars, $y_2, \ldots, y_m$, such that $R'(x_1, y_2, \ldots, y_m)$, and such that y_2 has the G^2s, $\ldots$, y_m has the G^ms.

To get this effect, the bundle theorist needs an attribution of comprence that is true just when, as we would ordinarily say, this last statement is true. The needed attribution can be symbolized thus:

R is compresent with $(\ldots F^1{}_i \ldots |\alpha; \ldots F^2{}_i \ldots; \ldots; \ldots F^n{}_i \ldots)$; R′ is compresent with $(\alpha; \ldots G^2{}_i \ldots; \ldots; \ldots G^m{}_i \ldots)$

The presence of the symbol $|\alpha$ after the $F^1{}_i$s, and the presence of α in place of the $G^1{}_i$s, indicates that those positions are to be linked. In this case only one position is linked, and so we could say more informally (as we did with (*) above):

R is compresent with$(\ldots F^1{}_i \ldots; \ldots F^2{}_i \ldots; \ldots; \ldots F^n{}_i \ldots)$, the first of which is such that R′ is compresent with (it; $\ldots G^2{}_i \ldots; \ldots; \ldots G^m{}_i \ldots)$

But in the general case we need the symbols α, β, etc., for clarity.[11] One might, for example, want to link quite a few positions in a pair of attributions of compresence. For definiteness sake, let R have three places, let R′ have four, and consider the following example:

R is compresent with $(\ldots F^1{}_i \ldots |\alpha; \ldots F^2{}_i \ldots |\beta; \ldots F^3{}_i \ldots |\gamma)$; R′ is compresent with $(\alpha; \beta; \gamma; \ldots G_i \ldots)$

This sentence would be true in cases in which, as we would ordinarily say:

there exist 3 particulars, x_1, x_2, x_3, such that $R(x_1, x_2, x_3)$, and such that x_1 has the $F^1{}_i$s, x_2 has the $F^2{}_i$s, x_3 has the $F^3{}_i$s

&

there exists a particular, y, such that $R'(x_1, x_2, x_3, y)$, and such that y has the G_is.

Still more generally, the bundle theorist will want to allow linkages between more than two attributions of compresence, for example:

R is compresent with (F and G$|\alpha$; H and I); R′ is compresent with $(J|\beta; \alpha;$ K, L and M); R″ is compresent with $(\beta; \alpha;$ N and O)

which would be true in just those circumstances in which, as we would ordinarily say:

there exist two particulars, x_1 and x_2, such that $R(x_1, x_2)$, Fx_1, Gx_1, Hx_2, and Ix_2

&

there exist two particulars y_1 and y_2, such that $R'(y_1, x_1, y_2)$, Jy_1, Ky_2, Ly_2, and My_2

&

there exists a particular, z, such that $R''(y_1, x_1, z)$, Nz and Oz

Moreover, linkages should be allowed within a single attribution of compresence, as in:

R is compresent with (F and G$|\alpha$; H and I; α)

which would be true in cases in which, as we would ordinarily say, there exist particulars x and y, such that $R(x, y, x)$, Fx, Gx, Hy, and Iy.

Call any sentence of the following form a *pure Ramsey sentence*:

There exist particulars $x_1, \ldots, x_n$ such that ϕ_1 & ... & ϕ_m

---

[11] Note that α, β, etc., are not variables standing for entities; they are syntactic devices for associating certain positions within attributions of compresence.

where each ϕ_i is an atomic sentence attributing some universal (perhaps a property, perhaps a relation) to some of the variables $x_1, \ldots, x_n$, and in which repetition of variables between and within the ϕ_is is allowed. (Note that this definition disallows the presence of negation symbols.) What we have seen is that for any pure Ramsey sentence, S, our revised bundle theory allows a sentence concerning the compresence of universals that is true in just those cases in which, as we would ordinarily say, S is true.

By allowing linkage within a single statement of compresence, our bundle theorist can now distinguish worlds w_1 and w_2 above:

$$w_1 : \quad \overset{\displaystyle R}{\underset{\displaystyle F}{\bullet \curvearrowleft}} \qquad\qquad w_2 : \quad \underset{\displaystyle F}{\bullet} \leftarrow R \rightarrow \underset{\displaystyle F}{\bullet}$$

Only in w_1 is it true that R is compresent with $(F|\alpha; \alpha)$, for only in w_1 is it true that, as we would ordinarily say, something bears R to itself. It might be surprising that the new bundle theory can distinguish w_1 and w_2, since the failure to allow distinctions between indiscernible objects is usually thought to be a defining feature of the bundle theory. But distinguishing these worlds is a natural extension of allowing the linkage one needs to distinguish between worlds like w_3 and w_4.[12] Moreover, if the example is changed so that each object in w_2 bears R to itself, the worlds can no longer be distinguished:[13]

$$w_{1a} : \quad \overset{\displaystyle R}{\underset{\displaystyle F}{\bullet \curvearrowleft}} \qquad\qquad w_{2a} : \quad \overset{\displaystyle R}{\underset{\displaystyle F}{\curvearrowright \bullet}} \leftarrow R \rightarrow \overset{\displaystyle R}{\underset{\displaystyle F}{\bullet \curvearrowleft}}$$

Thus, even the new bundle theory collapses certain possibilities involving indiscernible things.

One *could* modify the bundle theory even more, to distinguish even these possibilities. Imagine, in addition to the $|\alpha$ notation for linkage, adding notation for *anti-linkage*. Let:

R is compresent with $1(F|\text{-}\alpha; G)$; R' is compresent with $(H|\text{-}\alpha, I)$

---

[12] What if, despite this, the bundle theorist shies away from distinguishing w_1 and w_2, on the grounds that this smacks of belief in particulars, but still wants to invoke linkage to distinguish w_3 and w_4? She might claim that sometimes differences in claims of linkage correspond to no genuine ontological difference. She might, for example, claim that 'R is compresent with $(F|\alpha; \alpha)$' and 'R is compresent with $(F; F)$' are, as it happens, true in exactly the same possible circumstances. Such a bundle theorist ought to give a principled account of *which* differences in statements of linkage correspond to distinct possibilities, since, on her view, some do and some do not. We will not explore the issue further.

[13] A similar example: given linkage, the bundle theorist can distinguish a world containing (as we would usually say) a pair of indiscernible spheres separated by one foot from a world containing a single bi-located duplicate sphere that is located one foot from itself; for only in the second world is it true that *being one foot from* is compresent with $(\text{spherehood}|\alpha, \alpha)$. However, even linkage will not distinguish this second world from a world containing *two* bi-located duplicate spheres, each located one foot from itself, each located in exactly the same places as the other.

be used in cases in which, as we would ordinarily say, there exists an x_1 and x_2, such that $R(x_1,x_2)$, Fx_1, and Gx_2, and there exists a y_1 and y_2, such that y_1 **is distinct from** x_1, $R(y_1,y_2)$, Hy_1, and Iy_2. Marking two property-slots with ⊢α signifies, as we would normally say, *distinct* particulars that have the properties in question. Worlds w_{1a} and w_{2a} can now be distinguished: only in w_{2a} is it true that R is comprement with (F⊢α; F⊢α), for only in w_{2a} is there, as we would normally say, an F that bears R to a *distinct* F. In addition to capturing the content of what we normally express with pure Ramsey sentences, this doubly modified bundle theory captures the content of what we normally express with *impure Ramsey sentences*, which are like pure Ramsey sentences except that information about the numerical distinctness of the values of the variables may be added.[14]

Some might charge this doubly modified bundle theory of being the theory of particulars in disguise. This charge is to some degree unjustified since a believer in particulars is free to distinguish possibilities that share the same impure Ramsey sentences. The view that such possibilities can indeed be distinguished is sometimes called haecceitism,[15] and is not open to the doubly modified bundle theorist. Moreover, the doubly modified bundle theorist may insist that she does not believe in particulars, even though her beliefs about what is possible are isomorphic to those of the genuine believer in particulars. Still, some may remain alarmed at how close the modified bundle theorist has moved to believing in particulars. The question then becomes whether there is any principled reason to allow linkage and then stop, without going on to allow anti-linkage as well. If not, then so much the worse for the bundle theorist!—she can neither live with linkage (since that draws her too close to belief in particulars) nor live without it (since that violates too many ordinary modal intuitions). But we think that a bundle theory that allows linkage while disallowing anti-linkage is a reasonably motivated middle ground; it is that bundle theory we consider henceforth.

Allowing linkage is attractive for its modal consequences. But there is a serious cost. By admitting that sentences like (*) do not reduce to simpler predications of comprement, the bundle theorist adopts a sort of holism. Whenever there is a network of interrelated things, the facts cannot be captured by anything simpler than a single statement describing the entire organic whole. Suppose an F bears R to some G, which in turn bears S to something else with G, H, and I; suppose the F-thing stands in a three place relation to a G-thing and an H-thing, each of which bear relation R to . . . A new irreducible, complex locution of comprement will be needed to describe this entire situation. Any series of statements describing mere parts of the system will leave out the linkages expressed by locutions like 'the F-thing'. One is reminded of the nineteenth-century British idealists, who denied that the truth about the world could be broken down into facts about the world's components.

Indeed, the original bundle theory, which attributed relations with statements like 'Relation R is comprement with (F and G; H and I)', already implied a limited holism.

---

[14] If *all* impure Ramsey sentences are to be captured, a separate mechanism would be needed for expressing anti-linkage in statements of comprement that involve no relations.

[15] See David Lewis, *On the Plurality of Worlds* (Oxford: Basil Blackwell, 1986), section 4.4.

The holding of relations could not be attributed without specifying the properties of the things related. The totality of facts of a given case of R's holding could not be specified by anything other than a single statement mentioning all the monadic properties of R's *relata*. Moreover, the irreducibly plural nature of compresence is the source of more holism: the compresence of multiple properties does not reduce to pairwise compresence between properties taken two at a time.

Holism can be avoided if one accepts locations, in this case particulars, for locations provide linkages between distinct facts. This is the *raison d'être* of locations. When we say 'particular *a* is F, and bears relation R to particular *b*, which is G', and later go on to say that '*b* bears relation R to particular *c*, which is H', the two facts expressed are linked by the recurrence of the name '*b*'—we thereby say that the very same case of G mentioned in the first fact is related by R to a case of H.

What, exactly, is the worry about 'holism'? Holism, we have said, is a failure of complex truths to reduce to simpler truths. By 'reduce' we do not mean translation; everyone should agree that '∀xFx' does not translate any conjunction of simple subject-predicate sentences. We mean instead supervenience: complex truths ought to supervene on simpler truths. By 'complex' and 'simpler' truths we mean (what we would ordinarily describe as) truths about complex and simpler systems of objects. Thus, truths about a set of objects should supervene on truths about the properties and relations of subsets of that set. But this in turn requires clarification, for the holding of an *n*-place relation over *n* objects will not in general supervene on facts about subsets of those *n* objects. The objectionable holism implied by the modified bundle theory is that *no matter what the basic properties and relations are, truths about what intuitively count as complex systems involving just those properties and relations do not supervene on simple statements about those properties and relations.* To capture the linkages in complex systems involving a chosen set of basic properties and relations, complex statements that fail to supervene on simpler ones must be introduced. This is the neo-Hegelian holism we reject, or at least ridicule.[16]

Related to holism is an explosion of ideology. The modified bundle theory appeals to an infinite number of primitive locutions concerning compresence, for example:

> R is compresent with (F; G)
> R is compresent with (F; G|α); S is compresent with (α; H)
> R is compresent with (F|α; G); S is compresent with (α; H)
> R is compresent with (F; G|α); S is compresent with (H; α)
> R is compresent with (F; G|α); S is compresent with (α; H|β); R is compresent with (β; F) etc.

Each is an irreducible form, in the sense that the more complex forms are never definable in terms of the simpler ones. Thus, the re-use of the term 'compresence' in each is a bit of a cheat. Rather than containing a single notion of compresence, the primitive

---

[16] This holism also implies modal connections some might find strange. Necessarily, if (*) is true then R must be compresent with F and G (likewise, it is necessary that if (*) is true then R is compresent with G and H.) Thanks to Dean Zimmerman for this observation. (See p. 36.)

ideology of the bundle theorist now contains infinitely many locutions, each of which can be used to make a different sort of statement about universals.[17]

The burden could be shifted from ideology to ontology. Instead of saying:

R is compresent with (F; G|α); S is compresent with (α; H)

one could introduce a new relation, T, intuitively described as the relation holding between particulars x, y, z iff x and y stand in R and y and z stand in S; one could then say:

T is compresent with (F; G; H)

The complexities in ideology could be avoided if such complex relations were generally postulated. Whether or not this trade of ontology for ideology is significant, it does nothing to avoid holism, for the new relations remain irreducible to simpler relations. Further, despite this irreducibility, the instantiation of the new relations necessarily implies the instantiation of simpler relations. T's being compresent with (F; G; H) would necessarily imply, for example, that R is compresent with (F; G). Finally, one should not be too quick to trust these new relations, for they are not the ordinary 'complex relations' we all know and love. The instantiation of what one normally thinks of as a complex relation is just a matter of the instantiation of its 'constituents', whereas these new relations do not supervene on their constituents.

Set aside complex relations, and return to the theory that adds new locutions of compresence to ideology. Even with these additions, the bundle theory still threatens to preclude some possibilities involving infinitely many individuals.[18] Consider two cases, each involving an infinite series of F-things, each of which stands in a certain relation R to the adjacent members in the series but nothing else. The first infinite series has a beginning—a first thing that is F, as we would ordinarily say—but no end, whereas the second series is two-way, with neither a beginning nor an end:

One-way infinite series: F-R-F-R-F-R-F-R-F-...
Two-way infinite series: ...-F-R-F-R-F-R-F-R-F-...

In each case the same finite predications of compresence are true:[19]

R is compresent with (F; F)
R is compresent with (F; F|α); R is compresent with (α; F)
R is compresent with (F; F|α); R is compresent with (α; F|β); R is compresent with (β; F) etc.

---

[17] Might one regard each locution as involving a single highly flexible bit of ideology? Such a notion would be 'multigrade' in a very generalized way. One's sense of how to count bits of ideology breaks down. Alternatively, finitude might be restored using something like Quine's tricks for eliminating variables from quantification theory (see his 'Variables Explained Away' in his *Selected Logic Papers* (Cambridge, Mass.: Harvard University Press, 1966), pp. 227–35). Regardless of the relative merits of such an ideology, holism remains.

[18] Moreover, the examples we consider involve discrete infinities; we do not here consider the even more complex matter of how the bundle theorist will describe continuous infinite structures, for example space.

[19] We continue to assume a sparse conception of universals.

So the possibilities apparently cannot be distinguished. However, the bundle theorist might be willing to allow infinite predications of compresence, in which case the possibilities could be distinguished after all. The following would hold in the two-way series but not in the one-way series:

> ... R is compresent with $(\alpha_{-1}; F|\alpha_0)$; R is compresent with $(\alpha_0; F|\alpha_1)$; R is compresent with $(\alpha_1; F|\alpha_2)$; ...

This sentence involves a two-way infinite primitive locution of compresence, which is irreducible to finite locutions. Appealing to this locution implies more holism and bloats ideology, but at least it distinguishes possibilities that ought to be distinguished.[20]

Our discussion of the bundle theory has been very abstract. We described possibilities schematically, as involving universals 'F', 'G', 'R', etc., without specifying what those universals were. But a certain sort of bundle theorist would hold that our thinking about possibilities is tied to specific universals: spatiotemporal relations. According to this view, which we may call 'spatiotemporalism', the world is essentially spatiotemporal. Moreover, spatiotemporal relations are essentially *pervasive*, in that the world is necessarily a single spatiotemporal structure in which everything (as we would normally say) stands in spatiotemporal relations to everything else. Moreover, our modal intuitions are essentially intuitions about these spatiotemporal structures.[21]

Spatiotemporalism appears, initially anyway, to allow the bundle theorist to do without linkage, and thus avoid holism. Recall the first argument for linkage. Worlds w_3 and w_4 were not distinguished by our original bundle theorist:

$$w_3 : \text{F-R-G-R-H} \qquad \text{vs.} \qquad w_4 : \text{F-R-G} \quad \text{G-R-H}$$

Each world was to be ordinarily describable as containing an F-thing, a, standing in R to a G-thing, b, and a G-thing, c, standing in R to an H-thing, d; the difference was that the G-things, b and c, are identical in w_3 but not in w_4. But if R is a spatiotemporal relation, then the spatiotemporalist will claim, *additional* spatiotemporal relations will distinguish the worlds. Since $b \neq c$ in w_4, b and c must be at different spatiotemporal locations, which will generate differences from w_3. For concrete-

---

[20] Consider the following pair of worlds, in neither of which is any relation instantiated. The first contains (as we would ordinarily say) an infinite series of objects, the first of which has property F_1, the second of which has F_1 and F_2, the third of which has F_1, F_2, and F_3, and so on. The second contains just a single object that has infinitely many properties: F_1, F_2, F_3, ... This is another case showing the need for infinitary locutions: to distinguish these worlds we need the infinitary sentence 'F_1, F_2, ... are compresent with each other'.

[21] Suppose the spatiotemporalist admitted no primitive relations other than spatiotemporal ones. Then compresence could be replaced in ideology with spatiotemporal locutions, and spatiotemporal relations could be dropped from ontology. Instead of saying '*being five feet from* is compresent with (F, G and H; I, J and K)', one would say instead 'F, G and H are five feet from I, J and K'. Cover and O'Leary-Hawthorne ('A World of Universals') defend spatiotemporalism but take yet another approach: they drop compresence from ideology in favour of instantiation, and say that properties instantiate spatiotemporal relations (and perhaps a select few others, such as nomic necessitation).

ness sake, let R be the spatial relation *being five feet from*, and suppose the objects are linearly arranged as follows (ignoring time):

	F	G	H			F	G	G	H
		b							
w_{3a}:	*a*	=*c*	*d*		w_{4a}:	*a*	*b*	*c*	*d*
	$\leftarrow 5' \rightarrow	\leftarrow 5' \rightarrow	$			$\leftarrow 5' \rightarrow	\leftarrow 5' \rightarrow	\leftarrow 5' \rightarrow	$

Then it will be true only in w_{3a} that *being ten feet from* is compresent with (F; H), and it will be true only in w_{4a} that *being fifteen feet from* is compresent with (F; H). The spatiotemporalist thus claims that if R in the abstract descriptions of w_3 and w_4 is a spatial relation, then the worlds are impossible since spatial relations are pervasive. It cannot be that *only* R holds in these cases; other spatial relations *must* hold. Once this is taken into account, w_3 and w_4 become w_{3a} and w_{4a}, which can be distinguished.

At first glance, spatiotemporalism does not answer the objection when R is not spatiotemporal. Let R in w_3 and w_4 be a relation that is not pervasive in the way spatiotemporal relations are. The spatiotemporalist will insist that *some* spatiotemporal relations must hold. If the worlds are to remain indistinguishable by the bundle theorist then the same facts of compresence involving spatiotemporal relations must hold. Since *b* and *c* are identical in w_3, they must be spatiotemporally indistinguishable from each other in w_4; this may be achieved by letting them be spatiotemporally coincident. The resulting worlds, call them w_{3b} and w_{4b}, cannot be distinguished. For concreteness sake: suppose that in w_{3b}, *a* is F and is five feet from and bears relation R to *b*, which is G; then another five feet in the same direction we have another object, *d*, which is H, and such that *b* bears R to *d*. In w_{4b}, *a* is F and is five feet from and bears R to *b*, which is G; but in exactly the same place as *b* there is another G-thing, *c*. Object *d* is located exactly as before, and is H as before; but now it is *c* that bears R to *d*; *b* does *not* bear R to *d*:

	F	G	H			F	G	H
							a - R - *b*	
w_{3b}:	*a* - R - *b* - R - *d*				w_{4b}:		≠*c* - R - *d*	
	$\leftarrow 5' \rightarrow	\leftarrow 5' \rightarrow |$				$\leftarrow 5' \rightarrow	\leftarrow 5' \rightarrow |$

These worlds cannot be distinguished, for the facts of compresence involving spatial relations are the same in the two worlds, and in each case, R is compresent with (F; G), and R is compresent with (G; H). Pressure towards complex locutions like (*), and thus towards holism, has apparently returned.

But it would be in the spirit of spatiotemporalism to reject any genuine difference between these worlds. Since our concept of possibility is inherently spatiotemporal, and w_{3b} and w_{4b} have the same spatiotemporal distribution of universals (in some suitable sense), they are not genuinely different possibilities.

Thus, some of the bundle theory's restrictions on possibility can be accepted, and some holism thereby avoided. The limitation of possibilities to spatiotemporal possibilities will seem overly narrow to some, but at least the limitation is principled. However, other cases reintroduce the need for linkage. First, recall a case considered above:

$$F \overset{R}{\underset{S}{\underset{\rightarrow}{\rightarrow}}} F \qquad \text{vs.} \qquad F \overset{R}{\underset{S}{\underset{\rightarrow}{\leftarrow}}} F$$

In each case R and S hold between, as we would ordinarily say, a pair of objects that are F; in the first they hold in the same direction whereas in the second they hold in opposite directions. We pointed out that the cases have the same description: in each R is compresent with (F; F), and S is compresent with (F; F). To make the example acceptable to the spatiotemporalist, the cases must become spatiotemporal; so let the Fs in each case be spatiotemporally similar (separated by one foot in each case, say). Let R and S be non-spatiotemporal relations, holding as before. Then the cases still have the same description, but nevertheless seem distinct (even the spatiotemporalist ought to admit this, since the cases involve different spatiotemporal distributions of R and S).[22] The spatiotemporalist might be willing to reject the existence of R and S, perhaps by making the very strong claim that there can be no polyadic universals other than the spatiotemporal ones. Otherwise even the spatiotemporalist needs linkage.

Second, consider two cases, each involving an infinite line of F-things spaced evenly five feet apart. In the first case the line has a beginning whereas in the second the line is infinite in each direction. These in essence are the cases considered above:

One-way infinite series: F-R-F-R-F-R-F-R-F-...
Two-way infinite series: ...-F-R-F-R-F-R-F-R-F-...

in which relation R is taken to be *being five feet from*. The spatiotemporalist has no principled reason to refuse to distinguish these cases since they involve distinct spatiotemporal structures. But they share the same facts of compresence. In each case we have '*being five feet from* is compresent with (F; F)', '*being ten feet from* is compresent with (F; F)', and so on. The spatiotemporalist then faces the same choices as the bundle theorist: live with an unintuitive limitation on possibility, or accept linkage, and so holism.

3 SPACETIME RELATIONALISM

Spacetime relationalists deny the existence of spatiotemporal locations (or perhaps say that spatiotemporal locations are constructs of some sort, as opposed to *sui generis entities*). We will discuss a *pure* relationalist, who admits nothing whatsoever playing

---

[22] Another example, this time involving asymmetric relations; let each of the following cases involve three Fs spatially arranged in the same way:

$$F \leftarrow R \rightarrow F \leftarrow S \rightarrow F \qquad \text{vs.} \qquad F \overset{\leftarrow R \rightarrow}{\underset{\leftarrow S \rightarrow}{}} F \qquad F$$

the role of spacetime locations. Not only are *points* renounced; other spatiotemporally local entities such as temporal parts (whether arbitrarily small or instantaneous), events, and the like, are renounced as well. An especially pure spatiotemporal relationalist would not even admit *spatially* local entities, and so would reject the existence of arbitrarily small or point-like spatial parts. The world would thus contain spatially as well as temporally extended mereological atoms. Our relationalist is only temporally pure: while temporal parts are prohibited, spatial parts are allowed. (Discussion of the spatially and temporally pure relationalist would parallel what follows, but we will focus on a view more similar to currently popular views.)

Relationalism must be formulated precisely. The relationalist's ontology has no spacetime points, only enduring particulars—entities with no temporal parts—and properties and relations. (We do not here explore the combination of spacetime relationalism with the bundle theory.) The relationalist's ideology requires extensive discussion. The temporal facts must be described without invoking temporal locations. These temporal facts concern (i) qualitative change and (ii) relative temporal location.

Most who reject spacetime points have an easier time than our relationalist, for though they reject one sort of spatiotemporally local entity, they accept another: temporal parts.[23] Given temporal parts, the facts about relative temporal location emerge from the holding of binary temporal relations between temporal parts, relations such as *simultaneity* and *being n units after* for various *n* (we ignore the theory of relativity throughout). Enduring objects have temporal extent, and so stand in more complex temporal relations. Suppose one enduring object lasts from 1950 to 1970, whereas another lasts from 1960 to 1965; are the two objects simultaneous? Is one after the other? Neither description seems quite right: a new vocabulary is called for.[24]

Given temporal parts, the facts about qualitative change emerge from the intrinsic properties instantiated by the temporal parts of continuing things. A person changes from being short to being tall by having an earlier temporal part that instantiates *shortness* and a later one that instantiates *tallness*.[25] Those who reject temporal parts usually say instead that the person instantiates *shortness at* one time while instantiating *tallness at* a later time.[26] But this talk of instantiation *at* times presupposes the

---

[23] See Michael Friedman, *Foundations of Space-Time Theories* (Princeton: Princeton University Press, 1983), chapter VI, and Brent Mundy, 'Relational Theories of Euclidean Space and Minkowski Space-Time', *Philosophy of Science* 50 (1983): 205–226. Even Leibniz does not count as a pure temporal relationalist, given his acceptance of accidents.

[24] See Russell's (*op. cit.* pp. 122–127) temporal relationalism based on non-instantaneous temporal relata. Russell's relata—events—have temporal parts, which makes his task easier than the pure relationalist's.

[25] This presupposes the usual view that continuants are aggregates of temporal parts, but see Theodore Sider, 'All the World's a Stage', *Australasian Journal of Philosophy* 74 (1996): 433–453 and *Four-Dimensionalism*, chapter 5.

[26] Except for presentists (see Mark Hinchliff, 'The puzzle of change', in J. Tomberlin, ed., *Philosophical Perspectives, 10, Metaphysics* (Cambridge, MA: Blackwell, 1996) and Trenton Merricks 'Endurance and indiscernibility', *Journal of Philosophy* 91 (1994): 165–184). Interestingly, presentists avoid the difficulties considered here: the notion of the present, together with the metrical tense operators (e.g. 'it was the case 20 minutes ago that'), let the presentist in effect speak of properties had at particular instants of time. Our target relationalist is not a presentist.

existence of times. Our relationalist accepts neither temporal parts nor times, and so can make use of neither strategy for characterizing change.

The following strategy solves both problems at once. The usual notion of instantiation is expressed this way, given temporal parts:

x instantiates property F
x and y instantiate relation R

or this way, if temporal parts are rejected:

x instantiates F at t
x and y instantiate relation R at t (single-time relation)
x and y instantiate relation R at t, t' (cross time relation —'x as it is at
    t bears R to y as it is at t')

Instead, let the relationalist's ideology include notions expressed thus:

x instantiates F n units of time after/before
    y instantiates G
x instantiates F n units of time after/before   (single-time relation)
    y and z stand in R
x bears R to y n units of time hence/earlier   (cross-time relation)

These locutions are primitive, but may be clarified by saying how a substantivalist would interpret them:[27]

x instantiates F n units of time after/before y instantiates G :
    There exist times, t and t', such that t' is n units of time after/before t, x
    instantiates F at t', and y instantiates G at t

x instantiates F n units of time after/before y and z stand in R :
    There exist times, t and t', such that t' is n units of time after/before t, x
    instantiates F at t', and y and z stand in R at t

x bears R to y n units of time hence/earlier :
    There exist times, t and t', such that t' is n units of time after/before t,
    and x and y stand in R at t, t'

An example. In a situation in which object a is F for five minutes, then is G for another five minutes, the following statements would be true:

a is F one minute before a is F
a is F two minutes before a is F
a is F three minutes before a is F
a is F four minutes before a is F
a is F five minutes before a is F
a is G one minute before a is G

---

[27] A substantivalist who rejects temporal parts, that is.

a is G two minutes before *a* is G
a is G three minutes before *a* is G
a is G four minutes before *a* is G
a is G five minutes before *a* is G
a is F one minute before *a* is G
a is F two minutes before *a* is G
.
.
.

a is F ten minutes before *a* is G

Thus qualitative change can be characterized on this view.

Facts of relative temporal location also emerge from the facts stateable in this language. Certain properties and relations are *existence-entailing*. As a substantivalist would say, if an object has a certain mass at a time, then the object must exist then. If two objects are ten feet apart from each other at a time, then each must exist at that time. If *x* as it is at *t* causally affects *y* as it is at *t'*, then *x* must exist at *t* and *y* must exist at *t'*. (Some say that all properties and relations are existence-entailing, others that some properties, e.g. *being famous*, are not.) At any time a thing exists, it must surely have some existence-entailing property then, or stand in some existence-entailing relation then (whether cross-time or no). So the totality of facts about the instantiation of existence-entailing properties and relations fixes the relative temporal locations of all objects.

4 SPACETIME RELATIONALISM AND POSSIBILITY[28]

The bundle theory collapsed possibilities involving indiscernible things. In the simplest case, a world containing a single F-thing was identified with a world containing two F-things. The relationalist theory has analogous consequences. Contrast a world containing just a single time, at which a thing, *a*, is F, with a second world that contains two disconnected times—two times neither of which is any temporal distance from the other—such that *a* is F at each. The relationalist will describe each as a case in which *a* is F zero units before *a* is F. Relationalism does indeed preclude a distinction between these worlds, but relationalists may well be happy to deny that the second world is a genuine possibility.[29]

---

[28] This section shows that some temporally local entities should be postulated. One of us sees in this the starting point of an argument for temporal parts, on the grounds that the postulation of further enduring things would be ontologically redundant. See Sider, *Four-Dimensionalism*, chapter 4, section 8.

[29] Compare the disconnected spacetimes objection to modal realism discussed in Lewis, *Plurality*, pp. 71–73.

A slightly more complicated example of indiscernible objects was that of worlds w_1 and w_2:

$$w_1: \quad \overset{\text{R}}{\underset{\text{F}}{\overset{\frown}{\bullet}}} \qquad\qquad w_2: \quad \underset{\text{F}}{\bullet}\leftarrow \text{R} \rightarrow \underset{\text{F}}{\bullet}$$

But the analogous temporal case looks even less plausibly possible: w_1 contains a single time bearing temporal relation R to itself, and a is F at that time, whereas in w_2 two distinct times stand in R, and are such that a is F at each. But if R is simultaneity then the second world involves two distinct simultaneous times, whereas if R is, say, *being three minutes apart* then the first world consists of a single time that is three minutes apart from itself. Either way, one of the alleged possible worlds seems impossible.

A somewhat more plausible example of this sort involves circular time. Compare a world with two-way infinite linear time containing a single thing, a, that is F at each moment, with a world with circular time, in which a is again F at each moment. In the two-way infinite world, a is F n units before a is F, for any n. But the same is true in the circular world, for one can simply travel around the circle again and again until n units has elapsed. (One might argue that 'a is F n units before a is F' is true in the circular world only when n is less than the temporal circumference of the circle; perhaps so, but then the circular world cannot be distinguished from a world with a finite timeline of temporal length n.) These limitations concerning circular time constitute the most serious analog of the bundle theorist's limitations with indiscernible individuals. But it would take a bold metaphysician indeed to rest the case against relationalism solely on the belief in circular time as a distinctive possibility.

Other modal objections to the bundle theory carry over better. The relationalist's facts of property instantiation do not capture 'linkages' between distinct property instantiations. Suppose that a is F for an instant, then five minutes later is G for an instant, and then five minutes after that is F again for an instant:

$$w_5: \quad \underset{\text{F}a}{\bullet} \qquad \underset{\text{G}a}{\bullet} \qquad \underset{\text{F}a}{\bullet}$$

The relationalist will describe w_5 thus:

> a is F five minutes before a is G

and

> a is G five minutes before a is F

But, intuitively, this leaves out the fact that the case of a's being G mentioned in the second sentence is the very same as the case of a's being G mentioned in the first sentence.

One might worry that w_5 will be identified with another world in which a is F for an instant, then five minutes later is G for another instant; then, much later (say, 30 minutes later) is G for an instant, and then is F for an instant, five minutes after that:

$$w_6: \quad \bullet \qquad \bullet \qquad \leftarrow 30 \text{ mins.} \rightarrow \qquad \bullet \qquad \bullet$$
$$\qquad\quad Fa \qquad Ga \qquad\qquad\qquad\qquad Ga \qquad Fa$$

In fact, this is incorrect. The two sentences mentioned above are indeed true in each case; but further sentences distinguish the cases. For example, only in w_6 is it true that a is F 35 minutes after a is G. The pervasive character of the temporal relations makes the objector's work harder than with the bundle theory: in moving to w_6, the second case of a being G must be added to the timeline somewhere; that then adds temporal facts that distinguish the worlds.[30] Relationalism is analogous in this way to the spatiotemporalist version of the bundle theory considered above.

The victory is short-lived: more complicated worlds are identified by the relationalist theory. Suppose that world w_7 contains a single object, a, which is F for an instant, then a minute later becomes F and remains F for a minute; world w_8 also contains only a, which is F for 2 minutes solid:

$$w_7: \quad \bullet \qquad\qquad \rule{2cm}{6pt}$$
$$\qquad\quad Fa \qquad\qquad\qquad Fa$$
$$w_8: \quad \rule{4cm}{6pt}$$
$$\qquad\qquad\qquad Fa$$

(Let a exist, and have property G at all other times, in each case.) These worlds do have the same relationalist description. For each n between 0 and 2, it will be true in each world that a is F n minutes before a is F. In w_7, for values of n between 0 and 1 these statements are made true by the one-minute-long stretch of Fa; when n is between 1 and 2 the statements are made true by the single instant of Fa and various points of the one-minute stretch.[31]

What is left out of the description is linkage. Only in w_8 is there, for example, an instant of Fa followed 45 seconds later by an instant of Fa *which in turn* is followed 45 seconds later by another instant of Fa. That is, the very same case of Fa that precedes the final case by 45 seconds occurs 45 seconds after the first case. Talk of 'cases', though, is forbidden fruit: a 'case of Fa' would be either a temporally local event, or a temporal part, or an instant of time at which a is F. Can linkage be made acceptable?

Following our bundle theorist, the relationalist might complicate her ideology with new notions of instantiation, for example:

(**) a is F 45 seconds before a is F, then a is F 45 seconds after that

---

[30] One could stipulate that (i) the first and third times in world w_5 are temporally disconnected (despite each being temporally related to the second time), and that (ii) the third and fourth times in w_6 are temporally disconnected from the first two. But then the cases are not at all pre-theoretically possible.

[31] Though we continue to assume sparse universals, adding negative universals would not help: in each case, for example, a is $\sim$F ten seconds after a is F (remember that a continues to exist in w_8 after the two-minute long stretch of being F).

(More carefully, following the notation of section 2: '*a* is F 45 seconds before *a* is F|α; *a* is F 45 seconds after α'; we henceforth revert to informal notation.) (**) is to be true in w_8 but not w_7, and is therefore not reducible to the old 'binary' statements of the form ⌜ϕ *n* units before ψ⌝, since those statements do not distinguish w_7 from w_8. While it may appear that the word 'that' in (**) is a referring expression, referring to the second 'case' of *a*'s being F, the relationalist would claim that the sentence actually just makes a complicated statement about *a* and F, the general form of which is:

(***) predication(x, F_1, n, y, F_2, m, z, F_3)

where x, y, and z are particulars, F_1, F_2 and F_3 are properties, and n and m are numbers representing temporal separation in some chosen unit.

The relationalist cannot stop with (***). Consider two worlds, w_9 and w_{10} with discrete time, each containing a single thing, *a*, that has always been red in the past, and then at some point in time begins to alternate between red and blue. In w_9 the alternation looks like this: BRBBRRBBBBRRRBBBBRRRR... In w_{10}, the first two alternations are swapped: BBRRBRBBBBRRRBBBBRRRR... These worlds *can* be distinguished using a 'four-place' locution—'*a* is blue one instant before *a* is red, then *a* is blue one instant after that, then *a* is blue two instants after that' is true only in w_{10}—but not by the three-place locution (***). Neither will the relationalist want to stop with four-place locutions. New irreducible locutions corresponding to all the possible temporal patterns of instantiation of properties will be introduced, for example:

> *a* is F 1 minute before *b* is G, then *c* is H 3 minutes after that, then *d* is I 2 minutes after that.

> *a* is F 1 minute before *b* is G, then *c* is H 3 minutes after that, then *d* is I 2 minutes after that, then *e* is J 5 minutes after that.

> etc.

None of these forms will be reducible to conjunctions of simpler ones, for the same reason that (**) needed to be irreducible to binary statements: there is no way to link the property instances attributed by multiple simpler statements without appealing to temporally local entities.

As before, this results in holism: the world cannot be described as the sum total of simple facts, since the complex does not supervene on the simple. As before, the theory's ideology contains infinitely many distinct primitive notions.[32] Each consequence offends against the metaphysical aesthetic.

(A related ugliness may afflict even the unmodified relationalist theory. As mentioned, substantivalists about time who reject temporal parts say that objects have properties *at* times. David Lewis objects that this turns properties into relations.

---

[32] Might a single sentence operator ⌜ϕ *n* units before ψ⌝, capable of iteration (as in ⌜ϕ *n* units before ψ *m* units before χ⌝) replace the infinity of primitive locutions? This operator handles only ascriptions of properties and single-time relations; cross-time relations are more complex. But tricks like those mentioned in note 16 might well suffice.

Surely a certain metal bar is *just plain straight*, whereas the substantivalist endurantist must say that it is straight *at*, or with respect to, a time.[33] The relationalist theory also seems to turn properties into relations—in fact, relations to other *objects*. The bar's straightness is expressed in sentences of the form: ⌜the bar is straight *n* units of time after ϕ⌝, in which ϕ may mention other things. In *some* cases ϕ will mention only the bar, for example statements of the form 'the bar is straight *n* units after the bar is F' and 'the bar is straight 0 units after the bar is straight'. But all such statements equally well express the bar's straightness.)

Unless the enhanced ideology includes infinitary notions, the relationalist theory still conflates intuitively distinct possibilities. Suppose that in one world a certain light comes into existence at some time, and flashes red and blue every minute forever after, whereas in a second world it has existed forever and will continue to exist forever, flashing red and blue as before. Statements such as:

> the light is red one minute before it is blue,
> the light is red one minute before it is blue, then is red one minute after that
> the light is red one minute before it is blue, then is red one minute after that, then blue one minute after that
> the light is red one minute before it is blue, then is red one minute after that, then blue one minute after that, then red one minute after that
> etc.

will not distinguish the worlds; the following infinitary sentence is needed:

> ... the light is red one minute after that, then blue one minute after that, then red one minute after that, then blue one minute after that ...

As with the bundle theorist's infinitary locution, this sentence is irreducible to finite sentences; the predicational form:[34]

> ... then one minute after that, ϕ_{-1}, then one minute after that, ϕ_0, then one minute after that ϕ_1, then one minute after that ...

cannot be reduced to finite forms.

This epicycle recapitulates our theme. Bundle theorist and temporal relationalist alike purchase the modal differences we want with unfamiliar irreducible locutions. The cost is an unsightly ideology, and a holism unworthy of the name metaphysics.[35]

---

[33] Lewis, *Plurality*, pp. 202–204. See also Sider, *Four-Dimensionalism*, chapter 4, section 6.

[34] This form cannot distinguish a single two-way infinite time line from a pair of two-way infinite time lines laid end to end, but if these really are distinct possibilities then perhaps an infinite locution with an analogous structure will distinguish them. And handling these discrete cases is not the end of the story; the relationalist must introduce means to define such notions as temporal density, continuity, and the like.

[35] It is perhaps unduly harsh to withhold the label metaphysics from Parmenides, Hegel, Bradley, and some distinguished contemporaries. When arguments are lacking, rhetoric is called for. The lack of arguments is no fault of Tamar Szabó Gendler, Gilbert Harman, Brian Weatherson, and Dean Zimmerman, whom we thank for their helpful comments.

3

Plenitude, Convention, and Ontology[1]

[1] I am grateful to Tamar Gendler and Ted Sider for comments on an earlier draft of this paper, and to Cian Dorr, David Manley, and Timothy Williamson for helpful discussions.

1

I bring a watch to a watchmaker, who dismantles it. Two communities look on. When I go back to the watchmaker the following week members of one community say 'He is picking up his old watch', while members of the other say 'He is picking up a new watch, one made of the same pieces that his old watch was made from'. Which of them is correct? Many of us are inclined toward reconciliation, unable to take very seriously the thought that one of the communities is ontologically more attuned than the other. But there are different ways of justifying such an attitude. In what follows I shall compare and contrast two such ways.

Let me begin by briefly describing the two approaches I have in mind. One approach is that of the *Plenitude Lover*. According to this view, there are ever so many objects in the world, including many that are undreamt of in ordinary thought and talk.[2] Cars exist. But so do Eli Hirsh's In-Cars[3], where an In-Car is constituted by the presence of a car in a garage, shrinking gradually as that car leaves the garage, and passing out of existence when the car finally emerges. Tables exist and survive a change of colour. But when a table is painted, there is an object that up until that point is materially coincident with the table, but which is unable to survive a change of colour and so passes out of existence. And so on. Generalizing: let a *modal occupation profile* be a function from worlds to filled regions of space-time. The Plenitude Lover says that for every such profile there is an object whose modal pattern of spatiotemporal occupation is correctly described by that profile.

What of the original case? There was an object—call it a watch$_1$—that was on my wrist when I went to the watchmaker and that was given back to me after repairs were performed.[4] There was another object—call it a watch$_2$—that was on my wrist when I went to the watchmaker but which permanently passed out of existence when dismantled.[5] The watch$_1$ and the watch$_2$ were spatially and mereologically coincident

[2] That is not to say that they never fall within the domain of ordinary quantifiers.

[3] See Eli Hirsh, 'Physical Identity', *Philosophical Review* 85 (1976), p. 361.

[4] Of course, given Plenitude, there are many objects that survived dismantling and that were coincident during the relevant period (and even coincident during their entire actual world history). The Plenitude Lover will deploy her favourite theory of vagueness here.

[5] Those who think that every object is eternal and necessary can read 'existence' as 'concrete existence'. Cf. Timothy Williamson, 'Necessary Existents', in *Logic, Thought, and Language* (Cambridge: Cambridge University Press, 2002).

for a period of time, but were numerically distinct throughout. (Identity is not contingent or relative.) With this ontology in place, it is easy enough to reconcile our two communities: one means watch$_1$ by 'watch', the other watch$_2$ by 'watch'. Given their subject matter, both communities are correct. A plenitudinous background is important of course: it gives each community something to talk about veridically.

A second approach is that of the *Convention Lover*.[6] On this account, the key to reconciliation is that each community attaches a different meaning to 'there is': there is no semantic value—The Existential Quantifier—that is the common property of the two linguistic communities with which I began. Given what the first community means by 'there is', 'something', and related determiner phrases, it is correct for its members to say 'There is something (namely a watch) that was present at delivery and after pick-up'. But the meanings of 'there is' and 'something' in the second community's mouth prohibit any speech of that sort; hence their alternative speeches. On this picture, reconciliation is achieved by ascribing different linguistic conventions to the use of expressions that play quantifier roles in each language. We shall elaborate further on these ideas in due course.

2

To sharpen the debate, let us focus on a toy example. A world contains two angels, Gabriel and Michael. Gabriel says 'Only two objects exist, myself and Michael'. Michael says 'Three objects exist, Gabriel, myself, and the fusion of Gabriel and myself.' Let us consider their speeches from the perspectives of the Plentitude Lover and the Convention Lover.

Begin with the Plentitude Lover. From her perspective there are two candidate construals of Gabriel's remarks.[7] She might reckon Gabriel's speech false; or she might reckon Gabriel's speech as employing restricted quantification. Indeed, she will likely suggest that the toy example is underdescribed. *Timid Gabriel* uses domain restriction and says something true with the words 'There are only two objects', since the domain of his quantifier is restricted to exclude fusions. *Bold Gabriel* uses unrestricted quantification and says something false with those words.

---

[6] My Convention Lover is based upon Eli Hirsch's writings. See *Dividing Reality* (Oxford University Press, 1993), 'Quantifier Variance and Realism' in *Philosophical Issues* 12 (2002), 51–73 and 'Physical-Object Ontology, Verbal Disputes, and Common Sense,' in *Philosophy and Phenomenological Research*, Jan 2005, 67–97. I do not, however, claim a perfect match. (Private correspondence has made me even more cautious.) Hirsch has in turn been influenced by the writings of Rudolph Carnap (see especially 'Empiricism, Semantics and Ontology' in *Meaning and Necessity*, 2nd edition (University of Chicago Press, 1956), and Hilary Putnam (see, for example, *Reason, Truth and History* (Cambridge University Press, 1981), 'The Question of Realism' in *Words and Life* (Harvard University Press, 1994))).

[7] Indeed, the Plentitude lover will think there are *many* fusions of Michael and Gabriel, each with distinctive persistence conditions and/or modal profiles. (She will have no sympathy with the unique fusion axiom of standard mereology.) She will therefore worry about Michael's use of 'the fusion'. But for the purposes of this toy example, I shall put this to one side, since it is not important to the points that I wish to make. I also shall not fuss about the fact that unless 'object' is restricted in some way, there will certainly be more than three objects in any such world on account of the existence of events (thought episodes and so on).

Does Michael have extra expressive power *vis-à-vis* Timid Gabriel? To answer this requires a bit of terminology. Note that Timid Gabriel's quantifier has thus far been characterized only extensionally: the actual domain of that quantifier is the set of angels. But that doesn't tell us how to evaluate the sentence 'There are exactly two objects' relative to a given possible world. Suppose, for example, that a world contained two mindless atoms. Is Timid Gabriel's sentence false or true at that world? Perhaps false, if the domain of the quantifier is intensionally restricted to angels; perhaps true, if it is intensionally restricted to things without proper parts. To make our question answerable, let us assume the latter. (Let us also assume that in every possible world everything is composed of simples without proper parts).[8]

Two sentences are *intensionally* equivalent when they are true in exactly the same possible circumstances. Let us say that a language L1 has more *possibility-expressing power* than a language L2 just in case there is some set of worlds that provides the truth conditions of some sentence in L1 but not L2 (and not vice versa).

While the case is admittedly still underdescribed, it seems eminently possible to flesh out our description of Michael's and Timid Gabriel's languages in such a way that Timid Gabriel's language has no less possibility-expressing power than Michael's (assuming that Timid Gabriel's language had a sufficient stock of suitable predicates, plural quantifiers and so on).[9] On some such elaboration, the contrast between Michael's and Timid Gabriel's language would be in this respect disanalogous to the contrast between a rich physical vocabulary and one unable to mark presence or absence of, say, certain fundamental physical properties. Whereas the latter pair would not have equal possibility-expressing power, the former would.

Our intuitive notions of expressive power cannot be cashed out simply in terms of possibility expressing power. Epistemic possibilities may have no metaphysical possibility corresponding to them, and distinct epistemic possibilities may correspond to the same metaphysical possibility. Fancy mathematics has in some good sense more expressive power than baby arithmetic—but the extra expressive power is not

---

[8] Note that the notion of 'proper part' needs to be treated with care by someone who believes in Plenitude. If a proper part of *x* is a part of *x* that is not identical to *x*, then there are no simples (according to the Plenitude Lover), since every purported simple will be mereologically coincident with sundry objects that differ with respect to their modal profiles. For current purposes, think of a proper part of *x* as some *y* that is part of *x* and is such that there is some *z* that is part of *x* that does not overlap *y*.

[9] Note the importance of the assumption that every possible thing is a simple or composed out of simples. Suppose there is a possible world with atomless gunk. If Gabriel's quantifiers are intensionally restricted to simples, there is in that case no sentence in Gabriel's mouth that is intensionally equivalent to the sentence 'There are at least three things' in Michael's mouth. (We could of course imagine that 'there is' in Gabriel's mouth is restricted to simples in any world where everything is composed of simples, and unrestricted otherwise, though Gabriel had better not then say 'Necessarily nothing has proper parts'.) Michael's language would also enjoy greater possibility expressing power if it were contingent whether or not sets of things had fusions. If it that were so, then 'There are three things' in Michael's mouth would again divide possibilities in a way that Gabriel's language cannot. Equations of possibility-expressing power cannot be made in a metaphysical vacuum. Essay 12 raises, in effect, a further worry for the claim that Timid Gabriel's language has equal possibility-expressing power: what if the singular truths about composite objects do not supervene on the truths about simples?

a matter of having more possibility expressing power. In general, where epistemic progress depends upon the discovery of necessary truths, the epistemic progress cannot be characterized in terms of possibility expressiveness.

We have concepts of synonymy, expressing the same thought, and so on, with which intuitive notions of expressive power are bound up. Let us say that a theory is *hyperintensionally more expressive* than another if the former can express thoughts that the latter cannot, but not vice versa.[10] The notion is only as clear as the notion of 'same thought', but since the latter is reasonably serviceable, so is the current notion of expressive power.

It is natural for the Plenitude Lover to suppose than Michael has a thought—an 'insight'—that is expressed by 'There are three objects'. This thought flows from another thought that Michael believes necessarily true, expressed by 'Whenever there are two objects there is a fusion of them'. While Timid Gabriel lacks the resources to express that thought, Bold Gabriel has the resources to express it: he merely lacks the epistemic wherewithal to recognize that it is true. Bold Gabriel makes mistakes; Timid Gabriel, while making no mistakes, is hyperintensionally overpowered by Michael.

What will the Convention Lover make of Gabriel and Michael? The Convention Lover will insist that there are two possible meanings for 'something' in play. We might use different styles of variables in order to try to perspicuously describe what is going on by the Convention Lover's lights. What we have are two languages. Let us use '$\exists_m$', 'x_m', 'y_m', and 'z_m' to stand in for the existential quantifier and variables that are in use in Michael's language and '$\exists_g$', 'x_g', 'y_g', 'z_g' for those in Gabriel's language. At the world described by the toy example,

$$\exists_m x_m \exists_m y_m \exists_m z_m (\sim x_m = y_m \ \& \ \sim y_m = z_m \ \& \ \sim x_m = z_m)$$

is true, but

$$\exists_g x_g \exists_g y_g \exists_g z_g (\sim x_g = y_g \ \& \ \sim y_g = z_g \ \& \ \sim x_g = z_g)$$

is false.

What if someone—an 'ontologist'–comes along and asks 'But what is there *really*, two objects or three?' The Convention Lover considers the ontologist to be guilty of semantic indecision: he has failed to decide whether 'object' and 'there is' are to be tied to '$\exists_g$' or to '$\exists_m$'. She will consider the ontologist's refusal to recognize this indecision as flowing from false presuppositions about the questions that he is asking and about the kinds of meanings that are available.

It is important to notice that the Convention Lover need not eschew the intuitive notions of intensional and hyperintensional expressibility. My imagined Convention Lover agrees that Gabriel's and Michael's languages are equivalent in possibility expressing power. For example, the possibility expressed by '$\exists_m x_m \exists_m y_m \exists_m z_m$ ($\sim x_m = y_m \ \& \ \sim y_m = z_m \ \& \ \sim x_m = z_m$)' is the very possibility that is expressed by

---

[10] For current purposes, the Plenitude Lover might adopt something like the method for individuating thoughts implicit in standard semantics, according to which a thought is determined not simply by its modal profile (the set of worlds at which it is true), but the semantic tree of intensions via which its modal profile is determined. (This is not to deny that for certain other purposes we are interested in even more fine-grained notions.)

'$\exists_g x_g \exists_g y_g \, (\sim x_g = y_g)$'. But that is just to say that he reckons the pair to be intensionally equivalent.

What of hyperintensional expressibility? Here it is natural for the Convention Lover to claim symmetry: neither angel can express the thoughts of the other—since each angel uses quantifiers with distinctive meanings. Thus, if we are users of one of the languages and encounter a user of the other, we shouldn't hope for hyperintensionally satisfying translations; the best we can do is to aim for intension-preserving translations.[11]

It should be noted—and this will be important later—that the Convention Lover that I am interested in deploys a transcendent rather than an immanent truth predicate.[12] A language L that contains its own truth predicate deploys an *immanent truth predicate* iff the extension of that predicate includes only sentences that are hyperintensionally equivalent to sentences of L. A truth predicate is *transcendent* iff it is not immanent. Our Convention Lover allows Michael to deploy a truth predicate that can apply to sentences of Gabriel's language and, relatedly to make claims of intensional equivalence between sentences in his language and sentences in Gabriel's. So Michael's truth predicate is a transcendent one.

Is there any great ideological difference between the Plenitude Lover and the Convention Lover? *Prima facie*, the difference may seem minimal. For compare on the one hand, the pair Timid Gabriel and Michael, as depicted by the Plenitude Lover with the pair Gabriel and Michael, as depicted by the Convention Lover. In each case, intensional equivalence between the respective theories was claimed. So that does not separate the perspectives. Nor are the perspectives cleanly separated by the issue of whether the existential quantifier is univocal across the angels. After all, there is a good sense in which the quantifier has varying meaning, even from the perspective of the Plenitude Lover. For he admits that one quantifier has a different domain than the other (an extensional difference) and more generally a different domain relative to this or that world of evaluation (an intensional difference).[13] Nor is there a difference grounded in the fact that for the Plenitude Lover, Michael can say 'There are things that I talk about that Timid Gabriel is in no position to talk about.' For the Convention Lover will permit Michael to say '$\exists_m x_m$ I talk about x_m and Gabriel does not talk about x_m'.

Nonetheless, there are important ways in which the two views differ, and in the next few sections, I will explore three potential contrasts between them.[14] First

---

[11] Of course, if some such intension preserving translation became sufficiently internalized and familiar, it would in addition come to have the *feel* of being *a priori* correct.

[12] Note that Quine and Carnap preferred immanent truth predicates. My Convention Lover, like Hirsch, does not balk at ascribing truth to utterances made using what he regards as alien determiners.

[13] Granted, some may be inclined to call this 'context dependence' rather than flat out 'ambiguity'.

[14] There are other potential disanalogies that lie beyond the scope of this paper. Notice, in particular, that not every dispute can be resolved by an appeal to plenitude. Consider debates about the domain of abstracta; or about whether actual concrete objects would exist in worlds where they do not occupy any region of space time; or about whether there are multiple objects with the same

(section 3), I will consider the issue of Bold Gabriel. Recall that the Plenitude Lover is quite happy to admit the possibility of such a character, claiming that Bold Gabriel is simply making ontological mistakes. Admit that as a serious possibility and, as Michael, one can reasonably think one has made real epistemic progress, since a real epistemic risk—that of being like Bold Gabriel—has been averted. On such a picture it would be natural to think of one's commitment to a plenitudinous ontology as encoding something of a 'deep' metaphysical insight.

Second (section 4), I shall turn to the question of hyperintensional expressibility: here, the Plenitude Lover claims asymmetry between Michael and Gabriel (at least on the version of Gabriel that was speaking the truth), whereas the Convention Lover claims symmetry.

Finally (section 5), I shall turn at length to the matter of analyticity. The Plenitude Lover's sense of real epistemic progress is based, at least in part, on a conviction that the claims of plenitude in her mouth encode no mere analytic truths. The Convention Lover, meanwhile, may choose to pay lip service to a plenitudinous ontology, but will adopt a self-conception according to which its central claims are analytic.

3

Consider Bold Gabriel from the perspective of the Plenitude Lover. What is it that justifies one in thinking that when Bold Gabriel says: 'Only two objects exist, myself and Michael,' the domain of his quantifiers includes fusions (rendering his utterance false) rather than excluding fusions (rendering his utterance true)? After all, wouldn't it be more *charitable* to interpret someone who is allegedly bold as timid?

One answer to this kind of worry might make appeal to Ted Sider's suggestion (following David Lewis) that semantic value is determined by use plus naturalness (or 'eligibility').[15] Following this suggestion, let us suppose that an omniscient interpreter will, on the one hand, try to assign semantic values in a way that fits use, and, on the other, try to assign natural rather than unnatural properties as the semantic value of predicates. When these desiderata conflict—an interpretation that best fits use[16] may score poorly on 'naturalness'—the right interpretation will be the one that does suitable justice to both desiderata. (Of course, there may be borderline cases.)

modal profile; or about whether there are objects that are spatiotemporally but not mereologically coincident; and so on. Here the Convention Lover may feel he has more to say than the Plenitude Lover (after all it is not clear what an absolutely unconstrained plenitude principle would look like). I am sceptical, but will not pursue the matter here.

[15] *Four Dimensionalism* (Oxford University Press, 2001), p. xxii: 'the world comes 'ready made' with a single domain D of objects: the class of all the objects that there are. This class is the most eligible meaning possible for any symbol playing the role of the existential quantifier.' (For ease of expression, Sider is here treating meaning extensionally. I will at times do the same.) For Lewis's presentation of the idea, see 'New Work for a Theory of Universals,' and 'Putnam's Paradox', in *Papers in Metaphysics and Epistemology* (Cambridge University Press, 1999).

[16] I shall not fuss about the details of what 'fitting use' comes to.

How might this apply to the case at hand? Clearly, the desideratum of fitting use would be better served by interpreting Bold Gabriel as if he were Timid Gabriel. But it seems *existence* is a highly natural property and, correlatively, the universal domain is a highly natural domain. So if we try to find the best compromise between the two central desiderata, then our initial semantic profile for Bold Gabriel will be correct.[17]

Some might object that the justification feels tenuous: are we so confident that existence is so natural? And even if it is, mightn't it be that the property of being a simple is also highly natural, so that the restricted domain would also score very highly on naturalness?[18,19] In what follows I shall offer a sketch that does not rely so heavily on the naturalness of the property of existence and which helps us to better understand the difference between Timid and Bold Gabriel.

What is it about Gabriel's use that puts pressure on us to describe him as Timid? The answer is clear enough. Charity recommends that Michael treat Gabriel's utterance of 'There are only two things' as having a restricted domain, for then the utterance will be true rather than false. Is there pressure from use in the other direction? Well, there isn't direct pressure: presumably, Gabriel never says 'There are three things', and never says 'Simples might compose something'. But there may be indirect pressure that comes from Gabriel's semantic thoughts about the language of others. Suppose, for example, Gabriel fully endorses the following generalization about Michael's language:

Ref:[20] Sentences of the form 'That is F' as uttered by Michael, are true only if Michael refers to something by 'that'.[21]

Since Ref comes out false on an interpretation that reckons 'something' to have a domain restricted to simples,[22] Gabriel's commitment to Ref will put considerable

---

[17] Note that strictly speaking, implementing this idea requires some extension of the Lewisian framework, since that was contrived for providing an account of the semantic values of predicates, whereas we are here envisaging generalizing the view to other semantic types. Also note that the naturalness based account of wide quantifiers need not be based exclusively on the naturalness of existence. For example, a restricted set of referents for the bare plural 'tigers' (in 'Tigers have stripes') may be less natural than the set of all tigers. But once naturalness considerations secure an unrestricted interpretation of 'tigers', then it will not do to restrict the quantifier to a domain that includes less than all the tigers, because of obvious interactions between plurals and determiners.

[18] Moreover, we cannot let the 'existence magnet' be too attractive. After all, we also want Timid Gabriel to be possible too, and if existence is too magnetic, then there is a risk that any putative Timid Gabriel will turn out semantically Bold (if, for example, we let the magnet override certain features of use, including protestations to the effect 'I only meant to be talking about simples').

[19] Of course, Gabriel might say 'I am not restricting my quantifier by fiat to simples, even though I believe it is intensionally restricted to simples.' But it would not on that score violate any feature of use to assign an intension to the quantifier that made it intensionally restricted to simples. That still might be, for all Sider has said, the best combination of eligibility and fit, in which case it would not, as Gabriel says, be merely the product of fiat that his quantifier had a quantifiers intensionally so restricted.

[20] This follows from the standard Tarskian truth definition for atomic sentences, applied to Michael's language.

[21] We may imagine, moreover, that Gabriel has no unusual views as to which sentences uttered by Michael are of the form 'That is F'.

[22] Assuming we don't wish to attach deviant interpretations to 'Michael', 'true', and so on.

pressure on us to reckon 'something' in Gabriel's mouth as unrestricted. For suppose that 'something' in Gabriel's mouth was restricted to simples but that he had a transcendent truth predicate that was true of whichever utterances were true in Michael's mouth. Then while (without her realizing it) 'true' in her mouth would be true of 'That is the fusion' as uttered by Michael (demonstrating the fusion), her utterance of 'Michael refers to something by 'That'' will express something false. And the lesson generalizes: semantic talk about the languages of others puts considerable pressure against restricting the quantifier.[23]

Consider in this connection how incapable we are of doing semantics on the languages of others in settings where quantifiers are clearly restricted. If I am in a context where my quantifiers are restricted so as to render true my utterance 'Nothing is in the fridge', then I will not be in a position to generalize in the following way: 'That is in the fridge', said by an English speaker on some occasion, is true on that occasion only if there is something referred to by 'That' which is in the fridge denoted by 'the fridge'. For such a semantic claim, made using the restricted 'something', delivers the false prediction that someone who says 'That is in the fridge', pointing to a temperature gauge in his fridge, speaks falsely.

Thus, even leaving the eligibility of existence to one side, there may well be cases where a better overall fit for use is provided by the semantic profile associated with Bold rather than Timid Gabriel. Note further in this connection that the Plenitude Lover ought to weight charity in favour of those sentences that are reckoned obvious as against those sentences that are treated as epistemically insecure. Suppose that Gabriel utters Ref with utter confidence but utters 'There are only two things' with a fair amount of trepidation. In this case, a universal domain will be appropriate even granting no difference in eligibility as between a universal domain and the more restricted domain candidate.

Turn now to the Convention Lover. As I have characterized her, she contends that Bold Gabriel is impossible. Let us be clear about what this claim amounts to. There is a false theory that is frameable in Michael's language, one which notably includes:

$$S: \sim (\exists_m x_m \exists_m y_m \exists_m z_m (\sim x_m = y_m \,\&\, \sim y_m = z_m \,\&\, \sim x_m = z_m)).$$

So the denial of the possibility of Bold Gabriel comes down to this: there could not be a community whose theory of the world included S (or a sentence hyperintensionally equivalent to S). The reason, presumably, is that anyone who embraced a theory that apparently endorsed S would be more charitably translated as embracing a theory that endorses a different claim, say

$$S\#: \sim (\exists_g x_g \exists_g y_g \exists_g z_g (\sim x_g = y_g \,\&\, \sim y_g = z_g \,\&\, \sim x_g = z_g)).$$

The considerations just adduced apply here as well. Suppose someone came along with a semantic theory that included Ref. An important part of her theory of the world is its claims about how the thought and talk of others is related to her own. To insist on understanding the person's determiner phrases and variables as *g*-type rather than *m*-type would be to interpret the person in such a way that her semantic claims make no sense (or so as to render her hopeless at recognizing cases to which her linguistic categories—like 'subject term'—apply). Isn't it at least possible that in certain cases, the best interpretation will be one that interprets the person as making the false claim S and various true claims about intensional and/or hyperintensional equivalence between various target sentences and her home language? Given this, it does not seem that the Convention Lover should deny the possibility of a person who embraced S.

The Convention Lover might try to reply along the following lines: assuming an analytic/synthetic distinction, it seems clear enough that it is possible for someone to deny an analytic truth in a language that he understands, through carelessness, confusion or some other kind of noise. Perhaps the Convention Lover (who embraces a plenitudinous-looking language) can define his difference in attitude to Bold Gabriel by appeal to this category of mistake:

I agree that Bold Gabriel is possible. That is, I agree that someone could have S as part of his favourite theory. But I can only make sense of this possibility by understanding it as one of those occasions where someone denies an analytic truth. Correlatively, it is true that Michael avoids an epistemic danger when he embraces the denial of S rather than S, having recognized the truth of S: but the risk that is being avoided—albeit one that we sometimes face, especially as philosophers—is that of embracing a claim that is analytically false. You, the Plenitude Lover, think that your claims of Plenitude are true without being grounded in analytic truths, and correlatively think that your opponents make errors, but not, on that score, analytically false judgements. That in turn induces a sense of 'depth' to your debates, one that I will be no party to.

I shall pursue the Convention Lover's use of analyticity in due course. But note for now that, at least *prima facie*, the reasons sketched earlier for interpreting Gabriel as Bold rather than Timid did not require at all the sentences in his language that express the correct principles of mereology be somehow analytic. Even if the rules of his language were silent on the truth of those sentences, his commitment to such principles as Ref would make a Bold interpretation altogether natural.

4

Let us go back to the issue of hyperintensional symmetry, recalling that it seemed to our Convention Lover that when thoughts were conceived of hyperintensionally, neither Gabriel nor Michael could express the thoughts of the other on account of the fact that the quantifiers of each were semantically alien to the other. And let us again pay heed to the details of our angels' semantic theories. In particular, let us attend to Michael's perspective on Timid Gabriel. Consider the following sentence, which Michael accepts:

Ref 2: If Gabriel utters a truth by a sentence of the form 'That is F' then $\exists_m x_m$ ('that' refers to x_m)

Michaels acceptance of Ref2 is problematic for the Convention Lover. For if Michael is prepared to accept Ref2, then Michael will surely have to accept 'The quantifier phrases of Gabriel's language range over some$_m$ x_ms'. If we suppose further that Michael wants to be charitable towards Gabriel's ontological statements about simples and fusions, this will just be tantamount to treating Gabriel's quantifier as restricted to a subdomain of the domain of his own quantifiers, and hence to allowing that Gabriel's sentences are each hyperintensionally equivalent to certain sentences frameable in his own language. From the perspective of this, albeit minimal, piece of semantic theorizing, the proposed hyperintensional symmetry of the Convention Lover will collapse into precisely the hyperintensional asymmetry proposed by the Plenitude Lover.

Suppose that the Convention Lover sticks to her guns and insists that Ref2 is unacceptable since it is a mistake to suppose that the objects spoken about within the framework of Michael's conventions can be used to characterize the semantic structure of sentences in languages with different quantificational conventions.[24] This will make for the following broad difference between the Plenitude Lover and the Convention Lover. The Plenitude Lover will be willing to use his own language to characterize the semantic contribution of singular terms and quantifiers in the languages of others, speaking freely of 'the referents of proper names of other languages' and so on. (Note that this way of speaking requires that the denotata of other languages fall within the domain of the determiner phrases—in this case 'the referents'—of the home language.) The Convention Lover, by contrast (of the transcendent-truth-predicate type) will happily speak of the truth and falsity of sentences with superficially more restrictive ontologies. But she will not use the familiar kinds of apparatus to describe how those sentences get to be true; she will not use the concepts of domain, reference, extension, property, and so on in this connection, since such mechanisms require characterizing the semantic behaviour of alien sentences using one's home ontology. One normally thinks of the concept of sentential truth as forming part of a family, linked integrally to such concepts as reference, being true of, and so on. Retain the family and one will inevitably favour the Plenitude Lover over the Convention Lover.

Note further that this kind of Convention Lover will have to be very careful about her own claim that quantifier phrases in other languages have different meanings. For it is not clear how *meanings*, as she speaks about them, are to be construed. As a rough first pass, many of us think of the meanings of predicates as intensions that determine, relative to any possible world, a set of objects and of the meanings of quantifiers as functions from pairs of predicate-intensions to truth values. The Convention Lover just described cannot think of meanings in this way, since ascribing meanings of that sort will, in effect, be tantamount to describing the semantic behaviour of target languages in terms of one's home ontology. Indeed, she will be hard pressed to provide any satisfactory elucidation of the category of meaning.

So far we have seen little to recommend the perspective of the Convention Lover. She refused to use her own language to explain the semantic working of theories that

---

[24] Even putting it this way is a cheat by my Convention Lover's lights, since if I cannot use my ontology to characterize the semantic behaviour of alien languages, then the expression 'the objects spoken about within the framework of Michael's conventions' will appear problematic.

she wished to count as true but which have superficially more restrictive ontologies. But this hardly seems like a selling point. Perhaps Convention Loving will appear in more favourable light when we consider the idea that ontological frameworks are somehow analytic.

5

5.1

Assume for now an (albeit vague) analytic/synthetic distinction for sentences, understood as follows: a sentence S of some language L is *analytic* iff it is somehow a rule of L that one should accept S (at least if the question arises).[25] What should the Plenitude Lover make of someone who pays lip service to a plenitudinous sounding theory but who claims that various central claims of her theory are analytic?

It may well turn out, of course, that despite all the blustering, the so-called Convention Lover is merely one who refuses to engage in debate with various speculative ontologists. Suppose I think there are record collections. A philosopher comes along and says there are no record collections. I might play the philosopher's game, trying to justify the claim that there are record collections on the basis of some commonly accepted body of evidence and inchoate procedures of confirmation and justification. Or I might simply insist there are record collections and refuse to try to justify that claim on the basis of some thinner evidential base. If one began the day knowing there are record collections, one probably wouldn't lose the knowledge simply by one's dogmatic refusal to enter into the dialectical arena. We might think one would be betraying tendencies that will get one into trouble elsewhere. But if one's tendency is just to ignore metaphysicians, rather than adopt a general dogmatism, it is not clear that we should think this either. This person might sound very much like a Convention Lover: 'It is so obvious that there are record collections that it is pointless to discuss the matter', he will say. But such a person might, for instance, just be a dogmatic Plenitude Lover. He needn't define his disagreements, or meta-disagreements, by appeal to the category of analytic truth.

But suppose we take the Convention Lover at her word. Suppose she is indeed speaking a language in which she is right to say of the central claims of her mereology—formulated in her language—that they are analytic. How would she then be situated *vis-à-vis* the Plenitude Lover? The remainder of this paper is devoted to this issue.

Let us suppose that the Plenitude Lover is speaking a language in which quantifiers and variables are deployed in such a way that the central tenets of his mereological theorizing are neither analytically true nor analytically false. The Convention Lover may well be inclined to insist that the claims of mereology, couched in such a language, are indeterminate—neither true in that language nor false in that language.

---

[25] We can define up some derivative notions of analyticity for propositions. Here are some: a proposition is analytic iff it expressed by some sentence that is analytic in some language; a proposition is analytic$_L$ iff it is expressed by a sentence that is analytic in L. No significant dialectical progress can be made in the current context by recourse to such notions.

Her idea, presumably, is that if basic mereological axioms, couched in some language, are to be either true or false, then they must be settled by the analytic rules governing that language. It is instructive here to see how a simple-minded application of this kind of strategy can easily get one into trouble. Let us consider an analogous issue within philosophical logic.

5.2

Let us grant that a Convention Lover can speak a language C in which every instance of excluded middle is analytic. Let us imagine further that claims of bivalence also held analytically for sentences of C. Suppose a less conventional community S used a sign that looked like disjunction but that in their language, the counterpart of excluded middle was not analytically valid. Let me use 'or$_c$' for the convention lover's disjunction sign, 'or$_s$' for the second community's sign. Suppose, then, that

(i) There is an odd number of ants past present and future or$_c$ it is not the case there is an odd number of ants past present and future,

and

(ib) Necessarily (there is an odd number of ants past present and future or$_c$ it is not the case there is an odd number of ants past present and future),

are analytic truths[26], but not

(ii) There is an odd number of ants past present and future or$_s$ it is not the case there is an odd number of ants past present and future,

and

(iib) Necessarily (there is an odd number of ants past present and future or$_s$ it is not the case there is an odd number of ants past present and future).

Suppose I am a Convention Lover who uses 'or$_c$' and encounters someone who uses 'or$_s$' and utters (ii). Waiving questions of hyperintensional equivalence, should I say that (ii) shares the same intension as (i) (that is, the function that assigns truth at all worlds), or that it lacks an intension, or that it has an intension, but one that is different from that of (i)? On pain of stating the obvious, it is worth dwelling on the considerable costs of denying the first answer, since they carry over to the plenitude issue.

If I am such a Convention Lover, I shall presumably wish to say that 'There is an odd number of ants past present and future,' in the S-member's mouth has the same intension as 'There is an odd number of ants past present and future,' in my mouth (assuming there were no further oddities in the use of 'ant' etc.), and thus will hold that bivalence necessarily holds of that sentence as used by S-members (whether or not they realize it). Given that, it is clear that I will think that 'It is not the case there

---

[26] Where perhaps the analyticity of (ib) flows from the analyticity of (i) plus the analyticity of the rule of necessitation of modal logic (that says that logical truths are necessary).

is an odd number of ants past present and future,' as used by S members, has the same intension as its C-counterpart. It is clear that the latter sentence is false at any world where it is true that there is an odd number of ants and true at any world where it is false that there is an odd number of ants. And it is clear that from my perspective any world falls into one of those categories. Moreover, I shall presumably wish to say that the contingent 'There is an odd number of ants past present and future or$_s$ there is an odd number of bees past present and future,' has the same intension as 'There is an odd number of ants past present and future or$_c$ there is an odd number of bees past present and future.' Of course, the 'or$_s$' user may endorse a weaker set of inference for 'or$_s$' than I do for 'or$_c$'—perhaps he only endorses intuitionistically valid ones, or flirts with truth tables that deploy more two values (perhaps he deploys strong Kleene tables in his self-conception). But none of that will disincline me from treating the relevant pair of sentences inequivalent in intension. I don't recognize any world where any disjunct is neither true nor false, and on that basis I will confidently assign the value false to the 'or$_s$' disjunction when both disjuncts are false and true otherwise, thus aligning it with its 'or$_c$' counterpart in intension.

A Convention Lover who claims that (i) does not match (ii) in intension is thus in the strange situation of saying that while 'There is an odd number of ants past present and future or$_s$ there is an odd number of bees past present and future,' has the same intension as 'There is an odd number of ants past present and future or$_c$ there is an odd number of bees past present and future', the sentence 'There is an odd number of ants past present and future or$_s$ it is not the case there is an odd number of ants past present and future,' does not match its 'or$_c$' counterpart in intension.

There are various ways to reinforce the absurdity of this position. One is to appeal to considerations of charity in interpretation. One would expect the Convention Lover, like everyone else, to assign semantic values in a charitable way, unless there are marked countervailing costs. In this case it seems pretty clear that charity will incline assigning the value true to (ii) and that there are no marked costs to doing so. Second, we may appeal to compositional considerations. For any pair of sentences s_1 and s_2 such that one is not the negation of the other, one will assign intensions to $\ulcorner s_1$ or$_s$ $s_2 \urcorner$ in such a way that the intension of the whole will depend systematically on the intensions of s_1 and s_2 in a way that one can easily state in one's home language: the intension assigned to the whole delivers truth at a world iff the intension assigned to s_1 delivers truth at that world or$_c$ the intension assigned to s_2 delivers truth at that world. Given this, it is obvious that the most simple and natural set of rules for assigning intensions will extend assign to (ii) an intension that gives the value true at all worlds rather than no intension at all. Third and most obviously: while the rule of excluded middle might not be analytically valid for the user of 'or$_s$', certain rules may be analytically valid. So, for example, the rule of addition might be analytically valid for 'or$_s$'-users. Assuming that we wish to assign intensions in such a way that analytically valid rules take one from truths to truths, it will not do to reckon (ii) as differing in intension from (i) since we would then regard one of the following analytically valid inferences as at some world constituting a move from truth to less than truth:

There is an odd number of ants past present and future.
Therefore, there is an odd number of ants past present and future or$_s$ it is not the case there is an odd number of ants past present and future.

It is not the case that there is an odd number of ants past, present and future.
Therefore, there is an odd number of ants past present and future or$_s$ it is not the case there is an odd number of ants past present and future.

In conclusion then, the Convention Lover should admit that, even if (i) is analytic and (ii) not, (i) and (ii) are intensionally equivalent.

The situation is not quite analogous when it comes to the user of 'or$_s$' confronted with the project of assigning an intension to the sentences of the 'or$_c$' user. That is because there is a crucial difference in the epistemic spaces that the 'or$_s$' and 'or$_c$' users are each working with. Let a *coherent* set of sentences in a language L be a set of sentences that do not violate any of the analytic rules of L. Let a *maximally coherent* set be a set of sentences that are coherent and for which there is no coherent superset. At a first pass, we can usefully think of the epistemic space for a language user as given by the sets of coherent sets of sentences—points in the space are constituted by maximally coherent sets of sentences, epistemic possibilities by sets of such points. (The epistemic possibility associated with a coherent set of sentences S is then given by the set of those points that contain S.) Now when the user of some language L considers which intensions to assign to the language of another, he will have to run through the various epistemic possibilities compatible with whatever information he thinks he can rely on.[27] The user of 'or$_s$' will have an epistemic space that includes points that contain (ii) and (iib) (we can assume that neither is analytically objectionable)—but also points that contain neither (as well as points the contain just (ii)),[28] since they are not analytic in that language. Insofar as the 'or$_s$' user does not take himself to be able to rely on (ii) and (iib), he will find it natural to consider the question 'What do I reckon the intension of the 'or$_c$' user's utterance of (i) is on the assumption (iib) turns out not to be true?' Crucially, no analogous question arises for the 'or$_c$' user: he cannot ask himself 'What intension ought to be assigned to (ii) on the assumption that (ib) is not true?', since the untruth of (ib) is not a coherent epistemic possibility for him.[29]

What should the 'or$_s$' user think about the intension of (i) and (ib) when he considers as actual a point where (iib) isn't true? There are two main options open to him: first, he may take seriously the possibility of false or untrue analyticities—sentences

---

[27] Of course, I am pretending here—for the purposes of this toy model—that the person is calibrated so as not to question claims that are analytic in his language.

[28] Perhaps because of borderline cases of anthood coupled with a conception of borderline cases as undermining excluded middle.

[29] I am here making the simplifying assumption that the 'or$_s$' user will be able to describe certain epistemic points in this way. An intuitionist may, for example, refuse to assert that any given instance of excluded middle is not true at some world. For him, some points in epistemic space might lack each of (ii), its negation, the claim that (ii) is true, and the claim that (ii) is not true.

that are analytic by the standards of its users but are such that the world's non-compliance renders them false or untrue.[30,31] On this picture, the rules of 'or$_c$' make it a condition on competence that one does not deny (i) and (ib), but one or both are nevertheless false or (better) truth-valueless (on the assumption that (iib) is not true). Of course, 'or$_c$' users cannot themselves, on pain of incompetence, consider the possibility that (ib) is not true. That possibility can only seriously be considered from the perspective of a different epistemic space—such as that enjoyed by 'or$_s$' users. Relative to an 'or$_c$' user's epistemic space, this instance of the worry that the analytic conventions fail to secure truth trades on an epistemic impossibility.

When one considers as actual a point where (iib) isn't true, one might (instead of treating (i) as an untrue analyticity) contrive a deviant, *prima facie* unnatural, way of interpreting sentences like (i) so that they still come out as true. Thus suppose 'or$_c$' users had points in epistemic space where (ii) was neither true nor false on account of its disjuncts being neither true nor false: considering those points as actual, they might then choose to regard (i) as not being truth functional. Such an interpreter might think something like the following to himself: 'If it turns out that bivalence and excluded middle hold of metaphysical necessity, then (i) and (ii) express the same intension—the function that delivers true for all worlds. But if it turns out that I am wrong, and a certain coherent epistemic possibility turns out to be actual—one in which a deviant logic prevails (perhaps of necessity), then (i) and (ii) express different intensions.' On this approach, one institutes a stronger tie between analyticity and truth by making (i) come out as true come what may.[32]

5.3

Let us return, at last, to the case at hand. Imagine a world of two angels—Conventional Michael and Speculative Michael—that ostensibly agree about everything, except that while Speculative Michael is a Plenitude Lover, Conventional Michael is a Convention Lover.

Just as a claim of intension failure or contingency was radically undermotivated in the case of an 'or$_c$' user who claimed that (ii) lacked an intension, so it would be similarly unreasonable for Conventional Michael to claim intension failure or

---

[30] One thinks here of Arthur Prior's famous 'tonk' example: were a tribe to have a term with rules corresponding to 'tonk' it is arguable that sentences such as 'If P tonk Q then Q' would be untrue analyticities. See Prior, 'The Runabout Inference-Ticket', *Analysis* 21 (1960), pp. 38–39.

[31] Of course, if the notion of 'untrue analyticity' seems jarring, one can institute a definitional connection between analyticity and truth by fiat, adding truth as an additional stipulative ingredient to analyticity's requirements. But for current purposes it is useful to have some notion of analyticity that does not connect to truth by fiat but which rather reflects rule-governed bounds on the conceptual imagination of concept-users.

[32] What of the 'or$_c$' user's commitment to bivalence? The current strategy would recommend that the 'or$_s$' user not treat the 'or$_c$' user as meaning truth by 'truth' and falsity by 'falsity'.

contingency for some basic fusion axiom of mereology in Speculative Michael's mouth. General considerations of charity should positively incline Conventional Michael towards translating a given axiom into its natural counterpart in his home language. Moreover, it would be strange indeed to treat as intensionless all the various claims made by Speculative Michael that are ostensibly about contingent matters—for example, 'There is a composite thing containing Conventional Michael as a part,' and 'I am thinking about the composite thing now.' But having granted an intension to those, compositional considerations will render more or less mandatory the assignment of an intension to mereological axioms as well.

Conventional Michael ought thus to translate Speculative Michael's metaphysical claims homophonically. He cannot reasonably maintain that insofar as a general ontological claim (about the nature of part and whole and so on) is necessarily true, it will be analytic in the language in which it is expressed. Of course, Conventional Michael will still not himself take various mereological alternatives seriously—indeed, he will not be a position to coherently do so. That is because he operates within an epistemic space in which the central claims of mereology, as formulated in his language, are epistemically necessary.

Let us turn to the perspective of Speculative Michael. There are, of course, important differences between the kind of epistemic space that Conventional Michael and Speculative Michael find themselves in. The fusion axioms of Speculative Michael's preferred mereology are not epistemically necessary. Thus, when he considers the claim that some fusion axiom in his language has the same intension as its counterpart in Conventional Michael's language, he may have differing reactions to that claim depending on which points in the epistemic space he considers as actual. When he considers as actual points in which his preferred fusion axioms come out necessarily true, he will almost certainly reckon the sentences to have the same intension as their counterparts in Conventional Michael's language. But what should he think when considering as actual points in which his own mereological claims come out false? Suppose he considers as actual those points in which simples never compose complexes. What should he then think about the fusion axioms in Conventional Michael's language?

As in the disjunction case, there are two main reactions. One is to treat the relevant claims as analytic falsehoods. A second reaction is to find a deviant interpretation on which the relevant claims still come out true. One natural way to achieve this effect is to think that the correct semantics will vary drastically according to which points one considers as actual. Thus Speculative Michael might think to himself, 'If the world is one where the fusion axioms of my mereology are true of necessity, then Conventional Michael's quantifiers contribute to the truth of the sentences in which they occur in a way just like mine. But if the world is one where mereology is false, then Conventional Michael's language, while ostensibly like mine, will have a very different semantic profile. In that case, for example, when Conventional Michael says 'There is a composite object made out of Conventional Michael and Speculative Michael', he means roughly what I would mean by 'If there are composite objects, there is a composite object made out of Michael and Speculative Michael.'[33] Of course, whatever his semantic view about Conventional Michael when considering as actual the falsity of his preferred mereology, Speculative Michael will certainly believe that his claims are intensionally equivalent to those of Speculative Michael. For on the assumption that his axioms are necessarily true—which he believes they are—a claim of intensional equivalence as between those axioms and their counterparts in Conventional Michael's language will be irreproachable.

Let us sum up. Speculative Michael should expect Conventional Michael to regard him as speaking the truth when he, Speculative Michael, puts forward his ontological views, though he will not expect Conventional Michael to regard him as taking epistemic risks. Of course, Speculative Michael thinks that he is taking risks. That is an inevitable upshot of his epistemic space. Further, he will not suppose it a straightforward matter to induce the Convention Lover to move to an epistemic space like his. Such recalibrations cannot be brought about by normal updating, since updating within a Convention's Lover space will not alter its confines.

CONCLUSION

For the purposes of this discussion I have been concessionary about analyticity. In particular, I have allowed for a possible language in which analogues of the main general claims of Plenitudinous metaphysics are analytic. I doubt very much that any actual Convention Lovers speak such a language. Most likely they are dogmatists who misunderstand the working of their language and thought. Nevertheless, I have not claimed an analytic language of this sort is impossible. What should I make of the Convention Lover who uses such a language? Insofar as he claims that false metaphysics (e.g. Bold Gabriel's) is impossible, I would think such a claim unreasonable even by his lights. Insofar as he refuses to use his own language to semantically characterize the workings of singular terms in other languages, I would reckon him severely handicapped. But suppose he were to abandon those points of difference. Suppose the residual point of difference was that he remained bewildered as to why I was somewhat tentative about certain plenitudinous bits of theory on the grounds that the rules of his language did not permit him to question their counterparts in his language. Certainly, if someone could fashion an epistemic space out of such a web of analyticities, then it would be no easy matter to lure him out of it. But, in metaphysics as in logic, his pleas of analyticity would have little effect on those outside the web.

Philosophers who pay lip service to conventionalism are no doubt either operating within some such epistemic space or else (more likely) under a deluded self-conception that mistakes dogmatism for analyticity. Either way they can perhaps maintain some, albeit precarious, internal stability. But with or without the analytic garb, such dogmatism will not function as an effective deterrent to those of a more speculative temperament.

---

[33] For relevant discussion, see Cian Dorr, 'What we disagree about when we disagree about ontology', forthcoming in Mark Kalderon (ed.), *Fictionalist Approaches to Metaphysics* (Oxford University Press).

4

Recombination, Causal Constraints, and Humean Supervenience: An Argument for Temporal Parts?

with *Ryan Wasserman and Mark Scala*

According to the doctrine of four-dimensionalism, our world and everything in it consists of *stages* or *temporal parts*;[1] moreover, where an object exists at various times, it does so, according to the four-dimensionalist, in virtue of having distinct temporal parts at those times. While four-dimensionalism is often motivated by its purported solutions to puzzles about material objects and their persistence through time, it has also been defended by more direct arguments. Three such arguments stand out: (1) the argument from temporary intrinsics, (2) the argument from vagueness, and (3) the argument from recombination, Humean supervenience, and causal constraints. Not surprisingly, each of these arguments originates in the work of four-dimensionalism's most prominent modern defender, David Lewis.[2] The third of these arguments has received, by far, the least attention, critical or otherwise; it is now time to begin to address this imbalance.[3]

This chapter first appeared in *Oxford Studies in Metaphysics, vol. 1*, (Oxford, 2004), pp. 301–318. I am grateful for permission to republish it here.

[1] At any rate, this is the construal at work in the argument of Lewis's that we are examining. For the purposes of this paper, we take on board that construal. For an examination of other issues in the vicinity, see 'Three-Dimensionalism' (this volume).

[2] For Lewis's formulation of the argument from temporary intrinsics, see *On the Plurality of Worlds*, (Oxford: Blackwell, 1986), 202–5. Ted Sider develops the argument from vagueness in his 'Four-Dimensionalism', *Philosophical Review* 106 (1997): 197–231, pp. 197–231. Sider's argument is an extension of the argument for unrestricted composition that is presented in *Plurality*. Finally, for the argument from recombination, causal constraints and Humean supervenience, see Lewis, 'Postscripts to 'Survival and Identity'', in his *Philosophical Papers*, vol. I (Oxford University Press, 1983), pp. 73–7.

[3] Harold Noonan's recent commentary offers a striking endorsement of this argument. As he sees it, the three-dimensionalist will have to resist by rejecting the supervenience thesis underpinning the argument. But Noonan claims of that thesis, 'Apart from the incompatibility with three-dimensionalism that Lewis's argument exposes, [it] seems philosophically uncontentious' ('The Case for Perdurance', in G. Preyer and F. Siebeldt (eds.), *Reality and Humean Supervenience: Essays in the Philosophy of David Lewis*. Lanham, MD: Rowan & Littlefield, 2001: 128). As will become clear, this evaluation is somewhat misguided.

The argument in question makes its first appearance in Lewis's '*Postscripts to* 'Survival and Identity' '. Here is the bulk of the argument, as presented by Lewis:

First: it is possible that a person-stage might exist. Suppose it to appear out of thin air, then vanish again. Never mind whether it is a stage *of* any person (though in fact I think it is). My point is that it is the right sort of thing.

Second: it is possible that two person-stages might exist in succession, one right after the other but without overlap. Further, the qualities and location of the second at its appearance might exactly match those of the first at its disappearance. Here I rely on a *patchwork principle* for possibility: if it is possible that X happen intrinsically in a spatiotemporal region, and if it is likewise possible that Y happen in a region, then also it is possible that both X and Y happen in two distinct but adjacent regions. There are no necessary incompatibilities between distinct existences. Anything can follow anything.

Third: extending the previous point, it is possible that there might be a world of stages that is exactly like our own world in its point-by-point distribution of intrinsic local qualities over space and time.

Fourth: further, such a world of stages might also be exactly like our own in its causal relations between local matters of particular fact. For nothing but the distribution of intrinsic local qualities constrains the patter of causal relations. (It would be simpler to say that the causal relations supervene on the distribution of local qualities, but I am not as confident of that as I am of the weaker premise.)

Fifth: then such a world of stages would be exactly like our own simpliciter. There are no features of our world except those that supervene on the distribution of local qualities and their casual relations.

Sixth: then our world is a world of stages.[4]

The first step in this argument is an unobjectionable modal claim—here Lewis merely asserts the possibility of a short-lived object whose intrinsic history duplicates part of the intrinsic history of a possible person. The third step is merely an extension of the first two steps. The concluding step certainly follows from the previous five.[5] That leaves us with the second, fourth, and fifth steps as likely targets. These premises rely, respectively, on a combinatorial principle, a principle about what constrains causal facts, and a weakened version of Humean supervenience. In the following three sections, we will evaluate each of these premises, along with their motivating principles. As we hope to show, each step of the argument faces significant—and instructive—problems, and so the defender of three-dimensionalism needn't worry about Lewis's argument.[6]

---

[4] op cit., pp. 76–7.

[5] Standard four-dimensionalism claims that this world is a world filled with fusions of *instantaneous* beings. This is not strictly entailed by the conclusion. Further, standard four-dimensionalism assumes, with standard mereology, that any set of such instantaneous beings has a unique fusion. That is not strictly entailed by the conclusion either. But the conclusion does secure a good part of what the standard four-dimensionalist wants: in any given person's life, there are a series of short-lived objects, existing in succession, each of whose intrinsic character exactly matches the intrinsic character of the person for the short period that it exists.

[6] We note that Lewis himself writes that, 'I do not suppose the doubters will accept my premises, but it will be instructive to find out which they choose to deny' (p. 76). On this point we can all agree.

1 RECOMBINATION

The second premise of Lewis's argument may be read as a conditional: if two person-stages are possible, then two person-stages of that sort are *com*possible, and moreover they might exist one right after the other and without overlap. According to Lewis, this premise is motivated by a combinatorial principle:

I rely on a *patchwork principle* for possibility: if it is possible that X happen intrinsically in a spatiotemporal region, and if it is likewise possible that Y happen in a region, then also it is possible that both X and Y happen in two distinct but adjacent regions.[7]

Combinatorial principles come in different persuasions, depending on what sort of entity one wants to combine. One might, for example, defend a combinatorial principle for local intrinsic properties, or defend a principle for concrete material objects. Lewis, however, invokes a combinatorial principle for *events*—this, at least, is suggested by the word 'happen'. Let us take the notion of two events being *duplicates* as primitive.[8] We may then say that two regions are *event-wise duplicates* just in case the events that occur at those two regions are duplicates. We also help ourselves to the notion of adjacency: Two regions are *adjacent* if and only if they do not overlap, and the union of those regions is a continuous region. Then:

A Combinatorial Principle for Events (CPE): Let R_1 and R_2 be any pair of possible spatiotemporal regions. Then, for any way W of making R_1 and R_2 adjacent,[9] it is possible for there to be two non-overlapping spatiotemporal regions R_1^* and R_2^* such that (i) R_1^* and R_1 are event-wise duplicates, (ii) R_2^* and R_2 are event-wise duplicates and (iii) R_1^* and R_2^* are adjacent in way W.[10]

---

[7] Op cit., p. 77.

[8] The notion of duplication is intimately tied to the idea of an *intrinsic property* and there are several different accounts of this relation—and several different definitions of 'intrinsic'—in the literature. See, for example, Rae Langton and Lewis, 'Defining Intrinsic', *Philosophy and Phenomenological Research* 58 (1994): 333–45, p. 116–12). We do not think that the ideas in this paper are much affected by which definition (if any) we employ.

[9] The notion of 'a way of making a pair of regions adjacent' should be intuitive enough: given two rectangles, one by two inch, one way of making that pair adjacent is to form a four by one inch rectangle, another one of making that pair adjacent is to form a two by two inch square. The idea can be rigorized as follows: the *adjacency set* for a pair of regions R_1 and R_2 is a non-empty set of continuous regions; and a continuous region r is a member of that set if and only if r is the union of two adjacent regions R_1^* and R_2^* which intrinsically match R_1 and R_2 with regard to topology and metric. Let a mode of adjacency be any maximal subset of the adjacency set whose members are alike with regard to topology and metric. So, for example, the set of possible spherical regions that are three inches in diameter is a mode of adjacency as between a pair of regions, the first of which is a solid spherical region of three inch diameter (except for a fish-shaped hole), the second of which is a fish-shaped region that is exactly the size of that hole.

[10] For ease of exposition, we presuppose Lewis's commitment to Modal Realism so that we may meaningfully quantify over possible, non-actual entities like regions of space. Accordingly, we will also presuppose Lewis's counterpart theoretical analysis of *de re* modal claims (though nothing of import turns on this last assumption).

Invoking something like CPE at this stage of the argument is a bit puzzling, since all we are working with here are *person-stages* and it is at best tendentious to treat person-stages as events. Moreover, the nature of events—in particular, Lewis's theory of events—is extremely controversial.[11] A more neutral combinatorial principle is desirable.

Perhaps a combinatorial principle for local intrinsic properties, or *qualities*, for short, would do the trick. Roughly stated, the idea is that any distribution of qualities across the spacetime manifold is possible. More carefully, let p be any spacetime point. Then Q is a *quality profile for p* just in case Q is the set of all the qualities instantiated at p.[12] A point-by-point quality profile for an extended spatiotemporal region will then be a function of the quality profiles for all of the points of that region. Finally, let us also say that two regions R_1 and R_2 are *qualitative duplicates* just in case there is a one-to-one function f between the points of R_1 and R_2 that (i) preserves topological and metrical features[13] and (ii) if Q is the quality profile of some point x in R_1, Q will also be the quality profile of $f(x)$ in R_2.[14] We can now state our new combinatorial principle thus:

Combinatorial Principle for Qualities (CPQ): Let R_1 and R_2 be any pair of possible spatiotemporal regions. Then, for any way W of making R_1 and R_2 adjacent, it is possible for there to be two non-overlapping spatiotemporal regions $R_1{}^*$ and $R_2{}^*$ such that (i) $R_1{}^*$ and R_1 are qualitative duplicates, (ii) $R_2{}^*$ and R_2 are qualitative duplicates and (iii) $R_1{}^*$ and $R_2{}^*$ are adjacent in way W.

CPQ is superior to CPE with regard to neutrality about the metaphysics of events. But CPQ does no better than CPE as a ground for (2). Person-stages, whatever they are, are no more quality profiles than they are events. It is worthwhile to clarify exactly what the problem is. From the first step of Lewis's argument, we know that it is possible for there to be a spatiotemporal region, R_1, that is exactly occupied by a person-stage, and that it is also possible for there to be a spatiotemporal region, R_2, that is likewise exactly occupied by a person-stage. CPQ, then, licenses the following inference: it is possible for there to be two (non-overlapping) spatiotemporal regions, $R_1{}^*$ and $R_2{}^*$, that are qualitative duplicates of R_1 and R_2 and whose union is a continuous

---

[11] See Lewis, 'Events', in *Philosophical Papers*, vol. II (Oxford University Press, 1986), 241–69 for his theory of events.

[12] We have borrowed Lewis term 'instantiated at'—we trust that it well enough understood. Note that, in the relevant sense, a quality need not be instantiated by a point in order for it to be instantiated at that point (for example, it may be that the quality is instantiated by a particle that is located at that point). In what follows we follow Lewis in ignoring complications about haecceitistic properties. We also ignore complications connected with the fact that some three-dimensionalists take fundamental property instantiations to be temporally relativized. We believe that such complications at best point to issues of fine-tuning, not to fundamental difficulties with the argument.

[13] For example, if some metric relation holds between two points x and y in R_1, then it also holds between $f(x)$ and $f(y)$. The holding of this relation between x and y is intrinsic to R_1; highly extrinsic relations like 'being a third of the size of space-time' won't count.

[14] We assume that literally one and the same quality can be instantiated at multiple points. One who denied this—the trope-lover, for example—may wish to complicate matters further by invoking a duplication relation as between qualities.

spatiotemporal region. But that is not the inference made in (2). What Lewis wants is the possibility of there being *two person-stages* that exactly occupy regions R_1^* and R_2^*. That conclusion says something about *what objects* are located at these regions. But CPQ cannot deliver *that* conclusion—it can only tell us about the *quality distributions* at those regions. Taking note of this fact, the three-dimensionalist might say something like the following:

I grant the possibility of a person-stage exactly occupying some region, R_1, and I grant the possibility of some person-stage exactly occupying some other region, R_2. Moreover, I am perfectly willing to accept CPQ. So I think that there is a world—call it w—where there are two regions, R_1^* and R_2^*, which are qualitative duplicates of R_1 and R_2, respectively, and whose union is a continuous region. But I (consistently) deny that there are two person-stages at w, occupying R_1^* and R_2^*, respectively. Rather, there is one *enduring* object at w, exactly occupying the fusion of R_1^* and R_2^*.

The upshot, then, is that Lewis requires a stronger combinatorial principle—a combinatorial principle for *concrete material objects*. Let us say that two regions R_1 and R_2 are *object-wise duplicates* just in case (i) R_1 and R_2 are qualitative duplicates, (ii) there is a one-one function, f, from the objects and points in R_1 to the objects and points in R_2 such that, if some object x instantiates some quality F at some point y in R_1, then $f(x)$ instantiates F at $f(y)$, and (iii) an object x exactly occupies[15] a set of points S_1 in R_1 if and only if $f(x)$ exactly occupies the corresponding set of points S_2 in R_2, (where a set of points in R_2 corresponds to a set of points in R_1 just in case f provides a one-one mapping from the former to the latter). We can now state our combinatorial principle for objects as follows:

A Combinatorial Principle for Objects (CPO): Let R_1 and R_2 be any pair of possible spatiotemporal regions. Then, for any way W of making R_1 and R_2 adjacent, it is possible for there to be two non-overlapping spatiotemporal regions R_1^* and R_2^* such that (i) R_1^* and R_1 are object-wise duplicates (ii) R_2^* and R_2 are object-wise duplicates, (iii) R_1^* and R_2^* are adjacent in way W.

Here, finally, we seem to have a combinatorial principle that can do the work Lewis intends. Given the possibility of two person-stages, CPO allows us to infer the possibility of two distinct objects, each a duplicate of one of our person-stages, occupying adjacent spatiotemporal regions.

Now we have to ask: should the three-dimensionalist—which for current purposes can be construed as anyone who denies Lewis' plenitude of temporal parts—accept CPO? As an entering wedge, let us introduce a principle about parthood and spatial extension that is denied by several prominent three-dimensionalists.

The Doctrine of Arbitrary Undetached Parts (DAUP): Necessarily, for every material object M, if R is the region of space exactly occupied by M at time T, and if sub-R is any occupiable sub-region of R whatever, there exists a material object that exactly occupies the region sub-R at T and that is a part of M at T.[16]

---

[15] An object exactly occupies a set of points comprising a region if and only if it occupies all and only the points that belong to that set.

[16] Cf. Peter van Inwagen, 'The Doctrine of Arbitrary Undetached Parts', *Pacific Philosophical Quarterly* 62 (1987): 123–37, p. 123).

Rejecting DAUP does not, on the face of it, commit one to too much. All that is required for the falsity of DAUP is the *possibility* of a material object that doesn't have a material object as a part at *some* subregion of the region occupied by the object in question. However, some philosophers who deny DAUP would do so even if it were restricted to objects in the actual world. In fact, some would deny DAUP even if it were restricted to particular material objects like you. To take one concrete example: some philosophers who deny DAUP will go so far as to deny that there is a material object exactly occupying the region that we would normally say is occupied by your left arm. Perhaps such philosophers would even go so far as to say that it is, strictly speaking, *impossible* for there to be a region, R, that qualitatively duplicates the region you occupy and that has a subregion exactly occupied by an arm-shaped material object. Let us say that some region, R_1, *part-prohibits* some subregion R_2 of R_1 if and only if it is impossible that there be two regions R_1^* and R_2^* such that (i) R_2^* is a subregion of R_1^*, (ii) R_1^* qualitatively duplicates R_1, (iii) R_2^* qualitatively duplicates R_2, and (iv) there is an object exactly occupying R_2^*. The philosophers we are imagining hold that the region that you occupy part-prohibits the subregion in which common sense claims that there is a left arm. Such philosophers subscribe (among other things) to the following claim.

Part-Prohibition: It is possible that there exists an object, O, and regions R_1 and R_2 such that (i) O exactly occupies region R_1, (ii) R_2 is a subregion of R_1, and (iii) R_1 part-prohibits R_2.[17]

Of course, such philosophers could consistently allow that an arm-shaped object exists, even one with an intrinsic profile that matches the arm-shaped subregion in which it is said that your arm exists. Indeed, such philosophers could, consistently, subscribe to the following general claim.

Occupation: For any possible object, O, if R is a continuous subregion of the region exactly occupied by O, it is possible for there to be a region R^* such that (i) R^* qualitatively duplicates R and (ii) there exists an object that exactly occupies R^*.

One who subscribes to Part-Prohibition and Occupation ought not to subscribe to CPO. Here's why: take as a sample case someone who thinks that the region you occupy part-prohibits the arm-shaped region we would normally suppose your left arm occupies. Suppose that philosopher were to subscribe to Occupation: then it remains possible that there is an object exactly occupying a region that qualitatively duplicates the region occupied by all of you except (loosely speaking) your left arm. It is likewise possible for there to be an object exactly occupying a region that qualitatively duplicates the region we would normally say is occupied by your left arm. (We can imagine the first object to simply be a disfigured doppelganger of you, the second object to be an arm that is not attached to a living being.) According to CPO, then, it is possible for there to be two non-overlapping regions (of space, let us say) such that (i) one region is exactly occupied by a duplicate of your disfigured duplicate, (ii) one region is exactly occupied by a duplicate of the lonely

---

[17] And also to *Actual Part Prohibition*: there exists an object O and regions R_1 and R_2 such that (i) O exactly occupies region R_1, (ii) R_2 is a subregion of R_1, and (iii) R_1 part-prohibits R_2.

arm, and (iii) the regions are adjacent to one another in just the way that the left-arm-shaped region in your vicinity is adjacent to the rest-of-you-shaped region. In short, CPO gives us a region that qualitatively duplicates *you*, but which counts among its subregions one occupied by a left-arm-shaped object. And *that* is inconsistent with the thesis that the region that you occupy part-prohibits the region occupied by your left arm.

The above discussion focused on *spatial* parts. But we also have corresponding principles for *temporal* parts. To begin:

The Doctrine of Arbitrary Undetached Temporal Parts (DAUTP): Necessarily, for every material object *O*, if *I* is the interval of time exactly occupied by *O*, and if sub-*I* is any occupiable sub-interval of *I* whatever, there exists a material object that exactly occupies the interval sub-*I* and is a part of *O* at sub-*I*.[18]

While certain three-dimensionalists reject DAUP, it seems clear that *every* three-dimensionalist should reject DAUTP. For DAUTP is simply the claim that four-dimensionalism is a necessary truth.[19] Moreover, it would not be surprising if a three-dimensionalist were to believe that certain spacetime regions part-prohibit some temporally smaller subregions. For example, such a three-dimensionalist may insist that while it is possible that there be a short-lived object that duplicates the first three years of Descartes' life, it is not possible that there be a spacetime region that duplicates Descartes' entire life that contains such a short-lived object in its first three-year temporal segment. On this view, the spacetime region occupied by Descartes's life part-prohibits the subregion corresponding to the first three years of his life. Such a version of three-dimensionalism is not at all unnatural. And, for reasons analogous to those just considered, the proponent of such a theory will reject CPO and, with it, the second premise of Lewis's argument.[20]

What about those three-dimensionalists who do not subscribe to the combination of Occupation and Part-Prohibition? Well, it is certainly consistent, at least, for such philosophers to deny CPO.[21] The key point here is that such philosophers may still cling to weaker combinatorial principles such as CPE or CPQ in order to capture what is right about combinatorialism. However, we suspect that some three-dimensionalists may still find CPO appealing. Such philosophers, it seems, must accept the second premise of Lewis' argument. Must they also accept the doctrine of temporal parts? To answer that question, we must investigate the remaining premises of Lewis's argument.

---

[18] Cf. *ibid*, p. 137.

[19] Cf. Sider, 'Four-Dimensionalism', where something like DAUTP is defended as the proper articulation of the central thesis of four-dimensionalism. Some readers will no doubt believe that four-dimensionalism involves more than DAUTP. We shall not be engaging with such readers here. Cf. n. 5.

[20] Some of the ideas explored in this section are echoed in van Inwagen, 'Temporal Parts and Identity across Time', *The Monist* 83 2000: 437–59.

[21] Notice that even if Occupation does not hold with full generality, Part-Prohibition may still make trouble for CPO, so long as certain particular sorts of objects are possible. If the region occupied by Descartes' life part-prohibits the subregion occupied by the first three years of his life, then so long as it is possible that there be an object that intrinsically matches the first three years of his life and an object that intrinsically matches the rest of his life, then CPO will have to be rejected.

2 CAUSAL CONSTRAINTS

We said at the outset that Lewis's argument relies crucially on three different principles. We have already discussed the principle of recombination. Humean supervenience will be the topic of the following section. Here we discuss the fourth premise of Lewis' argument and the topic of causal constraints.

The premise in question says something like the following: if it is possible for a stage-world to be exactly like our world with respect to its distribution of qualities, then it is possible for a stage-world to be exactly like our world with respect to its distribution of qualities *and* its causal facts. As Lewis puts it, 'nothing but the distribution of local qualities constrains the pattern of causal relations'[22]. It is not exactly clear what the scope of this generalization is. For example, is Lewis requiring his opponents to accept that the laws of nature cannot put additional constraints on the pattern of causal relations beyond the distribution of local qualities? We need not pause to consider such issues here, since a restricted version of the principle will serve Lewis's purposes just as well. Put informally, this version of the principle states that boundary facts—facts about where the boundaries of objects lie—do not place additional constraints on the pattern of causal relations beyond those imposed by the distribution of local qualities. We develop this idea in what follows.

Let us say that the boundary profile, B, for a world is the set of regions that are exactly occupied by an object in that world. Let us say that causal profile, C, for a world is a set of pairs of spacetime points, such that a pair $<p_1, p_2>$ belongs to C if and only if there is a line of causal influence running from p_1 to p_2. (A line of causal influence connects p_1 and p_2 just in case the instantiation of some quality at p_1 is causally related to the instantiation of some quality at p_2.)[23] Recall that a point-by-point quality profile is a function from spacetime points to sets of qualities. Q is the quality profile for world w just in case the following is true: given any spacetime point p as an input, Q delivers as output all and only the qualities instantiated at p in w. We also need the notion of a Q-type quality profile, a B-type boundary profile and a C-type causal profile. First, say that two quality profiles are duplicates just in case there is a one-one function from values of the one to duplicate values of the other (one that preserves topological and metrical features). Duplicates of a quality profile Q form a class of *Q-type quality profiles*. Similarly, duplicates of a boundary profile B form a class of *B-type boundary profiles* and duplicates of a causal profile C form a class of *C-type causal profiles*. The principle that Lewis needs can now be stated as follows:

---

[22] 'Postscripts,' p. 77.

[23] Some readers may wonder why a causal profile is not done in terms of events. On some metaphysics of events, this will clearly not serve Lewis's purposes: suppose an event is individuated in part by which object undergoes it. Then, clearly, boundary profiles will be constitutively relevant to which events occur in a world, which, given an event-theoretic conception of causal profiles, will automatically render boundary profiles constitutively relevant to causal profiles. Once again, we steer clear in the text of tendentious issues concerning the metaphysics of events. We do freely acknowledge the possibility of a critique of Lewis's fourth premise based on the idea that the concept of causal influence cannot properly be ultimately understood in a way that is neutral as to which objects exist and where: if that is right, then our best efforts at reconstructing Lewis's premise will not be ultimately coherent.

A Principle Concerning Causal Constraints (PCC): For any quality profile Q, causal profile C and boundary profile B: if there is a possible world with a Q-type quality profile and C-type causal profile, and there is a possible world with Q-type quality profile and a B-type boundary profile, then there is a possible world with a Q-type quality profile, a C-type causal profile and a B-type boundary profile.

Here is how PCC licenses the inference made in step four. Let Q_A be the quality profile of the actual world and let C_A be the causal profile of the actual world. It is clear, then, that there is a possible world with a Q_A-type quality profile and a C_A-type causal profile, since the actual world is such a world. The third premise of Lewis's argument tells us that there is a possible world with the boundary profile of a stage-world and the quality profile of the actual world. Let us say that the boundary profile of such a world is a B_S-type boundary profile. The third premise then tells us that there is a possible world with a Q_A-type quality profile and a B_S-type boundary profile. Applying PCC we can infer that there is a possible world with a Q_A-type quality profile, a B_S-type boundary profile, and a C_A-type causal profile. In other words, there is a stage-world exactly like our world with respect to the distribution of qualities and the causal relation. This is exactly what Lewis wants.

The question now before us is whether or not the three-dimensionalist ought to accept PCC. We mention two possible sources of resistance (there may be others).

Some three-dimensionalists, if they are to be taken at their word, claim that there are no informative criteria of identity over time.[24] But most three-dimensionalists, we take it, are not in this camp. Most three-dimensionalists will say that there is an informative analysis available of what it takes for something at one time to be identical to something at another time. Others will believe that there are at least informative necessary conditions upon endurance. Whether providing an analysis or merely necessary conditions upon identity, three-dimensionalists typically have recourse to *causal* notions. In particular, as most three-dimensionalists see it, there will be certain causal requirements upon an object's enduring through time.

Presumably Lewis did not intend his argument to speak merely to those who believe that causal facts supervene on quality distribution. A good thing too: many three-dimensionalists would contest such an assumption. Let us suppose then that (i) there are causal requirements upon identity, but that (ii) causal facts—and, in particular, the kinds of causal facts relevant to diachronic identity—do not supervene on the distribution of qualities. Given these two assumptions, PCC is in trouble. According to the three-dimensionalist, our world is a world of enduring objects—persisting objects like you and I are 'wholly present' at each moment of our existence. Let us suppose, then, that we have an enduring material object, m, at region R_1 and an enduring material object, n, at region R_2. Let us also assume that m is identical to n. Assuming that there are causal requirement upon endurance, only certain possible causal profiles will be compatible with the fact that an enduring object occupies R_1 and R_2; others will be incompatible. Call the quality profile of the actual world Q_A. If we allow that the causal facts pertinent to diachronic identity do

[24] See, for example, Trenton Merricks, 'There are no Criteria of Identity over Time', *Nous* 32 (1998): 106–24.

not supervene on the quality distribution of a world, then it will come as no surprise there is some causal profile C compatible with Q_A such that C is incompatible with the existence of a single persisting object that occupies R_1 and R_2. We now have a counterexample to PCC. Call the actual boundary profile B_A. Q_A is compatible with B_A. Q_A is compatible with C. But, contra PCC, Q_A is not compatible with B_A.

The point can be even more vividly illustrated with a simple thought experiment. The three-dimensionalist will likely be happy to embrace a world w containing a single enduring particle.[25] The boundary profile B_w of such a world is simple enough: there is a single boundary corresponding to the life of the particle. Suppose one believes that some line of causal influence that traces the trajectory of the particle is a necessary condition upon such a boundary profile, and that this line of causal influence does not supervene on the quality profile. Since the line of influence is not supervenient, there are worlds where the quality profile of w, Q_w, is combined with a causal profile that is incompatible with that line of influence. Consider one such profile C. C is compatible with B_w. Meanwhile, from the description of the case, Q_w is compatible with B_w. If PCC is true, then B_w, Q_w and C are compatible also; but that is just what has been denied.

The previous line of thought relied on a conception of causation that is anti-Humean. A more Humean three-dimensionalist may face pressure from a different source. Let us assume that Lewis's view on the laws of nature is correct—laws are the simplest and most informative generalizations concerning the world. We now pose a simple question: might not boundary profiles bear on which generalizations are the most simple and informative? Two worlds w_1 and w_2 might be alike in their qualitative profile and yet, owing to different boundary profiles, enjoy differences such as the following. It is true in w_1, but not in w_2, that nothing persists once it is both F and G at the same time. It is true in w_1, but not in w_2, that nothing stops being H once it is H. It is true in w_1, but not in w_2, that as soon as something that is I passes out of existence, everything that is J turn to K. By Lewis's own lights, differences like this might make for differences in the laws of nature. And this, in turn, will make a difference to the causal facts. Consider the last of our list of contrasts. Owing to the difference, it may be that, in w_1, some K-event is caused, *inter alia*, by an I thing passing out of existence; but the corresponding K-event in w_2 has no such cause. Allow that differences in laws of nature are in turn constitutively relevant to the causal facts and we will be forced to deny that nothing beyond qualitative profile constrains the causal facts. Thus, PCC has to be rejected. Assuming Lewis' own conception of laws, PCC is a principle that should (i) only be accepted by four-dimensionalists, and (ii) should be restricted to the 'inner sphere' (assuming that the four-dimensionalist admits three-dimensionalist worlds in the 'outer sphere').

We have not shown that PCC is incompatible with three-dimensionalism as such. The combination of three-dimensionalism with a Humean conception laws may preclude commitment to PCC. Meanwhile, those who think that causal facts are irreducible but who also use those facts to describe certain purported necessary

---

[25] The general point obviously does not require that the three-dimensionalist believe that single particle worlds are possible. The toy example is chosen merely to illustrate the point at hand.

conditions upon diachronic identity will also reject PCC. But there may be certain three-dimensionalists who remain committed to both PCC and CPO. Such theorists must accept the second and fourth steps of Lewis's argument. So they should be very interested in the remainder of that argument.

3 WEAK HUMEAN SUPERVENIENCE

If we grant Lewis the first four premises of his argument, we grant the possibility of a stage-world that is exactly like our own world in its distribution of qualities and causal facts. What the fifth premise of Lewis's argument says is this: such a world is exactly like our world *simpliciter*. That is, a world of stages exactly like our world in its distribution of qualities and causal facts is exactly like our world in *all* respects. Lewis is not relying here on Humean supervenience, the doctrine that everything supervenes on the distribution of intrinsic, local properties; he merely requires that 'there are no features of our world except those that supervene on the distribution of local qualities *and their causal relations*' [italics ours].[26] Let's refer to this claim as the doctrine of *weak* Humean supervenience. If we grant Lewis weak Humean supervenience, along with CPO and PCC, the conclusion of his argument appears to be established.

But here the dialectical shortcomings of the argument are especially apparent. We wish to pursue two themes in this connection.

Our first theme concerns the contingency of Humean supervenience. According to Lewis, weak Humean supervenience (like strong Humean supervenience) holds at our world and worlds like ours. But the first four premises of Lewis's argument only give us the mere *possibility* of a stage-world like ours in its quality distribution and causal profile—they do not locate that world at the inner or outer sphere of possibility. Now, if the stage-world in question is located in the outer sphere, the appeal to weak Humean supervenience is out of place. If a stage-world is located in the outer sphere, then, it is straightforwardly *false* that such a world is like ours *simpliciter*. For, if such a world is located in the outer sphere, it is a world where weak Humean supervenience fails. So Lewis needs to claim that the stage-world under discussion is an inner sphere world—it is a world like ours. But this is a claim that the three-dimensionalist may well reject. She may insist that stage-worlds, while possible, are not 'worlds like ours' and will summarily reject Lewis's fifth premise. Noting that Lewis himself admits the possibility of an endurance-world can sharpen the point here:

[There] are worlds in which things persist through time not by consisting of distinct temporal parts, but rather by bilocation in space-time: persisting things are wholly present in their entirety at different times.[27]

---

[26] 'Postscripts', p. 77.

[27] Lewis, 'Humean Supervenience Debugged,' in his *Papers in Metaphysics and Epistemology* (Cambridge: Cambridge University Press, 1999), 224–47, p. 227.

Lewis, of course, is about as generous with possibility as one can get. So, if he grants the possibility of enduring worlds, we take it that he will also grant the possibility of an enduring world exactly like our own in its distribution of qualities and causal facts. But, given *that* admission, the three-dimensionalist should be free to argue as follows:

It is possible for there to be an enduring world exactly like our own in its distribution of qualities and causal facts. But, by weak Humean supervenience, there are no features of our world except those that supervene on the distribution of local qualities and their causal relations. So an enduring world is exactly like our world *simpliciter*.[28]

Sauce for the goose is sauce for the gander. The only response available to Lewis, it seems, is to claim that enduring worlds are outer sphere, so that the appeal to weak Humean supervenience is out of place. The three-dimensionalist may, of course, say the same thing about stage-worlds. So we seem to have reached an impasse.[29]

Perhaps the impasse can be broken. Lewis claims the doctrine of weak Humean supervenience is contingent. Some philosophers, however, are at least willing to consider the claim that weak Humean supervenience is a necessary truth.[30] What happens if we break with Lewis and endorse such a strong claim? Well, we no longer have to worry about locating our stage-world in the inner sphere since, if we take weak Humean supervenience to be a necessary truth, the inner sphere/outer sphere distinction is no longer relevant. So, if it is possible for there to be a stage-world exactly like ours in its distribution of qualities and causal facts, and if it is a necessary truth that any world like ours in those respects is like ours *simpliciter*, we can infer that our world is indeed a world of stages. The catch, of course, is that the necessity of weak Humean supervenience is a highly questionable matter. Since Lewis himself does not even endorse such a claim, it seems unreasonable to expect as much of the three-dimensionalist.[31]

---

[28] Michael Rea, 'Temporal Parts Unmotivated', *Philosophical Review* 107 (1998): 225–60, pp. 249–50 suggests a similar response to Lewis's argument.

[29] Lewis once believed that he had a way to make the distinction between inner and outer worlds that was independent of Humean supervenience: outer sphere worlds include alien properties, inner sphere worlds do not. Alien properties are properties that don't appear at the actual world. Now, if this is an adequate way of drawing the inner sphere/outer sphere distinction, the premise in question would be in much better shape. Here is why: the stage-world built up in the first four premises of the argument didn't include any alien properties—the stage-world, after all, is supposed to be a *qualitative duplicate* of the actual world. That, together with the claim that all outer sphere worlds have alien properties, puts the stage-world in the inner sphere. And once we have located the stage-world in the inner sphere, the appeal to weak Humean supervenience is perfectly legitimate. The problem, of course, is that the attempt to make the inner sphere/outer sphere distinction by way of alien properties fails. Or so, at least, says Lewis in 'Humean Supervenience Debugged,' p. 227. At the time that the argument we are discussing was proposed, Lewis had not properly reckoned with the possibility of endurance worlds, and in particular their bearing on the doctrine of Humean supervenience and the inner sphere/outer sphere distinction.

[30] See, for example, D. Robinson 'Matter, Motion and Humean Supervenience', *Australasian Journal of Philosophy* 67 (1989): 394–409.

[31] Those readers who are compelled by the thesis that weak Humean supervenience is a necessary truth may wonder whether there is any plausible version of three-dimensionalism that can be rendered compatible with that thesis. We shall not pursue the matter further here.

We briefly turn to a second theme. We noted earlier that only certain three-dimensionalists will be sympathetic to PCC; more specifically, that principle will appeal only to the kind of three-dimensionalist who believes that there are no causal conditions upon diachronic identity. But that kind of three-dimensionalist will likely have no sympathy at all for weak Humean supervenience. After all, a three-dimensionalist who thinks that there are no causal conditions on diachronic identity will almost certainly believe that worlds may differ from the actual one with regard to boundary facts while duplicating the qualitative and causal profile of the actual world. Consider, for instance, a particle in our world that endures from t_1 to t_2. There are other possible worlds in which that particle (or its counterpart) ceases to exist sometime between t_1 and t_2 and is immediately replaced by an exactly similar particle. A three-dimensionalist who believes that there are causal criteria of diachronic identity will insist that there is a causal difference between these two scenarios. But a three-dimensionalist who believes that diachronic identity is, so to speak, 'brute'—thus admitting of no causal criteria—will be prepared to concede that the pair of scenarios may be alike causally and qualitatively. She will, in that case, have no sympathy at all for weak Humean supervenience.[32] In sum, there simply are no clear-headed three-dimensionalists who will sympathize with the combination of PCC and weak Humean supervenience. There are thus no clear-headed three-dimensionalists whom Lewis' argument will embarrass.

4 CONCLUSION

In conclusion, let us review the responses to Lewis' argument that we advocate on behalf of the three-dimensionalist. If a three-dimensionalist upholds Part-Prohibition and Occupation, we say that she should reject the combinatorial principle required by Lewis's argument, CPO. In so doing, she may reject the second premise of his argument. Alternatively, if a three-dimensionalist does not count herself among those just mentioned, she may still feel free to reject CPO in favour of a more modest combinatorial principle like CPE or CPQ. Again, such a three-dimensionalist may reject the second premise of Lewis's argument. A three-dimensionalist may in any case have powerful reasons for rejecting PCC. That three-dimensionalist may reject the fourth premise of Lewis's argument. A three-dimensionalist who accepts the fourth premise of Lewis's argument may think that the world that it posits belongs to the 'outer sphere', in which case it fails to fall under the scope of weak Humean supervenience. That in turn can provide a basis for questioning the move from premise four to five. Moreover, three-dimensionalists who accept PCC ought in any case to have no sympathy for weak Humean supervenience (even as a contingent truth). This will also provide a basis for rejecting the move from four to five. What about the philosopher bent upon accepting CPO, PCC, and the necessity of

---

[32] Spinning disc thought experiments are also suggestive here. Particularly relevant is Dean Zimmerman 'Temporal Parts and Supervenient Causation: The Incompatibility of Two Humean Doctrines', *Australasian Journal of Philosophy*, 76 (1998): 265–88.

weak Humean supervenience? Such a philosopher will, indeed, have to reject three-dimensionalism. However, we know of no contemporary three-dimensionalist who has anything to fear from Lewis's argument.[33]

---

[33] Thanks to Tamar Szabo Gendler, Ted Sider, and Dean Zimmerman for helpful discussion and for comments on earlier drafts of this paper.

5

Three-Dimensionalism

0 INTRODUCTION

The term 'three-dimensionalism' has wide currency in contemporary metaphysical debates, yet it is far from clear what the term means. Often three-dimensionalism is explained using metaphors: objects are wholly present at a time, rather than 'stretched out' across time and partially present at each. Since the ideology of 'wholly present' and 'stretched out' is too unclear to carry all the explanatory burden, there remains the task of explaining in a perspicuous way what exactly is at stake. I shall distinguish a number of issues that lie in the vicinity of the debates and indicate a range of considerations that may be brought to bear. I shall not offer an 'analysis' of 'three-dimensionalism'. There are often better things to do than define a term of art.

1 A PLENITUDE OF TEMPORAL PARTS?

It is a platitude that things gain and lose parts. A car loses its front bumper and gains a new one. A living organism metabolizes food, part of whose matter then becomes part of the organism. When we reflect further we realize that it is also natural to think that things gain and lose coinciding parts—where x is a coinciding part of y at t iff x is mereologically coincident with y at t.

For clarity's sake, I shall work with a notion of coincidence defined in terms of overlap, where x overlaps y at a time just in case x and y share a part at that time. Let us then say that x *coincides* with y at a time just in case x overlaps everything that y overlaps at that time and vice versa. On certain natural assumptions, this gloss is equivalent to one framed terms of parthood, viz: x coincides with y at a time just in case everything that is part of x at that time is also part of y at that time. But the gloss in terms of overlap prevents unnecessary distractions from those who opt for certain non-standard views of parthood.[1]

Consider a statue that exists at a time, which is made of a certain lump at that time. It is clear enough that the statue overlaps everything that the lump overlaps and vice versa. So the statue coincides with the lump at the time in question. Someone might object that the arm of the statue is not part of the lump, or that the statue itself is not part of the lump. But such considerations—which encode non-standard views of

---

[1] For more on non-standard mereologies, see Peter Simons, *Parts: A Study in Ontology* (Clarendon Press, 1987).

parthood[2]—can be ignored so long as we have the overlap-theoretic notion of coincidence clearly in view. (After all, every part of the statue will have as parts atoms that are parts of the lump, and vice versa.[3])

Suppose the statue and the lump come into existence at the same time, and that the statue is subsequently destroyed in such a way that the lump is not. Then the lump coincides with the statue at some times but not others, but the statue coincides with the lump throughout the statue's career.[4] It is helpful to have a piece of terminology to encode facts such as these. Let us say that x is a *temporal part* of y iff x coincides with y at all times that x exists. In the scenario described, the statue is a temporal part of the lump but not vice versa.

Of course, not all metaphysicians will agree that the lumps can have statues as numerically distinct temporal parts, even in the sense defined. Some will think that statues don't really exist. Some will think instead that 'statue' is a phase sortal like 'lord mayor': the lump is a statue for a sub-period of its existence and is not numerically distinct from it. And some have held[5] that when the lump is crafted into a statue, the latter pushes the former out of existence by a sort of metaphysical trumping relation. But let us set these views aside and focus instead on the garden-variety three dimensionalist who will here join with 'four-dimensionalists' in allowing that things may have temporal parts in the sense just defined. Admittedly, the *expression* 'temporal part' may be anathema to card-carrying three-dimensionalist's vocabularic sensibilities, but when the expression is defined as above, the reaction is misplaced. As Ted Sider has emphasized, the preceding gloss on 'temporal part' offers an eminently natural way to define that term, perhaps even the only one available that is well understood. The slogan 'There are no temporal parts' is false for nearly everyone on the construal that we can all understand.[6]

---

[2] In particular, the quoted suggestions will have to deny the connection between parthood and overlap that one gets by adding time-indexing to standard mereology, viz: x is part of y at t iff $(\forall z)(x$ overlaps z at $t \supset y$ overlaps z at t).

[3] I ignore here various deviant views that would deny this, such as (i) the thesis that the statue has as a part a substantial form/statue-geist/immanent principle of organization that itself has no atoms as parts and which does not overlap the lump at all, and (ii) the thesis that atoms are not parts of the statue; only statue-atoms, which are a sort of shadow of the familiar atoms are genuine parts of the statue.

[4] Suppose the statue does not gain and lose material parts.

[5] See Michael Burke, 'Dion and Theon: An Essentialist Solution to an Ancient Puzzle', *Journal of* Philosophy 91 (1994): 129–139, and 'Preserving the Principle of One Object to a Place: A Novel Account of the Relations Among Objects, Sorts, Sortals, and Persistence Conditions', *Philosophy and Phenomenological Research* 54 (1994): 591–624.

[6] The preceding discussion assumed that mereological thinking can proceed using some univocal notion of overlap at a time that has general application. This might be challenged. Some will claim that the relation that we pick out when we say that the war had some battle as a part belongs to a different family of relations to the one that we pick out when we say that the person has an arm as a part. (Suggestive in this connection are Kit Fine, 'Compounds and Aggregates', *Nous* 28 (1994): 137–158 and 'Things and Their Parts', *Midwest Studies in Philosophy* 23 (1999): 61–74). For example, it may be claimed (first) that the battle/war relation is timeless, whereas the arm/person relation is time-indexed and then (second) insisted that one cannot define either in terms of the other. Thus, according to this line of thought, the relation that holds between the war and the

There is, however, a further thesis that so-called 'four-dimensionalists' are wedded to, but to which many so-called three-dimensionalists will object. The issue concerns how plentiful the phenomenon of temporary coincidence is. Following Sider, let us consider the defining claim of temporal parts theory to be that the world is 'made up of short lived temporal parts'.[7] While there are various metaphysical images that may be connoted by the expression 'made up' that we will consider later, let us for now consider two alternative glosses on the 'defining thesis':

Instantaneous Plenitude: For any object x and any instant t at which x exists, there is an object y such that y coincides with x at t and y only exists at t.

Gunky Plenitude: For any object x and any temporal interval of non-zero measure during which x exists, there is an object y such that y exists just in the interval and coincides with x at every time in the interval.

The theses are different. Both are reasonable ways to capture the idea that objects have short-lived temporal parts.[8]

A commitment to plenitude theses is orthogonal to the issue of whether a multitude of things (that may or may not be separated in time) always adds up to a further thing. This idea can once again be stated with the help of (time-indexed) mereological notions.[9] Let us say that an object x *fuses* a sets S at time t iff $\forall z$ (z overlaps x at t iff z overlaps at least one member of S at t). The relevant idea can now be stated as follows:

Universal Composition: For any set S, there is an object x that exists when and only when at least one member of S exists, and for every time t that x exists, x fuses at t that subset of S whose members exist at t.

Consider Attila the Hun and my laptop. If Universal Composition is true, there is an object, call it Lattila, that exists when and only when either Attila the Hun or my laptop exists, and which fuses the singleton set containing Attila the Hun at the times that Attila the Hun exists and the singleton set containing my laptop at the times when my laptop exists. Thus Lattila was coincident with Attila the Hun during the latter's lifetime, passed out of existence and then came back into existence during my

---

battle is a different relation from the relation that holds between a statue x and a lump y when x coincides with y at every time that x exists but not vice versa. One could envisage a debate between someone who thought that the relation between such a statue/lump pair was the very same relation as that which holds between a battle and a war, and someone who denied this, where both sides agree to attach the name 'temporal part of' to the relation between the battle and the war. Many of us are not willing to distinguish between 'temporal part of' (so defined) and the relation that holds between the statue and the lump, but do not thereby think that all the main issues connected to three-dimensionalism are thereby settled. We cannot frame the main debate in these terms.

[7] I take this turn of phrase from Sider's 'Temporal Parts', forthcoming in the *Blackwell Companion to Metaphysics*.

[8] Of course other glosses are possible, including the view that the world is made up of temporally short but non-instantaneous 'atoms'.

[9] As Sider himself is aware, it is helpful to frame the relevant debates in terms of time-indexed mereological notions, since they are acceptable to all parties.

laptop's lifetime, during which time it is coincident with the laptop.[10] Lattila's existence is not secured by the plenitude theses (even in combination): the latter theses secure various liberalisms about decomposition, not about composition.

Universal Composition is one idea that is frequently packaged together with a plenitude of temporal parts thesis, but which requires separate argumentation. In sections 2–4 below, I present some other ideas of this kind.

2 PERMANENT COINCIDENCE?

Can objects mereologically coincide? The question can be taken two ways. First, we can consider a *Thesis of Temporary Coincidence*: some pair of distinct objects mereologically coincides at some time. Second, we can consider the stronger *Thesis of Permanent Coincidence*: some pair of distinct objects mereologically coincide at all times that either exists. If there is a lump *x* that outlives a certain statue *y* and yet *x* and *y* are coincident at some time, then the first thesis is true; if there is a lump *x* that is distinct from some statue *y* and yet *x* coincides with *y* whenever either *x* or *y* exist, then the first and second theses are both true.[11]

As a matter of sociology, most of those philosophers who are committed to a plenitude of temporal parts (in either form stated) deny the thesis of Permanent Coincidence. Call this the *Standard Package*. It should be clear on reflection that the Standard Package is not mandatory: the plenitude theses are logically orthogonal to the thesis of Permanent Coincidence. Note, for example, that the Thesis of Instantaneous Temporal Parts does not say that for a given time *t*, there is *only one* instantaneous object that I am mereologically coincident with. Further, even if there were only one instantaneous object that is coincident with me at any given time that I existed, there might still be another object that is, for any given time, coincident with exactly the same instantaneous object as me.

Most philosophers who are committed to a plenitude of temporal parts take a counterpart-theoretic approach to modal discourse. But this is because they endorse the Standard Package. Take a case where a ship exists eternally and is eternally composed of the same steel throughout its entire existence. We naturally say that

---

[10] Note that the combination of Instantaneous Plenitude and Universal Composition does not entail that for any set of occupied spacetime points, there is an object that exactly occupies that set. There are thus some even more demanding plenitude theses in the vicinity.

[11] Some hold that all objects are eternal. On such a view, if a statue stops existing concretely, it still continues to exist. See, notably, Timothy Williamson 'Existence and Contingency', *Aristotelian Society*, sup. vol. 73 (1999): 181–203, and 'Bare possibilia', *Erkenntnis* 48, 2&3 (1998): 257–273. Arguably, even if the statue and lump coincide throughout their concrete existence, coincidence does not continue beyond concrete existence. Those drawn to such a view might wish to consider cases in which two coinciding objects are concrete for eternity. More pertinently still, advocates of such a view are likely to restrict plenitude and permanent coincidence theses to concrete existence. (Note, for example, that on the unrestricted view I certainly have no instantaneous temporal parts, construed as objects that coincide with me at some time but which only exist for an instant. Note also that it is dubious that there is some eternal object that is not Aristotle but that coincides with Aristotle at exactly this time of writing.)

the ship might have been destroyed at some time *t* in such a way that the steel that composes it would have survived. If we deny Permanent Coincidence we must also concede that there is only one eternal thing, not two (or more) permanently coincident things. But how can we make charitable sense of our modal verdicts?

Counterpart theory offers one well-known solution to the problem.[12] Without fussing about details, the key step involves treating 'might have survived crushing' as a context-dependent predicate. When predicated of the eternal object in a ship-salient context, the predicate expresses a property that the object lacks, but when predicated of the object in a steel-salient context, it expresses a property that the object possesses.

But there are alternative strategies that do not resort to such devious semantics. One who accepts the Thesis of Permanent Coincidence is free to take the relevant modal verdicts at face value since he discerns differing objects as the referents of 'the steel' and 'the ship' respectively. In that setting, we can reconcile 'the steel' might have been F and ~the ship might have been F' without appeal to context dependence, since no contradiction is induced by a context-invariant semantics.

Some four-dimensionalists think there is a puzzle concerning how two objects—say a statue and a lump—can be compresent in the same matter, and hold that a doctrine of temporal parts will be somehow important to resolving the puzzle. Now one reaction to the puzzle is to concede that there is indeed something outrageous in the vicinity—namely Permanent Coincidence—but to insist that Temporary Coincidence is in itself unproblematic. But we could disallow Permanent Coincidence while also rejecting plentitude. In that case we can still resolve the challenge in the way just indicated, without depending in any way on a doctrine of temporal parts. Meanwhile, we might endorse a plentitude of temporal parts and *also* allow Permanent Coincidence. In that case, we shall have to answer the challenge differently. The relevance of temporal parts to statue/lump puzzles is therefore unclear.

A further dimension to the issue is brought out in Sider's recent discussion.[13] Sider proposes a *fundamental* metaphysical insight—namely that objects are nothing over and above their parts—and that cohabitation is a *prima facie* challenge to that insight. On one natural gloss—and speaking with deliberate looseness—the insight is that big things are nothing over and above their smaller parts: for any big thing *x* there are smaller *y*s such that *x* is nothing over and above the *y*s. This gloss seems to require, for each big thing, that it decomposes into some set of smaller parts, and, correspondingly, that for each set of smaller parts, there is only one big thing it makes up. If there weren't the smaller parts, then the big thing would not resolve into smaller parts, and if there were two big things made out of the same small parts, then it would seem that each big thing would be something over and above the small parts into which

[12] See, notably, David Lewis 'Counterparts of Persons and their Bodies', *Philosophical Papers Volume I* (Oxford University Press, 1983), pp. 47–54.

[13] See his 'Temporal Parts', forthcoming in *Blackwell's Great Debates in Metaphysics*. This is one of many places where I am grateful for discussions with him.

it resolves. The statue-lump example now stands as a threat to the idea, for here we seem to have two big things made out of the same small parts.

Against this background, the standard combination of plenitude and a denial of permanent coincidence is attractive, since it provides way of regimenting the putative insight that allows its spirit to be retained:[14] plenitude provides the little things to make up the big things, and a denial of Permanent Coincidence ensures (at or least helps to ensure) that the big things do not take on a metaphysical life of their own. Of course, if we adopt this strategy, we need to read 'big' and 'small' as 'spatiotemporally big' and 'spatiotemporally small' (rather than as 'spatially big' and 'spatially small'), and we need a notion of composing that is not indexed to a particular time.[15] But with such an understanding in place, we find a plausible reading for the putative insight. Consider by contrast one who allows for the cohabitation of statue and lump but denies a plenitude thesis. The ordinary material particles that make up the lump are small enough to satisfy the desideratum that big things have smaller parts, but they overgenerate big things. Meanwhile, there are no other available understandings of 'small' and 'big' (assuming there are no short-lived temporal parts) to vindicate the thesis. I shall leave it to others to consider whether this line of thought lends significant strength to the package that blends plenitude with a rejection of permanent coincidence.[16]

3 TIME-INDEXING AND PERMEATION

The issue of whether the fundamental properties and relations are time-indexed or timeless is of central importance to our discussion. In this section, I shall consider that issue in some detail.

3.1

Suppose that something is red for a while and blue afterwards. In describing this state of affairs, we are not inclined to say 'The thing is both red and blue'—for in using a

---

[14] I note in passing that the restricted version of plenitude mentioned in n 11 would be of rather less use in this connection.

[15] An object x composes a set S iff for any time t that a member y of S exists, y is part of x at t, and for any time t that x exists, there is some subset z of S such that x fuses z at t.

[16] The putative insight can be taken in a somewhat different and, in some ways, more radical direction. Some appear to be gripped by the thought that the fundamental mereological relations of composition are *akin to* identity—that when we say that the xs are the y, that is strongly *analogous* to an identity statement of the form x is identical to y. While this is not the place to scrutinize the analogy in detail, it is worth noting that it will ring odd to those who think of the relation x *is part of* y as one derived from the time-indexed relation x *is part of* y *at* t: if identity is not time-indexed and parthood is, then how could they be analogous in the way required? Advocates of the analogy will be driven to endorse a plenitude of temporal parts, since only then can one regard a simple two place parthood relation as fundamental. (Suppose that an atom is part of a statue at a time. If there are no short-lived objects, there is no promising way to gloss that fact in terms of a putatively more fundamental atemporal parthood relation.) And advocates of the analogy will likely deny permanent coincidence in order to give substance to the analogy. (Why say that A is its parts if some numerically distinct B has the same parts?)

present tense 'is,' we would be saying of the time of utterance that the object is red and blue at that time. Rather, we are inclined to say that the object is red at some times and blue at some other times. These linguistic facts have analogues in the metaphysical realm: we cannot, it seems, capture the history in question using metaphysical resources that include only the object in question and two simple monadic properties, *being blue* and *being red*—for then we will have no way of capturing the temporal reference encoded by tense and by modifiers such as 'at such and such time'.

Let us consider three ways that one might enrich one's conception of the fundamental properties, relations and objects involved in order to accommodate these facts.[17] Consider first the most simple:

Type One: Time-Indexed. Being red is fundamentally a two-place relation between an object and a time. The object is *red-at* $t1$ and *blue-at* $t2$.[18]

Those who reject a plenitude of temporal parts typically embrace the time-indexed conception. The next two views are distinguished by appeal to the notion of a permeating property: a property P is *permeating* iff, necessarily, something has P iff every temporal part of x has P.

Type Two: Non-Time-Indexed and Non-Permeating.[19] There is a simple monadic property of *being red*. But it is not necessarily true that something is *red* iff every temporal part of it is *red*.

We shall be looking in due course at a few different ways of developing the atemporal non-permeating conception. For now let us opt for the most obvious though least interesting one: an object has the fundamental property of *being red* just in case it is red at some time or other.[20] English claims of the form 'x is red' will obviously express additional information beyond the claim that x *is red* (where the italicized 'is red' is used in the fundamental sense). Modifiers corresponding to 'now' and 'at t' may be introduced, that express functions from properties to properties. Some such function will take in properties like *being red* and deliver properties whose extensions are subsets of the original property's. Thus while *being red* is had of all the things that are ever red, *being red at t* is only had by those things that are red at t.

Can we do without these modifiers? Perhaps so. Consider a view that accorded itself Instantaneous Plenitude and that held that all the fundamental facts about redness could be captured using the simple non-permeating *being red* above, together with an *existing at* relation.[21,22] On this model, both the temporarily red and the

[17] In what follows I shall pretend that colours are fundamental.

[18] A variant: instantiation is fundamentally a three-place relation between an object, a time, and a property. Both variants can be adapted to modern physics by taking spacetime points as *relata*. As Delia Graff pointed out to me, the three-placed approach has an easier time vindicating the intuitive idea that a persisting object can have the very same property at different times.

[19] I am especially grateful to Ryan Wasserman here, who helped get me clear about the Type 2/Type 3 distinction.

[20] Note that structural complexity in the mode of expression need not correspond to structural complexity in the property itself.

[21] Matters are more complicated if one endorses Gunky but not Instantaneous Plenitude. See 'Gunk and Continuous Variation', this volume.

[22] The model needs to assume further that if x and y coincide at t then x and y cannot differ at t with regard to being red.

permanently red things will instantiate the fundamental property *red*, all the facts
about redness can be captured with *existing at* and *red*, with no need for modifiers.

Type Three: Non-Time-Indexed and Permeating. There is a simple monadic property of *being
red*, and it is necessarily true that if something is *red*, then every temporal part of it is *red*. When
a thing is red at a time, it does not follow that it has the property of *being red*, since it may
have a temporal part that is not red (and which does not exist at that time). However, when
a thing is red at a time, it will have a temporal part that exists at that time that instantiates
being red.[23]

For those who are not metaphysically stingy about properties, the pertinent issues
will in some large measure turn on which properties are fundamental and which not.
For example, each camp will recognize the two-place relation *being red at* posited by
the first camp.[24] But the second and third camps will think of that relation as less
fundamental than their own favourite.[25] (Of course, to the extent that these disputes
about relative fundamentality lack content, there may far less to disagree about than
some metaphysicians think.)

3.2

Most so-called four-dimensionalists typically opt for a type 3 conception of fundamental properties.[26] (Some may even think that fundamental properties are *thoroughly permeating*, where a property x is thoroughly permeating iff necessarily if

---

[23] Further complications arise when we realize that not all philosophers are eternalists. Consider
a presentist who believes that only the present time and its contents exist. He might think that if
something is currently red, then the relevant state of affairs can be can be captured by the simple
model with which we began: the thing has a simple monadic property of being red (where the 'has'
does not need to carry a tense modifier). Meanwhile, claims about past exemplification of redness
are to be understood in terms of temporal operators such as 'It will be the case that' and 'It was
the case five minutes ago'—so that ontological commitments to the contents of past time can be
avoided. I will set aside these issues in the discussion that follows.

[24] A possible qualification: one might argue that the type 1 view requires the reification of times
as entities whereas type 2 and 3 views do not.

[25] I would hope that questions about fundamentality of properties survive in some form for
nominalists too, but I shall not pursue the matter here.

[26] Suppose that it so happens in world w that every atom exists for only an instant and has
time-indexed properties. Even assuming a Humean account of laws, it is not clear that the laws at
that world need require that the atoms be short-lived. Nor would worlds in which atoms live longer
and do not have instantaneous parts require the instantiation of alien properties relative to w (on the
assumption that the actual ones are time-indexed). World w counts as a 'four-dimensionalist' world
by the lights of the plenitude-theoretic definition offered in Sider's *Four Dimensionalism*, but most
philosophers would not classify the case that way. One might think that in light of this example,
'four-dimensionalism' should be redefined as requiring *essentially* instantaneous parts everywhere
and always. But as Sider himself notes, 'Some four-dimensionalists might reject the assumption
that temporal parts are essentially instantaneous' (*Four Dimensionalism*, p. 67). In particular, as he
notes, friends of counterpart theory that allow for a flexible counterpart relation will be hesitant to
take on such a commitment. Notice in connection with this case that once type 3 properties have
been supplanted for a type of fundamental property that can readily attach to temporally extended
and changing things, then our willingness to use the language of 'four-dimensionalism' immediately
wavers. Thanks to Adam Sennet here.

something has x then all of its parts—spatial and temporal—do.)[27] They also tend to defend some version of each of the following theses:

The Occupation Conjecture: When a thing is intrinsically F for all or part of its career, the fundamental facts will involve nothing but the facts of part and whole, the facts of spatiotemporal occupation, and the pattern of instantiation of some combination of fundamental simple (i.e. non-indexed) monadic properties.

The Inheritance Conjecture: An object is intrinsically F at a time by virtue of having an instantaneous temporal part that exists at that time that instantiates some combination of fundamental simple monadic properties.

Obviously, this package of views—the combination of a type 3 conception of fundamental properties along with the Occupation and Inheritance Conjectures—is not mandated by an acceptance of Instantaneous Plenitude. In what follows, I will explore some alternative packages and highlight some important choice-points they present.

Suppose one believes in Instantaneous Plenitude. One might certainly combine this with an approach that treats permeating properties as fundamental and that endorses the Occupation and Inheritance Conjectures. But one needn't do so. Thus, for example, one might think that the time-indexed mass properties associated with the time-indexed view are fundamental and that atemporal mass properties (of type 2 or type 3) are derived:

x has permeating non-indexed mass of 15 kgs just in case x has mass 15 kgs at all times that x exists;

x has non-permeating non-indexed mass 15 kg just in case x has mass 15 kgs at some time that x exists.

The time-indexer might concede that whenever something has mass at a time, it is mereologically coincident with an instantaneous object that has 'mass 15 kgs simpliciter' (defined in one of the two ways above), but still deny that the defined properties are fundamental. Relatedly, he might disavow the Occupation Conjecture—on the grounds that the fundamental properties that make for intrinsic character are not simple monadic properties—and also question the use of 'by virtue of' in the Inheritance Conjecture. If both the instantaneous object and the long-lived object have the fundamental property of being 15 kgs at a certain time, what licenses the claim that the former has it by virtue of the latter having it? (More on this later.)

There are yet more radical tacks that are perfectly consistent with Instantaneous Plenitude. One might claim that while certain long-lived things bear the fundamental relation of *being conscious at* to this and that time, their shorter lived temporal parts do not stand in any such relation to any time. And one might even claim that while masses of matter have instantaneous temporal parts, those parts do not have the fundamental mass properties: if some mass of matter has some fundamental mass property of being m at t, its instantaneous temporal part at t does not have m at t (though it may have the derived property of being coincident at t with something that has m at t).[28] Such a view—which denies that fundamental mass properties are shared at

---

[27] I am of course using 'parthood' in an atemporal way here.
[28] This view is explored in 'Motion and Plenitude', this volume.

a time by coincident things—may be particularly natural if, for example, we think mass is essentially governed by a gravitational law. Waves of water and statues (unlike the masses of matter that they are coincident with) do not quite satisfy that law, owing to the fact that different masses of matter constitute the wave and the statue at different times. If the wave and statue do not move after *t* where the masses of matter that constitutes them move and the masses of matter do what the laws for massy objects tell them to do, then unless those laws have special clauses for statues and waves, we must withhold mass from the waves and statues—on pain of severing the assumed tie between fundamental property and law.[29]

We have been exploring ways that the advocate of Instantaneous Plenitude might embrace time-indexed properties as fundamental, departing from the more familiar combination of Instantaneous Plenitude and non-indexed permeating (type 3) properties. One might also, of course, combine Instantaneous Plenitude with a construal of fundamental properties as non-permeating and non-indexed (type 2). Such a proposal would lend support to the Occupation Conjecture. But it would lend no immediate credence to the Inheritance Conjecture, since those who adopt a non-permeating approach have no reluctance to allowing things that change over time to be the bearers of fundamental properties.

I have gestured at plenitudinous views that reject a type 3 conception. Here are two specific reasons why the Plenitude Lover might not be able to make do with type 3 properties as her fundamental properties of choice.

First, non-permeating properties may not even be available (let alone fundamental) to someone who accepts Gunky Plenitude but not Instantaneous Plenitude. Such a person might, for example, allow that something is red for only an instant, on account of the fact that it is changing continuously. She could not analyse this in terms of an object that had a permeating property of being red simpliciter, for on the gunky view, every temporal part of the thing is red for only a portion of its career.[30]

Second, suppose one combined Instantanous Plenitude with a tolerance for permanent coincidence. From that perspective, one might permit multiple *coinciding instantaneous* objects at a time. At this point one faces an important question: could coinciding instantaneous objects differ in their local intrinsic properties? Suppose one were to allow this. Then one could no long offer the familiar sorts of analyses of 'being F at *t*' in terms of 'being coincident with an instantaneous object that is F simpliciter'.[31] For consider some temporally extended thing *z* that has instantaneous

---

[29] Proponents of the radical ideas we have just been considering may have no patience whatsoever with the Inheritance Conjecture (even were it softened by substituting an 'if... then' for an 'in virtue of').

[30] And if she is willing to tolerate such singularities she will not be able to capture them either using the simple version of type 2 properties described earlier. A thing that is always blue apart from being red at each rational moment and a thing that is always red apart from being blue at each rational moment will have the same distribution of 'red at some time' and 'blue at some time' across the temporal parts posited by gunky plenitude.

[31] Of course, such analyses are only offered for a restricted class of rather basic predicates: it obviously could not be run on 'being 20 years old at *t*'. Such properties may supervene on the distribution of fundamental properties; but no analysis of the sort alluded to is available. It is also

temporal parts x and y at t. Suppose x is F and y is not F. Apply the analysis and one would be forced to say that z is both F and not-F at t. Confronted thus, one would face considerable pressure to add 'is F at t' to one's stock of fundamental predicates. Of course, such complications depend on a tendentious metaphysical thesis, namely that coincident instantaneous objects can differ intrinsically. But we should not think that mere commitment to one or other of the temporal parts theses outlined earlier requires some particular view on this thesis.

3.3

Four-dimensionalists like to find analogies between space and time. Such analogies may indeed encourage sympathy to plenitude. But such analogies may not at all militate in favour of a type 3 view of fundamental properties.

Consider first the spatial distribution of mass. I shall examine two models. Suppose, first, in accordance with a natural regimentation of classical mechanics, that extended bodies occupy continuous three-dimensional regions and are built out of uncountable numbers of point particles.[32] We cannot, in this setting, think of the uncountable particles as being the fundamental bearers of mass (with the mass of the fusions of these particles being determined by the mass of the particles),[33] for if we accord non-zero mass to the individual particles the bodies will be far too heavy (assuming countable additivity for masses). In this setting, then, one will likely think of the fundamental mass properties as being instantiated by certain fusions of particles.[34] (Of course, there will be interesting derivative properties that can be defined for the point particles themselves. In particular, there will be an interesting derivative property of mass density for a particle that can be recovered from considering sequences of smaller and smaller bodies containing the particle: in each case the mass density for the relevant body will be given by the mass divided by the volume, and the mass density of the particle will be given as the limit of the sequence. But it is crucial to note that on such a picture, the mass density at a point is a derived property, not a fundamental one.)[35] Clearly, were mass properties so distributed, fundamental mass properties would not be thoroughly permeating.

interesting to note that it could not be run either on modal properties (which many of us will think are intrinsic to objects at times).

[32] For such a regimentation, see C. Truesdell's *A First Course in Rational Continuum Mechanics* (Academic Press, 1977) and *Six Lectures on Modern Natural Philosophy* (Springer, 1966).

[33] Of course, one could say that a countable number of point particles had positive mass and the rest had no mass, but this represents an utterly implausible way of building bodies with smooth mass distributions.

[34] In a sense each instantiation will be derivative—the mass of a fusion will supervene on the masses of each countable decomposition. But the mass of the whole will not supervene on the masses of the particles, and—crucially—one will not be in a position to explain mass variation within the body in terms of mass variation of the particles themselves. Mass variation in the body—say that the left half is massier than the right—will be explained in terms of parts but not particles.

[35] And one that is extrinsic, though which supervenes on an arbitrarily small open region around the point. Of course, one could try out the view that it is, after all, mass densities that are fundamental. I shall not engage with that option in this paper. Frank Arntzenius has work in progress which pursues these matters.

Consider, second, a model (perhaps more plausible in the light of current physics) of a finite number of point particles each of finite mass. Suppose two particles x and y each had the fundamental mass property associated with being n kilos and a third, z had the fundamental mass property associated with being $2n$ kilos. Consider the fusion of x and y. Clearly, given the additivity properties for mass, that object will have the fundamental property had by z. In the face of the additive structure we all assume for mass properties it would be very hard indeed to insist that the fusion is just not the right kind of object to have the fundamental mass property possessed by z. So here again mass properties are not thoroughly permeating.

Having worked through this case, and taking seriously the analogy between space and time, one might wonder whether similar structures are to be found along the temporal axis. Assuming a plenitude of temporal parts, the first model is particularly suggestive here. Suppose a thing varies in charge. If the analogy with the first model held up, one would deny that the fundamental bearers of properties are instantaneous things: rather, for some fundamental magnitudes, the magnitude of a temporally extended thing would be determined by the magnitude of countable decompositions of the thing into things of lesser temporal extent, but this would not bottom out at a supervenience base of instantaneous things. Rather, one would define up derived properties for instantaneous things (recovered as the limits of properties exemplified by shorter and shorter things)—rather in the way that mass-density is a derived property in the spatial case. Here the fundamental magnitudes exemplified by the temporally extended objects would not be permeating: a type 2 model would appear natural. From such a perspective, notice, the Inheritance Conjecture will have to be discarded.

Are such speculations likely to be vindicated? Could it be that magnitudes aggregate over time in the way just indicated? Well, it certainly *could* turn out that way.[36] If we are to avoid the arrogance of those who aspire to predict the outcomes of fundamental natural philosophy from the armchair, we should at least have some healthy agnosticism about the project of analysing change in terms of instantaneous objects.[37]

3.4

What might be said against type one and two views? What might tell against regarding such properties as fundamental? Some appear to think that we can just *see* that the fundamental property in the vicinity of, say, *being square* is of the type 3 variety. Such claims to metaphysical vision are especially embarrassing when one recalls the frame-dependence of shape that one learns about in relativistic physics.[38] But natural science aside, is the claim even prima facie plausible? The insight could not arise from reflection on the superficial monadicity of the ordinary predicate 'is square', since any

[36] Good test cases are provided by various fundamental magnitudes of relativistic physics—notably stress-energy and charge-current

[37] Of course, the reflections of this last section do not in any way preclude analysing change in terms of variation of temporal parts that are non-instantaneous.

[38] Of course, relativistic physics does not tell us that there are no intrinsic properties in the vicinity.

ordinary deployment will also carry a tense marker.[39] Moreover, its predicability of long-lived things implies that the ordinary predicate does not semantically express a type 3 property. Perhaps one is supposed to directly lock on to the underlying attribute and see, independently of any reliance on one's language organ, that there is a fundamentally monadic intrinsic property that is manifest. (Thus, for example, one ought to be able to just see that the squareness of the block can't consist in its occupying a square region since that would make the fundamental facts about the block too relational.) I leave such metaphysical pretence to others.[40]

Here is a different reason for rejecting a type 1 or 2 view. Some philosophers hold a kind of combinatorialism for fundamental properties and relations, according to which there are no necessary connections between absolutely fundamental properties and relations, so that the holding of a fundamental relation R1 between *x* and *y* neither excludes nor requires the holding of any distinct fundamental relation R2. A commitment to this sort of combinatorialism may well render certain time-indexing views difficult to maintain. For suppose one took, say, having mass to be a fundamental relation between an object and a time (or spacetime region) and also took locatedness to be a fundamental relation between an object and a spacetime region. If one added a commitment to combinatorialism to the mix, one would be left with the result that one can stand in the *having mass* relation to a region that one doesn't even occupy! Accept time-indexing and the relevant version of combinatorialism may well have to be abandoned. (I myself doubt whether this is a significant cost.)

3.5

When we turn to relations, a set of issues similar to those discussed in 3.1–3.4 arise. Consider, for example, the *part of* relation. The stereotypical temporal parts theorist typically assumes that the fundamental mereological relations are not time-indexed, so that the notion of parthood at a time is a derived notion: *x* is part of *y* at *t* just in case *x*'s instantaneous temporal part at *t* is part of *y*'s instantaneous temporal part at *t*. But just as the temporal parts theorist needn't be committed to the fundamentality of time-free properties in general, so too she need not be committed to the thesis that the atemporal *part of* relation is somehow more fundamental than a time-indexed parthood relation.[41] Consider, for example, someone who defended a gunky plenitude thesis. Mightn't she allow that an atom is part of a house for only an instant (imagine, for example, that the atom and the house coexisted for only an instant)? In that case she might naturally allow that the atom is part of the house at a time, but deny that any part of the atom is part of the house simpliciter (recall that the gunky plenitude thesis does not posit instantaneous parts).[42]

---

[39] To be fair, there are *some* naked uses: to be square requires having four sides. But it is hard to see the type 3 advocate getting much leverage out of such uses.

[40] For more on the weakness of the so-called 'argument from temporary intrinsics', see Sider's *Four Dimensionalism* pp. 92–98.

[41] Of course, commitment to a time-indexed parthood relation is not yet a commitment to the time-indexing of identity. I have discussed the view that identity is time-indexed elsewhere ('Identity', this volume). It is not a promising view.

[42] Thanks for discussions with Dean Zimmerman here.

We should also note the permeating/non-permeating contrast can be made out for relations, where one can ask for each place, whether it is type 2 or type 3. A relation xRy, is *permeating in the y position* iff necessarily $(xRy \supset (\forall z \ z$ is a temporal part of $y \supset xRy))$, and *permeating in the x position* iff necessarily $(xRy \supset (\forall z \ z$ is a temporal part of $x \supset zRy))$.

Note that the standard four-dimensionalist, while typically favouring type 3 over type 2 properties, has a more complicated attitude to the fundamentality of type three relations, since the fundamental mereological relations that she favours are not permeating in both places. Likewise for the fundamental occupation relations, for neither the relation of occupation nor that of exact occupation is permeating in both places. (Whether this comprises the elegance of her metaphysical vision is a question that I leave for others to consider.)

4   ARE THE SHORT-LIVED THINGS MORE FUNDAMENTAL?

A commitment of most so-called 'four-dimensionalists' is that instantaneous things are metaphysically fundamental. And this commitment is certainly one of the key targets of three-dimensionalist picture thinking. But what exactly does the dispute amount to? Here are three ways of making the issue a little more precise:

4.1   Which Entities Are the Bearers of Fundamental Properties?

Suppose one adopted the type 3 view outlined earlier. One would then naturally think that instantaneous things were well suited to stand as the bearers of fundamental properties. However, even on a type 3 conception, it may be difficult to maintain that fundamental properties attach only to instantaneous things. Supposing existence is a fundamental property, it will attach to everything. And supposing that a long-lived object has mass of 15 kgs throughout its existence, one would have to appeal to considerations other than permeation in order to withhold from it the fundamental property of having mass 15 kgs simpliciter.[43] There is conceptual space, of course, to claim that even an unchanging but long-lived object would be unsuitable as the bearer of those fundamental properties common to its instantaneous parts. But such a position is not easy to justify. Unless the proponent of such a view denied the existence of long-lived things, he would presumably have to deny the fundamental status of such properties as *existence* and such relations as *identity* and *mereological coincidence*. It would be very strange, for example, to claim that while long-lived things exist,

---

[43] Note that there is no outright contradiction in allowing changing things with no temporal parts to have exclusively type 3 fundamental properties. On such a view, there will be no direct threat to permeation, since there will not be temporal parts. But absent temporal parts, it seems radically implausible that type 3 properties would provide a supervenience base for the world and hence not plausible that they could provide the stock of fundamental properties (unless one conceived of the fundamental type 3 properties as distributional properties that each encoded large quantities of information about the world (cf. Josh Parsons 'Distributional Properties', in Jackson and Priest (eds.), *Lewisian Themes* (Oxford: Oxford University Press, 2004), pp. 173–180)) and insisted that possible objects with temporal parts could not instantiate these properties).

there is a property in the vicinity of 'existence'—superexistence—that attaches only to instantaneous objects. And presumably, the proponent of such a view would have to say either that worlds with gunky plenitude but without instantaneous plenitude were impossible, or else that the objects at such worlds would instantiate alien fundamental properties. Finally, one wonders whether the temporal restriction of fundamental properties to instantaneous objects is at all plausible without a spatial restriction to pointy objects. But the latter will encounter trouble from any fundamental magnitudes with an additive structure (recall the case of mass above).

While some may be tempted to a picture according to which short-lived things are fundamental, it is not clear that they will find much appeal in the view that only short-lived objects instantiate the truly fundamental properties. It is worth considering other construals of the picture.

4.2 Does the Temporally Long Depend on the Temporally Short?

When giving voice to their favourite picture of the world, metaphysicians often appeal to notions of dependence other than ordinary causal dependence: even when x does not precede or (efficiently) cause y, we can ask whether y exists *in virtue* of x; and even when x's profile does not cause y's profile in the ordinary sense, we can ask whether y is such and such *in virtue* of x's being so and so. Though the relevant *in virtue of* relations have not received much by way of systematic examination in contemporary metaphysical discussions, they remain prevalent in our informal thinking about these topics. And they allow us to articulate some further issues not raised in their own right above. In particular, we can ask whether the temporally long-lived things exist in virtue of the short-lived things and whether the temporally long-lived things have their qualitative character in virtue of temporally short-lived things.

Note in this connection that one might take the 'in virtue of' that appears in the inheritance doctrine very seriously, and in such a way that it resists straightforward modal definition. Take a world w in which a lonely particle is red throughout its existence. Suppose one maintained a type 3 view. It would still be natural in this case to claim that the non-instantaneous parts of the thing (along with the instantaneous parts) instantiate the fundamental type 3 property of being red. Now any world where the instantaneous parts of that thing are the same with regard to their state of redness at w, the non-instantaneous parts are the same with regard to redness at w. But note that in this case, the modal facts appear symmetric: in any world where the redness of the non-instantaneous parts matches their state of redness at w, the redness of the instantaneous parts matches their state of redness at w. Does this symmetry mean that neither has primacy? Perhaps not: one might still find it altogether intuitive to insist that, even at w, the non-instantaneous things are red *in virtue of* the instantaneous things and not vice versa. A similar option holds for objects. One might hold that the *de re* facts about which instantaneous objects exist at a world are modally fixed by the *de re* facts about which long-lived objects exist at that world and yet still maintain that long-lived objects exist in virtue of simple objects and not vice versa.

Supposing we tentatively grant the intelligibility of such 'in virtue of' questions. It is far from clear that a plenitude of temporal parts ought to commit us to the view—

abhorrent to three-dimensionalists—that reckons the fundamental lines of dependence to run from the temporally short to the temporally long. Consider an electron
that persists for an extended period. And suppose the doctrine of instantaneous temporal parts is true. It follows that, at any time, the electron is coincident with at
least one instantaneous thing. But the questions of metaphysical dependence remain
unanswered. Of course, one *might* claim that the electron exists in virtue of the
instantaneous things and inherits its qualitative profile at any given time from the
instantaneous thing that it is coincident with at that time; but one might instead
adopt the perspective that it is the electron that is most fundamental. (If we allow
ourselves the metaphysical distinction between substances and derived objects, it is
open to us to reckon the electron a substance, and some instantaneous stage of the
electron a derived entity whose 'real definition' consists of an electron and a particular
time.[44,45])

Though these issues of dependence, real definition, and so on, are notoriously
difficult to retain intellectual control of, they are nevertheless difficult to dismiss
altogether. To the extent that we take such issues seriously, a commitment to
instantaneous temporal parts leaves much unresolved.

4.3 Does Everything Supervene on the Profile of the Short-lived Things?

The dependence question can also be given a modal gloss. One modal notion of
dependence that has received considerable attention has been that of supervenience.
The central idea is easy enough to grasp: A facts *supervene* on B facts just in case
(cross-world) duplication of B facts guarantees duplication of A facts. Let us say
that A facts *asymmetrically supervene* on B facts just in case A facts supervene on
B facts but not vice versa. One cannot adequately capture the intuitive notions
of metaphysical dependence in terms of asymmetrical supervenience: any necessary
truth will asymmetrically supervene on any given contingent fact, but it seems
nonetheless that it may not depend on that fact. Still, the concept of supervenience is
clearer than the other notions of metaphysical dependence, and if we help ourselves to
it, we can frame some tractable questions that lie in the vicinity of our current inquiry.
In particular, we might consider a supervenience version of the Inheritance Thesis:
do the facts about long-lived things supervene on facts about the intrinsic profiles of
instantaneous things, coupled with the fundamental relations holding between those
things?

As with previous versions of Inheritance, this supervenience thesis is not forced
on us by Instantaneous Plenitude (suppose, for example, that consciousness was

---

[44] This gives one reason to worry about Sider's plenitude-theoretic account in *Four
Dimensionalism*.

[45] Note in this connection that one might naturally classify someone as three-dimensionalist
were he to accept Instantaneous Plenitude but thought, for example, that momentary person-stages
were dependent entities—rather than in the way that Aristotle arguably thought that the singing
man an entity distinct from but dependent on the man. Kit Fine's work is an excellent resource for
these topics. Relevant here are his 'Acts, Events, and Things', in *Language and Ontology, Proceedings
of the Sixth International Wittgenstein Symposium* (1981), pp. 97–105, 'Essence and Modality',
Philosophical Perspectives 8 (1994), pp. 1–16, and 'On the Non-Identity of Material Thing and Its
Matter', *Mind*, 40 (March 2003), pp. 195–234.

fundamental and did not attach to instantaneous things). And one might accept it while still holding that the lines of metaphysical dependence described in 5.2 run from long to short. Consider a lonely electron world and suppose that there exist derivative instantaneous parts spawned by the electron (and not vice versa). Let us allow that both the electron and the corresponding short-lived temporal part instantiate the same fundamental intrinsic properties at a given time (imagine, say, a type 1 model for such properties). Suppose some essentiality of dependence doctrine were true for the short-lived thing: it could not exist except as a stage in the life of the long-lived electron. In this story, the short-lived things exist in virtue of the long-lived thing. Yet it is clear enough that the identity of the electron and its character supervenes on the identity of the short-lived entities and their character.

5 ARE POTENTIALITIES INTRINSIC TO EXISTING OBJECTS AT A TIME?

In this section and the next I present some ideas that are commonly found among so-called three-dimensionalists and which are invariably rejected by those who opt for a plenitude of temporal parts. Here again my main aim is to throw the conceptual terrain into sharper relief rather than to defend some package of views.

Suppose a statue and lump that exist at some given time are coincident but distinct entities. When asked what is distinctive about each, it is natural to answer that the potentialities of each are different: one can survive flattening, the other cannot; one can survive radical changes of parts (so long as the transformation is not too sudden), the other cannot; and so on.[46] To what extent does that answer take us to the heart of things? Opinions differ radically. Let us consider two kinds of packages (without pretending that they exhaust the logical terrain).

One view, prevalent among card-carrying three-dimensionalists, is that potentialities count among the fundamental characteristics of a thing and are, moreover, intrinsic to a thing at a time. (Intrinsicality is coordinate with duplication: a property is intrinsic if and only if it is shared by all possible duplicates.)[47] Now on the view that we are currently considering, the statue and the lump are not intrinsically the same at the time that they are mereologically coincident, because they have different potentialities.[48] This picture allows for potentialities to be genuinely explanatory in certain ways. That the lump persisted because of its potentialities can be a sort of genuine efficient causal explanation rather than the mere articulation of some sort of definition (along the lines of 'he is a bachelor because he is an unmarried man'). Even assuming that *fundamental* causal explanations should appeal to properties that are

---

[46] Of course, there may be other answers that one can give: perhaps some aesthetic characteristics belong to one but not the other; perhaps the intentional relations that we stand in to one are different to the other. But the modal, potentiality-based answer is perhaps the most popular. (Cf. Fine, 'The Non-Identity of a Material Thing and Its Matter') 195–234.

[47] Cf Lewis, 'Extrinsic Properties', in *Papers in Metaphysics and Epistemology* (Cambridge University Press, 1999) pp. 111–115.

[48] We have already raised the issue whether things that are coincident at a time are automatically intrinsic duplicates. This is one arena where the issue becomes particularly important.

intrinsic to a time, explanation via potentialities can, on this view, be fundamental. This picture also gives some support to such three-dimensionalist slogans as that the nature of a thing is immanent to each time that it exists, since the differing natures of the statue and lump are manifest in how they are intrinsically at a given time.[49,50]

A second package of views opts for a picture according to which, at a given time of mereological coincidence, the statue and lump are intrinsic duplicates. This implies, among other things, that the distinctive potentialities accruing to each are not reflected in their respective intrinsic makeup at the time in question. (One way to motivate such a view would be via a kind of modal reductionism whereby dispositional facts reduce to non-dispositional, mundane facts about the distribution of purely 'categorical' properties.[51] Assuming we further admit there is no intrinsic difference at the time with regard to the purely categorical facts, the reductionist is forced to reckon the difference in potentiality to be extrinsic.)

Suppose I crush the lump. The statue passes out of existence, while the lump survives, albeit transfigured. Think back to the time before crushing. There were two objects, call them Lump and Statue, that coincided. We might ask: 'What was it was about Lump that enabled it to survive and what it was about Statue that precluded it from surviving?'.[52]

Our two packages will offer very different answers to the questions that motivate this query. A proponent of the first package will deny that they were exactly alike prior to the time of crushing: 'This is to presuppose a brutish view of intrinsic character. The intrinsic nature of a thing at a time goes far beyond that which can be revealed by a photograph, even a photograph of unlimited resolution. The intrinsic potentialities of the lump, the intrinsic manifestation of its nature at a given time, are very different than the intrinsic potentialities of the statue, though this difference will not be revealed by a pair of photographs. And it is these potentialities that explain why one perishes in the face of crushing while the other soldiers on.'

The second package will likely resort to the following kind of therapy when posed with our question, exploiting putative analogies between time and space. Consider a lump that exactly occupies region R of space and a part of that lump that exactly occupies subregion R' of R. Both the lump and the lump-part occupy region R' but the lump extends beyond that region. Suppose we focus on R' and ask 'What is it about the lump that enables it to extend beyond this region while the lump-part does not?' In answering this question, we feel no temptation to identify some way that they differ with respect to R' that then explains why they are different elsewhere. According to the second package, one ought to adopt the same attitude to our main question.

---

[49] Conversations with Mark Johnston were helpful here.

[50] Assuming that natures, in the relevant sense, can be read off from the intrinsic potentialities. To the extent that natures are partly origin-theoretic, natures will still not be immanent.

[51] The claim that the statue and lump are the same categorically might be disputed. Relevant here is 'Plenitude and Motion', this volume. Of course, the cogency of the categorical/non-categorical distinction might also be disputed.

[52] This is the respectable version of a question that we may secretly pose to ourselves more colloquially: 'How does each know what to do at the time of crushing given that they were exactly alike?'

Just as the facts intrinsic to R' will not tell one why the lump but not the lump part extends beyond R', so the facts intrinsic to *t* will not tell one why the lump rather than the statue extends beyond *t* (the time after which crushing occurs). Insofar as the question presupposed an answer that adverts to the facts intrinsic to *t*, it has no answer. If, meanwhile, we are not constrained to answer by appeal to such intrinsic facts, then we need not resort to the picture thinking proposed by the first package in order to answer the question.

Does a commitment to the second package mean that there is no fundamental causal explanation of why the statue survives and the lump does not? Assuming the constraint on fundamental causal explanations mentioned above, this does follow. But perhaps statues are outside the domain of fundamental laws in the first place. If so, one can explain why the lump survives in terms of its intrinsic properties (plus the laws) without paradox (since the statue will fall outside the domain of the laws). The cost—if it be a cost—is that one cannot explain the evolution of an object from a time in terms of its intrinsic properties at that time in combination with a set of *unrestricted* laws of the form: 'If a thing has intrinsic property *p* at a time and its intrinsic environment is *e* then it will F.'

Returning to our familiar theme, we should note that a commitment to the plenitude of temporal parts is neutral on the competing perspectives just sketched. To say that I am coincident with one or more instantaneous objects at each moment of my existence is not yet to concede that I duplicate some instantaneous object at each moment. One could consistently maintain that, were God to restrict His gaze to a single moment, He would see different potentialities present as between me and this or that instantaneous thing coincident with me, potentialities that make my prospects for longevity far brighter. Such a combination is seldom entertained by proponents of plenitude, though it is not clear whether this is due to reason or fashion.

6 'WHOLLY PRESENT'[53]

Some may worry that I have not yet adequately addressed the ideas about *occupation* that drive certain three dimensionalists, especially those who take the 'wholly present' gloss as a thesis purely about occupation, not about parthood. Might it be that the discussion so far has neglected a key relation? Let me pose this issue in a somewhat neutral way. Insofar as we do not wish to cash out 'wholly present' in terms of the plenitude theses articulated above, or in terms of the intrinsicality ideas just alluded to, one might choose to deploy an ideological primitive of 'exact occupation' in one's metaphysic. *Exact occupation* is conceived here as a simple two-place relation between an object and a spatiotemporal region, such that (crucially) an object can stand in the exact occupation relation to distinct spatiotemporal regions. On this basis, we can articulate certain derived notions: an object *o occupies* a spatiotemporal region iff that region is a subset of a region that *o* exactly occupies. An object *covers* a region R iff R fuses a set of regions that it occupies. And an object *o maximally covers* a region R

[53] I am grateful for discussions with Oliver Pooley here.

iff *o covers* R and there is no region R' of which R a proper part and which is also covered by *o*.

With such an ideology in place one might frame one's three-dimensional commitment as follows:[54]

For any object *o*, there a set *S* of regions of zero temporal extent that are each exactly occupied by *o*, such that the region maximally covered by *o* fuses *S*.

We might then try to gloss four-dimensionalism as the view that an object exactly occupies a region iff it maximally covers the region. From such a perspective Instantaneous Plenitude is altogether silent on the key issue (similarly for the other theses discussed above). After all, this gloss allows for the cogency of combining Instantaneous Plenitude with three-dimensionalism.

Of course, those of us who do not buy into the framework presented above will not recognize as legitimate the questions that are being raised here. Suppose one denies the ideology just presented and works instead with a basic relation of occupation between objects and spatiotemporal regions—where *occupation* obtains between *x* and *y* whenever the proponent of the first package claims that *x* covers *y*—and a defined notion of maximal occupation (corresponding to maximal covering above), where an object *maximally occupies* a region R iff R fuses the set of regions that the object occupies. The advocate of such a view will naturally translate 'covers' by 'occupies' and 'maximally covers' by 'maximally occupies', but then will be left without any means by which to make sense of questions posed using the predicate 'exact occupation'.

Such is the way of many foundational disputes: the framework within which one party raises questions may have no counterpart in the framework of other parties. Those of us who work with the bare-bones 'occupation' and those predicates that can be derived from it will be forced to look elsewhere for interesting theses in the vicinity of disputes about three-dimensionalism.

POSTSCRIPT: SIDER'S ARGUMENT FROM VAGUENESS

In *Four Dimensionalism*, Ted Sider is interested in defending a package that combines a plenitude of temporal parts with Universal Composition. One of his master arguments for that package is his argument from vagueness. Suppose I am restrictive in my ontology. Perhaps, for example, I believe in statues, artefacts, organisms, and atoms, but have no patience for the plentitude of parts espoused by either Instantaneous Plenitude or Gunky Plenitude, nor for the liberalism of composition endorsed by the Universal Composition thesis. Then, as Sider sees it, I will be under pressure to concede that existence is vague. For consider a series of scenarios $s_1 \ldots s_n$ that are pairwise only slightly different from each other, such that (i) it is clear that in s_1 some atoms and a single composite object built out of some of the atoms are the only things

---

[54] I shall not worry here about formulating the thesis for relativistic physics. Note also that the proponent of the thesis might find it natural to treat events and objects differently. Perhaps an event occupies a region iff it maximally covers it.

that exist at a certain time t; and (ii) it is clear, owing to how that atoms are scattered, that in s_n only the atoms exist at t. At which point in the series does there stop being a composite object? This seems to be a vague matter. But then for various points in the sequence, the question 'How many objects are there?' has no determinate answer. But this make is for the undesirable conclusion that the unrestricted existential quantifier is itself vague.

The metaphysics that Sider proposes will never be faced with this sort of indeterminacy: give him a series of slightly differing cases with, say, a cat at one end and no cat at the other another, and he can say (supposing no fundamental particles come or go across the series) that there are the same number of objects in each case, and it is merely a vague matter whether some object or other is to count as a cat. One who thinks that atoms only compose things when they are suitably arranged cannot respond in this fashion.

Let us lay out the argument as clearly as possible. Suppose the sequence of cases s_1 to s_n is such that each definitely has 50000 atoms at t.[55] In s_1 there is definitely a single composite object and in s_n there is definitely no composite object. The proponent of the view that we are imagining will presumably concede that in each case it is definite that (there are 50001 things at t ⊃ there is a composite object at t) and definite that (there are 50000 things at t ⊃ there is no composite object at t). In standard logics of definiteness (following normal modal logics), definiteness distributes over the conditional (so that if (Definitely P ⊃ Q) then (Definitely P ⊃ Definitely Q)). We thus have

(i) (Definitely there are 50001 things at t) ⊃ (Definitely there is a composite object at t)

and

(ii) (Definitely there are 50000 things at t) ⊃ (Definitely there is no composite object at t).

Suppose we now claim that there is no vagueness in the number of things and thus for each case:

(iii) (Definitely there are 50000 things at t) or (Definitely there is 50001 things at t).

A simple logical consequence of these claims is that

Definitely there is a composite object at t or Definitely there is no composite object at t,

which contradicts a claim of vagueness for composition.

Sider's own position is that there is never vagueness of composition in a borderline case of, say, cathood, since vagueness of the latter sort will never make for vagueness as to whether some atoms compose something (they always do). But, to reiterate, such a view cannot be taken by someone who thinks (for example) that for every member of the series, it is definite that everything at a given time is an organism or an atom.

---

[55] I am using the notion of definiteness in a standard way, so that it is vague whether P iff it is not definite that P and not definite that not P.

How should the proponent a restrictive ontology respond? One interesting kind of strategy begins with the observation that, strictly speaking, the above argument was only an argument for the vagueness of 'exists at *t*' and not for 'exists' simpliciter.[56] Suppose it was determinate how many concrete things existed in the world overall, but that the spatiotemporal boundaries of some things was indeterminate. (Suppose, for example, that at some world *w*, it is determinate that a cat exists but indeterminate whether it is still in existence at *t*.)[57] On that assumption, one could coherently insist on the determinacy of the number of existing things, while conceding that at a given time, it is indeterminate how many things exist at that time. The determinacy of existence itself, and thus the non-vagueness of the unrestricted existential quantifier, would be safeguarded.

This package is not as stable as it might first appear.[58] Take a world where it is indeterminate whether a composite object comes into existence at all. (It would seem, on the face of it, that the proponent of the restrictive ontology would be embarrassed to deny that there are such worlds.) But then one cannot quarantine the indeterminacy to matters of spatiotemporal boundary.

Given certain metaphysical orientations, however, the second strategy can be patched up. Some have held that every object is necessary and eternal, holding that the apparent contingency of concrete objects consists in the contingency of being concrete.[59] A given cat will exist necessarily and eternally, though it will be concrete at some times and not others, and at some worlds and not others. Given a view of this sort, one can easily resist Sider's argument for the vagueness of the existential quantifier. Consider the world which we would naturally describe as one in which it is vague whether a cat comes into existence. From the perspective we are currently imagining, this will be redescribed as a world where it is vague whether a certain object ever has the property of concreteness (and, relatedly, whether it ever comes to have certain atoms as parts).[60] Determinacy can be retained for the existential quantifier. The relevant kind of vagueness is explained away in terms of the indeterminacy of concreteness.

What of those who are disinclined to the kind of metaphysical excess entertained in the last paragraph? After all, it would certainly be a victory of sorts for Sider if the humble 'common sense' ontologist was forced to resort to such excess in order to save his view. The *eternalist strategy* just outlined is likely to have limited appeal. Let me then mention a second strategy—the *epistemic strategy*—for answering Sider's challenge.

It is arguable that we sometimes confuse ignorance due to vagueness with ignorance that is due to a lack in our discriminatory powers. Let me cite two examples. First,

---

[56] I am grateful for discussion with Ryan Wasserman here.

[57] Note that if the location of atoms is determinate and it is determinate that a cat is where its atomic parts are, then the view will require vagueness is the 'part of at *t*' relation.

[58] Sider is aware of this.   [59] See fn. 11 above.

[60] Which object? Which of the many possible tables will be indeterminately concrete? Well, that depends on the world. Just as there are qualitatively duplicate worlds in which numerically different atoms swirl in the void, so there are qualitatively duplicate worlds in which numerically different tables are indeterminately concrete.

there are cases where a pair of experiences are pairwise indiscriminable with regard to phenomenal character, but where we hesitate over the question whether the characters are identical or not. Now we may naturally describe this as a case of vagueness, but on further reflection we become unsure whether this is a profitable way of viewing things. An equally promising way of viewing the matter, it would seem, is that the experiences in question determinately did or determinately did not share the same phenomenal character, and our ignorance stemmed from a simple epistemic incapacity on our part to compare them (this is especially natural if the experiences are separated in time or else at distant ends of our visual field).[61] Granted, one can construct a 'Sorites' series of cases that gradually moves from an experience wildly dissimilar in character to some target experience *e* to an experience that one cannot discern to be different in character from *e*. But does this really show that 'identical in phenomenal character' is a vague predicate? Many of us would hesitate to draw that conclusion.[62] Consider next an admittedly recherché—though in some ways more relevant—metaphysic according to which there are extended simples. We encounter a spherical object and realize that the question arises as to whether is a single extended simple or else whether it is composed of two hemispherical extended simples. We may casually say that it is 'vague' which answer to the question is correct. But on reflection it seems odd to describe this as ignorance due to vagueness. Isn't our ignorance here due simply to an inability to detect the boundaries of objects?

What goes for spatial boundaries on the extended simples case goes for spatiotemporal boundaries on the envisaged ontology. Suppose there are atoms and organisms. When we are presented a series of cases, each only slightly different, with an organism at one end, and none at the other, it is indeed quite natural to claim that the cases where we do not know are cases of vagueness. But it might be argued that reaction is wrong in just that way that it is arguably wrong in the cases just considered. What is really going on is that we misdescribe a series of cases that manifest our limited discriminatory power as a vagueness-revealing Sorites series.

Now it is clear enough why Sider is uncomfortable with this sort of reply. His concern is that a picture like that just adumbrated would posit a sharp cut off in a series of cases that is 'metaphysically arbitrary', and would in that sense make the macroscopic 'autonomous' from the microscopic.[63]

This rhetoric points to a deep methodological issue: is the naturalness of a divide suitably revealed by describing that divide in terms of the language of fundamental microphysics? Sider, like many of us, believes in some objective ranking of properties on a scale of naturalness, with perfectly natural properties at one end and utterly gerrymandered properties at another. But he also tacitly accepts another commitment—namely that a property's naturalness is given by its ease of definability

---

[61] See Williamson, *Identity and Discrimination* (Cambridge: Blackwell, 1990) for an extended discussion of these issues.

[62] I think that even if one is an epistemicist one should be reluctant to count this as a case of vagueness, but I shall not pursue the matter here.

[63] P. 124. He is explicit that the defender of this kind of 'autonomy' could consistently claim that the macroscopic was supervenient on the microscopic.

in terms of fundamental microphysics. This is far from obvious. It may well be possible to motivate that kind of autonomy outside the province of the specifically ontological debates with which Sider is concerned. Many of us accept that consciousness supervenes on the physical. Perhaps naively, we are also inclined to accept that consciousness is not vague: for any being it is determinate whether or not that being is conscious (in the sense that there is something that it is like to be it). Now we can imagine a series of cases that are pairwise very close microphysically, at one end of which is a definitely conscious being, at the other end of which is definitely a non-conscious being. Suppose that the cut-off is, without our knowing it, at case x. The difference between cases to the right of x and cases to the left of x can be described in terms of the language of fundamental microphysics. But when so described the difference between cases to the left of x and cases to the right of x will seem to be no more important than the difference between cases to the left and right of some other arbitrarily chosen member of the series. But should this convince us that the line between the conscious and the non-conscious was, after all, of no great metaphysical significance?

Of course, someone could try to run Sider's concern of metaphysical arbitrariness: 'How could it be such a big deal that the cases are divided by a tiny physical discrepancy such as distance or charge?' And sure enough, if the importance (that is, naturalness) of any divide correlates with its importance when viewed through the lens of microphysics, we will be thrown back on conceding that the conscious/non-conscious divide is, despite appearances, a gerrymandered, metaphysically unimportant distinction. But it is far from clear that this is the right reaction.

Another possible reaction to the series is to turn panpsychist: embarrassed to posit lines that look unimportant through a microphysical lens, we might give everything a bit of consciousness and eliminate the line. Interestingly, not many of us are tempted to that reaction in this case, despite the fact that it is the structural analogue of Sider's recommendation in the composition case.

Might the threatened 'autonomy from the microphysical' be due to a naive assumption that the conscious/non-conscious divide is not vague? Our sense that the conscious/non-conscious distinction is natural *could not be rescued* from Sider's autonomy charge simply by insisting that it is vague—for on no precisification would a vague conscious/non-conscious divide appear natural when redescribed microphysically.

On reflection, then, it is clear that a key step towards maintaining the importance of the conscious/non-conscious divide is to deny that the naturalness of a divide is always suitably revealed by describing that divide in some canonical microphysical language. In this sense, Sider is right: by insisting that the naturalness of macrophysical divisions cannot be calibrated by their (perhaps infinitary) microphysical definitions, we are giving (consistently with supervenience) a certain kind of metaphysical autonomy to the macrophysical.[64]

The following thought experiment helps to crystallize the debate. Imagine that a Martian was endowed with a purely microphysical language and represented the

---

[64] I note in passing that it is arguable that cats can be realized by complexes that instantiate alien universals and so the property of being a cat resists (even infinitary) microphysical definition.

world using that language.[65] He records the various continuous changes in the world. He notes nothing especially important at time *t*. We who look on with our macrophysicalist lens see *t* as a profoundly important time in the history of the cosmos. Perhaps *t* was the first time there was something that it was like to be anything. Or *t* was the first time a living thing came into existence.

One diagnosis of what is going on is that the macrophysicalist is under a sort of metaphysical illusion—he mistakes changes which are significant relative to the modes of description with which he is familiar for changes which are significant *sub specie eternitatis.*

A second diagnosis is that the martian's cognitive resources, while adequate to describing a supervenience base for the world, are inadequate to capturing all the important objective similarities and dissimilarities manifested in the world, particularly, those grounded in higher-level natural properties. Those of us who opt for the first diagnosis will be utterly sympathetic with Sider's complaints of untoward macrophysical autonomy and arbitrariness. Those who opt for the second diagnosis will not. Philosophers like myself who have learned to live with the relevant autonomy may yet have various good reasons for disliking a restrictive ontology, and for embracing Instantaneous Plenitude and Universal Composition. But the argument from vagueness should not compel us. If that was the only serious challenge to a more restricted ontology, the epistemic strategy affords a compelling defence.

Fortunately for the Plenitude Lover, there are more compelling arguments than the argument from vagueness. For his own part, Sider has another, somewhat distinct, complaint about restrictive ontologies that ought to be sharply distinguished from the argument from vagueness: isn't it anthropocentric to suppose that the ontology of the world matches (more or less) exactly what human speakers have words for? Barring a kind of anti-realism that none of us should tolerate, wouldn't it be remarkable if the lines of reality matched the lines that we have words for? The simplest exercises of sociological imagination ought to convince us that the assumption of such harmony is altogether untoward, since such exercises convince us that it is something of a biological and/or cultural accident that we draw the lines that we do. If we are to be charitable towards ourselves without being unduly chauvinistic, it seems that we should posit ever so many more objects than we habitually talk about, in order not to credit ourselves with too much luck or sophistication in successfully hitting ontological targets most of the time. But once we are on this track, is there any reasonable stopping point short of positing a plenitude of temporal parts in combination with universal composition?

Those who are not so charitable to ordinary folk will not be swayed by this kind of argument. If someone claims that dogs but not kennels exist, or that magnetic fields but not cornfields exist, he can hardly be accused of anthropocentrism.[66] But what about those who wish to add to but not subtract from commonsense ontology? Is there any reasonable stopping point short of where Sider indicates? The challenge is a difficult one, and it is certainly not clear that it can be met.

---

[65] I am grateful to Jose Benardete for this way of putting things.

[66] See, notably, Peter Van Inwagen, *Material Beings* (Cornell University Press, 1990).

6

Motion and Plenitude[1]

0 INTRODUCTION

Many of us are drawn to an ontology that postulates an abundance of mereologically coincident concrete objects. But very often, not all the objects postulated will sit easily with our favoured dynamical laws: while certain of the postulated concreta will have strong prospects for satisfying the laws concerning matter in motion that are delivered by our best physics, others will have few such prospects. Yet we are not inclined to conclude on that score that our physics is wrong. Rather, we wish to say that only a subdomain of the totality of objects is the proper concern of dynamical laws. But we are then faced with the challenge of saying, in a moderately principled way, which objects fall within the purview of dynamics and which do not. We need to distinguish between those cases in which an object in the world stands as a counterexample to some putative law of dynamics from those cases in which an object falls outside its scope. Call this the *restriction problem*.

It will be helpful for what follows to restate the problem in the following way. Let us call the set of spacetime points of the world that are occupied the 'occupation profile' of the world. Let us call the objects of interest to those formulating dynamical laws 'quality objects', the remaining objects 'junk objects'. (Of course, what counts as junk from the purview of dynamics might not count as junk relative to some other perspective.) The project is to say something systematic about what determines which subregions of the occupation profile are occupied by quality objects.

Let me introduce a second problem. Quite often an abundant ontology threatens to collapse pairs of possibilities that appear to be quite distinguishable in thought. The problem tends to have the following shape: we seem to be able to imagine in thought a certain pair of possible worlds with the same occupation profile, but where a certain pattern of motion is imagined as being present in one world and absent in the other; and yet the abundant ontology tells us that for any world with the relevant occupation profile, there will be both objects that enjoy that pattern of motion and objects that lack it. It then begins to seem that when we imagined a world with the relevant pattern of motion in it, we failed to spot certain objects that lacked that

[1] I am most grateful to Tim Maudlin, Oliver Pooley, Ted Sider, Ryan Wasserman, Timothy Williamson, Dean Zimmerman, audiences at Oriel College and Rutgers University, and especially Frank Arntzenius and Jeremy Butterfield, for helpful comments and discussion.

pattern. And when we imagined a world without that pattern, we failed to spot one or more objects that manifested it. Call this the *collapse problem*.

The two problems are closely related, in that an answer to the restriction problem should be of considerable help with the collapse problem. Suppose we identified some quality Q that was distinctive of quality objects. We might then attempt to resist the collapse problem by exploiting the fact that not all objects that are mereologically coincident at a time enjoy Q. Perhaps for any world with some occupation profile O, there is one object with motion pattern M and another one that lacks M. But it does not follow that for any such world there is both a quality object with M and a quality object that lacks M. Perhaps, then, our original modal intuitions are vindicated by distinctions between quality objects. Of course, the restriction problem, as stated, concerns the actual world. By contrast, the collapse problem, as stated, concerns modal space. Answers to the restriction problem will be of greater or lesser use depending on their shape. If our answer to the restriction problem relies heavily on contingent features of the actual world, it may be of less help than anticipated in solving the collapse problem.

My project here is to describe how the restriction problem and the collapse problem arise within the context of various ontological frameworks and to make some preliminary remarks about the relative prospects of various abundant ontologies for resolving them. I do not plan to offer any definitive conclusions concerning the prospects for this or that plenitudinous ontology. But I do hope to get clear about some of the difficulties that lie ahead, and also to provide some motivation for preferring certain kinds of plenitudinous ontologies over others.

1 RESTRICTION

1.1

I have stated the problems abstractly. Now for some examples.

Let us begin with a commonsense metaphysics that postulates artefacts, living things, restaurants, cricket teams, and so on. The metaphysics that I have in mind alleges that such objects are mereologically coincident with various other material objects at various times, but not identical to them. For example, a restaurant might be mereologically coincident with a building at a time but not identical to it. From within the relevant framework, one reminds oneself that the 'persistence conditions' of a restaurant are not that of the building, and so, whether or not the actual occupation profile of the restaurant is that of the building, the former is not identical to the latter. One tells oneself similar stories for buildings in relation to masses of matter, statues in relation to lumps of clay (and perhaps lumps of clay in relation to certain aggregates of fundamental particles), and so on.

Now one does not have to be a specialist in physics to realize that restaurants and statues are not going to satisfy the dynamical laws that physicists are likely to settle on. Suppose one signs a legal document such that prior to the signing, Johnny's

Restaurant is constituted by one building, and then after the signing, it is constituted by another. Numerically different buildings, numerically the same restaurant. The restaurant, it would seem, has moved along a discontinuous path, has travelled faster than the speed of light, and so on.

More mundanely, think of the vicissitudes of a statue. It loses a part and its centre of mass shifts discontinuously. Later, the lump that constitutes it gets flattened and the statue vanishes into thin air. The 'worldtube' that describes its profile of spatiotemporal occupation grinds to an abrupt halt at the point of flattening. All of this will make trouble for the straightforward application of laws concerning matter in motion to the statue.

We are faced, *inter alia*, with the challenge of saying why statues and restaurants and so on do not stand as counterexamples to this or that dynamical law. We can dismiss some answers straight away.

It might be suggested that the statue gains and loses parts, and that physics is about things that don't gain and lose parts. In the context of discussing persisting things it will often be natural—and less tendentious—to use a time-indexed notion of parthood, so I shall be operating henceforth with talk of parthood at a time, as opposed to parthood simpliciter.[2] The current suggestion is that the things that physicists are interested in are not such as to have some part at one time but not another.

Let us recall the standard mereological conception of parthood, according to which x is part of y just in case anything that x overlaps is also overlapped by y. Adapted to the time-indexed conception, we get:

Parthood principle: x is part of y at t iff everything that overlaps x at t overlaps y at t.

Assuming the true mereology is not a deviant one with respect to the parthood principle, we can now see that the quality objects of physics do gain and lose parts. Suppose a body of the sort that our dynamics is interested in is mereologically coincident with a statue at one time but not at a later time, owing to the vicissitudes of its shape, or else accretions around its surface. Assuming the parthood principle, it is clear enough that the body loses a part, namely, the statue. Similarly, various larger bodies of which our original body is a part will lose the statue as a part.

By way of distinguishing them from quality objects, it won't do either to say that our statues and restaurants are too big too be of interest to the physicist. There are two obvious problems with this proposal. First, the laws of motion are usually conceived as governing, *inter alia*, big things. For example, it is wrong to say that Classical Mechanics is *really* just about point particles.[3] That particular mechanics concerns extended things that collide. Even supposing there are point particles, it is dubious whether they fall within the ambit of Classical Mechanics (after all the

---

[2] I am of course well aware that certain theorists will take an unrelativized notion of parthood as fundamental, defining time-indexed parthood notion as follows: x is part of y at t iff x's temporal part at t is part of y's temporal part at t.

[3] I am grateful to Jeremy Butterfield here.

concept of collision cannot be applied to them),[4] let alone that they are its exclusive subject matter.[5]

Second, artefacts and so on can in principle be very small. (I shall not bore you with extended stories of nano-sculpting; fads in 'stud' earrings constituted of an unusual single molecule that irradiates lots of light; nano-successors to horse racing; and so on.)

One aspect of the restriction problem, then, is to ensure that living things and statues and restaurants do not turn out to be quality objects.

1.2

Let me briefly raise and then set aside a somewhat technical cluster of issues.[6] (Readers who skip this section will have no trouble following the thread of discussion in the rest of the paper.) The problem is to evaluate a universal fusion axiom for quality objects in the light of one's preferred measure theories for the fundamental magnitudes. Here is the fusion axiom:

Universal Quality Fusion (UQF): For any set of quality objects at t, there is a quality object existing at t that fuses that set.

Now of course not *any* fusion of quality objects is a quality object. A statue fuses a set of molecules at any given time. But that does not make it a quality object. A natural idea is that any *mereologically rigid fusion* of quality objects is itself a quality object (where a fusion f of a set s is a mereologically rigid fusion of s iff for any time and world where f exists, f fuses s at that time in that world. Note that something can be a mereologically rigid fusion of a set and still gain and lose parts that are not members of the set.) Combine this idea with the plausible principle that any set of objects has a mereologically rigid fusion and UQF follows.

The following mereological principle is also natural:

Quality Difference (QD): If x and y are quality objects and x is a proper part of y, then there is a quality object that is a proper part of y that does not overlap x.

On a closer look, however, UQF and QD are not so compelling. To illustrate the potential difficulties, assume a world of uncountably many point particles and assume that the point particles count as quality objects.[7] Some fusions of those point particles will occupy a region whose volume is undefined. On fairly natural assumptions about the outlines of a measure theory for mass, the mass of some fusions will be undefined too.[8] Objects with undefined mass threaten to make a hash of laws about the

---

[4] As Butterfield points out, it will not do either to count interpenetration as collision. Newtonian gravitational theory goes haywire for collision so understood, since kinetic energy goes to infinity by the time of collision. See 'On The Persistence of Particles' (*Foundations of Physics*, forthcoming).

[5] See Clifford Truesdell, *A First Course in Rational Continuum Mechanics* (Academic Press, 1977) for a rigorous presentation of Classical Mechanics with continua as subject matter.

[6] Thanks to Frank Arntzenius for discussions that helped with the next few pages.

[7] As noted above, such an assumption is not unproblematic.

[8] Two models: (a) Take mass properties to be basic, assume each point particle has zero mass, and assume a standard kind of measure theory for mass. Such a measure theory will leave one with

relationship between mass and motion. Similar problems confront allowing objects with undefined volume within the ambit of one's laws. One might thus feel strongly inclined to exclude them from the purview of serious dynamical laws.[9]

But which principles are to provide the basis of a restriction? At least one pertinent issue is the status of QD. Suppose we allow only fusions of point particles that occupy regular open or regular closed regions to count as quality composite objects.[10] Then QD fails (subtract the interior of a regular closed region from that region). If we are wedded to QD, the proposal will have to be rejected. Suppose instead we only allow fusions of point particles that occupy open regions to count as quality composite objects. QD still fails owing to the fact that there are pairs of open regions, one of which is a proper part of the other, and which are such that there is no proper part of the larger region that is both open and which fails to overlap the smaller.[11] We might insist instead that only composite objects that can occupy regular open regions are quality composite objects. But one is then potentially embarrassed by the fact that certain fusions of regular open regions are not regular open, which, *inter alia*, has the result that a number of quality objects that enjoy a quality fusion can be rearranged so that they continue to exist but no longer have a quality fusion. This is a kind of death by rearrangement that may well be undesirable for quality objects, since it may provide unwanted violations of the laws. Even more obviously, on the assumption of an uncountable point particle physics, it is likely that nothing will, strictly speaking, occupy regular closed or regular open regions—owing to the fact that any composite object will have lots of 'gaps'. (Of course, classical continuum mechanics sets such issues to one side, but if one is thinking hyperrealistically about the matter, such possibilities cannot straightforwardly be discounted.)

I shall not be pursuing this second aspect of the restriction problem in any detail here. If one does assume a background of uncountably many point particles, then the natural course, it would seem, is to restrict one's laws to those mereologically rigid fusions with volumes of well-defined measure—'well-defined object' hereafter. We would then reject UQF, though we may accept the principle that *countable* sets of quality objects have a quality fusion (since well-defined objects are closed under countable additivity). QD would hold, since the mereological difference between any two overlapping well-defined objects is a well-defined object.

There may be residual worries, however. Objects can deform. What should we say about an object that occupies a well-defined region at one time and then deforms so as to occupy a region with undefined volume at a later time? Wouldn't it make

---

very many fusions whose mass is undefined. (b) Take mass-density as the basic quantity, allowing point particles to enjoy mass densities, deriving the mass of a fusion by integrating the mass-density over the volume. Once again, very many fusions will have undefined masses owing to undefined volumes or undefined average mass-densities.

[9] Of course, one could opt for laws sufficiently convoluted as to allow for objects of undefined mass/volume etc. to fall within their domain. I do not mean to settle the issue here.

[10] The closure of a set of points is the set plus its boundary points. The interior of a set is the set minus its boundary points. A regular open set is one that is identical to the interior of its closure. A regular closed set is one that is identical to the closure of its interior.

[11] Thanks to Frank Arntzenius here.

trouble for our laws if an object might be a quality object at one time and not another, falling within their domain at one time and not another? There are two subcases to worry about. (a) The occupation profile is covered by a countable set of objects each of which occupies a well-defined region at every time. (Of course, there may be plenty of other objects that don't occupy well-defined regions.) In this case it is natural enough to insist that quality objects are the ones that permanently occupy well-defined regions. (b) There is no countable set of objects, each of which occupies a well-defined region at any time that it exists, and whose fusion covers the occupation profile. It seems to me that this is the more difficult case. If the actual world is really this way (happily, physics thinks it isn't), then it strikes me as much more difficult to say which objects are the quality ones.

Our general line of concern *may*, of course, be needless. The concern over UQF, as I have developed it, only arises if we think of the actual world as containing uncountably many point particles. Assume that there are finitely many point particles, each of finite mass, abandon a collision-theoretic dynamics, and the puzzles I have gestured at will not arise.[12] I shall not be discussing the merits of UQF as regards its relation to measure theory any further. As a simplifying assumption, I shall assume in what follows that mereologically rigid fusions of quality objects are quality objects.

1.3

Returning to our main thread, it is important to see that certain plenitudinous ontologies make our problems particularly pressing. Let the thesis of *plenitude* say that for any subset of the occupation profile, there is at least one object that exactly occupies that set. This thesis is associated above all with the standard temporal parts theorist, who holds that for any subinterval, no matter how small, and no matter how gerrymandered, of an object's career, there is an object that exactly occupies that interval, and which is mereologically coincident with that object throughout that interval. Extend that doctrine in a natural way to the spatial case (where it is less controversial), assume a universal fusion axiom (stated now in terms of an atemporal notion of parthood), and we can deduce the thesis of plenitude.

The plenitude thesis might also be endorsed by some whom it would be tendentious to call standard temporal parts theorists. A good representative of the kind of theory I have in mind here is that proposed by Fine,[13] and inspired by Aristotle. On that account, there are *substances* and, in addition, there are *qua objects* whose real definition is given by a substance in combination with a *gloss*, and also complex qua objects that are aggregates of qua objects. Example: the combination of Socrates plus the gloss *singing* gives us the qua object, *singing Socrates*, that comes into existence when Socrates sings and passes out of existence when Socrates ceases to sing. Second example: suppose a hammer is first made of one portion of stuff, then another. Simplifying somewhat, we can say that the hammer is an aggregate of two qua objects,

---

[12] The worry may be needless for another reason. Perhaps the true theory has a 'gunky ontology' of quality objects whereby any quality object has smaller parts. See 'Gunk and Continuous Variation', this volume.

[13] 'Acts, Events, and Things', in *Language and Ontology, Proceedings of the Sixth International Wittgenstein Symposium* (1981), pp. 97–105.

one of which defined by the first portion of stuff in combination which a gloss that appeals to various shape/functional role properties (pick your favourite definition of a hammer) and the second of which is defined by the same gloss but different stuff. With this kind of picture in place, and assuming a suitable liberalism about glosses, it is natural to suppose for any subset of the occupation profile, we can find some suitable qua object or fusion of qua objects that exactly occupies that subset. (This style of metaphysics will be important to us later.)

It is not hard to see the force of the restriction problem, as it arises for the defender of plenitude. Consider an object O that is a fusion of two objects, one of which exactly occupies the spacetime region occupied by some particle up to t, the other of which exactly occupies the spacetime region occupied by some other particle after t. O does not move continuously, and at one point moves faster than the speed of light. But one would have thought none of that should stand as a potential counterexample to our favourite laws of motion. Similarly, consider some object O that is the fusion of a number of objects each of which is mereologically coincident with the post-oxidation careers of more mundane objects. Call this object 'Phlogiston'. It would seem that when an ordinary object gets oxidized, a portion of Phlogiston becomes part of it. (And while Phlogiston does not quite have negative weight, it certainly doesn't add extra weight!) None of this should provide any encouragement whatsoever for the old defenders of phlogiston.

1.4

As we ordinarily conceive of things, the distinction between space occupied by matter and space which isn't is a pretty fundamental feature of our world. But it is not clear that this is the right metaphysical picture. Descartes, Quine, and others have taken seriously the idea of *identifying* matter with certain regions of space-time (well, in Descartes's case, it was space, not space-time).[14,15]

Why might one be so inclined? Here is one reason. Perhaps the fundamental physical landscape is a world of space-time with various field values. Since fields vary continuously, there is no deep distinction coordinate with the intuitive filled/non-filled contrast (though of course fields may spike in certain regions and talk of particles may be explained by this).

On this view, there are no distinct entities that stand in occupation relations to the points of space-time. Rather, talk of physical objects is a handy way of selecting out some particularly interesting regions. Talk of regions being occupied cannot now be taken at face value. Relatedly, the concept of being occupied now no longer serves as a primitive piece of our ground-floor ideology: we now have to *earn* the distinction between occupied and unoccupied regions. (Unless, that is, we are Descartes, who, having identified matter with space, declared that there is no empty space whatsoever.) And of course we know in advance that given a metaphysic of

[14] See Descartes, *Principles of Philosophy* (1644) and Quine, 'Things and Their Place in Theories', in *Theories and Things* (Harvard University Press, 1981), p. 16.
[15] This is also a speculative program in physics. Jeremy Butterfield (in correspondence) cited Clifford in the nineteenth century and John Wheeler's geometrodynamics programme in the 1950s.

space-time with continuously varying field values, a distinction between an occupied and an unoccupied spacetime point will be inevitably vague and likely quite difficult to make out. (When is the spike in field values sufficiently large to count as 'being occupied by a particle'? At which point does such and such a spike begin?)

This perspective identifies quality objects with regions of spacetime. Within such a framework, our central challenge in the current context would be to say what it is about a region of spacetime that makes it deserve to be called a particle, and so on. It will be natural enough for this perspective to identify statues and restaurants with spatiotemporal regions as well, though those regions would not (except in unusual cases) be quality regions. Call this approach spatiotemporalism.

There is another perspective that, with the spatiotemporalist, disavows the fundamental metaphysical significance of the filled with matter/not filled with matter contrast. The spatiotemporalist denies that, strictly speaking, any region is occupied at all. We might instead retain a version of plenitude—call this perfect plenitude—that maintains that *every* region is occupied.[16,17,18] Such a view has the potential advantage (*vis-à-vis* the spatiotemporalist) of being able to take modal talk about ordinary objects at face value (these being a subset of the very many objects that there are), while (with the spatiotemporalist) eschewing the fundamental significance of the contrast between regions that are filled and regions that are not.[19]

As we proceed, the reader may wish to consider the problems discussed from the perspectives of the spatiotemporalist and the perfect plenitudinarian. However, I am not in these pages primarily concerned to evaluate the distinctive merits and costs of those approaches.

---

[16] The perfect plenitude thesis comes in a bold modal version as well: for any function from worlds to spatiotemporal regions, there is an object whose modal occupation profile is given by that function. It is this version that is best suited to taking ordinary modal talk at face value.

[17] There are also intermediate views. We might allow that every spacetime point that has some field value or other is occupied. (Note that it is relevant here whether having zero value for some range is crucially different from the absence of value in that range.)

[18] One might take the further step of not treating occupation as fundamental. The statue and lump are mereologically coincident. Perhaps they are also mereologically coincident with a spatiotemporal region. Occupation can then be defined in terms of mereological relations to regions. And just as we typically picture the statue as inheriting certain properties—weight and so on—from the lump by mereological coincidence, we can here think of various objects as inheriting various magnitudes associated with fields by mereological coincidence with spacetime regions which in turn are the fundamental bearers of field values.

[19] One version of perfect plenitude worth considering is one that allows for a layer of reality below that of dynamics (and in that sense perhaps treats some field-theoretic physics as more fundamental than dynamics), but insists that there are all sorts of extremely natural properties that emerge at the level of dynamics—ones whose naturalness is not to be calibrated by looking at their field-theoretic supervenience base. This, in effect, replays some familiar ideas about the special sciences (with a metaphysical spin), in the context of treating some favoured version of dynamics as, roughly, a special science.

2 COLLAPSE

The Kripke/Armstrong rotating disc puzzle[20] is a paradigm of the collapse problem. We seem to be able to imagine a possible world where a homogeneous disc spins, and another possible world where a homogeneous disc does not spin. Assume plenitude. In each world, there will be a decomposition of the disc into objects whose worldlines—the timelike curves through spacetime corresponding to their trajectory—are distinctive of particles caught up in a rotating disc, and also a decomposition of the disc into objects whose worldlines are not thus distinctive. The distinction between the disc spinning and not spinning threatens to be a distinction without a difference. After all, a natural way to make sense to ourselves of the difference between the pair of possibilities is in terms of the behaviour of the disc's parts. In one world the disc parts spiral though spacetime, in a second world they do not. Given plenitude, it seems that a homogeneous disc is bound to have both parts that spiral as well as ones that do not.

It is clear here that an answer to the restriction problem will probably be of service. Distinguish the quality from non-quality objects in a way that has application not only to the actual world but to the possible worlds in question; we can now say that the disc is spinning iff its *quality* parts spiral in the ways distinctive of a spinning object. And not otherwise.

Note that there are two styles of response that can be adopted by the advocate of plenitude when confronted with a collapse puzzle. First, one can respond with *respect*: there is indeed the relevant pair of possibilities, which can after all be captured within the favoured plenitudinous ideology. Second, one can respond with *dismissal*: the modal distinction is illusory, an artefact of an ideology that is to be jettisoned.[21]

We should note that it is important to keep verificationist concerns at bay, or at least not to raise them without being explicit that one is doing just that. It is clear enough that the pairs of possibilities that figure in various versions of the collapse problem are often not easily distinguishable by crude observation, and sometimes not even by subtle observation. But this is not the point. The point is that the ideology in which we naturally conceive of modal space generates pairs of possibilities that threaten to be collapsed by the plenitudinous ontology. Being no verificationist, I very much doubt the cogency of a position that adopts the attitude of dismissal whenever pairs of possibilities are not discriminable by observation.

---

[20] Kripke (unpublished lectures) and David Armstrong, 'Identity Through Time', in van Inwagen (ed.), *Time and Cause* (Dordrecht: Reidel). Related insights are at work in Leibniz' 'On Nature Itself' (1698, section 13), though there Leibniz is primarily concerned to challenge the at-at theory of motion on the grounds that it makes facts of diachronic identity primitive and inexplicable.

[21] Relevant here is Craig Callender, 'Humean Supervenience and Rotating Homogeneous Matter', *Mind* 110 (2001), 25–42.

That is not to say that an attitude of dismissal is *never* justified. But we cannot easily say in advance when it is justified. For the plenitudinous ontologist, the restriction question is compulsory. It just will not do to eschew the distinction between quality and junk altogether.[22] Candidate answers to the restriction question will be evaluated in part according to the pattern of respect and dismissal they encourage. In some cases, dismissal may actually conflict with our best physics. In that case such an attitude will be particularly extreme, since it will carry within it a recommendation for restructuring physics. But in some cases dismissal may be our best all-things-considered option. What remains unlikely though, is that knee-jerk verificationism—with blanket use of complaints like 'I cannot make sense of facts of diachronic identity and difference that are unverifiable' and 'Positing facts of diachronic identity requires an occult substratum metaphysics'—is going to be much of a substitute for hard work.

The importance of homogeneity to the rotating disc puzzle can be overstated. It may be useful to consider the following variant of the spinning disc thought experiment: suppose that discs sometimes constitute illuminated paintings by being made of bulbs that are lit by different colours. The same bulbs can constitute two different paintings by being illuminated in radically different ways at different times. And the same bulbs can constitute a spinning painting by changing colours in coordinated ways, so that the overall pattern is the same modulo the angle between some feature of it—e.g. the line of a painted nose—and some fiducial spatial line. We can thus distinguish four subcases: the painting spins and the disc spins; the painting spins and the disc does not; the disc spins and the painting does not; neither spins. The spin of the painting has to do with whether certain junk objects spin. The spin of the disc has to do with whether certain quality objects spin. Part of the answer to the question 'By virtue of what does the disc spin?' has to involve not merely the fact that certain quality objects that are parts of the disc rotate but also that it is the movement of those parts that, in the case of the disc (but not the painting), are the test for its spinning.

The painting example illustrates the fact while some set of parts may count as the test for whether some object *o* spins, they may not count as the test for whether some object mereologically coincident with *o* spins. But more importantly, it reminds us of the fact that it is *not* crucial to the Kripke–Armstrong puzzle that the matter be homogeneous. Suppose a disc enjoyed qualitative variety, say of colour. We seem to be able to imagine a pair of worlds, one in which the colour of the matter is constant, and the disc spins, another in which the disc stays still but wherein the matter changes its colour over time in order to produce an illusion of spinning. (In the latter scenario, it may well be that a non-quality object actually does spin—witness the painting above—but the matter does not.)

Let us now broaden our perspective beyond rotating disc puzzles. That is merely one example of the collapse problem. The disc puzzle crucially trades on pairs of possible worlds with matching occupation profiles but allegedly different motion profiles for the occupying matter. There are other pairs that exploit the same theme:

[22] Unless, that is, one thought that successors to dynamical laws will concern field values of space-time and not any of the objects that occupy it. I shall return to this idea briefly in the text.

In w_1, a straight strip of homogeneous matter that is infinitely long, with no end and no beginning, lies still. In w_2, a strip of the same width moves from left to right.

In w_1, two point particles approach each other, interpenetrate for an instant, and then continue in the same direction as originally. In w_2, two point particles approach each other, interpenetrate for an instant and then 'bounce', each travelling in the same direction as was originally taken by the other.

In w_1, a point particle moves continuously along a path. In w_2, a point particle pops out of existence and is replaced by another particle which continues along the same path.

In w_1, two point particles move continuously along a pair of paths. In w_2, two point particles jump so that the second continues along the path that was being taken by the first, and vice versa.

In w_1, a point particle moves continuously along a path. In w_2, two point particles interpenetrate during their entire existence and together move along the same path.

In w_1, there is a plenum of matter (every spacetime point is occupied) that has motion profile X (insert any motion profile at all). In w_2, there is a plenum of matter that has motion profile Y.

And so on.

When we philosophers articulate such thought experiments, we often rely on a fairly unsophisticated array of folk physical concepts about space, time, matter, motion, and contact. Someone blessed with a more sophisticated understanding of current physical theory might then question the terms in which these thought experiments are framed. For example, and notably, the contrast between rest and motion that forms the backdrop of certain of these thought experiments might reasonably be questioned. For example, if it makes no sense to identify points of space from one time to the next—consider, say, the so-called Galilean picture of space-time as opposed to the Euclidean one—then the contrast between a moving river and one at rest makes no sense without relative motion to other bodies. Nevertheless, in very many cases, it would seem that similar thought experiments can be rearticulated in a way that depends less crucially on a crude folk physics. Thus we can replace the contrast between an infinite moving river and a still river with the contrast between an infinite river moving at constant velocity and one that is accelerating, or between an infinite moving river that always moves in the same direction and one that switches its direction of motion at regular intervals. And, following Jeremy Butterfield, we can upgrade the spinning disc thought experiment by replacing the contrast between a disc that is at rest and one that is rotating with the contrast between two discs that are rotating in opposite directions and two discs that are rotating in the same direction (which in turn secures world matching with regard to the accompaniments of rotation, like stress and oblation).[23]

For each version we can ask two questions. Does the thought experiment so articulated still rely on a way of thinking about space-time that we deem acceptable by

---

[23] See 'On The Persistence of Homogeneous Matter' (in preparation); cf. Dean Zimmerman, 'Temporal Parts and Supervenient Causation: The Incompatibility of Two Humean Doctrines,' *The Australasian Journal of Philosophy* 76 (1998), pp. 268–269.

the lights of our preferred physics? (Thus, for example, a refashioned infinite river thought experiment that contrasts constant velocity with acceleration may be straightforwardly acceptable to one who was happy with Galilean space-time, but not to one whose preferred framework was the space-time of General Relativity.) But second, what kinds of spacetime frameworks do we think are *possible*? Suppose, for example, we thought that there are *possible worlds* that admitted an absolute contrast between rest and motion. Then, even granting the relevant facts about actual physics, we might wonder to ourselves what distinguishes pairs of worlds contrived using one of the above thought experiments and which have a spacetime of that sort. Assuming a suitably modalized version of plenitude, we would have to solve versions of the restriction problem for other possible worlds. While the philosopher might allow himself to be bullied concerning the actual spatiotemporal lay of the land, it is less clear to what extent he should allow himself to be bullied concerned the modal lay of the spatiotemporal land.

I admit, however, to finding myself slightly embarrassed by too heavy a reliance on distant possible worlds as a topic for these puzzles.[24] Fortunately, we need not treat them as our exclusive topic of concern. In very many cases, the plenitudinous philosopher should certainly not be amenable to any attempt to dismiss the relevant worries on straightforwardly scientific grounds. Consider, for example, worries that involve particles that jump in a discontinuous way. Assuming plenitude, there *are* jumping objects. I take it that one cannot easily dismiss plenitude by casual appeal to scientific theory. So one cannot dismiss jumping objects by appeal to it. There is thus no straightforwardly scientific escape from the version of the restriction problem that inquires why some discontinuous object is not a quality object.

Here is another example. It is well known that as a matter of fact discs tend to become oblate when they rotate. One might naturally complain that the rotating disc story takes no account of this. Suppose now that to pacify such critics, we focus our concern upon the difference between a world in which a disc becomes oblate by rotation and one where it becomes oblate by certain small outward motions of small parts—which subsequently stay still—but where there is no rotation. Here, once again, we can find an interesting point of contact between the restriction problem and the separation problem. For assuming plenitude, an actual spinning disc *has* parts that move in the way imagined for the non-spinning world. We are forced once again to confront the question as to what makes those objects non-quality, a question that cannot be settled by casual appeal to scientific theory.

Final example. Suppose I wish to distinguish a disc whose small parts are changing colour (for 'colour', read your favourite magnitude/quality) and that does not rotate from one that rotates rapidly. Now it won't do to just say that according to our best physics no point particles can change their colours in that way. That is not engaging with the issues at the right level. Whatever our willingness to be liberal in our modal thinking, we are faced with the restriction problem. Suppose that the particles in the disc change colour and do not move. Given plenitude, it would seem that there are

---

[24] For one thing, it is not altogether clear that we have enough intellectual control over the distinction between the impossible and the distant but possible to warrant such investigations.

also objects that move but do not change colour. We need to know what disqualifies those objects from being quality objects.

3 SOME STRATEGIES FOR THE FOLK-INSPIRED ONTOLOGIST

My primary interest is in the challenges raised by restriction and collapse for explicitly plenitudinous ontologies. But it will provide a helpful backdrop to consider the range of strategies available to those metaphysicians with a more mundane vision. Let us thus see first how the issues look from the perspective of someone who operates with a workaday physical ontology of particles, masses of matter, artefacts, and living things, together perhaps with a few categories of institutional objects—nations, corporations, and so on—but who eschews the gerrymandered inventions of other more unfettered metaphysics (hereafter the folk-inspired ontologist). I shall not fuss about the precise shape of the view. But I shall assume that according to this ontologist, both small and large things can mereologically coincide with other things throughout their careers: statue and lump, particle and tiny artefact, and so on.

For expository clarity let us focus on the challenge to the folk-inspired ontologist of saying what it is by virtue of which an object falls into the category of *particle*. With this in place she can—as a good first pass[25]—think of the dynamical laws as applying to particles and to certain mereologically rigid fusions of them. Let us call objects belonging to this latter category 'masses of matter'. Meanwhile, insofar as an object is, say, a statue or a restaurant or a country, it will be disqualified as a subject for the straightforward application of dynamical laws, i.e. it will not be a quality object.

One strategy has to be dismissed right away by the folk-inspired ontologist. Let us call any continuous line though space-time in the occupation profile, each point of which is filled, 'a filled worldline'. Call a filled worldline that is not a proper part of another filled worldline 'a maximal filled worldline'. A folk-inspired ontologist might claim that point particles are the occupants of the maximal filled worldlines. (Call this 'the continuity answer'.) Four problems beset a view.

First, given that she doesn't subscribe to plenitude, there is no guarantee that a maximal filled worldline will mark the career of *any* single object. Second, since she allows that many things can mereologically coincide throughout their careers, she will presumably have to allow that on occasion two objects may occupy the same maximal filled worldline. If one of them is a particle, the other an artefact, then presumably only one of them is the fit subject of dynamical laws. Third, it may be that the only object that occupies a maximal filled worldline is the wrong kind of object to serve as the object of physics. (Suppose a maximal filled worldline is occupied by an earring that is constituted by one glittering point particle during its earlier and then a second glittering point particle during its later career.) Fourth, one wonders whether it is legitimate to rule out by fiat a scenario in which a particle moves discontinuously and thus does not occupy a maximal filled worldline.

---

[25] Though we have seen that this may only be a first pass.

Of course, none of these considerations shows decisively that the continuity answer is not going to be an extensionally correct answer to the restriction problem. Supposing that, as a happy accident, the particles are all and only the occupants of maximal filled worldliness. (Perhaps there is nowhere any plenum and the particles never jump and so on.) Then the continuity answer will have no actual counterexamples. But such an answer may not be philosophically illuminating. Other extensionally equivalent (but intensionally different) answers may do much better on that score. Relatedly, if the continuity answer was only correct as a happy accident, it would not be a useful basis for answering various versions of the collapse problem, since the continuity answer would not be projectable from the actual world. Let us agree, then, that the folk-inspired ontologist would do well not to place her faith in a continuity answer to the restriction problem. What other answers are available to her?

First, she may give a straightforwardly *modal* answer, one that appeals to the *persistence conditions* for each kind of thing. Statues cannot endure being flattened. Masses of matter can. These kinds of modal properties disqualify statues for being the fit subject of dynamical laws. We should note one complication right away: certain strands of our intuitive persistence conditions may be circular. When we are trying to get clear on what a mass of matter is in the first place, we cannot simply rely on the claim that masses of matter cannot lose those parts that are masses of matter, but statues can. The claim is not uninformative, since it puts a real constraint on a solution. But such claims cannot do all the work.[26]

Those who think that modal profiles must have a categorical base will be unimpressed by the modal answer. The speech is a familiar one: 'If there is a difference in persistence conditions, that must have a basis in the actual nature of the objects in question.' (Only some will be pacified by the reply 'But the propensities I am talking about *are* actual.') Others will think the modal answer too shallow. Why should physics be interested in objects with these but not those persistence conditions? (I do not propose to evaluate those complaints here.)

Second, she may give a *causal* answer. One version: the real pushing and pulling is done by masses of matter and not statues or living things. Strictly speaking, only a subset of the actual objects do any pushing and pulling at all. And it is those objects that the laws are about. Second version: when a particle survives, there is a *special* causal relation between the particle at one time and that very particle at a later time. Call that *immanent causation*.[27] The particle immanently causes itself to be around at a later time. But statues and living things do not survive by immanently causing their own survival.

Third, she may give a *qualitative* answer: certain magnitudes that define the scope of dynamics attach to some objects and not others. The former are the quality objects. Example: strictly speaking, only particles (and certain fusions of them) have *mass* and undergo *stress* and so on. It is only in a relaxed sense that we can speak of the masses of and stresses upon statues and so forth. Of course, if one takes a so called 'at-at' view of velocity, then one isn't well placed to adopt such an attitude towards velocity vectors.

---

[26] Note that we cannot say that particles never change their parts—for the reason given earlier.

[27] See Dean Zimmerman, 'Immanent Causation', *Philosophical Perspectives* 11 (1997), 433–471.

On this view, there is nothing more to velocity—metaphysically speaking—than the standard textbook account which treats it as the first derivative of position. Since it is hard to deny that both junk and quality objects have location, it is hard—on that construal of velocity—to deny that they both have velocity (except at times when it is undefined). So one who adopted a qualitative answer will either maintain that there is more to velocity than facts of location over time, or else defend the answer by way of magnitudes other than velocity.

(We may note that it is in principle open to the defender of the qualitative answer to allow that, say, objects with mass are not at the metaphysical ground-floor, in that objects with mass enjoy their mass properties by virtue of certain properties attaching to objects which lack mass, objects that are even more basic than those that fall within the province of dynamics. For example, it might be maintained that while spacetime regions do not have mass, they have certain properties on which the existence of objects with mass supervenes. Even more radically, one might think that space-time itself emerges from a yet more fundamental network of objects enjoying certain kinds of algebraic relations that are not spatiotemporal.[28] One might even maintain that there are *no* fundamental objects—that for each magnitude, there is a more fundamental metaphysical level of objects lacking that magnitude but determinative of it, maintaining—against Leibniz—that there is no metaphysical ground-floor.)

Note in passing that certain versions of the qualitative answer have a natural affinity with certain versions of the second answer. After all, we naturally associate certain causal profiles with mass. In classical mechanics, mass has an inertial aspect, associated with Newton's second law, and a gravitational aspect, associated with the law of gravitation. We thus naturally think of bodies with mass as responding to forces on account of their mass and exerting forces on account of their mass. If a statue does not strictly speaking have mass, it is not directly caught up in the fabric of forces (although it will assuredly be carried along for the ride, so to speak), which may give some justice to the rather less technical idea of it lacking *oomph*. I believe that the most promising versions of a causal answer would proceed along these lines and thus be intimately connected with a qualitative answer. (Note, however, that versions of the qualitative answer that concede that the objects of dynamics are derivative from a yet more fundamental layer of objects are rather less conducive to the causal answer.)

Fourth, she may give an *inheritance* answer. Example: there are two subcases of having mass. First, an object can *inherit* it from one that it is mereologically coincident with. Second, one can have it without it being so derived. The quality objects are the ones whose mass is not derived. To avert confusion, let us distinguish two kinds of inheritance. First, there is the case of a thing inheriting some magnitude from its spatially smaller parts. Call this *small-to-large inheritance*. Those magnitudes that are historically known as extensive magnitudes are thought of as subject to additivity principles whereby the magnitude of a certain object will equal the sum of the magnitudes of countable sets of disjoint smaller parts that make it up. We would of course expect small-to-large inheritance of, say, mass, in the case of masses of matter

---

[28] Some of my friends in philosophy of physics appear to be drawn to this proposal as their best-guess fundamental metaphysics.

(excepting those masses of matter without smaller parts). A second kind of inheritance concerns a thing which inherits a magnitude from something that it is mereologically coincident with. Call this *coincident inheritance*. To bring matters into sharp focus, let us think about an earring constituted by a single particle. Insofar as the earring has such a magnitude as mass, it is altogether quite natural to think of the earring as inheriting its mass from the particle that it is mereologically coincident with. (I do not say that it is absolutely obligatory to think of things this way, only that it is quite natural to do so.) Supposing there are such lines of inheritance, it seems quite reasonable to make use of them in answering the second problem: the quality objects do not inherit their magnitudes at a time by coincident inheritance (though they may do so by small-to-large inheritance).

Some measure of reconciliation may be possible between the third and fourth answers. Suppose there is a very fundamental property—*mass*—which could divide things that are mereologically coincident. There would then also be another somewhat less fundamental property—call it *mass**—of being mereologically coincident with something that had *mass*. A statue would have *mass** by virtue of being mereologically coincident with a lump that had *mass*. With this ideology in place, we can pay lip service to an inheritance answer, having given a qualitative one. Suppose instead that there is a fundamental property, *mass* that is sometimes but not always inherited by coincident inheritance. Then we can define up a property, *mass**, that is the property of *having mass but not by coincident inheritance*. Then we can pay lip service to a qualitative answer, having given an inheritance one.

Fifth, she might give a *primitivist* answer. It is a primitive fact about an object that it is a mass of matter and not something else. There is a primitive quality of the thing—being a mass of matter. An answer in the same spirit would say that it is a basic fact of the world, incapable of further explanation, that the laws of nature are about some things and not others; the masses of matter are just those things that the laws are about. I take it, though, that such an answer is something of a last resort.

4 THE LEWISIAN PACKAGE

Let me turn next to the standard four-dimensionalist package, associated above all with David Lewis.[29] (I do not want to say that this package of theses defines 'four-dimensionalism'. Indeed, I wish here to set aside the questions of whether such a term of art is worth defining and, if so, how to do so.)

The package combines *plenitude* with the following theses:[30]

(i) *Extensionalism.* If x and y are mereologically coincident at all times that either exist, then x is identical to y.

(ii) *Anti-essentialism.* The *de re* modal profile of a thing has to be relativized to some way of thinking about it, which determines a counterpart relation between it and other possible things.

---

[29] See *Philosophical Papers Volumes I and II* (Oxford University Press, 1983 and 1986), and *On The Plurality of Worlds* (Blackwell, 1986).

[30] They are obviously not all logically independent of each other.

(iii) *Stage primacy.* The most basic intrinsic properties attach to instantaneous objects—which are stages in the life of longer-lived objects. Suppose some property—say being bent simpliciter—attaches to the stage. We can then define a derived property—having a stage as a part that is bent simpliciter—that attaches to certain long-lived objects that have the stage as a part. But the long-lived object does not have the fundamental property of being bent simpliciter.

(iv) *Causal Humeanism.* (i) Causal facts are not fundamental. Rather they are facts that are supervenient on the mosaic of qualities. (ii) Causal facts do not mark necessary connections between intrinsic goings on. How things are intrinsically at one spacetime region places no necessary constraints on how things are intrinsically at disjoint regions.

(v) *The worm view.* The objects that we talk about in ordinary life and in science are fusions of temporally short-lived things. Such objects inherit their occupation profiles from the occupation profiles of their shorter-lived constituents.

(vi) *Humean supervenience.* The facts about the world supervene on the spatiotemporal distribution of local intrinsic qualities, qualities that are intrinsic to an object that exactly occupies a spacetime point—or perhaps to the spacetime point itself.

Against this background, a certain answer to the question 'What makes something a particle?' is slightly more promising, though still not promising enough. We found four reasons to reject the continuity answer. Two of them no longer hold. The commitment to extensionalism removes the worry that only one of a number of objects that mereologically coincide throughout their career may count as a quality object. The commitment to plenitude removes the worry that there may be no object corresponding to a maximal filled worldline. But the third and fourth worries remain. First, we may wish to allow for particles that do not occupy maximal filled worldliness. For, once again, it seems unreasonable to rule out *a priori* discontinuously moving particles. (From the current perspective, we may put the issue as follows: there are all sorts of discontinuous objects; what gives us the right to categorize them as junk?) Second, we may wish to allow for objects that occupy maximal filled worldliness that do not count as particles. Thought experiments involving continua (qualitatively homogeneous or not) make this concern vivid. For if we imagine all the maximal filled worldliness that we can draw within the worldtube corresponding to a continuum (let is be rotating, or moving in a straight line, or whatever), it is unlikely that we will want to count the occupant of each such worldline a quality object. To do so would, *inter alia*, allow that particles are constantly undergoing fusion and fission within continua, and moreover, threatens to remove the basis for a distinction between rotating and non-rotating continua, as well as the basis for assigning a direction of rotation to continua (since on this picture disc-shaped continua will have particles going every which way). Thought experiments involving crossing worldlines also make trouble for the continuity answer. If we imagine two crossing filled worldlines, that will make for four maximal filled worldliness. It is far from obvious that in such a case we wish automatically to conclude that there are four particles. The continuity answer, while faring better in this ontological environment, does not fare well enough.[31]

I think it is instructive to see how various aspects of the Lewisian package deprive its proponent of certain of the other strategies available to the folk-inspired ontologist.[32]

The modal answer seems unsatisfying from the point of view of this perspective, owing to its commitment to anti-essentialism. A thing's 'persistence conditions' turns on a selection of a counterpart relation: one cannot ask after a thing's persistence conditions simpliciter. This feature of the view is not easily dispensible either, given the commitment to extensionalism. Suppose a lump and a statue are coincident for their entire career. In that case, given extensionalism, we are committed to their identity. How then can we rescue our intuition that the lump can survive squashing but not the statue? As Lewis well knew, anti-essentialism is the answer here:[33] The lump conception selects out a counterpart relation R1 such that the worm in question has counterparts whose later stages are symptomatic of squashing. The statue conception selects out a counterpart relation R2, such that the worm is not related by R2 to any 'squashed' worms. But none of this plausibly gets to the heart of the restriction and collapse problems.

Meanwhile, stage primacy makes trouble for the qualitative and inheritance answers. For if stage primacy is right, then the quality objects of physics are not the fundamental quality bearers.[34] Junk and quality objects are alike in lacking the fundamental magnitudes. And as for derived qualities of being such and such at a time, both junk and quality objects have them via the same route, namely, by having temporal parts with the relevant basic properties. Consider a gerrymandered fusion that fuses a set containing a stage that is bent simpliciter together with various other stages that are spatiotemporally disconnected from the original and each other. Compare that with a quality object that contains the said stage. Neither are bent simpliciter. Both are bent at the relevant time, by having a part that exists at that time that is bent simpliciter.

What of primitivism? Let us consider the most straightforward version of the view. Let us posit a fundamental property of *being interesting*, and postulate that the worms that are of interest to physicists are the ones with that quality. (Alternatively, we can posit a fundamental and transitive relation of *being interestingly related*, which we might call *genidentity*, and try to specify what it takes to be a quality object in terms of such a relation; most naturally, quality objects are maximal sets of objects that each of whose instantaneous stages stand in the *genidentity* relation.) There are two versions

[31] See David Lewis, 'Zimmerman and the Spinning Sphere', *Australasian Journal of Philosophy* 77 (1999), 209–212 for his views on the spinning disc problem.

[32] Cf. Dean Zimmerman, 'Temporal Parts and Supervenient Causation: The Incompatibility of Two Humean Doctrines'.

[33] See 'Counterparts of Persons and Their Bodies', *Philosophical Papers Volume I* (Oxford University Press, 1983), pp. 47–54.

[34] Except perhaps in the special case where a body does not change over time with respect to a fundamental quality. We may wish to allow that if every instantaneous stage of a body has the fundamental property of being F simpliciter, then so does the body.

of this view. On one version, the facts of being interesting/being related by genidentity do not supervene on the sets of local qualities. Hold the local qualities fixed and the genidentity relation could have gone any old way. This violates Humean supervenience.[35] On another version, the facts of genidentity/being interesting supervene on local facts, but there is nothing systematic at all to say about the way that the former supervene on the latter. This position is consistent with the package laid out above, but seems deeply unsatisfying.[36]

Let us turn, finally, to the causal answer. Some versions of that answer violate Humean supervenience. Since point particles inevitably have causal influence on their neighbours, lines of mundane causal influence cannot be used to cordon off the quality objects from the junk. Suppose that one held that it is the lines generated by a distinctive immanent causation relation holding between certain instantaneous stages that define the quality objects.[37] Given that such stages are densely ordered, we can presume that any immanent causal connection between a pair of stages will supervene on yet more local immanent causal connections. Whatever one thinks of the infinitely descending structure that emerges, it is certainly not one available to the proponent of Humean supervenience, since he will not tolerate primitive non-spatiotemporal relations that fail to supervene on the perfectly local quality distributions.

5 SIDER AND THE LEWISIAN PACKAGE

Ted Sider has produced a version of the causal answer that is consistent with the Lewisian package as it stands.[38] He relies upon the neo-Humean picture of laws that Lewis proposes, one according to which the laws that govern the actual world are those true generalizations that offer the best compromise between strength and simplicity. Given plenitude the interesting dynamical generalizations had better be restricted in their domain. The quality objects are the ones that fall within the domain

---

[35] It also gives one pause—and not merely crude verificationist pause—about placing one's hopes on genidentity. Take, for instance, a world where the genidentity relation is scattered in odd ways but some other natural relation was scattered the way genidentity is actually scattered. By what right can one say that ordinary concepts of persisting particulars, as applied to those worlds, would track the genidentity related things? One has to earn the right, in this case, to suppose the occurrence of 'identity' in 'genidentity' is not like the occurrence of 'cat' in 'catastrophe'. Matters are different when possibilities are articulated *using* the concept of identity. In that case, the possibility is expressed using an ordinary concept and no question can sensibly be raised—on that score—about the relation between the theorist's language and the ordinary conceptual scheme.

[36] Moreover, this approach will have a problem in principle with any cases of the collapse problem that involve worlds that match in their local properties but not in their motion profiles.

[37] One wonders whether there is much that separates a genidentity based primitivism from the immanent causation view. What makes genidentity deserve the name 'immanent causation'? Both sides would agree that a particle can only survive from one time to the next when a genidentity relation holds. What more is at stake then when it comes to labelling the genidentity relation 'immanent causation'?

[38] See his *Four Dimensionalism* (Oxford University Press, 2001), p. 224ff. David Lewis, 'Zimmerman and the Spining Sphere', 209–212 contains some related ideas, as does Jeremy Butterfield, 'On the Persistence of Particles'.

of that set of dynamical generalizations that are the best compromise of simplicity and strength:

Consider various ways of grouping stages into physical continuants. Relative to any such way, there are candidate laws of dynamics. The correct grouping into physical continuants is that grouping that results in the best candidate set of laws of dynamics; the correct laws are the members of the candidate set.

As Sider argues, this approach to the restriction problem, when applied modally, can help a good deal with the rotating disc puzzle.[39] An illustration: let us call a max-imally filled worldline a worldstrand just in case there is some open region of space-time that contains that worldline and that is otherwise empty. In effect, worldstrands are worldlines that are surrounded by empty spacetime. Now suppose that world-strands in environment of type X take helical paths through spacetime. Suppose now there is a homogeneous disc in some environment of type X. Some of the maximally filled worldlines in the worldtube occupied by the disc are helical; others are not. If we allow only the helical ones to count as particles, then we are afforded a good candidate for a Humean law, namely a law which says (or entails): particles in X environments take helical paths.

(One might think of environment X as an environment in which a flashing red light is visible; perhaps there is a law that particles near a flashing red light take helical paths. But we might instead put scientific flesh on these bones by thinking of environ-ment X as a certain spacetime curvature profile; the law says that particles in a region with that profile take helical paths.)

Of course, for certain pairs of putatively possible but distinct cases, Sider will have no option but to take what was earlier called a dismissive attitude.[40] Descartes believed in a plenum where there were no vacuums and where parcels of matter[41] enjoyed various differing motions, this being the basis for the qualitative variety that we see in the world. In modern parlance, he thought that all the physical facts about the world supervened on the facts of motion and extension. But assuming perfect plentitude, a plenum will exemplify all motions. If there is no further qualitative variety at the ground-floor, there will be nothing to ground a preference for one restricted domain of quality object/law package over another. Indeed, the best combination of simplicity and strength would seem to be an unrestricted domain of continua for the laws whose content is tantamount to a thesis of plenitude for the physical objects. From this perspective then, the Cartesian vision of worlds that differ only in their patterns of motion (the occupation profile and all else qualitative being the same) is chimerical.[42]

---

[39] He is also aware of the possibility of handling the rotating disc puzzle by appeal to worlds where the Lewisian metaphysic is not true. (Perhaps there are worlds where plenitude is false.) He does not primarily wish to rely on such moves, however.

[40] Or perhaps more cautiously, to admit collapse except in 'distant' worlds where plenitude is false.

[41] Which he identified with space: in effect the Cartesian corporeal world is one of moving space and nothing else.

[42] This is relevant to Dean Zimmerman. 'One Really Big Liquid Sphere: Reply to Lewis', *Australasian Journal of Philosophy* (1999) 77, 213–215.

The same goes for pairs of worlds containing a homogeneous disc and nothing else upon which to ground a preference for one restriction over another.

Now the Humean is traditionally willing to concede that we are subject to systematic illusions concerning the space of worlds in which certain laws hold. For example, we find it easy enough to imagine a world where a single particle moves at a constant velocity, where there is nothing else going on, and where the full panoply of classical mechanical laws is in force. For the Humean this is an illusion: given such paucity in the mosaic, there is nothing in that world to make it true that the laws of classical mechanics hold. Within the current perspective, this kind of illusion will carry over to the question as to which objects are the fit subjects for dynamical laws. For someone who has learned in general to bite Humean bullets, these consequences may not constitute all that much of an additional embarrassment.

It does bear emphasizing, though, that in simple worlds the account is likely to deliver radical indeterminacy as to which objects are the quality objects. An illustration: consider a world which we might at first blush be inclined to describe in the following way: two point particles exist and move continuously. They are intrinsically F and G respectively until a time when the F particle becomes G and the G particle becomes F. The current perspective tells us that we should not be so quick to describe this world in such a way. For there is a different candidate law/quality object package. Call the objects described by the first story 'Janet' and 'John'. There is a pair of objects Jonet and Jan, each of which are F and G respectively throughout their existence. Jonet is composed of the F temporal part of John and the F temporal part of Janet, Jan is composed of the G temporal part of John and the G temporal part of Janet. Relative to this package there will be an elegant continuity law of quality—'Things don't change their intrinsic character'—that counteracts the unqualified continuity law of motion delivered by the first package. Each package has compensating virtues. In simple worlds like this there is likely to be no fact of the matter as to which objects are the quality objects. I freely admit, though, that this kind of result is the least of a Humean's worries—or at least a long way from the greatest of her worries.

Another interesting point to note is that in certain cases, the account will yield the result that nothing that is the spatial size of a point counts as a quality object. For suppose the world were such that maximally filled worldliness were never worldstrands, and that in particular the occupants of maximally filled worldlines were clumped together into small homogeneous continua. Then it may very well turn out that the laws would generalize over the continua, not the occupants of worldlines. This would not be a physics of point particles. It would be a physics of continua, in which point-sized parts were junk objects. An interesting consequence of the account, to be sure. But no deep embarrassment.

I do not wish to pass final judgement on the account. But I do want to bring out the ways it which it requires a very unusual perspective on the question of which objects are quality objects. Let me briefly discuss three topics in this connection: disorder, chance, and determinism.

Consider, first, a world in which maximally filled worldlines come in two varieties, which I shall label 'red' and 'blue'. The red ones predominate and are well behaved in their trajectory. The blue ones are rare and disorderly both in their trajectory—some come to abrupt halts, some indulge in Lucretian swerves—and are also disorderly in their relationship to red worldlines. We can well imagine that the best continuant/law package for such a world counts only the objects occupying the red worldlines as particles/quality objects. This is especially so if what I have called 'red' and 'blue' worldlines have no distinguishing mark apart from the facts of orderliness.[43] Maximally connected sets of blue stages will not count as particles. Indeed, nothing composed of blue stages will count as a particle. Now one would have thought that if a spacetime point is occupied by an object X, then it would be obligatory for the physics to say that *some* physical object occupied that point. Of course, it wouldn't be obligatory to talk about X. Supposing X is a statue the physics will talk about another object that occupies that point. But this scenario is stranger: the point is occupied and yet, on the current proposal, the physics does not recognize anything as occupying that point.[44]

The theme can be generalized a little. Suppose the actual world is much as we imagine it, except for a pocket of horrid disorder: a truck vanishes into thin air. How should we think about this from the current perspective? Suppose, to keep things simple, all the maximally filled worldlines are worldstrands. Consider two sets of objects: (i) the set of all the exact occupants of the worldstrands. Call that Big. (ii) The set of all the exact occupants of the worldstrands apart from those that run through the truck. Call that Small. There are two corresponding packages of laws/physical continua. One package is restricted to Small. In certain respects, it has a richer set of generalizations about patterns of motion, since Small contains no worldstrands that come to an abrupt halt, etc. But of course there are costs: if we only recognize the occupants of Small as particles, we may miss out on interesting generalizations that depend, at least in part, on the relationships between certain members of Small and those objects that are in Big but not Small.

Now even if it turns out that a pretty good case can be made for an all-things-considered preference for Big, it is worth emphasizing how bizarre it is that, in this locally disordered world, we have to earn the right to think that the truck is made of particles by working through a complicated Humean profit-and-loss account. And we can well imagine that the trade-off will favour Small in a case where, on the best set of Humean laws, the pocket of disorder is nomically irrelevant to the goings on elsewhere. Take a very orderly world with a vacuum in region R. Now consider a second world that duplicates the first in its distribution of local qualities except that it has an intrinsic duplicate of a 12-minute period in the life a fully operational grocery store in R. We can imagine that the smoothest set of generalizations in the new world will

---

[43] If they really did have colours, then we can more easily imagine that the best set of Humean laws would recognize both as particles and then have additional laws of the form 'the red particles do such and such'.

[44] Of course the spatiotemporalist might not quite see things this way. Perhaps I am misdescribing the world by saying that the so called blue lines are 'occupied', as if the concept of occupation had primitive application. (The defender of perfect plenitude will have different but related complaints.) I shall not pursue this thread here, though in Sider's defence it is worth noting that he is sympathetic to spatiotemporalism.

be those that held of the original world and will thus not count any of the occupants of R as physical continuants at all.

(We may note in passing that these worries may yield surprising counterfactuals. Assume the standard account, whereby counterfactuals take you to worlds where a small miracle—by the lights of the laws of the actual world—makes the antecedent is true.[45] Suppose then I enunciate a counterfactual of the form 'Had particle x gone on path y, then. . .'. At the worlds in question, a small miracle occurs. The counterparts of the particle at those worlds will not of course be exceptions to the laws there. Yet we cannot assume without argument that the particle will be a particle at those worlds! For it might be that the best set of Humean laws at some such world exclude the counterpart from their domain in order to achieve the best combination of simplicity and strength. Yet we would hardly be comfortable with such counterfactuals as 'If particle x had gone on path y then it wouldn't have been a particle.' The Lewisian has resources here, however. Perhaps, *for some purposes*, we would do better to identify the real particles at a world not by asking whether they fall within the domain of the laws at that world, but whether they are counterparts of the objects that fall within the domain of the real laws here. I shall not pursue the matter further here.)

Let me turn next to chance. This is a topic that Sider explicitly sets to one side, but it does make potential trouble. Suppose the laws of dynamics are chancy. Then it is going to be much harder to handle collapse problems by the proposed account. Return to our toy environment X example. Suppose that the laws say something like 'When in environment X there is likelihood Y of the particles taking a helical trajectory.' Suppose now we have a homogeneous disc in environment X. Consider a generalization/continuant package that takes a helical set of disc constituents as the physical continuants versus a package that takes a non-helical set. The one package may include the candidate law 'When in environment X it is 98 per cent likely that particles will take a helical trajectory', while the second package may assign a slightly different probability (or perhaps not if there are enough things around). It seems that it will be very hard to adjudicate between the packages. The likely result is that it will turn out to be indeterminate, once again, whether the disc is rotating, since it will be indeterminate which package gives the laws. Once again, I do not pretend this is a decisive consideration—it merely points out that once we move to probabilistic laws, the ability of this approach to handle collapse cases with respect rather than dismissal may be compromised.

Finally, let us turn to our third theme, determinism. One would have thought that it was an interesting empirical question whether the world is deterministic or not.[46] But Sider's account seems to provide us with an *a priori* argument against determinism. Following Lewis, let us take it that the world is deterministic iff any world free of alien universals that has the same laws as this world and which duplicates this world at one time duplicates this world at all later times[47]. Consider a world that duplicates

---

[45] See Lewis, *Counterfactuals* (Blackwell, 1973).

[46] At least in its qualitative version (see 'Determinism De Re', this volume).

[47] See e.g. 'New Work for a Theory of Universals', *Papers in Metaphysics and Epistemology* (Cambridge University Press, 1999), 32–33.

this world now, but which at a later time has a junk object that has no duplicate in our world, but which is outside the domain of the best Humean law package for that world. The existence of the junk object at that world is no obstacle, then, to supposing that the laws that govern that world are the same as the laws that govern this one. We have a recipe for constructing worlds which have the same laws, which duplicate this world at one time, and which diverge at some later time: make the other world have a junk object (all of whose parts are junk) at a later time and have laws that are just like ours (which handle the offending object by leaving it outside of their domain). It seems that counterexamples to determinism will be just too easy to come by. It does not help that we have formulated determinism using worlds in 'the inner sphere' in which there are no alien properties (perfectly natural properties that are not instantiated at this world).[48] For it is not required that the offending junk object have alien properties. And it will not do to weaken the thesis of determinism to one that says that if a world duplicates this one at a given time and has the same laws, then there will be duplication of *quality objects* at all future times. After all, if we learned that a world 'free of alien intrusions' could share our laws of nature, duplicate this world at a given time, but then diverge *in any way whatsoever*, that would lead us to conclude that determinism is false.

I offer none of this as decisive. If the actual world is, as Lewis thinks it is, a mosaic of local qualities instantiated by point-sized stages (or spacetime points themselves), then something along the lines discussed above may be the best that can be done by making sense of both our ordinary conception of matter in motion and of dynamical science. And if the local qualities are orderly in certain ways—suppose for example that spacetime contains a neat finite number of worldstrands that never criss-cross—its application to the actual world may proceed fairly smoothly. In such a setting, the limited application of the approach to various other possible worlds, and even the incoherence of determinism, may not seem like a great price to pay for the advantages of a Humean desert. Moreover, there may be one way of significantly improving upon Sider's proposal. Let us call a domain of continuants a *covering domain* if and only if every occupied point is occupied by some member of the domain. Let us call a set of dynamical laws a *covering set* just in case its domain is a covering domain. One might require of a set of dynamical laws that they be a covering set, so that the dynamical laws turn out to be that covering set with the best combination of simplicity and strength.[49,50] Might not this go a long way to remedy the problems concerning disorder and determinism?

[48] The language of 'inner sphere' and 'alien intrusions' is taken from Lewis. For relevant discussion, see 'New Work for a Theory of Universals'.

[49] Of course, this approach is not so readily available for the spatiotemporalist, since he cannot take the facts of occupation as input to the theory of dynamical laws.

[50] One might instead allow that in certain cases the generalization that a domain is a covering set itself counts as a covering law. As Hilary Greaves pointed out, the admission of such generalizations as laws could be justified by the Lewisian conception of laws as generalizations with the best blend of simplicity and predictive power, and moreover, such laws could then be used to rescue Lewis from the anti-determinism argument given above.

We should also be aware that our assumption that the laws of nature are cast over physical continuants is not sacrosanct.[51] Suppose the best combination of simplicity and strength is a set of laws that quantify only over spacetime points and which describe the developments of field values. Then, many of the current concerns disappear, or at least need serious rethinking. Consider a case (described earlier) which we might naturally describe as one of two point particles colliding, and where we ask what makes it true to say that the point particles bounce rather than continue on their way. If the fundamental physics is field theoretic, then the laws describing how things evolve over time may prescind altogether from selecting out a pair of 'quality particles' from the candidates, resting content with a set of laws that predict and explain a certain pattern of criss-crossing in the pattern of distribution of field values. From such a perspective, the Lewisian solution will not consist in providing the resources from distinguishing the junk from the quality continuants, but rather in showing that fundamental physics can do without that distinction. Such an approach was hinted at in our discussion of spatiotemporalism above. It is certainly of interest. Yet it seems premature to place all our faith in field-theoretic dismissals of our current line of inquiry.

6 RETREATS FROM THE LEWISIAN PACKAGE

If one is uncomfortable with Sider's approach (I have offered no final verdict), one will probably not wish to keep the Lewisian package as it stands. Even as plenitude lovers, many of us will find that this package does sufficient violence to our take on the world—as well as to our modal understanding—to motivate us to seek out other answers to our puzzles. Note, for example, that those of us who are not happy with a counterpart theoretic account of *de re* modality will feel much more inclined to allow for multiple occupancy of a given spatiotemporal region. We will then still be left wondering how one rather than another occupant gets selected out as the fit subject for dynamical laws.

Relaxing some of the features of that package can open up new strategies for handling the restriction and collapse problems. In what follows, I wish to consider some departures from the Lewisian package that I find particularly interesting. The first has been proposed by Jeremy Butterfield. The second is the kind of view that I favour.

6.1 Butterfield

Consider a point particle. Lewis says that for any temporal interval that is a subinterval of the particle's life, there is an object that exactly occupies that interval. This is true for any temporal interval whatsoever, including instantaneous intervals. But suppose that we are not quite so liberal. Suppose that we concede that for any subinterval of non-zero extent,[52] there is a temporal part of the particle that occupies that

---

[51] I am grateful for discussions with Frank Arntenius and Tim Maudlin here.

[52] I am oversimplifying somewhat here: we may also deny the existence an object that exists for the first five minutes and then some isolated later instant in the life of the particle, even though the putative object would have non-zero temporal extent. For further discussion, see 'Gunk and Continuous Variation', this volume.

interval, but deny that there are instantaneous temporal parts. We can still retain much of what is important in the Lewisian view. We can keep extensionalism and anti-essentialism. We can keep the worm view. We can, if we wish, maintain with the Humean that all the fundamental intrinsic qualities are local.[53] And we can endorse a close cousin of stage primacy. Of course, we can no longer think of temporally long things as inheriting their properties from temporally instantaneous things. But we can still claim that, in general, temporally long things inherit their properties from temporally shorter things. There will not, of course, be ultimate bearers of properties on this view: there will be a descending chain, with no bottom, of temporally longer things inheriting their properties from temporally shorter things. It will be a matter of dispute whether this cousin of the stage primacy view is significantly inferior to stage primacy in its original form.[54]

While this view keeps much of the Lewisian package, Butterfield has seen that it may have something distinctive to say about the restriction and collapse problems.[55] The reason is that the view does not go so far as to endorse plenitude. Imagine that a disc rotates. Consider the helical worldlines that are described by the point particles that make up the disc. Given plenitude, there will inevitably also be objects that occupy the non-helical trajectories that would be expected of a non-rotating disc. One then has to say why such objects are junk rather than quality. But on the current view there will not be such junk objects. Without the instantaneous building blocks, there will be no mereological route to the troublesome junk objects from the respectable ones. This view can maintain, it seems, that any object that occupies a maximal filled worldline is a quality object. On the current approach, supposing there is a continuum of point particles whose mereological structure is as Butterfield envisions, there just won't be objects that occupy those maximal filled worldliness that the Lewisian fills with junk.

Butterfield's account of the mereological decomposition of objects means that despite endorsing the universal fusion axiom, there is still no guarantee of an object for each maximally filled worldline. Suppose a set of maximal filled helical worldlines in a continuous worldtube are each occupied. Suppose each finite subinterval of each such worldline has an exact occupant. Suppose every object is the fusion of some set of those objects just mentioned. Then there will be plenty of maximal filled worldliness that have no occupant. This view thus has no problem in providing ideological

[53] On the Lewisian view if we say, for each spacetime point, whether or not it is occupied and say which local qualities are had at it, we fix the world. Not so on this view. Thus Humean supervenience cannot quite be right on this view. Cf. Butterfield, 'On the Persistence of Homogeneous Matter', section 7.3. Here is not the place to engage with such issues.

[54] That will depend in large part on how pressing one thinks the problem of temporary intrinsics is (as applied to intrinsic monadic properties and intrinsic relations). Local qualities will no longer be had *simpliciter*. Suppose some particle varies continuously over time along some qualitative dimension, and has some particular quality at some spacetime point. The possession of the quality by the particle has to be indexed to the spacetime point, or else made sense of by some yet more elaborate strategy (see 'Gunk and Continuous Variation', this volume).

[55] I do not mean to imply that he is operating with quite the same taxonomy of the problem space as the one I am working with here.

resources for distinguishing homogeneous discs whose point-sized parts take helical trajectories from homogeneous discs whose point-sized parts do not.

What is wrong then with a version of Butterfield's view that builds quality objects out of quality point particles, and defines a quality point particle as an object that occupies a maximal filled worldline?[56] Let me raise a cluster of concerns.

First, we should note that some of the original concerns about the continuity answer carry over to this account. One of the problems arising for the continuity answer turned on the concerns about maximally filled worldliness that are only filled by junk objects. One way of generating such junk objects was via continua. That route is now successfully blocked. But another way was via interpenetrating particles. If two particles interpenetrate and then go along their way, we can generate two junk objects by combining the early stages of one with the late stages of another. That construction did not depend on instantaneous stages. It does not go away. Another of the problems turned on the concern that one should not require by fiat that particles occupy continuous paths. That worry survives unscathed.[57]

Second, it is worth noting that in certain special cases, Lewisian strategies for handling the objects of folk ontology can no longer be applied. Suppose a lump is a statue for a while, and the statue is only ever made from that lump. On the Lewisian account, we say that what is really going on is that statue is a temporal part of the lump. Meanwhile, if the lump is a statue only for an instant, we identify the statue with an instantaneous part of the lump, and in the case that the statue exists for a period but is constituted by that particular lump for only an instant, we analyse this situation by saying that the statue has an instantaneous part that is part of the lump. These last ideas get disrupted on the current view. If a mass of matter is part of a statue for only an instant, we cannot make sense of this in the standard Lewisian way.

Third, it is at least worth noting that the issue of spatiotemporalism matters a good deal here. Presumably, Butterfield does not wish to deny the existence of spacetime points. If objects are identified with spatiotemporal regions, then we are in no position to assert that they lack instantaneous parts.

Fourth, one wonders how Butterfield can justify differing attitudes to the spatial and temporal dimensions of matter. Why admit point-sized parts spatially, but only arbitrarily small parts temporally? If, meanwhile, he adopts a similar attitude to the spatial dimension, then the central idea that I have presented no longer has force. It is correct that one cannot construct junky continuous point particles out of a continuum of quality point particles if one only has the point particles and their non-instantaneous parts to work with (and the point particles never interpenetrate). But suppose that nothing was spatially point sized: everything occupies a worldtube, not

[56] Butterfield himself is a little more cautious. I do not want to be represented as saddling him with this view. Yet this is a view that is certainly suggested by some of his recent writings on the subject. See especially 'On the Persistence of Homogeneous Matter', and 'The Rotating Discs Argument Defeated' (in preparation).

[57] To be fair, Butterfield is fully aware that 'jumping particles' are not handled. See 'On the Persistence of Particles', section 4.2.2. Some of the ideas about particle identity in the latter paper do not, I should note, rely on the main idea discussed in the text, and are instead rather more in line with Sider's thinking on the matter.

a worldline. Suppose one now tried to institute the analogue of Butterfield's idea, disallowing instantaneous slices of worldtubes, but allowing for exact occupants of arbitrarily small chunks of any exactly occupied worldtube. One would no longer have grounds for ruling out junky objects corresponding to this or that continuously filled worldtube, since one could construct such objects out of the materials provided by the new requirement (imagine drawing a 'junk' worldtube across a row of adjacent 'quality' worldtubes, and then building an object out of the objects defined by each area of intersection).[58]

6.2 Neo-Aristotelian Plenitude

Let me return to the neo-Aristotelian theory, mentioned earlier, in order to advocate a very simple idea. Certain issues of fine-tuning that arise within neo-Aristotelian metaphysics do not concern me here. Instead, I wish to dwell on a particular contrast, one that I think is of great significance. In the Lewisian package, temporally extended worms are not metaphysically fundamental. The thesis of stage primacy tells us that stages and not worms are the bearers of fundamental properties. The qualitative character of temporally long things is analysed in terms of that belonging to temporally short things. However, plenitude does not require such privileging of the temporally short. It is quite clear that, for Aristotle, singing Socrates is metaphysically less fundamental than Socrates himself. What if we opt for a version of plenitude that abandons stage primacy, privileging certain temporally long things for the purposes of making out a quality/junk divide?

There are two natural ways of underscoring the derivative nature of a certain short-lived object *vis-à-vis* a certain long-lived object that it mereologically coincides with, ways that correspond to the qualitative and inheritance answers canvassed earlier.[59,60]

Turning first to the inheritance answer, we might say the path of inheritance goes from the long-lived thing to the short-lived thing and not vice versa. Imagine that a body, call it 'Body', is highly charged for a short period. There will be a derived object, Charged Body, that exists only during the period that Body is highly charged. In a perfectly good sense, Body will be made of some collection of short-lived objects of this sort: for some such set, Body will be mereologically coincident with at least one member at any time, and at every time any member exists, it will be mereologically coincident with Body at that time. Notwithstanding all this, the lines of property inheritance will run from Body to those short-lived objects and not vice versa. In a very natural sense, then, he 'begets' them and not they him.

---

[58]   Thanks to Frank Arntzenius here.

[59]   Of course, it is not part of the view that a quality object is never short-lived. An atom might, unluckily, be annihilated after a very short life.

[60]   There are other ways of attempting to cash out the derivative nature of the shortlived object that I shall not pursue here. Insofar one believes in 'real definitions', one might say that while Socrates will be mentioned in the real definition of singing Socrates, no mention of singing Socrates will figure in a real definition of Socrates. One might also (or alternatively) insist that singing Socrates has an extra dimension of mereological complexity, containing singing as a part (while Socrates merely enjoys singing as a property). One would then, of course, have to slightly qualify the claim that there are times when Socrates is mereologically coincident with singing Socrates.

This way of privileging the temporally long over the temporally short relies on an ideology of inheritance. As it is being used here, such ideology cannot easily be cashed out in terms of the bland modal relation of supervenience. After all, for all that has been said, it may be that the qualitative facts about the long lived 'substances' supervene on the qualitative facts about the shortlived 'qua objects'. The point is a familiar one: modal facts about supervenience are unsuitable to capturing lines of metaphysical dependence. Some may think this a reason to dismiss the alleged facts of inheritance as scholastic and unusable. The proponent of this view will think of it as a reason to think the tools of standard modal ontology too impoverished to capture the metaphysical structure of the world. This is too large a topic to pursue further on this occasion.

The neo-Aristotelian view will likely recommend that we treat the fundamental properties as somehow time indexed (or perhaps, better, spacetime indexed).[61] Returning to Lewis's toy example of bentness, this view needs to treat as fundamental the two place relation of bentness that holds between an object and a time. For if an enduring substance is the ultimate bearer of bentness, and that bearer is bent at one time and not another, then one had better not require—as Lewis does—that the basic properties be index free. (None of this is to deny, of course, that one can define up the property of being bent at all times that one exists out of the more natural relation of *being bent at*.)

Let us turn now to the qualitative answer, one that will also rely on the time-indexed conception of fundamental properties. Return to our pair of Body and Charged Body. There is a fundamental, natural relation—called it 'Being Charged+ at' (which is a relation between certain objects and certain spacetime points)—that is possessed by Body and that is not possessed by Charged Body. However, recalling our discussion of *mass** above, there is a slightly less fundamental relation—of being mereologically coincident at t with something Charged+ at t—that is entered into by Charged Body and Body (since Body is mereologically coincident with itself). A similar story will be advanced for, say, the fundamental property Mass+ in connection with some body and some statue that it constitutes. Note that the Lewisian can hardly complain that, on this view, we don't ordinarily ascribe the fundamental property of Mass+ and Charge+ to an object when we predicate 'mass' and 'charge' of it. For, after all, we do not do so either on his view, since the subjects of ordinary predications are the worms (at least according to Lewis), and the bearers of the fundamental properties are the stages.[62] In general, I see no good 'argument from ordinary language' against the qualitative view.

Both of the views just sketched are committed to privileging certain long-lived objects which we might, following a long tradition, call 'the substances'. On one view, the substances are those that are the bearers of fundamental magnitudes; on

---

[61] Actually, there are some other options (see 'Three-Dimensionalism', this volume). What is clear, though, is that the Lewisian picture of the fundamental properties has to be replaced.

[62] For the Lewisian, when we say that an ordinary object has mass, we are saying that it has a temporal part that has the fundamental property of mass simpliciter, where 'mass simpliciter' is a term of art for the fundamental property.

the other, the substances are the things that have fundamental magnitudes but not by coincident inheritance. Substance-theoretic views of this sort, while agreeing with the Lewisian with regard to plenitude, might depart from him on a number of issues of basic metaphysical significance. We have already seen that they need not subscribe to mereological extensionalism: a statue that begins and ends its life with the lump may be reckoned distinct from and yet mereologically coincident with the lump throughout its career. They need not think of all the fundamental qualities as local. They need not have any patience for counterpart theoretic treatments of *de re* modality. And they need not endorse a Humean attitude to the facts of causation. Clearly, then, a number of the strategies mentioned earlier for engaging with the restriction and collapse problems are in principle open to one who endorses a version of plenitude with this kind of shape. However, there is a very natural kind of answer to such problems that is suggested by their rejection of stage primacy, one that appears to be a very promising avenue for engaging with those problems.

It is out of the question for the Lewisian to maintain that the objects that dynamics is interested in providing laws for are the fundamental bearers of the physical magnitudes. And that is because the fundamental bearers are instantaneous objects but the targets of the laws are a subset of the worms. But Aristotelian plenitude lovers, while accepting plenitude, need have no patience with stage primacy. They are thus free to insist that the fundamental bearers of the magnitudes *are* the quality objects. They are thus free to endorse either a qualitative answer or an inheritance answer to the restriction problem and to various versions of the collapse problem.

Let us take a simple case which puts the matter into sharp relief. Given plenitude, what would the world have to be like for it to be correct to conceive of it as one in which two point particles move discontinuously, switching places at a certain time, so that each continues along the extension of the erstwhile path of the other from that time? Plenitude tells us that in such a scenario there will be two objects that move continuously. Why not call them the particles? Suppose, to simplify, that there is one basic physical quantity, mass. Both the qualitative and the inheritance perspectives have the resources to distinguish two scenarios: (1) There are two continuously moving substances which have Mass+ primarily (which for the qualitative view amounts to having Mass+ rather than merely being coincident with something that has Mass+, and which for the inheritance view amounts to having Mass+ but not having Mass+ by coincident inheritance). There are various particulars that do not have Mass+ primarily, including various particulars that move discontinuously. (2) There are two substances—objects that have Mass+ primarily—that move discontinuously. There are also various dependent particulars, two of which move continuously but which do not have mass primarily.

What is so good about the account? We must take care here not to stray into verificationist criteria of success and failure. The project was never to find some way of looking to see whether particles move discontinuously or not. That (1) and (2) can never be discriminated by observation is a desirable result, not an undesirable one. For of course, if we are unlucky enough to be in a world where things jump, we may well be in no position to tell that this is so.

So what are the rules of the game here? First of all, the metaphysics should provide some answer to the restriction problem and, except in cases where the collapse problem turns out to rely on conceptions of space and time that are deemed impossible, one would hope that an answer to the restriction problem would provide some guidance. Second, one would think that, other things being equal, an attitude of dismissal to collapse problems is best avoided. Third, one would think it preferable that a metaphysics does not merely 'tack on' extra ideology designed to solve the problems of restriction and collapse. In natural science we are suspicious of ad hoc additions to a theory that are specially designed to account for some local problem. Much better that a solution flow from the general structural features of a theory rather than special purpose solutions. The same is true in metaphysics. One who tried to have a solution to problems of restriction and collapse that invoked special relations of immanent causation and genidentity that had no previous life at all, but which we introduced as special purposes fixes, can reasonably be viewed with a certain amount of suspicion. (This last ground rule is inevitably somewhat inchoate, and vague in its application: but it does have real intellectual force in theory choice nevertheless.)

Supposing something like these ground rules are roughly correct, the neo-Aristotelian does very well. He has natural answers to the restriction and collapse problems that do not at all encourage attitude of dismissal (as (1) and (2) above make clear). The Lewisian plenitude lover is forced into dismissal in cases where the Humean mosaic lacks sufficient richness to ground a solid preference for one law/object package over another. The neo-Aristotelian need not do so.

We may note in passing that there are fundamental differences between Sider and the current view on the relationship between quality objects and laws. Suppose a smoother set of laws about, say, mass, can be obtained by eliminating some object *o* from their domain. On the current view, a primary bearer of mass cannot simply be ignored when it comes to formulating the laws. If some such object violates some simple generalization, one has to say 'So much the worse for the putatively nomic generalization' and not 'Keep the nomic generalization but restrict the domain a little bit'. The current view is, I submit, the more intuitive of the two.

My own preference, I should say, is for the qualitative version of the view. That view is certainly less of an ideological strain—it does not require a primitive notion of inheritance.[63] And it coheres very nicely with certain of the ideas that motivated a causal answer. Presumably the laws of nature will be about Mass+, not the property of being coincident with something with Mass+. On the qualitative perspective, it will be altogether natural to see statues as exempt from the dynamical laws of nature: they quite simply do not have the properties that the laws of nature are about.

Some will resist the qualitative view on the grounds that it is committed to the thesis that things can be mereologically coincident at a time and yet not share the same intrinsic properties at that time. It is indeed so committed, yet no worse for that. Views that hold that intrinsic properties are automatically shared at a time

---

[63] Nor does it require a fundamental distinction between small-to-large inheritance and coincident inheritance. Might that not get problematized in a setting that eschews absolute simultaneity? (The relevant notion of coincidence, after all, was coincidence at a time, not permanent coincidence.)

by mereological coincidents rely, I suspect, on a kind of photographic model of the intrinsic in their metaphysical picture thinking, one that is not metaphysically defensible. (This is especially obvious once we take *de re* modality at face value. It is strange to think of the *de re* modal potentialities of a thing as extrinsic: yet they are certainly not shared by all of the things it is mereologically coincident with.)

I have tried to motivate a simple idea, that the quality objects are the primary bearers of the basic physical magnitudes, a thesis that is unavailable to the Lewisian. The substance theoretic picture makes room for instantaneous objects but reverses the order of primacy, paving the way for endorsement of the simple idea. Let me end by noting some variants on the picture just sketched. The core idea was that the province of dynamics is the primary bearers of physical magnitudes. This idea can be detached from the thesis that the domain of dynamics is the set of all the genuine substances (as opposed to metaphysically 'second rate' objects). There are various reasons why one might wish to deny this latter thesis. First, that thesis relies on the idea of the domain of dynamics as fundamental. But as noted earlier, one might think that the objects of dynamics depend on yet more fundamental objects and magnitudes—waves, fields, certain categories of objects currently unknown to us. Second, one might think, with Aristotle, that certain 'higher-level' objects—Socrates, for instance—are metaphysically first rate. One might, for example, be led to such a view if one thought that there was a distinctive range of highly natural, non-gerrymandered properties—say, mental properties—that belonged to a category of objects to which Socrates belonged and which did not attach primarily to the objects of dynamics. Faced with these various pressures one might wish to relax the boundaries of substancehood. One obvious proposal is this: let a substance be any object that has some family of highly natural properties in a primary way (where primary is glossed according to the qualitative or the inheritance answer, depending on what one favours). We can then imagine that the province of dynamics is defined by a certain family of interconnected properties: the objects that form its domain are then the objects that have *those* primarily. An underlying metaphysical layer might boast a domain of objects with a very different set of properties—ones that are no fit subject for the kind of laws concerning matter in motion with which dynamics deals, but which may be a fit subject for some other branch of fundamental physics. And some overlying layer might boast a domain of objects which have some properties from a different family non-derivatively.

Such views are obviously very schematic—awaiting, *inter alia*, some suitable elucidation of the concept of 'family of properties that define the concerns of dynamics'. I think it best to avoid excessive *a priorism* here. When seventieth-century natural philosophers ventured forth various laws about bodies, statues and restaurants were certainly not things that made trouble for those laws. We suppose that there is a broad natural kind of entity—that they called '*bodies*'—that was the object of their study, but that is not to suppose that we possess some *a priori* definition of what membership in that kind consists in. This natural kind is a broader one than figures in standard philosophical discussions of natural kinds, but much of the lessons wrought there can be transposed to this case. Of course, one can imagine that the world is not amenable: one can describe bleak scenarios in which it is only by grossly idealizing that one can suppose that there is a domain of entities to which some successor dynamical theory provides a correct nomic profile. (But note that the mere hypothesis that the level of dynamics is not the level of truly fundamental physics does not yet vindicate such a bleak conclusion.)

Supposing there is such a natural kind as *body*, there are various hypotheses as to what natural properties play a constitutive role *vis-à-vis* that kind. One is that bodies are those entities that have *location* primarily.[64] Another is that bodies are those entities that have *velocity* primarily. A third is that bodies are those entities that have the properties associated with *mass* (or *mass density*) and *stress* primarily. It may even turn out that the most plausible 'real definition' of the domain of dynamics proceeds by way of properties far different to those with which the casual dabbler in Newtonian physics is acquainted. The abstract questions with which I have been dealing—centred upon the metaphysical thesis of stage primary—are silent on many of these important questions of detail.

---

[64] I realize that some will balk at a qualitative version of this view, according to which there is a fundamental relation of being located at+ that is lacked by statues, who only get to stand in slightly less natural relations to spacetime regions.

7

Gunk and Continuous Variation[1]

with *Frank Arntzenius*

1 INTRODUCTION

Let us say that a thing is gunky just in case every part of that thing has proper parts (i.e. parts that are not identical to it). The idea that all physical objects are gunky seems sufficiently sweeping, interesting, and plausible that it is worth examining. However, there is a difficulty. The features of an extended object can surely vary continuously (in time and/or space). If an object is gunky then it cannot have point-sized parts which have no further parts. But how can one conceive of a continuous variation in features other than as the obtaining of different features at different point-sized locations?

Addressing this matter will require us to get clear about which distinctions the gunk lover will wish to respect, and which to abolish. In section II we make some preliminary remarks about gunky conceptions of the natural world. In section III we introduce our focal problem, paying special attention to its history. In section IV we sketch four strategies for handling this problem that we do not find satisfactory. In section V we develop a pair of rather more promising strategies. We conclude by noting some interesting analogies between our development of gunk theory and relationalism about space and time.

2 GUNK

Begin with a *Barebones Gunk Thesis* about some object O:

Every part of O has proper parts.

Suppose now that O is a gunky chocolate bar. The Barebones Gunk Thesis provides us with some information about the chocolate bar, but leaves many questions unsettled. For example, as stated, the Barebones Gunk Thesis does not rule out that the chocolate bar has point-sized parts. It merely entails that if it has point-sized parts, then these in turn have to have proper parts. One might wish to object that a point has volume 0, and nothing can have a volume that is smaller than 0. However, being a

This article first appeared in *The Monist* (Oct. 2005). I am grateful for permission to reprint it here.

[1] We would like to thank Dean Zimmerman, David Manley, and Ted Sider for discussions.

proper part does not entail that one must have a strictly lesser volume. (For example, consider a region, and that region minus a point: the second region is a proper part of the first, but it has the same volume.)

Now of course, we would not naturally think of the gunky chocolate bar as having point-sized parts; nevertheless, the Barebones Gunk Thesis, unsupplemented, is neutral on the matter. More generally, the Barebones Gunk Thesis does not tell us which subregions of the chocolate bar mark out parts of the chocolate bar. For example, it is compatible with the Barebones Gunk thesis that every part of the chocolate bar has the same height as the chocolate bar itself. (Suppose, for example, that each part has the same height but contains proper parts of lesser widths.) Such considerations make it clear that when philosophers give voice to a gunky conception of some class of extended things, that conception encodes background assumptions about the class that go well beyond the sparse content of the Barebones Thesis. Often these background assumptions are not properly articulated, checked for coherence, and systematically applied. As a prelude to a disciplined treatment of our main puzzle, it will be useful to lay out the conception of gunk with which we are operating and to indicate some motivations for that conception.

One key component to any gunky conception ought to be some background set of mereological assumptions, i.e. assumptions about the structure of part-whole relations. A key decision here is whether to adopt the standard mereology, or instead one or other deviant mereology.[2] Our mereology will be the standard one. Of particular note for what follows will be the following claims of standard mereology:

Universal Fusion: For any set of objects s, there exists some object that fuses that s (where x fuses y iff every object that overlaps x is overlapped by a member of y and every object that overlaps a member of y is overlapped by x).

Remainder: If x is a part of y and not identical to y then there is some z that is part of y that is discrete from x, such that y is the fusion of x and z (where x is discrete from y iff there is no part that x shares with y).

A second key component of a gunky conception will be one's measure-theoretic assumptions. Gunky objects will have volumes, or sizes. (By the 'size' of an object we will, in this paper, mean its volume, i.e. not its shape, not its full set of metric features, merely its total volume.) Fusions of those objects will also have sizes. If x fuses a class of objects, how does the size of x relate to the sizes of the members of the class? We make the standard measure theoretic assumption that size is countably additive:

Countable Additivity: For any countable set of objects C whose members are discrete from each other, the size the object that fuses C is identical to the sum of the sizes of the members of C.

Note that Countable Additivity implies Finite Additivity: the size of a discrete finite set equals the sum of the sizes of its finitely many members. Countable Additivity

---

[2] See e.g. Peter Simons, *Parts: A Study in Ontology* (Oxford: Clarendon Press, 1987) for an account of standard and non-standard mereologies. We shall not fuss here about the possible need to relax standard mereology so as to allow for the coincidence of statue and lump etc.

may seem so obvious as to be scarcely worth announcing. Yet it will be helpful in what follows to make it explicit.

If one looks back at early modern discussions and seeks to extract motivations for a gunky conception of objects, the primary motivation that one will discern is the following measure theoretic one:

No Zero: There are no objects whose volume is zero.

Return to our chocolate bar. Assuming No Zero, we can say that there are no parts of the chocolate bar with the dimensions of a point, no parts of the chocolate bar with the dimensions of a line, and none with the dimensions of a plane. Moreover, when No Zero is combined with our mereological assumptions, further results follow. In standard point set topology, we can distinguish an open region from its closure.[3] Typically, each has the same volume, since the latter differs from the former only by including the boundary points of the former.[4] Can the Gunk lover admit a distinction between such closed and open parts of the chocolate bar? Assume for reductio there is some open piece, call it Open, that is a proper part of some closed piece, call it Closed, each of the same volume. Remainder tells us that there will be a part x of Closed that does not overlap with Open, such that Closed is the fusion of x and Open. Assuming Countable Additivity (Finite Additivity is all we need here), it follows that x has zero measure, violating No Zero. So, once No Zero is assumed, we cannot admit the standard distinction between open and closed regions.

Many people find No Zero compelling. One famous defence is provided by Arnauld and Nicole's Port-Royal Logic:

Finally, nothing is clearer than this reasoning, that two things having zero extension cannot form an extension, and that every extension has parts. Now taking two of these parts that are assumed to be indivisible, I ask whether they do or do not have any extension. If they have some extension, then they are indivisible, and they have several parts. If they do not, they therefore have zero extension, and hence it is impossible for them to form an extension.[5]

The purpose of these remarks is, *inter alia*, to show that extended things cannot be composed of points. What Arnauld and Nicole say explicitly to this end is that any two purported entities of zero magnitude would together have zero magnitude. But it is clear that they are implicitly endorsing a generalization of that thought, viz that the sum of the magnitudes of any set of entities of zero magnitude is zero. Indeed, this line of thought is often found in casual conversation, as well as in the writings of distinguished philosophers from the past. The conclusion is that things of finite magnitude could not possibly be composed just out of things of zero magnitude, even if there were infinitely many such zero magnitude things.

---

[3] Well, some regions are open as well as closed. But this does not matter for what follows.

[4] We say 'typically' because, perhaps surprisingly, one can prove that there are regions (in standard continuous spaces) whose boundaries have non-zero (Lebesque) measure.

[5] Antoine Arnauld and Pierre Nicole, *Logic or the Art of Thinking* (Cambridge: Cambridge University Press, 1996; first published in French in 1662), 231–232. See also page 245: 'the point is not part of a line'. Note that this line of thought is represented not as something novel but as part of what geometry has made clear.

The standard modern response to this worry is *not* to claim that adding infinitely many 0's can yield a number that is not 0. Rather, one starts by getting clear on what it means to add infinitely many numbers, and one concludes that no sense can be made of the notion of adding up uncountably many numbers. Here is some more detail.

The standard conception of the sum of infinitely many numbers is that number, if there be such a number, that one gets closer and closer to as one adds more and more numbers from a list of numbers which eventually lists every number in the set. This has several consequences. In the first place, sums of infinite sets are generally only defined relative to an *ordering* of that set into a particular sequence.[6] In the second place, the sequence of partial sums may not converge to any number, in which case the infinite sum does not exist (is not well defined). In the third place, and most importantly for our purposes, this notion of infinite addition is only defined for sets of numbers which are such that there exists a list which eventually lists every number in that set, i.e. for countable sets. Of course, Cantor has shown that the real numbers are not listable, i.e. that there are uncountably many real numbers. And, of course, according to the standard conception of space there are as many points as there are (triples of) real numbers. So the modern response to Arnauld and Nicole's argument is that the notion of adding the sizes of all the points in a region just makes no sense whatsoever, so that their argument cannot even get off the ground.

One may consider this a perfectly satisfactory response. However, note that it is a consequence of the standard modern view of geometry that the size of a region is not determined by the sizes of its ultimate parts, namely the points in that region. There is a sense, then, in which the standard modern view makes size a holistic notion: sizes of regions do not supervene on the sizes of their ultimate parts. While this kind of holism clearly is not inconsistent, one may find it unattractive or implausible. One might hope that, instead, a gunky conception of the world can validate the following principle:

Summing: For any x and any class c of discrete things, if x fuses c, then there will exist a well-defined sum of the magnitudes of the members of c that is identical to the magnitude of x.

This, of course, prohibits any part-whole structure that permits the decomposition of an entity into an uncountable infinity of discrete (i.e. non-overlapping) things, since in such a case there will not exist a sum of the magnitudes of the set into which the entity is decomposed. If Summing is true, and the chocolate bar is not gappy, then the chocolate bar cannot be composed out of point sized entities.

Summing is certainly one motivating springboard for a gunky conception of the world. But there are others. A feature of contemporary measure theory, as applied to pointy space, is the admission of regions whose measure is undefined. This in turn yields some well-known results that are apt to strike one as paradoxical upon first inspection—notably the Banach–Tarski paradox, according to which the volume of the fusion of a finite number of disjoint regions (or objects) can be altered by rearranging them without stretching or distorting the shape of each region (or object). Thus

---

[6] The sum will be independent of an ordering if it consists only of non-negative numbers.

a natural motivating desideratum for the gunky conception is the desire to eliminate objects of undefined measure:

Definition: The volume of every object, and of every region, is well defined.

Assume Definition and we can motivate No Zero. For once we allow point-sized parts and Universal Fusion, we will be forced to admit regions of undefined measure. To be a bit more precise, one can prove in standard measure theory, which assumes Countable Additivity and Universal Fusion, that continuous spaces, spaces that contain an uncountable collection of zero-sized points, must contain regions that have no well-defined measure.[7] Definition thus constitutes a second motivating springboard for the gunky conception.

A third motivating springboard is provided by the observation that, according to the standard pointy conception of things, there will be pairs of objects that are of the same magnitude, one of which is part of the other. Thus if one takes an open sphere and its closure, one will be a proper part of the other and yet the pair are of exactly the same measure. Isn't this perhaps unnecessary overpopulation? It would be nice if there were never a zero measure difference between any part and whole, viz:

Difference: If x is part of y and not identical to y, then the magnitude of x is less than the magnitude of y.

Assume Difference, and No Zero follows: for the sum of an object x with an object of zero measure would be an object of which x was part but of equal magnitude to x.

One important decision point, suppressed so far, concerns the scope of one's gunk theory. The moderate gunk lover embraces a gunky conception of material objects, like chocolate bars, but a pointy conception of space/time/space-time itself, restricting his favourite motivating axioms (Summing, No Zero, etc.) to material objects.

We anticipate that the marriage proposed by the moderate gunk lover will likely be an unhappy one. Consider the region of space occupied by the chocolate bar. The moderate gunk lover, we have seen, cannot allow both that some open subregion is exactly occupied by a part of the chocolate bar and also that its closure is exactly occupied by a part of the chocolate bar. He must thus embrace a theory according to which at most one of those regions is occupied by a part of the chocolate bar. The theory risks untoward arbitrariness. If we are to restrict the Difference thesis to material objects, we need some reason for tolerating zero measure differences in the domain of spatiotemporal objects while prohibiting them within the realm of the material. We are not aware of any such reason. We shall thus assume that the most promising version of gunk theory applies not merely to physical objects in space but to space and time (or better: spacetime) themselves.

3 THE PROBLEM

It is clear enough that standard presentations of physics represent point size entities as the bearers of magnitude. Consider, for example, the standard representation of a

---

[7] Standard Measure Theory also assumes the Axiom of Choice, which is required for the proof.

field as a function from points to field values. This tendency is by no means new. Isaac Barrow, Newton's predecessor as Lucasian Professor at Cambridge, cited the words of Proclus[8] as providing *prima facie* motivation for treating points as the movers and shakers:

But let us hear Proclus' Elogium concerning a point: The centers, say he, in respect of energy, do sustain the composition of the spheres to which they belong, bounding their distances, comprehending their powers, and uniting them together into themselves.[9]

Citing support from his contemporary physics, Barrow notes that:

The moments of bodies do consist about a Point, viz the Center of Gravity; in it they gather and unite their powers; are in some sort supported and sustained by it.[10]

And of particular relevance to our present concern is the following remark:

Rest is often peculiar to them [i.e. points] ... as ... to the center of a wheel.[11]

The line of thought underlying this last remark is clear enough. Consider a wheel rotating around a centre. We attribute rest to the centre of the wheel. Rest cannot be a property attributed to anything larger than the centre point itself, since any such thing will have moving parts.

This in turn generates a worry for the gunk lover. Consider a gunky wheel that is rotating. How do we represent the fact that the centre is at rest? We cannot attribute rest to any extended portion of the wheel, since any such part will have moving parts.

Now Barrow does not accept the conclusion recommended both by Proclus and by a face value reading of his contemporary mechanics. While noting the superficial attractions of treating points as real, he tells us that he does not think that surfaces, lines, and points 'possess any existence or proper efficacy from themselves' and that 'every Magnitude consists of Magnitudes homogenous to itself, a Line of Lines, a Superfice of Superfices, and a Body of Bodies; but not a Line of Points, or a Superfice of Lines or a Body of Superfices', for Points 'are nothing else but Negations of further extension and do scarce obtain anything Positive'.[12] But one is left wondering how exactly the argument concerning the centre of the wheel is supposed to be answered.

The argument just alluded to turned, we should note, on a case in which there was continuous variation along a certain magnitude—in this case velocity. The point that Barrow raised for the centre of the wheel could be raised for any given point. For at any point there is a velocity that obtains there and not elsewhere within the neighbourhood. We thus have a general case for admitting point-sized bearers of the relevant velocities.

This pressure was astutely noticed by Leibniz in his 1676 dialogue 'Pacidus to Philalethes: A First Philosophy of Motion'. Pacidus, Leibniz' spokesman, engages with Descartes's view that while space was composed *ad infinitum* of extended parts,

---

[8] Who died AD 485, famous for his commentary on Euclid.

[9] Isaac Barrow, *Mathematical Lectures* (London, 1734), p. 144.

[10] Ibid, p. 143.   [11] Ibid.   [12] Ibid, pp. 144–145.

it did not have extensionless parts (extension being of the essence of non-mental substance). In particular, he gets Charinus, his interlocutor (whom Pacidus is instructing) to recognize that Descartes seemed to have no good means of blocking the decomposition of extended substance into points. In this connection, Pacidus asks Charinus to imagine a circular vessel in which a solid body is set off centre, and around which a liquid is made to flow. He notes that the velocity of the liquid at any point will be different to that at any other, and then remarks

Hence it seems to follow that matter is divided into points: for it is divided into all possible parts, and thus into minima. Therefore body and space will be composed of points.[13]

Charinus then chimes in:

[Descartes] ought to have at least explained how in this case matter is not resolved into a powder, so to speak, consisting of points, when it is clear that no point will be left cohering to any of the others, since each one will move in its own right with a motion different from that of any other.[14]

A similar problem arises along the temporal dimension. Suppose an object changes continuously with respect to a certain scale of values. Suppose that this object's temporal parts have a gunky make-up, and that in particular it lacks instantaneous temporal parts. Suppose that the object has some value V instantaneously. Then it is not clear what the bearer of V should be, since none of the gunky temporal parts can be properly described as being V. Let the scale be colour, and V some particular shade of crimson. No gunky temporal part is that shade. And yet no instantaneous part is available to bear that shade.

How then are we to represent continuous qualitative variation without the benefit of point-sized bearers of qualities?

4 FOUR UNSATISFYING APPROACHES

The gunk lover should not, one would hope, wish to dispute the fact of continuous variation along this or that qualitative axis. Things do move continuously, electromagnetic fields vary continuously, and so on. The point lover has a natural way to model such variation, namely by a continuous function from point-sized (or instantaneous) bearers of values to the values they possess. This way of thinking about continuous variation is not, it would seem, available to the gunk lover. How then should he think of the relevant facts? In this section we sketch four solutions to the problem just raised, ones which, by our lights, are ultimately unpromising. We then sketch two superior approaches in section 5. Before we start let us say that since our focal problem is the question of how one can have continuous variation of properties in a gunky space, we are going to assume that there exists a satisfactory account of the geometric structure of gunky spaces.[15]

---

[13] G. W. Leibniz, *The Labyrinth of the Continuum* (New Haven: Yale University Press, 2002), p. 184.

[14] Ibid., p. 185.

[15] For some details of such an account, see F. Arntzenius, 'Gunk, Topology and Measure', http://philsci-archive.pitt.edu/archive/00001792.

4.1 Approach A

One might deny the existence of point-sized objects, and deny the existence of point-sized regions of space, and yet 'construct' set theoretic entities that can stand proxy for spatial points, and point parts of objects, when it comes to the possible properties of gunky regions and gunky objects. For instance, suppose one has a gunky space in which there exist nested sequences of spheres, whose sizes converge to 0. Following Whitehead, one could let such sequences of nested gunky spheres stand as surrogates for the points of standard point set topology.[16] Let us call such set theoretic constructions out of gunky regions 'pseudo-points'.[17] One might now claim that such pseudo-points, rather than gunky regions, are the fundamental bearers of magnitudes.

Consider, for example, the chocolate bar that varies continuously in shade. We can construct pseudo-point-parts of the chocolate bar. The suggestion would then be that it is these pseudo-point-parts that are the bearers of colour properties of the bar. That is, one might suggest that the possible colour properties of the bar correspond to all the possible colour distributions over its pseudo-points. What should one think of this suggestion?

Well, in the first place it seems strange to suppose that the relevant set theoretic entities are the fundamental bearers of physical magnitudes: once sets of objects are allowed in the back door as bearers of properties, why not sets of sets, and so on? Second, and relatedly, it destroys much of the point of being a gunk lover in the first place. With a bit of work, one can show that the standard point-set topology, complete with an open-closed contrast for sets of pseudo-points, can be defined over pseudo-points, provided one started with a suitable gunky space. If one then claims that the pseudo-points are the fundamental quality bearers, then there will be no prospect at all of any gain in simplicity or explanatory virtue for *this* style of gunk theory *vis-à-vis* the standard pointy approach. Indeed, such an approach to gunk seems to merely amount to the claim that extended regions (spheres) should be regarded as, in some sense, 'more basic' or 'more fundamental' than points, rather than the claim that point-sized objects and regions do not exist. This then, does not seem to be an interesting approach to gunk, or, at least, it seems not to have any connection to the motivations for gunk that are at issue in this paper.

4.2 Approach B

Consider a temporally gunky particle that varies continuously over time. There is no instantaneous temporal part to paint a particular shade of crimson. But it might seem that one can readily avail oneself of the standard ways of accommodating change within a metaphysical framework that eschews instantaneous parts. Most notably,

---

[16] See Alfred North Whitehead, *An Enquiry Concerning the Principles of Natural Knowledge* (Cambridge: Cambridge University Press, 1919).

[17] The suggested construction of point surrogates makes use of metric structure: whether a region is spherical or not depends on the distances between points. One can also construct surrogates for points without presupposing metric structure. Which route one takes matters not for our purposes.

one can treat being such and such shade, not as a simple monadic property, but as a relation to a time. The particle is crimson at t, but not crimson at any other time. The approach can be extended to spatial variation. Suppose a chocolate bar is only crimson at one spot. Why not then treat being crimson as a relation to a place? Thus the chocolate bar (as well as the myriad parts of it that cover the place in question) bear the relation of *being crimson at* to the place in question.

This kind of approach is perfectly well available to the moderate gunk lover who places gunky objects in a pointy spacetime. But, as we have said, we reckon the most interesting version of the gunky conception to be one that extends to space and time (spacetime) itself. Suppose we allow it to do so. Then the current proposal cannot get off the ground, there being no points in space (or instants of time, or spacetime points) to serve as the relata of the postulated relations.

4.3 Approach C

Consider a pointy chocolate bar, with a colour specified for each of its pointy parts. Corresponding to every possible distribution of colours there will be a very complicated property had by the bar itself. Within this framework, it is natural to think of the colours of the points as basic, and the distributional properties of the chocolate bar as derived. But what if we allow the distributional properties to be basic as opposed to derived?[18] Then, it would seem, we can solve our problem. The chocolate bar has a distributional property (and each of its parts has a distributional property), which characterizes all its colour properties. On this way of thinking, the gunky chocolate bar has exactly the same set of possible distributional colour properties as the pointy chocolate bar. The only difference is that in the gunky case the distributional properties are not treated as supervenient upon a base of pointwise colour instantiations, since there are no points.

One might hope that even though the distributional properties of a region R do not supervene on a base of pointwise colour instantiations, they will nonetheless supervene on the distributional properties of any set of subregions $\{R_i\}$ the fusion of which is R. Unfortunately, that is not true. Consider a gunky line L which stretches from $x = -1$ to $x = 1$. Suppose it has the distributional property which corresponds to the single point $x = 0$ being red and all the other points being blue. Now, for any integer n, define gunky region L_n to be the gunky region that stretches from $x = -1$ to $x = -1/n$, and the gunky region R_n to be the region which stretches from $x = 1/n$ to $x = 1$. Now, for any n both R_n and L_n should have the distributional property of being entirely blue (or else our supervenience claim is in big trouble right off the bat). But the fusion of all the gunky regions R_n and L_n (for all finite n) just is the gunky line L. But the distributional properties of the gunky regions R_n and L_n can not possibly determine that L has the distributional property that corresponds to containing a single red point. So it is not true that the distributional properties of a region R always supervene on the distributional properties of any collection of regions the fusion of which equals R.

[18] For an example of this kind of approach, see Josh Parsons, 'Distributional Properties', in Jackson and Priest (eds.), *Lewisian Themes* (Oxford: Oxford University Press, 2004), 173–180.

Let's move on to an even more basic objection to the distributional view. Why remove points and point-like differences from the geometry of the world, if one is going to re-introduce such differences at the level of properties? Why saddle the space of possible properties with distinctions that are exactly the kind of distinctions that arguments and intuitions in favour of gunk tell one to get rid of? Moreover, by removing these differences at the level of space and time, but reintroducing them at the level of properties, one also loses the possibility of understanding these differences in terms of combinations of atomic differences, and one loses the possibility of generating all possibilities from a set of atomic possibilities via simple combinatorial principles.

And it gets worse. In the pointy case there are distributional properties that only open regions can have, and there are distributional properties that only closed regions can have (and ones that neither can have). For instance, a closed sphere of radius 1 (the set of all points which are distance 1 or less from some given point x) might be white everywhere except for the points on its outermost surface (the points that are exactly distance 1 from x) which are black. An open sphere of radius 1 (the set of all points which are less than distance 1 from some given point x) cannot have this kind of distribution of colours. For the open sphere does not have an outermost surface of 0 thickness, so it cannot have anything like the indicated colour distribution. What are we now to say about the possible colour properties of a gunky sphere? Should it have both possible colour distributions? Or is only one a possible property of any given gunky sphere? Let us look at both possibilities, in turn.

First, suppose we say that if a given gunky region can have an open colour distribution then it cannot have a closed one (or indeed any non-open one). Consider such a region. Ask: why can it only have open colour distributions? The natural answer would be: because the set of points that compose it is an open set. But, of course, since space is gunky, we cannot say this. So it is presumably just some primitive fact about that region's possible colour distribution properties that they just have to be open. How about other distributional properties of that region? Consider, say, its electric field strength properties. Could that very same region have a closed electric field distributional property? If we answer 'yes', then we have generated more possibilities than even the point lover has. For in a pointy space one can, of course, not have a region that has an open colour distribution and also a closed electric field distribution. But creating even more possibilities than the point lover is the last thing the gunk lover wants. So let's answer 'no'. Then we have imposed not only unexplained impossibilities in colour distributions, we additionally impose unexplained correlated impossibilities in all types of distributions of all possible features. The lack of an underlying geometric explanation of such co-variation then becomes even more glaring.

And how about the possibility of contiguity between regions that have such primitive restrictions on their distributional properties? In the pointy case, a region which has a closed colour distribution cannot be contiguous to another region which has a closed colour distribution. For closed regions must either overlap, or be a finite distance apart. What are we to say in the gunky case? Are we, yet again, going to impose unexplained constraints on possibilities, or are we, yet again, going to allow for more possibilities than the point lover does? Neither is appealing.

Suppose now, instead, that any gunky region can have both open and closed colour distributions. It would then seem plausible that any such region could have an open colour distribution and a closed electrical field distribution at the very same time. If so, again, we have created too many possibilities. And if not, why not? Does it just so happen that the possible distributional variations of different properties of a given region must co-vary in time? If so, what relation does that bear to the contiguity properties of the regions? And why?

Let's abandon this craziness. Approach C amounts to theft rather than honest toil. Worse: it's theft of distinctions we were trying to rid ourselves of in the first place.

4.4 Approach D

Let's try a rather obvious approach to the colour properties of gunky objects. Let's say that all the colour facts about gunky objects (regions) supervene on all facts of the following type: 'Gunky part (region) X has colour Y', where Y is some exact colour. Fine, but what do we mean to convey by such claims? When we say 'The flag is red' do we mean to say that the flag is red all over? If so, we would not get very far. For if an object has a continuously varying colour then no extended part of it has any exact colour all over, and all assertions of the form 'Part X has colour Y' would be false no matter what. That's no good.

So let us say that when we say 'Gunky object, or region, X has exact colour Y' we express a primitive monadic property that can be informally glossed as 'X has colour Y somewhere' (but which officially has no structural analysis). Let us now consider some problems for such a view.

Here is a problem. Given that all gunky regions are extended, it should be possible that every region (other than the Null region) is red ('somewhere') and is blue ('somewhere'), and that all other colour attributions are false. One might immediately object that such colour facts would not distinguish between many distinct corresponding pointy distributions of blue and red. However, this by itself hardly constitutes an objection: the gunk lover, after all, wants to get rid of some of the distinctions that the point lover can make. For instance, the point lover can distinguish the case where the rational points are blue and the irrationals are red, and the case where all but one of the rational points are blue. On the current approach to gunk one cannot, and that seems a good thing. However, gunk lovers presumably do want to make a distinction between the case in which measure 1 of space is blue and measure 0 is red. But on the current approach the gunk lover cannot make such a distinction, for all the facts are given once one has said that every region is both red and blue, and these facts are compatible with any assignment of measures which add up to 1.

Here is another problem. Consider a countable sequence of regions X_i such that for all n, region X_n contains region X_{n+1}, and their size converges to 0 as n goes to infinity. For each X_i let X_i^C be its complement. Now suppose that for each X_i we have it that 'X_i is red' is true, that 'X_i is blue' is true, and that all other colour attributions to each of the X_i are false. And suppose that for each of the complements X_i^C we have that 'X_i^C is blue' is true, and all other colour attributions to the complements are false. The natural way to understand this is that only the region to which the regions X_i converge is red, and that everything else is blue all over. But, of course, the gunk lover does not think there is a region of size 0 to which the regions X_i are converging, let alone that it can have a colour property that the rest of space does not have. Now, one might deny that what we just called the natural way to understand the facts is the correct way to understand these facts. But one cannot deny that the currently suggested fundamental colour property facts allow one to make the kind of distinctions that the gunk lover set out to be rid of. So let us be done with it, and move on.

5 TWO MORE PROMISING APPROACHES

The gunk lover's sensible response to the above problem is to say: of course we can't make do just with facts regarding which exacts colours obtain where, we also need basic facts as to where *extended* ranges of colours obtain, or, instead, we need basic facts as to which are the *average* colours associated with gunky regions or gunky objects. Let's consider these strategies, beginning with facts about extended ranges of values of quantities such as colours.

5.1 Approach E: Containment

Let us represent each exact colour as a point in the space of all possible colours, which we call the 'colour value space'. In a pointy physical space a continuous variation of colour from location to location then amounts to a continuously varying function from points in physical space to points in colour space. Consider now the relation C where we say that a set of colour values stands in the relation C to a region R iff R is the largest region that does not stray outside that range of colour values. Call this relationship Containment. Since each set of colour values stands in the relation of Containment to a single, unique, region, this relation amounts to a *map* from sets of colour values to regions. In the pointy case this Containment map is definable in terms of colour values at points: a set S of colour values Contains a region R just in case every point in R has a value belonging to S and no other point has a value belonging to S. From this definition, it follows that the Containment map has certain nice properties: it maps unions of sets to unions of regions, intersections of sets to intersections of regions, and it maps complements of sets to complements of regions.

If space (or extended objects) is (are) gunky one cannot define a Containment map in terms of the colour values that obtain at points. Our fifth gunky strategy is to therefore take the Containment map as primitive. That is to say, according to this approach, the fundamental facts about colours of regions (or objects) are given by a Containment map C from sets of colours to gunky regions, which has to satisfy the following requirements:

(1) It has to map the complement of a set S of colours to the complement of the region R that S gets mapped to.

(2) It has to map a countable union of sets of colours to the countable union of the regions that the sets get mapped to.

(3) It has to map a countable intersection of sets of colours to the countable intersection of the regions that the sets get mapped to.

These requirements mean that the Containment map is a (countable) *homomorphism*. The restriction to *countable* join and meet is important. For suppose that colours in fact vary continuously, and in particular that no region is one specific colour all over. Then, roughly speaking, the Containment map will map each precise colour to nothing, for there is no region that has all and only that colour. Speaking more precisely, each specific colour value will get mapped to the unique so-called 'Null region'. (The 'Null region' is introduced for reasons of mathematical simplicity. It corresponds to the null set in point set topology. Note that the Null region is part of every region, and that it is the only region that has size 0.) In any case, assuming that every extended (i.e. non-Null) region is coloured, the Containment function had better assign something other than the Null region to at least some non-denumerable sets of the shades. And that means that the Containment function cannot respect uncountable union.

Admittedly, treating containment as primitive takes a bit of getting used to. This is so, however, with many metaphysical views which locate a mismatch between what is first in order of knowing and what is first in the order of being. Obviously, Containment is not prior in the order of understanding when we learn about a value range. But that is no decisive barrier to a natural philosophy that puts it at the metaphysical ground floor.

It is worth noticing how this approach obliterates certain distinctions that are natural from within a pointy perspective. Given that the Containment function is a homomorphism, it will have the following feature: supposing that a value set S gets assigned to region R, and a certain value V gets assigned to the Null region, then the union of S and V will also get assigned to R. Matters are different in the pointy case. Suppose, for example, that a region R was shade S1 all over except at a point where it was shade S2, and that nothing else was either S1 or S2. S2 would not Contain R, but the doubleton set of S1 and S2 would Contain R. In our new framework the contrast does not arise. But of course, this is how things should be: given our stated desiderata of collapsing 0 size differences, one should hope *not* to be able to raise the question of whether such singularities as the one just described are there or not. Indeed, the gunk lover should hope that the colour homomorphism should not be able to capture differences in colour distributions that amount to differences only at single points, or amount only to differences in colours of regions that have size 0.

In fact one can prove exactly that. That is to say, one can prove that corresponding to every homomorphism H from a (well-behaved) continuous value space there is at least one pointy function F from the corresponding pointy space (or spacetime) to that value space. Moreover, every well-behaved (i.e. measurable) function corresponds to some homomorphism. And finally, if pointy functions F and G correspond to the same homomorphism H, then F and G can differ in their values at most on a set of points in space (or spacetime) of measure 0.[19] This is great. Differences of functions on sets of points of measure 0 are exactly the kind of differences that the Gunk lover wants to be rid of. But everything else *can* be captured on the current

[19] See H. L. Royden, *Real Analysis* (New York: MacMillan, 1968), chapter 15.

gunky strategy. In particular: one can specify a homomorphism H from colour sets to the gunky parts of a chocolate bar such that H entails that a chocolate bar has a colour that varies continuously, e.g. at a constant rate everywhere, across the bar. Problem solved. Now let us conclude the discussion of the current approach with two cautionary remarks.

First, one should be careful not to rely on casual intuitions when it comes to the question of which kinds of choppiness in value distributions are coherently articulable from within this picture. Think back to the pointy picture. Differences in value assignments that make for non-zero measure differences in the corresponding value functions will be differences that carry over to the gunky framework that we are proposing. Consider in particular the 'Cantoresque' region that is delivered by removing from the chocolate bar one-quarter from the middle, one-sixteenth from each of the two middles of what remains, one sixty-fourth from each of the four middles of what remains, and so on. The total removed adds up to one half of the volume of the chocolate bar (assuming standard measure theoretic assumptions). There will thus be a gunky region that is what remains when one removes the aforesaid from the chocolate bar (assuming the mereological Remainder principle noted earlier). This region will be everywhere divided. Suppose one precise shade of red Contains exactly this region. Then that shade of red will be distributed in a surprisingly choppy way, one that one might not readily anticipate as a gunk lover. The key point is that while one eschews zero measure distinctions, the existence of such strange regions of non-zero volume guarantees that there will be no route from gunk theory to even stepwise continuity in one's qualitative manifold.

Second, the reader will have noted that while we have been operating with a gunky conception of space, we have clung to a pointy conception of the relevant quality spaces. What if one dispensed with the latter assumption? Suppose we think of colour space itself as gunky, and gave the fundamental facts of colour in terms of a Containment homomorphism from gunky regions of colour space to gunky regions of space (or space-time)? One thing is immediately clear: one could then not capture the idea that a region is a precise shade of red all over. Perhaps more disconcertingly: one could not have a constant valued electric field in some region. Well, of course, one could construct the equivalent of Whiteheadian pseudo-points in value and then recover constant exact functions, but that would go against the spirit of the assumption of a gunky value space. No, presumably one is only going to be interested in something like a gunky colour space if one really thinks that it makes no sense whatsoever for the colour of anything to be some exact shade throughout some region. But even if one embraces this idea, there remain technical obstacles to the idea that one can represent the colour features of regions in space (or spacetime) by a homomorphism from a gunky colour space to gunky space (or spacetime). For in that case the existence of a (countable) homomorphism H from the gunky value space to gunky space no longer guarantees existence and uniqueness of the corresponding pointy functions up to measure 0 differences.[20] So the idea of a gunky value space seems less promising.

---

[20] One can guarantee existence and uniqueness up to differences of measure 0 if in addition to H there exists a homomorphism H' from gunky space to gunky value space such that H∘H' is the

Let's now look at another promising approach to the characterization of varying qualities in a gunky space.

5.2 Approach F: Average Values

Suppose we ask after the average mass density of an object. According to the standard pointy conception this value is determined by integrating over the mass density values at points. On this conception then, the average mass density is derived from the point-local mass densities. But one needn't understand things in this way. Suppose instead we took average mass density as primitive. Then we have a means of handling our focal problem from a gunky perspective: the fundamental facts about some value space would be given by the instantiations of average values, call them 'A-values', by gunky objects.

Of course there will be necessary connections between the A-values of a gunky object and the A-values of its parts: it will not do to allow, say, that an object have an A-value V, but that it decomposes into some set of objects each of which has A-value V′ which is different from V. (See the appendix for a statement of the relevant constraints. The constraints that we impose turn out to be rather simple and natural when formulated in terms of integral values rather than average values. To avoid technicalities which cloud the basic issues we will keep talking about average values, rather than integral values, in the main text.) Perhaps certain radical combinatorialists would be unhappy with such constraints on combinations of fundamental quantities. However, it seems plausible to us that some natural and simple constraints on the fundamental quantities of the world will be unavoidable, and we will therefore not dwell on this type of objection.

Let us now discuss the extent to which average values might be thought to underdetermine the local facts. Start with the pointy case. It should be clear that all the facts about the average values (for all regions of well-defined non-zero measure) of a given function do not serve to fix the value of the function at all points, or, indeed, at any particular point. For consider two functions F and G that take identical values everywhere except at one point. These functions will have the same integrals, and hence the same average values, over any region of non-zero measure. So the average values cannot serve to determine the value of a corresponding function at any specific point.

This should hardly serve as an objection to an approach in which one takes average value assignments to gunky regions as primitive. For such differences on size 0 regions are exactly the kind of differences the gunk lover wants to be rid of. Indeed, one might hope that average value assignments determine the value features of gunky regions (or gunky objects) in exactly the same sense that the homomorphisms of the previous approach do. That is to say, one might hope that average value assignments to gunky

identity map on gunky space (where 'H∘H″' means 'compose H with H″', where H is applied after H′). See H. L. Royden, *Real Analysis* (New York: MacMillan, 1968), p. 329. However, assuming this amounts to assuming that the corresponding pointy function is monotonically increasing or monotonically decreasing. This, of course, is implausible as a general constraint. One might nonetheless try to salvage the approach by building non-monotonic functions up from pieces that are monotonic. However, this business is beginning to look rather desperate and unnatural.

regions determine pointy value functions from the corresponding pointy space up to differences of measure 0. In the appendix we show that this is so.

There is one final objection to be considered. For some value ranges it is natural to associate some objective notion of distance between members of the value range. Consider mass densities. There are objective facts of the matter as to the ratios between the mass densities at different locations. For magnitudes of this sort, the notion of an average magnitude can be defined. But not all value ranges are intuitively of this sort. Consider colour, as intuitively understood. It is not clear at all that we can make objective sense of such questions as whether the distance from this shade of blue to that one is the same as that between this shade of pink and that one.[21] In such a case there will be no unique objective notion of the colour average of an extended region or object: different, equally good numerical coordinatizations of the colour space will yield different colour integrals and different colour averages.

Precisely how much trouble this makes for the current approach depends on one's conception of the fundamental magnitudes. We all know (certain philosopher-mystics aside) that colour is not really fundamental, that facts about colour supervene on facts about wavelength, spectral reflectance, and so on. Indeed, it seems plausible that the fundamental quantities of physics allow for an average value treatment. And so long as a supervenience base for the world can be provided by A-values, the gunky natural philosopher need have little to fear from the fact that, say, colour cannot be handled directly in terms of average colour.[22]

6 CONCLUDING REMARKS

We end with an analogy that some readers may find helpful. Think back to the Leibniz–Clarke debate. Clarke (speaking for Newton) worked within a framework that generated a space of what might be called structural possibilities, ways that the world could be that were compatible with the basic ontological framework that was claimed for the actual world. If one were to claim further that certain of those structural possibilities were physically impossible, it would be because the laws of nature prohibited certain of those structural possibilities from being actualized. For example, the Newtonian framework allows for distinct possible states of motion of the entire universe: all matter in the universe might be moving at one or other constant speed in one or other direction; the material universe might even be rotating at one or

---

[21] Of course, we can make sense of this relative to some projection of the colours onto the colour wheel, but the issue is whether the distances on the colour wheel correspond to anything objective in colour space.

[22] Even if not all fundamental quality spaces have sufficient structure to determine unique average values, all hope is not lost. One might suggest that in such a case, the fundamental quality facts are given not by a single homomorphism but by a set of homomorphisms, where this set of homomorphisms corresponds to a set of pointy functions (up to differences of measure 0) which differ from each other by transformations which amount to changes in quality distances, but leave the topological and differential structure of the quality space intact, or, more generally, by transformations which leave intact whatever structure one takes it that the quality space in question has.

other speed in one or other direction. If some such possibilities were to be ruled out, it would have to be by natural law. By contrast, the mere structure of the Leibnizian framework rules out such distinctions in the possible states of motion of the material universe.

Now of course, the metaphysical possibilities may outstrip the structural possibilities. Suppose, for instance, that in fact the world contains absolute space. Perhaps it is nonetheless metaphysically possible that relationalism is true. Similarly, suppose that space in fact is gunky. Perhaps pointy space is still metaphysically possible. There is nonetheless something intuitive and important about the distinction between something that is physically impossible because it is structurally impossible versus something that is physically impossible only because certain laws prohibit it. (Call the latter a mere nomological impossibility.) For instance, we have empirical evidence that the universe as a whole in fact does not rotate. Within the Newtonian framework one might account for this by saying that the initial conditions of the universe just happened to be such that the universe did not, and hence does not, rotate, not even one whit per aeon. But what a coincidence that would be. In view of this one might be inclined to add a law to the Newtonian framework, one forbidding the rotation of the universe. Yet this does not seem as satisfactory as the relationalist account, which makes a rotation of the universe a structural impossibility. The absolutist generates a set of possibilities and then needs to call upon a law to steer the actual world one way rather than another. The relationalist embraces a framework within which the relevant possibilities cannot be distinguished in the first place, and thus does not require a nomic steering wheel to plot our path.

A similar distinction can be made for certain putative possibilities of discontinuity, as they relate to the debate between the gunk lover and the point lover. Suppose one represents the qualitative array via a point-to-value function. One then admits the structural possibility of all sorts of local discontinuities that confine themselves to regions of zero measure. Similarly one allows for the structural possibility of all sorts of haphazard pointwise assignments so as to make the relevant magnitude for an extended object undefined. (Consider, for example, an assignment of local mass densities to a chocolate bar that is not integrable and thus delivers an undefined mass for the chocolate bar.) If the point lover is to maintain that we should not fear such a scenario, he will have to posit special purpose laws of nature that enforce the relevant kind of desired continuity. Such discontinuities are at best mere nomological impossibilities. But if one is a gunk lover of the stripe that pursues strategies E or F above then one will offer an altogether different diagnosis of why we should not fear such scenarios. For they turn out to be structurally impossible: the actual world lacks the kind of ontological structure needed for such scenarios to be intelligible. And this is because the very distinction between smooth quality distributions and local jumps of non-zero measure cannot be made sense of within the gunk lover's framework. What the point lover prohibits by law the gunk lover prohibits by structure. There is, we submit, something rather compelling about the recourse to structure rather than law to handle the relevant putative possibilities. Now, of course, intellectual history following the Leibniz–Clarke debate revealed that there are more options under the sun than simple-minded, full-blooded Leibnizian relationalism and simple-minded, full-blooded Newtonian absolutism. Similarly, there are, or course, many different versions of gunkology and pointillism. Our own tentative assessment is that gunkology enjoys some interesting and important theoretical advantages over pointillism.

APPENDIX: AVERAGES, INTEGRALS, AND GUNK

Let's start with an ordinary pointy space. (The relevance for gunky spaces will become clear as we move along.) Could we take as our fundamental quantities 'A-maps', A(R), which are maps from pointy regions R to real numbers, instead of the usual functions $f(x)$ from points (n-tuples of real numbers) to point values (real numbers)? Can we recover an ordinary function completely from all the facts about its average values in all regions, or is there some information lost when we only have facts about its average values? For reasons of mathematical simplicity, let us turn to a slightly different question. Let us ask the analogous question about integrals. (The relation between integrals and averages is simple: the average value of a function in a region is the integral of that function in that region divided by the measure of the region. An integral is undefined if, intuitively speaking, it converges to positive infinity or negative infinity, or if it does not converge because it oscillates too much.) Let us now be more precise.

Define an I-map to be a map from all measurable regions to real numbers which satisfies the following axioms:

(1) Any I-map maps every measurable region to a real number or to 'undefined'

(2) $I(R) = \Sigma I(R_i)$, whenever R_i is a countable partition of R (where 'undefined' plus anything is 'undefined')

(3) $I(R) = 0$ when $M(R) = 0$.

Now we can pose a precise question: is there a 1-1 correspondence between I-maps satisfying constraints 1–3, and measurable functions? (A measurable function is a function that sends measurable regions to measurable value ranges. Non-measurable functions cannot be integrated, and are presumably not needed in science.)

The way in which to answer this question is to note that an I-map behaves *almost exactly* like a countably additive measure, one which (by axiom 3) is absolutely continuous with respect to Lebesque measure. Now if I-maps behaved *exactly* like ordinary measures, then we would be pretty much done. For the Radon–Nikodym theorem says the following: if a measure I is absolutely continuous with respect to Lebesque measure M then there exists a non-negative measurable function f such that $I(R) = \int_R f dM$, for any measurable region R. Since measurable functions which differ at most on a region of measure 0 give rise to exactly the same integrals, we would then have the nice result that each I-map determines a measurable function which is unique up to differences of Lebesque measure 0. So we would have then shown that the average value approach to gunk is effectively equivalent to the Containment (homomorphism) approach. Unfortunately, I-maps do not behave exactly like ordinary measures, for integrals can have negative as well as positive values, while (ordinary) measures cannot take on negative values.

A way in which to solve this problem is as follows. Any measurable function f is the sum of two unique measurable functions f^+ and f^-, where f^+ is non-negative and f^- is non-positive, and each has value 0 whenever the other has non-zero value. Each of these functions, by the Radon–Nikodym theorem, corresponds to a unique I-map. (The I-map corresponding to f^- is just the I-map corresponding to $-f^-$.) So one might simply suggest that fundamental quantities are ordered pairs of I-maps. This, however, is too simplistic as it stands. For there are many distinct pairs of I-maps that correspond to the very same measurable function. For instance, suppose that I_1 corresponds to f_1, that I_2 corresponds to f_2, that I_3 corresponds to $f_1 + 5$, and that I_4 corresponds to $f_2 + 5$. Then the ordered pair $\langle I_1, I_2 \rangle$ corresponds to $f_1 - f_2$, and the ordered pair $\langle I_3, I_4 \rangle$ corresponds to $(f_1 + 5) - (f_2 + 5) = f_1 - f_2$. Thus two distinct ordered pairs of I-maps correspond to exactly the same measurable function.

The problem is that we have not imposed a condition on the I-maps which insures that each of the two I-maps in a pair corresponds to a function that has value 0 when the function corresponding to the other I-map has non-zero value. So let us do that. We cannot simply demand that whenever $I_1(R)$ is non-zero then $I_2(R) = 0$ (and vice versa). For if one integrates a function f over a region R where f takes both positive and negative values, then both $I_1(R)$ and $I_2(R)$ should be non-zero. Rather, we should demand that any pair of I-maps $\langle I_1, I_2 \rangle$ has the property that one can partition the total space into a collection of subregions R_i, each of which has non-zero measure, such that for each R_i either $I_1(R_i) = 0$ or $I_2(R_i) = 0$. If we then identify quantities in a gunky space with pairs of I-maps satisfying the above demand, then there will be a 1-1 correspondence between quantities in a gunky space and measurable functions in the corresponding pointy space. In short, this Average Value approach to gunk is effectively equivalent to the Containment approach.

There is in fact also a slightly different way to go about the Average Value approach. One need not identify a quantity in a gunky space with a *constrained pair* of I-maps. One could instead choose to identify it with a *single* I-map, while merely demanding that such an I-map *can* be expressed as a sum of a non-positive I-map and a non-negative I-map. Here is how.

Define an I*-map to be a map from all measurable regions to real numbers which satisfies the following axioms:

(1′) It maps every measurable region to a real number or to 'undefined'

(2′) $I^*(R) = \Sigma I^*(R_i)$, whenever R_i is a finite partition of R (where 'undefined' plus anything is 'undefined')

(3′) $I^*(R) = 0$ when $M(R) = 0$

(4′) There exists a non-negative I-map I^+ and a non-positive I-map I^- such that $I^* = I^+ + I^-$.

In short, an I*-map is a *finitely* additive I-map that can be written as the sum of a (countably additive) non-positive I-map and a (countably additive) non-negative I-map. (The reason why we only demand that I* be *finitely* additive is that the sum of a countably additive non-negative I-map and a countably additive non-positive I-map sometimes is not countably additive, but will always be finitely additive.) For essentially the same reasons as before, there is a 1-1 correspondence between I*-maps in a gunky space and measurable functions in the corresponding pointy space.

We leave it to the reader to judge how plausible it is that fundamental quantities should satisfy the above suggested sets of axioms.

8

Vagueness and the Mind of God[1]

How ought we to conceive of an omniscient mind in light of the phenomenon of vagueness? Working within the framework of one of the more promising approaches to vagueness—supervaluationism—this chapter explores the mind (and language) of God. In section 1 I sketch the barebones of supervaluationism, familiar to most readers. Section 2 is concerned with how the supervaluationist ought to define omniscience. Section 3 describes, from a supervaluationist perspective, how the divine mind would engage with a Sorites series. Finally, in section 4, I address a thought experiment concerning omniscient speakers offered by Timothy Williamson, designed to support the view that there are epistemically inaccessible hidden boundaries associated with ordinary vague predicates. I conclude by noting the broader philosophical significance of the themes explored here.

1

The supervaluationist traces the existence of vagueness to the phenomenon of semantic indecision. Consider a simple example from David Lewis:[2] It is vague whether an external carport is part of a house. Let us call the fusion of the main body of some house with its external carport 'Big', the body of the house 'Little'. It is plausible to suppose that the English language delivers no verdict as to whether it is Big or Little that merits the predicate 'is a house'.

That indecision of this sort exists will often not matter. If I say 'The house is majestic', that may well be unobjectionable on either way of making the predicate 'is a house' precise, for both Big and Little may be eminently majestic. The supervaluationist suggests that we semantically evaluate sentences beset by semantic indecision by examining admissible ways of making such sentences precise.[3] A sentence is supertrue just in case it is true on all admissible ways of making it precise.

This article first appeared in *Philosophical Studies* 122 (2005), pp. 1–25. I am grateful for permission to reprint it here.

[1] Thanks to Cian Dorr, Mark Scala, Ted Sider, audiences at the University of Arizona and King's College, London, and especially Tamar Szabo Gendler and Timothy Williamson for comments and discussion.

[2] See 'Many, But Almost One,' in *Papers in Metaphysics and Epistemology* (Cambridge University Press, 1999) p. 172. The expression 'semantic indecision' is his.

[3] Lewis' advice to think of a precisification as a way of 'making the unmade semantic decisions' is helpful here. See 'Many, But Almost One', p. 172.

A sentence is superfalse just in case it is false on all admissible ways of making it precise. Clearly, some sentences will be neither supertrue nor superfalse. According to the supervaluationist, we can make sense of the phenomenon of borderline cases using this semantic machinery: a borderline case of say, baldness, is one where an ascription of the predicate 'is bald' is neither supertrue nor superfalse.

As Kit Fine urged in his seminal paper on the topic,[4] the main interest of this approach is that it can validate logical connections between sentences that, taken individually, are neither supertrue nor superfalse. Thus if Joe is a borderline case of baldness, it may nevertheless be supertrue that if Joe is bald then he is not bald and supertrue that either Joe is bald or Joe is not bald. If a carpet is borderline between yellow and orange, it is nevertheless supertrue that if it is yellow it is not orange (since the semantic decision that 'yellow' and 'orange' cannot be simultaneously true of an object *has* been made) . . . and so on. This already makes for a big advantage over any approach to vagueness grounded in any of the standard truth tables for many valued logics, since the latter do not validate logical connections between vague sentences. Of particular note is the fact that the supervaluationist is able to embrace classical logic, on the grounds that classical valid sentence forms will have all and only supertrue instances.[5]

Supervaluationism is motivated by the idea that when there is semantic indecision, there is no inscrutable hidden boundary, accessible only to God (or worse still to no possible being). Of course, the world often contains boundaries that are hidden to us. We were at one point altogether unable to detect the joint in nature that separates fool's gold from gold, and which separates Parkinson's disease from other superficially similar degenerative disorders. But borderline cases do not, according to the supervaluationist, point to a whole new range of hidden boundaries. This motivation puts further constraints on the shape of supervaluationist semantics: if we are, as semanticists, to avoid positing boundaries of which we are in principle ignorant, we must inevitably deploy a vague metalanguage. Just as there is no sharp line between the people that are bald and the people that are not, so there is no sharp line between the properties that are acceptable precisifications of 'is bald' and the ones that are not, and so on. Formal models have been developed suitable to the intuitive picture of 'vagueness all the way up,' built by analogy with modal logics that deny the S4 axiom.[6]

It is often noted that supertruth and superfalsity do not obey the disquotational schemas standardly held to be canonical for truth and falsity: one cannot accept

> If 'u' means P, then ('u' is supertrue iff P)[7]

or

---

[4] 'Vagueness, Truth and Logic,' *Synthese*, 30 (1975), 265–300.

[5] It may be, however, that certain classically valid *inference patterns* cannot be recognized as valid by the supervaluationist. See Williamson's *Vagueness* (Routledge, 1994), chapter 5. The arguments in the text do not trade on the disputable inference patterns (which accounts for their longwindedness in some cases).

[6] See, for example, Fine's 'Vagueness, Truth and Logic' and Williamson's 'On The Structure of Higher-Order Vagueness', *Mind* 108 (January 1999), 127–143.

[7] After all, 'P' may be borderline and yet "'u' is supertrue' may be superfalse, in which case there will be some precisifications on which 'P' is true and yet "'u' is supertrue' is false.

If 'u' means P, then ('u' is superfalse iff ∼P).

This renders pressing the issue whether or not to identify truth and falsity with supertruth and superfalsity and correlatively whether or not to abandon the standard axiom schemas for truth and falsity. On this issue—a real trouble spot for supervaluationism—the following discussion will remain neutral.

2

How should the supervaluationist characterize omniscience? As we shall see, the issue is both delicate and instructive. There seem to be three alternative conceptions available. The first conception opts for the following definition:

(1) $\forall x$ (x is omniscient iff $\forall P$ ((x knows P iff x believes P) and (x believes P iff P)))[8,9]

(The more straightforward '$\forall x$ (x is omniscient iff $\forall P$ (x knows P iff P))' has the drawback of allowing an omniscient being to *believe* certain falsehoods.)

Supervaluationists standardly introduce an operator 'definitely' into their language, governed, inter alia, by the schema: 'if 'u' means P, 'u' is supertrue iff definitely P'.[10] This permits the acknowledgement of borderline cases without resorting to semantic ascent. Thus, the claim that there is no sharp line between bald and non-bald people can be expressed by

∼$\forall x$ (definitely x is bald or definitely x is not bald)

A second conception of omniscience can be articulated using such an operator, viz:

(2) $\forall x$ (x is omniscient iff $\forall P$ ((x believes P iff x knows P) and (x believes P iff definitely P))).

Since the schema

P iff definitely P

is unacceptable, conception (1) and (2) cannot be regarded by the supervaluationist as equivalent.

A third conception is motivated by the idea that an omniscient being only has thoughts that involve precise ingredients: a belief ascription that involves a vague singular term or a vague predicate cannot be true of an omniscient being. Now there are plenty statements that are definitely true that involve either vague singular terms or vague predicates. For example: if I am bald, then I am bald. The third conception contends that if 'that P' involves any vague terms or predicates, then any belief ascription using it will be false of the omniscient being.[11] In short: only where 'P' is

---

[8] Those that hold that there can be knowledge without belief will obviously want to do things a little differently.

[9] I shall use propositional quantification throughout. Here is not the place to defend its cogency.

[10] Assuming that we allow that a language can contain its own supertruth predicate. If not, the definiteness operator will have to be explained slightly differently. The relevant technical issues do not bear much on the topic of this paper.

[11] Relevant here is the discussion of supervaluationism and propositional attitude attributions that follows shortly.

both precise and supertrue can we use it to describe the contents of God's mind. Let us introduce an operator 'precisely', governed by the schema,

If 'u' means P, then (precisely P iff ('u' is supertrue and all the constituents of 'u' are precise)).[12]

We can now articulate the third conception as follows:

(3) $\forall x$ (x is omniscient iff $\forall P$ ((x believes P iff knows P) and (x believes P iff precisely P))).

Given that nearly all of our predicates are vague, we can, on this view, make very few positive knowledge attributions to God that are correct. Whatever its merits, the shortcomings of the third approach are obvious: it entails, for example, that while *we* know that bald people are bald, an omniscient being does not know any such thing.[13] Before retreating to such a compromised conception of omniscience, we should at least investigate whether either of the first two conceptions can be made to work. (I shall not be exploring the third conception any further in this paper.)

Which of the first two conceptions is preferable? Return to the toy example with which we began. The supervaluationist is committed to each of the following:

(4) It is indefinite whether Big is a house.[14]

(5) It is indefinite whether Little is a house.

(6) Either Little is a house or Big is a house.

If it is indefinite whether P, for some P, then it would not seem that I am in a position to know that P. Knowledge is unavailable in a borderline case. Thus, given that Little and Big are both borderline cases of being a house, the following pair of claims seem right:

(7) I don't know that Little is a house.

(8) I don't know that Big is a house.

With (4)—(8) in view, it is easy enough to recognize the costs of our first two conceptions. Supposing we embrace the first conception and claim that God is omniscient. We are forced to the conclusion:

(9) Either (Little is a house and God knows it and I do not know it) or (Big is a house and God knows it and I do not).

That seems bad. As far as Big and Little's claim to be houses goes, it doesn't seem that God knows any more than I do. But (9) suggests he does. Against (9), it seems intuitively clear that God doesn't know that Little is a house (and that he doesn't

---

[12] Of course, more work would need to be done to convince us that the 'precisely' operator is coherent.

[13] Notice, moreover, that since our semantic and psychological concepts—means, refers, believes, loves and so on—are vague, we could not on this view coherently think of God as believing that we mean anything, refer to anything, believe anything, or love anything. I note for the record that in conversation the third conception nevertheless proved attractive to many interlocutors.

[14] Here 'It is indefinite whether P' has its standard meaning, abbreviating '~definitely P and ~definitely ~P'.

know that Big is a house). And if you asked Him why, say, he does not know that Little is a house he would tell you: it is because the concept house does not definitely apply to Little. So it seems that

(10) God doesn't know that Little is a house

and

(11) God doesn't know that Big is a house.

Combine (10) and (11) with (9) and contradiction ensues.[15]

Further if we combine the first conception of omniscience with (4), (5) and (6), we get the bizarre

(12) Either (it is indefinite whether Little is a house and God knows that Little is a house) or (it is indefinite whether Big is a house and God knows that Big is a house).[16]

Initially, the second conception may seem to raise equally serious problems for the supervaluationist. If (2) rather than (1) is taken as the proper characterization of omniscience, and we assume that God exists, then we are compelled to accept

(13) (Either Little is a house and God does not know that Little is a house) or (Big is a house and God does not know that Big is a house).

Prima facie, this is disturbing, for it suggests that there is something that God does not know. Recall, however, that supervaluationists must already be willing to tolerate:

(14) Either (Little is a house and it is indefinite whether Little is house) or (Big is a house and it is indefinite whether Big is a house).

If one has learned to live with (14), (13) is likely to strike one as less disturbing. So while (13) is surprising at first, it does not seem to offer grounds for abandoning the second conception that are nearly as compelling as those that were offered for abandoning the first. So I suggest, albeit somewhat tentatively, that of the three candidate characterizations of omniscience, it is (2) that best accords with the supervaluationist's other commitments. Since definitions are, plausibly, supertrue, we can now endorse

(15) Def[17] $\forall x$ (x is omniscient iff $\forall$P ((x knows P iff x believes P) and (x believes P iff Def P))).

---

[15] I assume here and elsewhere that the supervaluationist embraces modus ponens and conjunction introduction as inference rules, and that she accepts as valid all the classically valid sentence forms. (That supervaluationism may not license certain classically valid inference rules (see Williamson, *Vagueness*, p. 151ff) is thus not relevant.)

[16] Those supervaluationists who wish to identify supertruth with truth can offer a further consideration against the first conception. Knowledge entails truth. That is: $\forall$P$\forall x$ (x knows that P $\supset$ It is true that P). If truth is supertruth, this is equivalent to: $\forall$P $\forall x$ (x knows that P $\supset$ definitely P). Combine this with the first conception and we get $\forall x$ (x is omniscient $\supset$ $\forall$P (P $\supset$ definitely P)) This is clearly unacceptable, unless we intend our conception of omniscience to be so crafted that it be blatantly infelicitous to believe that something is omniscient.

[17] Henceforth I shall abbreviate 'definitely' by 'Def'.

To lend further support to this choice of definition, let me address another objection to the second conception. Supervaluationists have said little about how supervaluations work for terms as they occur within belief contexts. But in choosing among the candidate definitions of omniscience, it matters crucially how belief contexts are treated. We have imagined that there are two precisifications of 'house', one which holds of Little (and not Big), the other of which holds of Big (and not Little). Call these precisifications house[1] and house[2] respectively. Let us agree that God believes that Little is a house[1] and that he does not believe that Little is a house[2]. It might now be suggested that any that-clause involving 'is a house' is beset with semantic indecision. Since propositions themselves are never indefinite, the line of thought runs, it must be that the ascription is vague as to which proposition is being ascribed as the object of belief. One precisification of 'God believes that Little is a house' is 'God believes that Little is a house[1]'; another is 'God believes that Little is a house[2]'. Accordingly it will be suggested (contrary to the second conception) that it is indefinite whether God believes that Little is a house, since that belief ascription is correct on one precisification, incorrect on another.

This model is hardly faithful to how ordinary belief ascriptions work. We can all agree that Clinton believes that he has a house. According to the model just adumbrated, the latter has two precisifications—Clinton believes that he have a house[1]; Clinton believes that he has a house[2]—each being required to hold in order for the original belief ascription to definitely hold. But we are not nearly so willing to accept either precisification as we are the original belief attribution! Something is wrong with the model.[18]

A more promising supervaluationist approach to belief attributions maintains that the vague concept *house* is definitely distinct from the precise concept *house[1]* and that one may have a belief involving the latter and not the former (and vice versa). That one concept is an acceptable sharpening of another does not require that the concepts are indefinitely distinct. In passing,[19] Kit Fine remarks that the claim 'Casanova believes that he has had many mistresses' can be taken in two ways: as a 'precise report of a vague belief or as a vague report of a precise belief'[20] (say, that he has had more than 15 mistresses). I take it that the first use is more typical: it would in most contexts be misleading to use the ascription if Casanova believed he had more than 15

----

[18] As a way of trying to salvage the model criticized in the text, it may be suggested that there are various ways of precisifying the binary predicate 'believes'. On each way of precisifying 'believes' there is a particular class of precise propositions that count as the objects of thought. So perhaps 'believes 1' is one precisification of 'belief', 'believes 2' another 1 and Clinton believes 1 that he has a house[1] and believes 2 that he has a house[2] (the latter two claims being the acceptable precisifications of 'Clinton believes that he has a house'). We can now maintain consistently that it is indefinite whether Clinton believes that he has a house[1] (since this is only true on one precisification) and definite that Clinton believes that he has a house. I leave further exploration of such a view to others. I note in passing that a satisfying supervaluationist account of belief ascription will have to be coordinated with an account of the 'means that' construction, given the intuitive link between accepting a sentence and believing a proposition, viz: if S accepts sentence 'u' and 'u' means that P then S believes that P.

[19] See 'Vagueness, Truth and Logic', p. 289.

[20] Or at any rate, more precise.

mistresses but had no idea as to whether more than 15 mistresses was a lot of mistresses. To avoid confusion, we should not lapse into the second use without warning. Adhering now to the first, more standard use, we should insist that while the predicate 'is a house' expresses a vague concept in that it admits penumbral cases, the claim that I believe I have a house serves as a perfectly precise report of my state of mind.[21] Meanwhile, ordinary people definitely don't believe that they own a house^1, since they don't have the concept *house*^{1}. And God definitely does not believe Little is a house, since, while he ascribes the concept *house*^{1} to Little, he definitely does not ascribe the concept *house* to Little. (Of course he definitely does not ascribe the complex concept *not a house* to Little either.) It is a happy consequence of the second conception that God's omniscience is not compromised by such failures to believe.

Let me end by noting how the second conception makes trouble for a much discussed proposal concerning propositional attitude ascriptions. It is sometimes maintained that proper names occur transparently within the scope of attitude ascriptions, and thus that coreferring proper names are (surprisingly) substitutable salva veritate in attitude contexts.[22] Proponents of such a thesis will endorse the following schema (henceforth 'the transparency schema'):

S knows *a* is F iff ∃*x* (*x* = *a* and S knows *x* is F)

But this schema cannot be accepted by a proponent of the second conception. Assume with such a proponent that ∼God knows that Little is a house. Suppose further that the house figuring in our focal example has a proper name, say 'Balmoral'. It is clear enough that we want to say that (i) definitely, Balmoral is a house (ii) it is indefinite whether Balmoral is identical to Little and (iii) it is indefinite whether Balmoral is identical to Big. Now we should not reckon valid any schema that allows us to derive a claim that is not definitely true from a set of claims that are definitely true. But the transparency schema, in combination with the second conception, allows us to do just that. As follows:

Given that definitely, Balmoral is a house, we should agree that:

(16) God knows Balmoral is a house.

Applying the transparency schema we now get

(17) ∃*x* (*x* = Balmoral and God knows *x* is a house).

The following is a logical truth:

(18) ∃*x* ((*x* = Balmoral and God knows *x* is a house and Balmoral = Little) ⊃ ∃*y* (*y* = Little and God knows *y* is a house)),

---

[21] As the beginnings of a toy theory, let us imagine with Frege that when 'house' occurs within belief contexts, what is normally its sense serves as its reference. In ordinary contexts, its reference might in indeterminate, there being a range of extensions that serve as acceptable precisifications of that predicate. But in the context of belief attributions, its reference might be determinate, namely to a particular sense that admits borderline cases.

[22] For an introduction to the topic, see Kripke 'A Puzzle About Belief', reprinted in Peter Ludlow, *Readings in the Philosophy of Language* (MIT, 1997), esp. 906–9 (reprinted from Margalit (ed.) *Meaning and Use*, Reidel 1979). For a recent extended discussion and defence, see Scott Soames, *Beyond Rigidity* (Oxford University Press, 2002).

which, assuming the transparency schema, is equivalent to:

(19) $\exists x\, ((x =$ Balmoral and God knows x is a house and Balmoral $=$ Little) $\supset$ God knows Little is a house)).

But we have agreed that, given the second conception

(20) $\sim$God knows Little is a house.

From (18), (19), and (20), we can now derive

(21) $\sim$ Little $=$ Balmoral.

But (21) is not supertrue. Something has gone wrong. Assuming the second conception, we should not endorse the transparency schema. There is a more general point to be made, of course: if knowledge is absent in borderline cases, we should not endorse the transparency schema. (After all, the above derivation could have been run for anyone that clearly knows that Balmoral is a house but clearly does not know that Little is a house.) It thus seems that considerations of vagueness, as applied to proper names, provide compelling grounds to give up the transparency schema. Some no doubt will be inclined to run the argument in the other direction, arguing that if I know that Balmoral is a house, then at worst it is indefinite whether I know Little is a house. That diagnosis seems less plausible, refusing as it does to acknowledge that vagueness brings a lack of knowledge in its wake.

These matters are admittedly very delicate; I cannot pursue them further here. Having motivated the second conception, I shall adhere to it in what follows. Some readers will no doubt be unconvinced. Fortunately, they should have little trouble seeing how the remarks that follow might be adapted to fit the first conception.

3

Recall that a key motivation for supervaluationism is the idea that vagueness does not generate hidden boundaries. On such a picture, suitable reflection would enable us to know all there is to know about how, say, the concept *bald* pertains to some Sorites series. If there is nothing that we are not in a position to know about such a series (at least in connection with questions to do with baldness), we should not, it seems, find any great conceptual strain in allowing an all-knowing being to come into the picture.[23] Further, if there is nothing to know about baldness that can't be known by us, then it doesn't seem that we could learn anything from such a being that we couldn't, in principle, learn by inquiring into the matter for ourselves.

It turns out that matters are rather more complicated than this initial picture would suggest. There are two key points that are easy to overlook but which are vital to a proper understanding of the matter. I shall present them in turn.

---

[23] Cf. Williamson, *Vagueness*, p. 198ff, whose discussion inspired this paper. I shall discuss Williamson's treatment in detail in Section 4.

3.1

Suppose that we have encountered a being—God—who definitely fits the second conception of omniscience. And so, abbreviating 'definitely' by 'Def':

(22) Def God is omniscient.

We have adopted the following conception of omniscience:

Def $\forall x$ (x is omniscient iff $\forall P$ ((x knows P iff x believes P) and (x believes P iff Def P)))

Let an omniaccurate being be one that meets the following weaker characterization:

(23) Def $\forall x$ (x is omniaccurate iff $\forall P$ (x believes P iff Def P))

God, let us assume, is no mere borderline case of omniaccurateness. And so:

(24) Def $\forall P$ (God believes P iff Def P).

In what follows, we shall focus on the implications of omniaccurateness: the additional requirements of omniscience will not matter. I shall assume throughout the following standard rule for logics of definiteness:

(25) $\vdash$ Def($\alpha \supset \beta$) $\supset$ (Def $\alpha \supset$ Def β),

and also that any logical truth is definitely true.[24]

Suppose we sit God down and run through a familiar Sorites series, removing one hair at a time from a person that is, at the outset, clearly not bald, asking at each step 'Is he bald?' How are we to describe what goes on?

It is important to notice that in order describe this situation in detail, we need to make some decisions about the nature of God's language (or more precisely, the relevant fragment of language that is being put to use in conducting this test). In particular, we need to decide whether or not the language in question is 'slippery' or 'pristine'. An utterance type u is pristine just in case it is always a sharp matter whether or not u has been uttered by God. An utterance type u is slippery just in case it is not pristine.

What would it be like if God deployed a slippery language? Consider the following story. I say to God: 'Ok, I'm going to take away one hair at a time and at each step tell me if the person in front of me is not bald.' God replies: 'Ok I'll draw a picture of a bald person if and only if the person is bald.' As I remove progressively more hairs, God draws increasingly hair-free depictions. After a while, it will be plausible to say that God has stopped drawing pictures of people who are definitely not bald. And a

---

[24] So here, for example, is how to derive (24) from the assumption that (24A) Def God is omniaccurate. We have (24B) Def ($\forall x$ (x is omniaccurate iff $\forall P$ (x believes P iff Def P)) $\supset$ (God is omniaccurate iff $\forall P$ (God believes P iff Def P))), since the claim within the scope of the main Def operator is a logical truth. We can now derive (24C) Def (God is omniaccurate iff $\forall P$ (God believes P iff Def P)) from (24B) and (23) (using (25) and modus ponens), and in turn (24) Def $\forall P$ (God believes P iff Def P) from (24C) and (24A) using (25) and modus ponens. A derivation of (24) from (22), the claim that Def God is omniscient, is similarly mechanical and straightforward.

while after that, it will be plausible to say that God has started drawing pictures of people who are definitely bald. As for drawings made during the intervening period, we will say on each occasion that God has drawn a picture of someone who is neither definitely bald nor definitely not bald. The utterance type which is used to say that the person is bald is the act of drawing a bald person. Obviously there will be cases in which it is indefinite whether the utterance is performed. A slippery language is in play.

Such a story seems intelligible enough. But it does seem rather unsatisfying. Our natural conception of a Sorites-related conversation with God is one where God uses a pristine language—so, for example, supposing that 'yes' is part of the language fragment in use, it is sharp matter whether or not God utters 'yes' in response to a question.[25] (I shall return to slippery languages later.)

Suppose I take someone—call him 'Dave'—and remove one hair from his head at 11 a.m. each day. Let's imagine further that at least it is a sharp matter whether the noises: 'Dave is not bald yet' has been uttered by God at any given time. (Suppose that the time of the utterance is given by when the utterance is completed). So for any time, either it is definite that 'Dave is not bald yet' has been uttered by God at that time or else it is definitely not the case that 'Dave is not bald yet' has been uttered by God at that time. So, for example,

(26) Def God utters 'Dave is not bald yet' at noon on Tuesday or Def ∼God utters 'Dave is not bald yet' at noon on Tuesday.[26]

We haven't yet given those noises semantic significance. But now we tell God what to do with the noises—we explain to him a fragment of the language that we want him to use in talking to us. The rule is simple: utter 'Dave is not bald yet' at noon on a given day iff David is not bald at noon on that day. Each day, at about eleven a.m., we remove a hair and await God's pronouncement.

Can God use the language in accordance with our directive? Suppose he definitely accepts the instructions. Then, definitely, God believes that he will utter 'Dave is not bald yet' at noon on Tuesday iff Dave is not bald yet at noon on Tuesday. So we have

(27) Def God believes (God utters 'Dave is not bald yet' at noon on Tuesday iff Dave is not bald yet at noon on Tuesday).

It follows that

(28) Def (God utters 'Dave is not bald yet' at noon on Tuesday iff Dave is not bald yet at noon on Tuesday).

(From (24) and (27) using (25) and Modus Ponens.[27])

---

[25] Or at any rate, our natural way of envisaging the Sorites engagement is one where we suppose that slipperiness plays no essential role in the story. We shall see in due course whether this supposition can be maintained.

[26] Let 'noon' stand for 'noon Greenwich mean time'. I assume that it is a sharp matter whether a certain time is noon Greenwich mean time.

[27] There is no special worry about the universal instantiation step—see, by analogy, n25.

Combine (28) with (26)—the assumption that there are no borderline cases of uttering 'Dave is not bald yet'—and we get the conclusion that

(29) Either Def Dave is not bald yet at noon on Tuesday or Def ∼Dave is not bald yet at noon on Tuesday.[28]

This is a terrible result for our supervaluationist. Tuesday might well be one of the days when Dave was a borderline case of bald.

What is the supervaluationist to say? Let's retrace our steps and see what has given rise to the situation. Reflection reveals that the problem has arisen from two sources working in tandem. First, we assumed that the relevant fragment of the language God was speaking was pristine. Second we assumed that God definitely believed that his use of the fragment would conform to a certain biconditional of the form

(30) God will say 'u' at t iff a certain condition C obtains at t.

Call the first assumption—that it is sharp whether or not the relevant utterances in the story are made—*Pristinity*. Call the second—that the relevant utterances are believed by God to conform to certain biconditionals of form (30)—*Tracking*. Simultaneous commitment to Pristinity and Tracking is tantamount to a commitment to sharp boundaries. (This is the first of the two key points that I wish to bring out.)[29] So if we are committed to a condition C's admitting of borderline cases, and we wish to maintain our commitment to a being who definitely satisfies the second conception of omniscience, then we must abandon our commitment to that being's simultaneous conformity to Pristinity and Tracking. We have already seen how abandoning Pristinity can help in this regard. Let us see how the same holds for the abandonment of Tracking. Suppose, for example, that God merely intends (and believes) that he will conform to the rule:

(31) God utters 'Dave is not bald yet' only if Dave is not bald yet.

Then, even with a commitment to Pristinity and borderline cases, no incoherence ensues. For God could conform to (31) by staying silent throughout the entire event,

[28] We have 28A Def ((God utters 'Dave is not bald yet' at noon on Tuesday iff Dave is not bald yet at noon on Tuesday) ⊃ (∼God utters 'Dave is not bald yet' at noon on Tuesday iff ∼Dave is not bald yet at noon on Tuesday)) since the claim within the scope of the Def operator is a logical truth. From (28A) and (28) using (25) we get (28B) Def (∼God utters 'Dave is not bald yet' at noon on Tuesday iff ∼Dave is not bald yet at noon on Tuesday). Applying (25) to (28) and (28B) we get (28C) Def (God utters 'Dave is not bald yet' at noon on Tuesday) iff Def (Dave is not bald yet at noon on Tuesday), and also, (28D) Def (∼God utters 'Dave is not bald yet' at noon on Tuesday) iff Def (∼ Dave is not bald yet at noon on Tuesday). It is a logical truth that 28E (((Def God utters 'Dave is not bald yet' at noon on Tuesday or Def ∼God utters 'Dave is not bald yet' at noon on Tuesday) and (Def God utters 'Dave is not bald yet' at noon on Tuesday iff Def Dave is not bald yet on noon on Tuesday) and (Def ∼God utters 'Dave is not bald yet' at noon on Tuesday iff Def ∼Dave is not bald yet at noon on Tuesday)) ⊃ Def Dave is not bald yet at noon on Tuesday or Def ∼Dave is not bald yet at noon on Tuesday)). From 26, 28C, 28D and 28E, by modus ponens, we get (29).

[29] Notice that (unlike the point to be made in 3.2), this point depends simply on the assumption of borderline cases and some simple rules for the definiteness operator, not on any other details of supervaluationist semantics.

or by uttering 'Dave is not bald yet' on a couple of occasions of definite baldness, staying silent the rest of the time. But, as before, Tracking offers a natural gloss on what it would take for an omniscient being to conform to the conversational maxim of being maximally informative. If God is to use 'Davis is not bald yet' as a vehicle for conveying the information that Dave is not bald yet and is to be maximally informative, then we would not expect Him to be silent or to be sparing in his utterance of 'Dave is not bald yet' If so, however, then the supervaluationist's God must give up on Pristinity: if there are vague boundaries of the sort the supervaluationist claims there are, then an omniscient being who intends to be maximally informative will find a pristine language unusable.

Note that what goes for God's language also goes for God mind. Omniaccuracy gives us:

(32) Def (God believes Dave is bald on Tuesday iff Def Dave is bald on Tuesday).

Assume that God's state of mind is sharp, that it is definite whether God has some given belief on not. This gives us

(33) Def God believes Dave is bald on Tuesday or Def ∼God believes Dave is bald on Tuesday.

We can now derive

(34) Def (Def Dave is bald on Tuesday) or Def ∼(Def Dave is bald on Tuesday).

Where does this all leave us? As we noted in the opening sketch, supervaluationists wish to make room for second order vagueness. There will be cases where it is indefinite whether definitely P. If there is definitely an omniaccurate being and his belief states are sharp, then we can rule out second order vagueness for any given P by a derivation of the sort just given. Thus a supervaluationist who wishes to accommodate a being who is definitely omniaccurrate will take care not to assume that God's mind is sharp. (In effect, we deny pristinity for God's language of thought.) Supposing it is indefinite whether Def Dave is bald on Tuesday, the supervaluationist will insist that it is also indefinite whether God believes that Dave is bald on Tuesday.

3.2

Let me pursue a further complicating thread that has been kept out of view thus far.

To begin, we should remind ourselves that if 'P' is true on some precisifications and 'Q' is false on some precisifications, it does not follow that there is some precisification on which 'P and not Q' is true. This is because there may be logical/conceptual connections between 'P' and 'Q'—what Fine calls 'penumbral connections'[30]—that must be respected by any precisification of that sentence. To take a simple example, 'That is a pale shade of red' might be true on some precisifications, 'That is red' may be false on some precisifications, but 'That is a pale shade of red and that is not red' will not be true on any way of making that sentence precise, since the inferential

---

[30] 'Vagueness, Truth, and Logic,' especially sections 1 and 3.

connection between 'is a pale shade of red' and 'is red' must be respected by any way of making the complex sentence precise. Our supervaluationist theist must similarly hold that there is a penumbral connection between 'God believes that Dave is not bald on Tuesday' and 'Definitely Dave is not bald on Tuesday'. Suppose that it is indefinite whether Def Dave is not bald on Tuesday and also indefinite whether God believes that Dave is not bald on Tuesday. By supervaluationist lights, there will in such a case be precisifications on which 'God believes that Dave is not bald on Tuesday' is false and there will be precisifications on which 'Def Dave is not bald on Tuesday' is true. If there is no penumbral connection between the relevant pair of sentences, there will be no reason to deny that there is a precisification on which 'God believes that Dave is no bald on Tuesday iff Def Dave is not bald on Tuesday' is false. But if there is such a precisification, then God cannot, after all, be definitely omniscient or definitely omniaccurate since

(35) Def (God believes Dave is not bald at noon on Tuesday iff Def Dave is not bald at noon on Tuesday)

will not hold. So a penumbral connection between the belief ascription in (35) and the definiteness claim to the right of the biconditional in (35) will have to be instituted.[31] If no such penumbral connection can be made coherent, then the supposition of a being that is definitely omniscient (as opposed to one that is indefinitely omniscient) will begin to look suspect. (I leave it to others to explore this issue further.)

Analogous points can be raised in connection with various stories that invoke definitely omniscient beings that deploy slippery languages. Consider the following story: 'A definitely omniscient being is subjected to a Sorites series. He agrees (and believes) that he will issue a loud clap of thunder at noon on any given day iff Dave is not bald on that time. On a certain day—say Tuesday—we think to ourselves that Dave is a borderline case of bald. We listen for guidance and notice that the clap of thunder we hear is only borderline loud.' The story seems at first glance coherent by supervaluationist lights. But it is not so clear that it is. Suppose that on Tuesday Dave is a borderline case of bald. The story had it that

(36) Def (God issues a loud clap of thunder at noon on Tuesday iff Dave is bald at noon on Tuesday)

(since God is definitely omniaccurate and also believes the claim embedded by the 'Def' operator in (36)). Meanwhile, we are supposed to think that on Tuesday it is indefinite whether God issues a loud clap of thunder and also indefinite whether Dave is bald. But there is no special logical or conceptual connection between the loudness of thunder and the baldness of a person. So there would seem to be some ways

---

[31] As a rough model for such a penumbral connection, we might think of God's mind like a mirror. A borderline case of baldness is reflected in the mirror. The claim that God's mind contains a belief that the person is bald is treated by analogy with the claim that baldness is reflected in the mirror. For consider: the precisifications on which the case is one of baldness will be precisifications on which it is also true that baldness is reflected in the mirror.

of making precise the biconditional 'God issues a loud clap of thunder at noon on Tuesday iff Dave is bald at noon on Tuesday' such that on those precisifications, the biconditional is false. But in that case, (36) cannot hold, contra the assumption of the story. What we learn—and here is the second key point—is that if God is to speak a slippery language and Tracking is to hold, then some penumbral connection has to be in force that connects that question whether the relevant utterance has been performed to the question whether the relevant condition holds. Notice that in the earlier, picture-drawing story, such a penumbral connection did hold—and one can no doubt tell other such stories. But without a penumbral connection between utterance and condition, our story risks lapsing into incoherence. Notice, once again, that if we merely assume that God is a borderline case of omniscience (or Omniaccuracy), no threat of incoherence will arise. But if he is to be definitely omniscient, and to satisfy Tracking, then the language he uses will have to be subject to very special strictures: it will have to be slippery, and there will have to be a penumbral connection between utterance and condition.

4

Timothy Williamson has observed that omniscient speakers make for something of a puzzle for those, like the supervaluationists, who claim that nothing epistemically elusive is marked by ordinary vague predicates. The puzzle that he raises is the following. Consider an omniscient speaker, asked at each step in a Sorites series whether or not a certain condition holds—for example, suppose he is presented with a progressively diminishing pile of sand grains, and asked at each step whether the grains in front of him form a heap. We are sure that the being will say 'yes' to 'Is it a heap?' when confronted with, say, ten million grains (suitably arranged)—and we are similarly sure that He will not say 'yes' to that question by the time we are down to a single grain. So it seems that God would have to stop at some point—and that we are in no position to know where that point will be. Moreover, it is hard to believe that such a stopping point would lack semantic significance. After all, it seems that one could be confident that if we ran the series again, He would stop at the same place. As a result, Williamson suggests, we should conclude if that there must, after all, be a hidden boundary associated with any given vague predicate. Here is Williamson's statement of the puzzle:

> On the view that nothing is hidden, it should be harmless to imagine omniscient speakers, ignorant of nothing relevant to the borderline case. Such a hypothesis of itself carries no commitment to bivalence or excluded middle. It is supposed, for example, that if TW is thin, then the omniscient speaker knows that TW is thin, and that if TW is not thin then the omniscient speaker knows that TW is not thin. It is no part of the hypothesis that TW is thin or TW is not thin. . . . .

> Accompanied by an omniscient speaker of English, you remove grain after grain from a heap. After each removal you ask 'Is there still a heap?' The omniscient speaker is not required

to answer 'Yes' or 'No'; she can say 'That is indeterminate' or 'To degree 0.917' or 'You are asking the wrong question' if she likes. If there is nothing to say, she will remain silent. She will not say 'I don't know', nor will she hesitate, unsure of the best answer. You can ask her not to mumble. She is determined to be cooperative and as relevantly informative as she can.

After the first few removals, what is left remains quite clearly a heap. The first few times you ask 'Is there a heap?', the omniscient speaker answers 'Yes'; she may say other things too, but whatever else she says, on those first few occasions she says 'Yes'. She is not an obscurantist. After sufficiently many of the grains have been removed, she does not say 'Yes'. She is not a liar. For some number *n*, she says 'Yes' after each of the first *n* removals, but not after *n* plus 1. You do not know the value of '*n*' in advance. Yet on the view in question, her stopping point cannot represent a hidden line between truth and something less than truth. How can that be?

You repeat the experiment with other omniscient speakers, starting with exactly similar arrangements of grains in exactly similar contexts, then removing the grains in exactly the same way. The trials are independent; there is no collusion between the omniscient speakers. If they all stop at the same point, it evidently does mark some sort of previously hidden boundary, although it may be a delicate matter to say just what it is a boundary between.

... You can instruct the omniscient speakers how to use their discretion. For example, you can instruct it to use it conservatively, so that they will answer 'Yes' to as few questions as permissible ....

... Now if two omniscient speakers stop answering 'Yes' at different points, both having being instructed to be conservative, the one who stops later has disobeyed your instructions, for the actions of the other show that the former could have used her discretion to answer 'Yes' to fewer questions than she actually did... Thus if all are instructed to be conservative, all will stop at the same point. You do not know in advance where it will come. It marks some sort of previously hidden boundary...[32]

The discussion contains a slip that is easily corrected. The idea of running independent trials on omniscient speakers makes no sense. For how is one to keep the results of various trials a secret from an *omniscient* being! One could, however, run the thought experiment with beings whose omniscience was restricted to matters having to do with heaps,[33] the rest of the details being essentially unchanged. So this hardly takes us to the heart of the issue.

With section 2 in mind, the supervaluationist might also object to the initial characterization of omniscience. Williamson seems implicitly to appeal to the first conception of omniscience—but as we have seen, the supervaluationist would do well to insist on the second conception, defining omniscience in terms of what is definitely the case.

One might also object to Williamson's failure to address the possibility that the instruction 'Be maximally conservative' is itself vague owing to borderline cases of maximal conservativeness.

---

[32] *Vagueness*, pp. 199–201.
[33] And about what 'Yes' means and so on. Admittedly, it is a slightly tricky matter to specify the requisite domain. I shall not press the concern here.

More importantly, though, I want to suggest that, once accepted in their own terms, the preliminary materials of the thought experiment—prior even to the invocation of a multitude of speakers and an instruction to be conservative—already wreak havoc for the supervaluationist. Three features of the thought experiment stand out, corresponding to the untenable trio identified in Section 3.1:

(a) It is clearly being taken for granted that our omniscient speaker is no mere bor-derline case of omniscience—that is, that our omniscient speaker is definitely omniscient.

(b) The 'no mumbling' clause is, in effect, an instruction to presume that the utter-ance of 'yes' is pristine: the story has it that the omniscient speaker, being cooper-ative, is not to mumble in such a way that it is not clear whether or not he has said 'yes'.

(c) The suggestion that the omniscient speaker is to be 'cooperative' and 'as relevantly informative as she can' induces us into supposing that the omniscient speaker is determined to utter 'yes' after a removal if and only if a heap remains after that removal.[34] That is, the story seems to presuppose that the speaker is committed to Tracking.

After all, we are being in effect told that for any removal r:

(37) (A heap remains after removal r and she does not say 'yes' after r) ⊃ she will not be relevantly informative and cooperative (she would be an obscurantist).

and

(38) (A heap doesn't remain after removal r and she does say 'yes' after r) ⊃ She will not be relevantly informative and cooperative (she would be a liar).

For one who accepts the validity of classical logic—as the supervaluationist does—this amounts to the information that

(39) ∀r (She is relevantly informative and cooperative ⊃ (A heap remains after removal r iff she says 'yes' after r)).

Given that it is part of the description of the case that the omniscient speaker is determined relevantly informative and cooperative, we are forced to assume that the speaker is determined to make it the case that

(40) ∀r (A heap remains after removal r iff she says 'yes' after r).

To assume that the omniscient speaker accepts (34) is to assume that Tracking is in force. We are now, already, caught in incoherence.

---

[34] I note in passing that extra complications are created in connection with this suggestion by the dynamical conception of vague predicates enunciated, *inter alia*, by Delia Graff, Hans Kamp, and Scott Soames. (See Graff, 'Shifting Sands: An Interest-Relative Theory of Vagueness', in *Philosophical Topics* 28 (2000), 45–81; Kamp, 'The Paradox of the Heap', in Monnich (ed.) *Aspects of Philosophical Logic* (Reidel, 1981), pp. 225–277; and Soames, *Understanding Truth* (Oxford University Press, 1999), chapter 7. I lack space to take account of such views here.

Perhaps the later stages of the thought experiment will be important to those who reject classical logic. But the supervaluationist cannot accept even the initial terms of the thought experiment insofar as it involves a determinately omniscient speaker, Pristinity and Tracking.

The earlier result holds: insofar as a determinately omniscient speaker uses a pristine language, he cannot coherently take himself to be governed by the sorts of biconditionals that we would naturally associate with being maximally informative. The result may be surprising to some, admittedly: but I do not see it as a cogent basis upon which to convict the supervaluationist of incoherence.

A variant on Williamson's thought experiment is worth considering,[35] one which makes important use of a multitude of omniscient speakers, while dropping the tracking assumption. Suppose that each of, say, ten thousand definitely omniscient speakers is given the following pair of instructions: say 'heap' only if what is in front of you is a heap. Say 'no heap' only if what is in front of you is not a heap. An omniscient speaker who remained silent throughout would obey the instructions (they being merely of the 'only if' variety). But presumably many would offer sundry 'heap' and 'no heap' utterances. One could keep track of which cases received some 'heap' responses, which 'no heap' responses, which neither. As we ran more and more trials, evidence would accumulate. True enough, different speakers would have different levels of reticence with regard to their willingness to offer 'heap' and 'no heap' verdicts. But after ten thousand trials, two lines would have emerged—one between those cases that received at least some 'heap' verdicts and those that received none, a second between those cases that received at least some 'no heap' verdicts and those that received none.[36] We could not easily anticipate in advance where these two lines would appear. Wouldn't they then, plausibly, mark a pair of semantically significant hidden boundaries? Of course, there is no logical guarantee of such. We could imagine our multitude to conspire to refuse *en mass* to offer a 'heap' verdict in certain clear cases of heaphood. But wouldn't we have at least accrued considerable evidence of semantically significant hidden boundaries in such a case? And absent some kind of conspiracy, isn't it obvious that such multiple trials will cumulatively reveal hidden boundaries?

I suspect that the force of this last thought experiment relies on our forgetting that the divide between omniscient and non omniscient speakers (whether or not we are considering omniscience simpliciter or omniscience regarding some restricted subject matter) may itself be vague. Without pretending to offer a final word, I offer the following, countervailing, intuition pump. Suppose a tribe contains some contingently omniscient speakers. We know that if a member of such tribe drinks ten pints of beer he or she is definitely sufficiently impaired as to cease to be omniscient. Meanwhile, we know that if a member of the tribe drinks one pint of beer he or she is definitely still omniscient. We run trials on groups of tribemembers in varying

---

[35] I am very grateful here to conversations with Timothy Williamson.

[36] Note that our supervaluationist will not tolerate the idea that the 'heap' verdicts would give out at exactly the point at which 'no heap' verdicts kick in. Assuming the second conception, we can be secure that a definitely omniscient being will not give either verdict in a clear borderline case.

states of inebriation using the same protocol as above, deploying a Sorites series on heaphood and the same pair of instructions. No instance in the Sorites series will be immune from any given verdict. But we will notice that some cases will not receive, say, a 'heap' verdict from any tribesperson that falls short of a certain level of inebriation. Would we now be able to detect some sharp hidden boundary of semantic significance? Only if some level of inebriation clearly marked the transition point from omniscience to less than omniscience. But if that transition point is not sharp, we could not very well extract a hidden boundary from our various trials. Look back to our original ten thousand trials, described in the previous paragraph. Various tribepeople in our new trial will certainly have given a 'heap' verdict in other cases. Call these the 'deviants'. Assuming that omniscience, as well as definite omniscience, is no sharp matter, we would be in no position to assert that all the deviants are to be classified as not omniscient, or even not definitely omniscient. But insofar as we are in no position to assert *that*, we are in no position to claim that the pair of lines described in the preceding paragraph are semantically significant.

In conclusion, then, it remains unclear whether any thought experiment involving omniscient speakers makes real trouble for the supervaluationist who denies the existence of inscrutable hidden boundaries associated with vague predicates. Certainly, Williamson's thought experiment is inconclusive; nor is any in the vicinity clearly more decisive.

AFTERWORD

The wider relevance of the preceding remarks should not be overlooked. Even those unsympathetic to the metaphysical possibility of an omniscient being will take seriously the possibility of local omniscience[37] about some restricted, though still Sorites susceptible, subject matters. Not only do we idly recognize such possibilities. As philosophers, we frequently invoke some counterfactual idealized being (or else an idealized 'limit of inquiry') as a tool in philosophical analysis. Certain ethicists have suggested that x is good iff x would be reckoned good by an ideally reflective agent. Some philosophers of modality have suggested that P supervenes on base Q just in case $(Q \supset P)$ would be a priori for an idealized agent. And so on. Many of the preceding puzzles and concerns have analogues in connection with those philosophical analyses. Consider a simple illustration. In a borderline case of goodness, should we suppose that there would be no fact of the matter as to whether an ideally reflective agent would accept a goodness ascription in that case? Or should the proponent of the ethical analysis just mentioned retreat to

$\forall x$ Def x is good iff x would be reckoned good by an ideally reflective agent,

---

[37] Even perhaps by a human, if the subject matter is sufficiently restricted.

(in effect supplanting the first conception of (restricted) omniscience by the second)? Relatedly, in a case where it is definite that either x is good or x is not good but indefinite whether x is good, should we learn to live with the problematic disjunction:

Either (an ideally reflective agent would reckon x good and it is indefinite whether x is good) or (an ideally reflective agent would reckon x not good and it is indefinite whether x is good)?

Obviously, this is not the place to pursue these connections further.

9

Epistemicism and Semantic Plasticity[1]

0

I shall endeavour to make vivid a kind of puzzle that arises when Timothy Williamson's epistemicist machinery[2] is applied to borderline cases of (i) personhood and (ii) semantic properties. My aim will be to raise some concerns about his development of the epistemicist view, and then to explore an alternative way of thinking about epistemicism. What follows is very much a progress report on unfinished business, but I hope there is enough progress to warrant the report.

1

Consider a Sorites series in which a subject S has his hair removed, one hair at a time, beginning with a full head of hair, ending with no hair at all. At the beginning, S is clearly not bald. At the end, S is clearly bald. However, there will be occasions where S is neither clearly bald, nor clearly not bald: at those times, S is a borderline case of baldness. Williamson's epistemicism combines the following theses about borderline cases of baldness:

(1) The relevant instances of excluded middle hold. Supposing that our subject is now a borderline case of baldness, it is nevertheless true that
S is bald or ~S is bald.

(2) Bivalence holds for any baldness ascription to S. Thus, whether or not S is now a borderline case of baldness,
'S is bald' is true or 'S is bald' is false.

(3) If S is a borderline case of baldness, then we are unable to know whether or not S is bald.

(4) Not all ignorance is due to vagueness. In borderline cases, vagueness has a distinctive source, namely: if we had used the word 'bald' ever so slightly

This essay is also printed in *Oxford Studies in Metaphysics II*, pp. 289–322. I am grateful for permission to reprint it here.

[1] I am grateful for conversations with and comments from Cian Dorr, Hartry Field, Kit Fine, Hud Hudson, David Manley, Stephen Schiffer, Ted Sider, Ryan Wasserman, Peter van Inwagen, Dean Zimmerman, audiences at Oxford, MIT, NYU, and Syracuse, and especially Timothy Williamson.

[2] See his *Vagueness* (Routledge, 1994).

differently, we would have picked out a different property by 'bald'. We are insensitive to the ways that slight differences in usage make a difference to the semantic values of our terms. When ignorance is due to that kind of insensitivity, we suffer ignorance that is due to vagueness.

How does the kind of insensitivity in (4) make for ignorance? Well, suppose 'bald' is true of S, but it is also true that if we had used the term 'bald' ever so slightly differently, 'bald' would have been false of S. If we are insensitive to the ways that slight differences in usage makes for a difference in semantic value, then insofar as we actually believe S is bald, there will be close worlds in which we make a mistake in a relevantly similar situation. Thus even if we believe that S is bald and get it right, we do not *know* that S is bald.

In a borderline case of baldness, (a) there are a plurality of candidate semantic values, where a semantic value is a candidate for 'bald' insofar as, for all we are able to know, it is the actual semantic value of the term 'bald', (b) one of the candidates is the actual semantic value, which in turn determines the actual truth value of the relevant baldness ascription, and (c) some of the candidates hold of the case at hand, and others do not. Here is a bit of terminology: let us say that a term is 'semantically plastic' when (a) slight differences in usage make for differences in semantic value and (b) we are insensitive to the ways in which difference in usage makes for a difference in semantic value.

2

Assuming that persons are material beings, it is natural to think that the predicate 'is a person' is vague. Here are four relevant considerations:

(i) There is vagueness about when a person comes into existence. Even if, for example, one is convinced that a person begins with conception, there will be vagueness at the beginnings of personhood owing to vagueness as to when conception actually takes place. (Think of the trajectory of sperm, slowly approaching and entering the egg. It is clearly a vague matter when conception occurs.) In general, all views about the beginnings of personhood use vague predicates in the favoured criterion. Thus, even granting any given one of those views, vagueness along the temporal dimension will not disappear.

(ii) And unless one believes that persons enjoy life (or at least existence) everlasting, there will be vagueness as to when a person's existence comes to an end. Once one remembers that such predicates as 'dies' and 'is braindead' and so on are vague, the relevant thesis about persons should be obvious enough.

(iii) Further, there is vagueness as to where the spatial boundaries of a person lie. There are, for example, certain atoms in the vicinity of my surface such that it is a vague matter whether or not they are parts of me.

(iv) There is vagueness as to whether various less sophisticated beings count as people.

3

Suppose that there is a speck of dirt—call it Tony—such that it is a vague matter whether or not the sentence 'The person sitting down has Tony as a part' (hereafter S1) is true. Let us try to describe the vagueness of this case using epistemicist machinery. What we should say, it seems, is that there are a multitude of candidate semantic values for the term 'person' such that the truth value of S1 differs according to which of those candidates is adopted as the interpretation of 'person'. The point presumably extends to personal pronouns. It will thus presumably also be a vague matter whether or not the sentence 'He has Tony as a part' (pointing at the person in the chair) is true (hereafter S2). And this will be because there is a range of candidate semantic values for 'he' such that the sentence differs in truth value according to which semantic value in the range is adopted. Suppose S2 is true. There will be a meaning that could very easily have been given to 'he' such that S2 is false.

This semantic picture invites us to posit a plentitude of overlapping objects in the vicinity of the chair. Only one of them falls within the extension of 'person'. Only one of them is the referent of the personal pronoun 'he'. Insofar as the object in question has Tony as a part, then S1 and S2 are true. But owing to semantic plasticity, there are a variety of candidate semantic values of 'person', each of which associates some object or other with the definite description 'the person in the chair'. While some of the candidate semantic values associate an object containing Tony as a part with the definite description 'the person in the chair', others will not.

Let us focus on two of the candidates, one containing Tony as a part, the other not. Call them Grubby and Clean. Suppose Grubby and not Clean falls within the actual extension of the term 'person' in English (though of course we would be unable to know this). Then S1 and S2 are both true. But there is a possible tribe that uses the word 'person' ever so slightly differently, so that Clean and not Grubby falls within the extension of the term 'person' in their mouths and S1 and S2 in their mouths are false. Such a tribe might even be actual. Pretend that there exists a tribe of Twinglish speakers that uses 'person' in such a way that 'person' is true of Clean and not Grubby. Then when a Twinglander says 'The person sitting in the chair has Tony as a part' he will express a false proposition even though we say something true.

There are a variety of overlapping objects on the chair. Only one of them is a person. That is, only one of them falls under the extension of the actual semantic value of 'person'. The same holds, presumably, for such predicates as 'thinks', 'talks', and so on. Only one of the objects thinks. Only one of them talks. The one that is the person is also the one that thinks and talks. Others of the overlapping objects fall within the extension of candidate semantic values for 'thinks', 'talks', and 'is a person' (in the sense of candidacy explained). Suppose Grubby thinks and talks. If our use of 'think' and 'talk' had been ever so slightly different in certain ways then 'think' and 'talk' would have applied to Clean. Let us say that an object thinks* iff it falls within the extension of one of the candidate semantic values for 'thinks'. We could similarly introduce the predicates 'person*' and 'talks*'. There are many objects that on the chair that are persons*, which think* and which talk*. But only one of them thinks, talks, and is a person.

Why do I insist that only one of the objects is a person? Well, I take it that a feature of our usage we do not allow that many objects at a time are people when those objects mereologically overlap almost entirely. If semantic values are going to respect that aspect of usage then each candidate semantic value for 'person' will allow only one of the objects on the chair to fall within its extension.[3]

What makes, say, Grubby and not Clean the thinker? If we could know the answer to that question then (says the epistemicist) it would not be a vague matter whether Tony is part of the person. We cannot know what it is about our use of 'thinks' that determines one of the candidate semantic values to be the actual one. Our knowledge of semantic relations is incapable of extending that far. And that is precisely why ignorance arises in the case at hand.

Call the approach just sketched the 'Simple Epistemicist Treatment of Persons'.

4

There is a problem for the simple epistemicist treatment. Let me illustrate it by an example. Suppose a Twinglander is sitting in a chair. Suppose that the Twinglander uses 'thinks' and 'person' ever so slightly differently (and is otherwise very much like an ordinary English speaker), so that the semantic value for 'thinks' and 'person', as used by the Twinglander, is different from ours. In particular, let us suppose that Grubby and Clean are both in the chair, our use of 'person' is such that it is true of Grubby and not Clean, and the Twinglander's use of 'person' is such that it is true of Clean and not Grubby.

Here are some very obvious truths:

(1) The Twinglander is the person sitting on the chair.

(2) The person sitting on the chair is the only thing on the chair that is able to talk and think.

(3) When the person sitting on the chair says 'I' the person is referring to himself.

(4) If the person sitting on the chair says something of the form 'a is F' then that claim is true iff the predicate 'F' in the mouth of that person is true of the thing referred to by 'a'.

Let us add to these obvious truths the added facts provided by our epistemicist-driven description of the scenario

(5) Grubby is the person sitting on the chair (and Clean is not);

(6) 'is a person' in the mouth of the Twinglander is true of Clean and not Grubby.

---

[3] Even if one goes against that aspect of usage and counts many of the objects sitting on the chair each as a person, some of the issues that follow will arise. For even if there are many persons on the chair, there will presumably be certain objects for which it is vague whether or not those objects are persons at all.

Suppose the Twinglander says 'I am a person'. We can deduce: (i) Grubby says 'I am a person', (ii) Nothing else on the chair says 'I am a person', (iii) Grubby is referring to himself, (iv) 'I am a person' as uttered by Grubby is true iff 'is a person' in the mouth of Grubby is true of Grubby, and (v) 'is a person' in the mouth of Grubby is not true of Grubby. All of this leads us to conclude that when the Twinglander says 'I am a person', the Twinglander expresses a false proposition and that nothing in the vicinity says something true. The same argument could have been run, *mutatis mutandis*, for 'I think' and 'I talk'. We should now conclude further that if our use of 'person' and 'think' had been ever so slightly different, then the sentences 'I think' and 'I talk', in our mouths, would have been false. This casts a sceptical shadow over the actual world: on a safety-driven conception of knowledge, the presence of mistakes at close worlds undermines knowledge at the actual world. Clearly, something has gone terribly wrong.

Let us get a bit clearer about the source of the problem. As things have been set up, it is *our* standards for 'person', 'thinks', 'talks', and so on that determine which of the candidate objects is an object that is self-referring, but it is an object's own, potentially different, standards that determine the extension of 'is a person', 'thinks', 'talks', and so on in its own mouth. It is our own standards that determine which objects are objects that are capable of engaging in the activity of drawing boundaries. In short, our standards determine which objects are boundary drawers. But it is the potentially different standards of the boundary drawer that determine where the extension of 'thinks' and 'person' in its mouth are to fall. Suppose the set of boundaries corresponding to 'person' that are drawn by a boundary drawer do not include its own boundary. Than were that boundary drawer ever to self-ascribe that predicate it would make a mistake.

Let us say that a person uses a close variant of 'person' iff the semantic value of 'person' in the mouth of that person is a candidate semantic value for 'person' in English. Assuming that 'person' is semantically plastic, it seems very easy for a variant of 'person' in the mouth of a boundary drawer to be false of the boundary drawer. That is just to say that it is easy for a person to be such that she uses a close variant of 'person' in a way that is false of that person. The same holds for 'thinks'. The trouble is that we do not want to say that there are close variants of 'thinks' and 'person' such that those predicates are falsely self-ascribed. For it is all too easy to self-ascribe those predicates—'I' thoughts will do the trick.

The simple epistemicist model needs supplementation or revision. I shall explore three approaches.

5

Strategy A: One response is to deny that self-ascription is easy for close variants of English. One might insist that when the Twinglander says 'I think', the Twinglander is not referring himself by 'I' but is referring to, say, Clean. On this model 'I think' in the mouth of the Twinglander is much more like 'he thinks' than it may first appear. In brief: whenever a person uses a close variant of 'thinks' in such a way that the person does not fall within the extension of that predicate, then the person will have no readily available device for self-reference and in particular will not self-refer when that person uses what would naturally be taken as a cognate of 'I'.

This view may not be as bad as it first appears. In particular, it is worth bearing in mind a certain potential symmetry between me and the Twinglander. For on this view the Twinglander may point in my direction and say 'He cannot refer to himself', where 'he' in the Twinglander's mouth refers to something that mereologically over-laps me, but which is not identical to me, and that satisfies 'person', 'talker', 'thinker', and so on in *his* mouth. So the proponent of this view can do something to deflate the suggestion that we are really special by being able to self-refer.

We should also bear in mind that, almost inevitably, the epistemicist is going to have to learn to live with a mass of strange counterfactuals. Suppose I want not to be bald. It seems at first blush to be true that if I had gone to the pub last night, I would still have wanted not to be bald. But suppose that if I had gone to the pub, the evening's conversation would have induced slight differences in use that shifted the meaning of 'bald' ever so slightly. Then it would seem that, strictly speaking, the counterfactual is false, since at the closest world where I go to the pub I do not stand in the desire relation to the proposition actually expressed by 'I am not bald'.

All that said, I remain unimpressed by the view that self-reference fails in close variants of English. There is something exceedingly strange about a view according to which, at close worlds, many people (perhaps most people) do not have linguistic devices of self-reference. Relatedly, it is extremely natural to think that if a pronom-inal device has the conceptual role of the first-person pronoun in a person's cognitive life, then that pronoun will be a device of self-reference. The thought is a little rough-and-ready, owing to the rough-and-ready nature of the concept of 'conceptual role', but has some force nevertheless. 'I' thoughts in the Twinglanders belief-box will have stereotypical roles in practical reason and so on that make it utterly natural to suppose that they are devices of self-reference. While the meaning of 'bald' may be fragile, 'I' does not seem to be so easily purged of the character that Kaplan described for it.[4]

6

Strategy B: Return to the case of the Twinglander. Suppose that by the standards of the Twinglander, 'person' is true of Clean. In short, Clean is the object that counts as the utterer of 'I'–talk by the standards of the Twinglander. Perhaps the concept of a person is distinctive in that it defers to the self-conception of people: an object can only count as a boundary drawer insofar as its draws its own boundaries *at* its own boundaries.[5] On the hypothesis that Grubby is a person, Grubby counts Clean but

---

[4] See 'Demonstratives', in J. Almog *et al.* (eds.), *Themes from Kaplan* (Oxford University Press, 1989).

[5] This is not to say, of course, that a person cannot radically misdescribe himself. He may think himself an immaterial being when in fact he is material. And so on. The point is that we must allow questions of who the person is to march in step with questions about what is picked out by 'I' in the person's mouth. Thus once we concede that, overall, the pattern of usage in the person's mouth privileges x over y as the referent of 'I', it is no longer an option to nevertheless reckon y as the person/thinker/utterer.

not Grubby as the referent of 'I'. That counts as a reductio of the idea that Grubby is a person at all.

Example: suppose there is an Englander and a Twinglander each in a chair. The intrinsic environment is pretty much the same for each. There are, *inter alia*, two objects Grubby$_E$ and Clean$_E$ in the Englander's chair and two objects Grubby$_T$ and Clean$_T$ in the Twinglander's chair. Suppose the Englander's self-descriptions (without him knowing it) privilege Grubby$_E$ and the Twinglander's self-descriptions (without him knowing it) privilege Clean$_T$. Then 'person' in the Twinglander's mouth is true of Grubby$_E$ and Clean$_T$. Something analogous holds for the Englander. Each defers to the other's self-description as the prime semantic determinant of which object is the referent of 'I' thoughts and, in turn, of which object falls within the extension of 'person'. (I am here abstracting away from the question as to what it takes to be a person beyond being a thinker that can self-refer.)

Our simple epistemicist position claimed, in effect, that people could very easily have used the term 'person' in slightly different ways such that they did not fall under the extension of 'person' in their mouths. Our revised position denies this.

7

Let us turn to the diachronic case. Suppose I begin life with the self-conception of a Twinglander and towards the end of my life move towards the self-conception of an Englander. (Of course, the shift my not be epistemically obvious to me: in fact if the shift is around borderline cases, it will not be.) Suppose my earlier self is sitting in a chair and my earlier self's usage privileges Grubby (where now let Grubby be an object that always has Tony as a part)[6] and not Clean (which never has Tony as a part) as the referent of 'I' thoughts. My later self however privileges Clean but not Grubby as the referent of 'I' thoughts. The natural way to apply the deferential conception is thus: my earlier self refers to Grubby with his 'I' thoughts and my later self refers to Clean with his 'I' thoughts. But this can't be right. My earlier self *is* my later self! But Grubby is not identical to Clean. When I look back on my earlier self, I want to say 'I was referring to myself when I said 'I am hungry' '. If I am Clean then it cannot be that my earlier self refers to Grubby by 'I'. The problem is analagous to the earlier one. The ascribee's usage puts semantic pressure to count one thing as the referent of its 'I' thoughts, whereas the ascriber's standards on who is to count as a thinker in the first place puts semantic pressure towards a different thing to count as as the referent of 'I' thoughts. Where the target and the ascriber take themselves to be one and the same person, the 'to each his own' deferential strategy cannot be made to work.

At this point the epistemicist can appeal to externalist themes. Return to the case of 'bald'. It is wrong to think that the extension of 'bald' in my mouth is simply a matter of how *I* use 'bald'. My own use creates various semantic pressures, but I am a member of a linguistic community. The usage of others also contributes to the extension of the term in my mouth. Indeed, one reason—though not the only one—why

---

[6] Let us assume that Tony remains within the close vicinity of the surface throughout the life of the individual.

I cannot know which value is the semantic value of 'bald' in my mouth is the fact that I am not privy to all the details of others' usage. Now what goes for my semantic relationship to others in the linguistic community may go for my later or earlier self. The extension of 'person' in my mouth—and relatedly, the referent of 'I'—may be constitutively determined by the usage of my later or earlier self. Suppose, to simplify, a community consisted of two individuals A and B. A's usage of 'bald' may favour a cutoff at seventeen hairs. Roughly speaking: if A was the only member of the community, then the extension of 'bald' in his mouth would include all and only people with seventeen hairs or less. Suppose, meanwhile, B's usage favours a cutoff at fifteen hairs. This does not mean that B and A have different semantic values for 'bald'. The fact that they translate each other homophonically and use their own word to report the others mental states creates semantic pressure against such a resolution. If God were to interpret them he would likely say that their terms have the same semantic value, adopting some appropriate weighting of the various semantic pressures at play.[7] We cannot know how the weighting would proceed, of course—our lack of knowledge of the details of the relevant laws of semantics is what gives rise to the phenomenon of vagueness (says the epistemicist). Similar remarks apply, *mutatis mutandis*, to the case at hand. If the earlier usage favours Grubby, the later Clean, but there is considerable semantic pressure for uniformity of semantic value across uses, then the matter is resolved by some (we know not what) weighting of semantic pressures to yield a uniform semantic value. Perhaps the usage that favours Grubby loses out to the usage that favours Clean. In that case, both the early and later self use 'person' in such a way that the extension of 'person' includes Clean and not Grubby. In that case no utterance of 'I am a person' gets to be false: on both occasions, it is Clean that makes the utterance. Grubby is not a person at any time. Both utterances come out true since Clean is always, Grubby never, included in the extension of 'person'.[8]

8

I have sketched a picture. Does it fit with the barebones epistemicism I began with? It is of course perfectly consistent with excluded middle, with bivalence, and with the

---

[7] We cannot say that God would respond that way in every such case. If we imagine a community that gradually shifts over time from being disposed to favour a cutoff that is at fifteen hairs to favouring a cutoff that is at 1015 hairs, we will not tolerate the conclusion that the first means the same as the last, despite the fact that, from one time to the next, the shift in use is small and the homophonic pressures towards semantic uniformity great (we can imagine each without hesitation translates the utterances of recent community members in a homophonic way). We are faced here with a familiar situation: a relation R1 that might initially be thought to be sufficient for a relation R2 cannot be quite treated that way owing to the fact that the former is intransitive and the latter transitive. Intriguing versions of the same problem seem to arise for longlived persons with evolving self-conceptions, though I shall not attempt to delve into the matter here.

[8] And perhaps the use favours a third object that has Tony as a part early on but has Tony slightly beyond its mereological boundaries later on. If the pattern of use described can induce that kind of extension then the relevant changes in use would have the effect of making the person shrink. It would be odd were diets of this kind possible.

thesis that borderline cases are beset by ignorance. What is less clear on this picture is that there is semantic plasticity in borderline cases. More specifically, it is not clear that the intension associated with 'person' could easily have been different. To make this vivid, consider a world W containing nothing but a Twinglander sitting in a chair. If 'person' is deferential in the way described and the Twinglander's usage favours Grubby, then I should say that Grubby is the person in that world. Could the intension of 'person' have easily been such that it did *not* deliver Grubby as the extension taking W as its argument? (I am operating here with a standard conception of intensions as functions from worlds to extensions.) It would seem that a word that was not deferential in the way described would not be a close variant of 'person'. But that inclines me to think that there is no close variant of 'person' that does not deliver the set containing Grubby as its value, taking W as argument. We want to say that it is a vague matter whether the person in W has Tony as a part. But it is not at all clear that the ignorance can be explained as a matter of semantic plasticity.

9

(An aside: suppose one adopts the epistemicist picture sketched thus far. Given the plenitudinous ontology in the background and the willingness to defer to self-conceptions as the determinants of boundaries, it is at least natural to extend the picture to allow that some people have wildly different boundaries simply on account of wildly different self-conceptions. To make this vivid, consider a community of Eggers. An Egger believes that he or she came into existence as a human Egg. An Egger will say that fertilization made him or her gendered (and in general a lot more interesting). But on an Egger's self-conception, his or her existence began with an egg. Embrace the plenitudinous ontology suggested by epistemicism and it is very natural to suppose that there is at least an object—don't ask yet whether it is a person—that comes into existence at the time that the egg does, endures for seventy or eighty years, and has all the intrinsic requirements for thought later in life. Assume the deferential perspective and it becomes very natural to say that these are the objects that the Eggers refer to by means of their 'I' thoughts. Some people, then, come into existence prior to fertilization. Not us, perhaps.[9] But the Eggers do. Is this a *reductio* of the deferential conception of persons? I shall not try to settle this matter here.[10])

10

Strategy C:[11] One might say in these cases that vagueness in spatiotemporal boundaries does not, despite first appearances, have its source in any vagueness associated with

---

[9] I shall not investigate the delicate issues of transworld identity here.

[10] A few people have raised the following puzzle: what of someone whose usage favoured the cosmos as the preferred boundary (and who thus thought of himself rather on the model of a many-headed hydra)? While we might defer to the Egger we will not be so ready to defer to the Cosmos. I leave the issue as a puzzle for the deferentialist.

[11] Thanks to Mark Johnston, Ted Sider, and Timothy Williamson for urging me to consider this strategy.

the term 'person' (and in the associated personal pronouns), but rather in vagueness associated with other pieces of vocabulary. Suppose it is a vague matter when I came into existence. It might be claimed that there is some particular object o, such that it is definite that 'person' is true of o, and definite that 'I' in my mouth refers to o, but that the location of o is indefinite owing to vagueness associated with the term 'occupies'. Now in the case of mereologically complex objects such as myself (assuming the falsity of Cartesianism), it seems clear that the location of the whole is derivative upon the location of the small parts. It would thus be strange to suppose it is a sharp matter as to whether any given atom is or is not part of a mereologically complex thing at each time but that the location of the thing is vague, unless there is vagueness in the location of particular atoms. But the latter is *not* plausibly the source of indeterminacy in my boundaries. So as far as I can tell, then, the most promising development of the current strategy will require positing vagueness in the concept of parthood: it is vague for various pairs x, y whether, at some given time, x is part of y. Assuming semantic plasticity, this will require that we posit a variety of candidate semantic values for 'is a part of', ones that differ intensionally.

Some will consider this an extremely radical tack, almost as radical as the idea that 'exists' is vague. I think this reaction can likely be traced to a tendency to think of mereology as part of logic, and thus a tendency to think that 'part of' enjoys purity of the kind possessed by existence and identity. This will be reinforced insofar as one adopts an extensionalist mereology according to which x is identical to y iff x is part of y and y is part of x.[12] For then it will be particularly difficult to maintain vagueness for 'part of' in combination with precision for 'is identical to'.

I do not find such abstract logical considerations very pressing myself: I am not particularly drawn to extensionalism, nor to a logicist thesis about mereology. There is a more local problem, however. For consider a case in which it is vague whether or not a person comes into existence at all (imagine the room blowing up just as the sperm is entering the egg). In that case it seems extremely difficult to explain the vagueness of the case in terms of vagueness in 'part of', since here it is vague whether 'person' is true of anything at all. Similarly, consider a world where there is an explosion that renders it vague whether I come into existence. (Imagine the world is just like the actual world up to the freak explosion.) If it can be vague whether I exist at that world then there had better be something that exists there that is a candidate semantic value for 'I'.[13] Let us use 'Johnny' as a precise name for that object. It now appears that 'I am Johnny' is indefinite. But it is hard to see in this case how the vagueness can be blamed on 'part of'.

I can think of only one promising escape. In other works, Timothy Williamson has defended a necessitarianism about objects according to which any object exists eternally and necessarily.[14] If one adopts that view, it is no longer coherent to suppose

---

[12] And allayed insofar as one thinks that it is the time indexed 'is part of at t' and not the time-less 'part of' that is fundamental.

[13] I assume, reasonably enough, that the unrestricted existential quantifier cannot itself be vague.

[14] See, for example, 'Existence and Contingency', *Aristotelian Society*, sup. vol. 73 (1999), 181–203.

that there is a world where it is vague whether I exist at all. It is of course coherent to suppose that there is a world where, at some time, it is vague whether I am concrete. Further, it is coherent to suppose that there is a world where it is vague whether I am ever concrete. But this kind of vagueness *can*, perhaps, be blamed on 'part of'. Suppose that for one of the candidates for 'part of', there is a world w where I never have atoms as parts, but that on another precisification of 'part of', I do have atomic parts at w. On this conception, there are worlds where, while I definitely exist, it is vague whether or not I ever, so to speak, descend into the atom-filled void. Acknowledging a restricted use of 'exists' to mean 'concretely exists', there is a sense in which it is vague whether I exist at that world, though the vagueness can be placed squarely on the shoulders of 'part of'.

I recommend strategy B to non-necessitarian epistemicists. However, strategy C may very well turn out to be preferable if we assume a necessitarian setting. Strategy B makes trouble for the semantic plasticity component of Williamson's view. Strategy C does not. Considerations of personal identity thus appear to forge an interesting bridge from his version of epistemicism to necessitarianism. (Not that one needs to rely on such a bridge in order to motivate necessitarianism.)

11

The issues I have raised are far from unique to epistemicism. Consider the main competing theory of vagueness,[15] supervaluationism. The supervaluationist uses supertruth and superfalsity as her primary concepts of semantic evaluation. A sentence is supertrue iff it is true on all precisifications, superfalse iff it is false on all precisifications. A borderline case is one where the relevant sentence is true on some precisifications, false on others. Suppose 'He has Tony as a part' is a borderline case (where 'Tony' is precise). That will be because there are various precisifications of 'he', some of which contain Tony as a part, others not. Here too we have a plenitude of objects required by the semantics. Suppose further that we embrace the analogue of semantic plasticity: small shifts in use generate small shifts in the range of acceptable precisifications of a term. Suppose now a Twinglander has a slightly different set of acceptable precisifications for 'person' than I do. Now the competing pressures described above will arise. On the one hand, I want to say that the Twinglander self-refers by 'I'. This encourages me to treat all and only the acceptable precisifications of 'the Twinglander' in my mouth as acceptable precisifications of 'I' in the Twinglander's mouth. But suppose some of the acceptable precisifications of 'the Twinglander' in my mouth are not acceptable precisifications of 'person' in the Twinglander's mouth. Then there is a threat that 'I am a person', in the mouth of the Twinglander, will not come out supertrue. (Similarly for 'I think'.) Such a sentence will have to be reckoned borderline. This result is intuitively unacceptable. The same theme is in play. We have competing pressures on the reference of 'I', generated on the one hand by my conception of a person and on the other hand

---

[15] See Kit Fine, 'Vagueness, Truth and Logic', *Synthese* 30 (1975).

by the self-conception of another. It is thus relatively straightforward to recast the issues just discussed within the alternative semantic framework of supervaluationism. A shift from epistemicism to supervaluationism will thus not make the problems go away, so long as semantic plasticity is maintained.

12

I now turn to the case of semantic predicates. Williamson is happy to suppose that his picture extends to such predicates as 'refers' and 'is true'. Thus, in a reply to a commentary by Stephen Schiffer, he writes:

> ... semantic ascent preserves vagueness. For example, since it is clear that something is bald if and only if it is in the extension of 'bald', 'bald' has the same borderline cases as 'in the extension of "bald" '.

> My general explanation of the ignorance that constitutes vagueness extends to semantic terms. Although someone may judge truly 'Baldness is the property of having fewer than 3832 hairs on one's scalp', the judgement does not express knowledge, for whatever produced a judgement in those words could very easily have done so even if the overall use of 'bald' had been very slightly shifted (as it could very easily have been) in such a way that it referred to the property of having fewer than 3831 hairs on one's scalp, in which case the judgement then made in those words would have been false. What produces the judgement does not produce true judgements reliably enough to produce knowledge. . . . To extend this explanation of our non-semantic ignorance to an explanation of our semantic ignorance, note that in the envisaged counterfactual circumstances the sentence ' 'Bald' refers to baldness' naturally still commands assent (clearly, 'bald' refers to baldness). In those circumstances, the false judgement in the words 'Baldness is the property of having fewer than 3,832 hairs on one's scalp' goes with a false judgement in the words ' "Baldness" refers to the property of having fewer than 3,832 hairs on one's scalp'. Although someone may use the latter words to make a true judgement in the actual circumstances, the judgement does not express knowledge, for what produces it does not produce true judgements reliably enough to produce knowledge. Thus the account explains equally why we are not in a position to know that 'baldness' refers to the property of having fewer than 3,832 hairs on one's scalp.[16]

I think that this passage obscures an important distinction. Let us distinguish semantic plasticity—the phenomenon whereby the intension associated with a term could easily have been different—from extensional plasticity—the phenomenon whereby the extension of a term could easily have been different. Suppose I am moody. I fall under the extension of 'happy at noon, 15 April 2004'. Being moody, I could very easily have failed to fall under the extension of that predicate. Thus, there are close worlds where the extension of that predicate is different to what it actually is. But *that* phenomenon obviously does not by itself indicate that 'happy' is semantically plastic. Now if 'bald' is semantically plastic in the way that Williamson envisages, that certainly means that, say, 'expresses' (conceived of as a relation between a noise token and a property) is extensionally plastic. A noise token may in

---

[16] 'Reply to Commentators' *Philosophy and Phenomenological Research* 57(4) (December 1997), 947–8.

this world express a property *p*, baldness, and yet at a close world that noise token not express that property. (Similarly, if we allow '*c* means *p* by noise type *n*' to express a three-place relation between a phonetic or graphemic type, a community, and a property, then the semantic plasticity of 'bald' will make for extensional plasticity with regard to that ternary predicate.) Moreover, it is plausible enough to think that such extensional plasticity, coupled with our insensitivity to the ways that slight shifts in use make for differences in semantic value, will undermine the possibility of knowledge of the propositions expressed by the relevant metalinguistic claims in borderline cases. The words ' "baldness" refers to the property of having fewer than 3,832 hairs on one's scalp' could easily have expressed a falsehood. And given our insensitivity to the shifts in semantic value, one who accepted that sentence would not plausibly express knowledge thereby. But none of this shows that semantic terms are themselves semantically plastic. And thus none of this shows that ignorance in the metalinguistic claims can be traced to the semantic plasticity of one or more terms that are used in them. If we assume with Williamson that vagueness requires semantic plasticity, then while we may grant that semantic ascent preserves ignorance, we are still owed a justification of the passage's opening claim that semantic ascent preserves vagueness.

13

We have seen that the considerations adduced by Williamson in the quoted paragraph do not demonstrate that semantic terms are semantically plastic. But is there any positive reason to think that they are not? Interestingly, the puzzle adduced earlier can be reproduced here. We generated havoc earlier by allowing our standards for what counts as a person to draw boundaries in different places to cognate terms (terms used at close worlds with almost indistinguishable conceptual roles) used by various counterfactual people themselves. What happens if we allow, say, the predicate 'true' to draw boundaries in a way that fails to match the boundaries drawn by people at close worlds who use a term with a conceptual role that bears the hallmark of our use of 'true'? Havoc similarly results.

Let us suppose that 'true' is semantically plastic, so that its intension at close worlds differs from its actual intension. Here, I am thinking of 'true' as a predicate of utterance tokens, so that its semantic value will be a function from worlds to sets of utterance tokens.[17] Suppose, then, that at a nearby world *w* the semantic value of 'true' was slightly different, so that each utterance of a particular sentence S by a particular community C fell under the extension of the semantic value expressed by our term 'true' (given *w* as argument), but did not fall under the extension of the semantic value of 'true' as used at *w*. Let us assume, as required by the Williamson picture, that at that world the use of 'true' is only ever so slightly different, so that the fundamental

---

[17] The ontology of words is obviously a tricky business. The points that I am making can, however, be recast in terms of other different semantical frameworks, including, for example, one that takes 'true' as a predicate of utterance types—where an utterance type is individuated by a combination of phonemic/phonetic considerations and a specified context of use.

features of its conceptual role at our world—in particular the behaviour gestured at by the 'T-schema'—are intact.

Consider now an utterance of

'S' is true iff S

made by an inhabitant of *w*. By hypothesis the right-hand side of the biconditional is true. How about the left-hand side? By hypothesis, 'S' does not fall within the extension of 'true' as used by the community at that world. Thus, the community would be saying something false by the left-hand side. Thus, if the community were to utter the relevant biconditional, the left-hand side would be false, the right-hand side true. The biconditional would be false. Assuming semantic plasticity, we have been led to conclude that at close worlds, certain counterparts of the T-schema are false! This seems just as bad as conceding that at close worlds people do not self-refer by 'I'. Note that in both cases we supposed that a certain conceptual role is accompanied by a certain semantic achievement: a pronoun with the conceptual role of 'I' has self-reference, a predicate with the conceptual role of 'true' will yield true instances of the associated T-schema. In both cases, semantic plasticity induces a detachment between the relevant conceptual role and the associated semantic achievement.[18]

As in the case of 'I', one might try to soften the blow. 'After all,' it may be said, 'while counterparts of the T-schema are false at close worlds, they are true*, where the property of being true* is the property expressed by 'true' at close worlds.' But I take it that this is not satisfactory. Truth is the norm by which we evaluate both our actual and counterfactual selves. The response requires us to think that at nearby worlds truth doesn't really matter. As such, it is not acceptable. (Consider an analogous conversation in ethics, where one tries to let one's counterpart off the hook by combining a concession that he is cruel with the observation that he is not cruel*, where cruel* is what he means by 'cruel'.)

Untoward results can also be reproduced for 'refers', 'expresses', 'designates', and so on. Suppose, say, that 'refers' is semantically plastic, so that while tokens of some counterfactual name *n* refer to *x*, the pair <*n, x*> does not fall under the extension of 'refers' as used at that (nearby) world. Consider now the claim

'*n*' refers to *n*

as used at that counterfactual world. That claim is true just in case the pair picked out by the flanking singular terms falls under the extension of the binary predicate. The referent of '*n*' is the name itself. By hypothesis the referent of '*n*' is *x*. By hypothesis the pair <*n, x*> does not fall under the extension of 'refers', as used by members of the counterfactual community under consideration. Thus certain instances of the 'disquotational schema for reference' come out false at nearby counterfactual worlds. Once again, an intolerable result.

---

[18] Some people have suggested to me a salvage that goes by way of reinterpreting 'iff' at close worlds. It does not seem plausible that logical operators are semantically plastic in the relevant respect. Moreover, one can redo the puzzle so that instead of considering a statement ' "S" is true iff S', we consider an *inference* from 'S' to ' "S" is true' (where the paradoxical result is that at close worlds the inference is invalid).

The lesson, I take it, is that we should be very cautious about positing semantic plasticity for semantic vocabulary. Not only does the quoted passage from Williamson fail to provide any reason for embracing it; there are powerful reasons for rejecting it.

14

Insofar as we are sympathetic to epistemicism, we are left with a residual problem. What exactly is distinctive of the ignorance due to vagueness? I have argued that it is implausible that our ignorance concerning the boundaries of personhood can be traced to semantic plasticity. But this does not seem to be a good reason for denying that in some very reasonable sense, 'person' is vague. We should similarly allow that in some very reasonable sense, certain claims of the form

'bald' is true of people with less than N hairs

are borderline, even though the vagueness of such claims cannot be traced to the fact that certain terms occurring in them are semantically plastic. (Even if 'bald' is semantically plastic, that does not mean that "bald" is.) Now we have noted that semantic terms may well be beset by extensional plasticity in borderline cases. But we cannot say that, in general, ignorance due to extensional plasticity makes for the kind of ignorance associated with borderline cases. Suppose a particle moves rapidly between point A and B—so rapidly that we cannot in principle discern whether, at a given time, the particle is at location A or B. Consider the claim, 'The particle is at A at noon'. There is extensional plasticity, sure enough. Suppose 'is at A at noon' is true of the particle. That predicate could easily have been false of the particle. But this case does not in any way have the feel of a case in which there is ignorance due to vagueness.

So let us re-examine the question as to what the epistemicist should say about the ignorance that is distinctive of borderline cases. Let us begin with an epistemicist picture of the metaphysics of semantics. It would be very strange indeed to deny that semantical facts (and propositional attitude facts) supervene on a groundfloor comprised of a certain distribution of fundamental properties across spacetime (which will be microphysical, assuming that some broad naturalistic picture is correct). The epistemicist is thus happy to believe that there is some sort of function from fundamental distributions to semantical facts. Call that function 'F'. Meanwhile, semantical ignorance about a certain noise type may have at least two different sources. On the one hand, we may be ignorant of various facts about the groundfloor which serve as input to F. Such facts will, let us suppose (or pretend[19]), straightforwardly encode this or that fact about how the noise type is used by some member of the community, by fellow members of the community, the causal relations of that noise type to this or that feature of the world, and so on. Let us call this source of ignorance about semantic facts *groundfloor ignorance*. On the other

---

[19] This involves a bit of oversimplification, since facts about macro-organisms, words, and causal relationships to other macro-objects will not themselves really be fundamental.

hand, we may have a rather incomplete grasp of F itself, so that even if one were (idealizing now) to have a full grip on the array of fundamental facts, one would still not be in a position to discern the semantical facts on the grounds that one's grasp of how the latter depends on the former is radically incomplete. Let us imagine that the nature of F could be captured by a set of semantical laws that describe how semantical facts depend on the groundfloor. Insofar as we didn't know what the semantical laws were, we would have ignorance not traceable to groundfloor ignorance. Let us call the second kind of ignorance _semantico-nomic ignorance_.[20]

Now it is quite clear that in a borderline case, Williamson supposes the ignorance not merely to be rooted in groundfloor ignorance: even if one knew all of the relevant groundfloor facts, one would not be able to make the ignorance go away. Suppose that the groundfloor facts are captured by P, and that Q includes the relevant semantic facts about the extension of some predicate. The problem is not merely that we do not know that P. It is that we are in no position to know that $P \supset Q$, even though that material conditional is presumably a necessary truth. Groundfloor omniscience would not remove our insensitivity to the true semantic mechanisms.

Notice now that this picture provides a plausible epistemicist account of ignorance due to vagueness that does not proceed by way of semantic plasticity: in cases which we call 'ignorance due to vagueness', we have a sentence that expresses a proposition P such that our principled inability to know whether P is rooted in semantico-nomic ignorance. Even if, say, some claim of the form

(1) Tokens of 'big number' as used by community C are true of any number greater than 154

are not semantically plastic, we may have a principled ignorance of their truth value that is rooted in semantico-nomic ignorance. Hence our ignorance of (1) will count as 'ignorance due to vagueness'.

One might worry that the picture just sketched disrupts a safety-based conception of knowledge according to which belief is knowledge just in case there is no danger of error—that is, no error at 'close worlds'.[21] Suppose someone dogmatically believed some claim S of the form (1) above. Clearly such a person would not know that S even if it were necessarily true. Williamson provides us with a vision of how semantic plasticity explains ignorance in borderline cases: suppose someone were to accept dogmatically a borderline claim S. Even if S is true, then, owing to semantic plasticity, S would express a falsehood at 'close worlds'. Thus, at close worlds, the dogmatist could make a mistake. His actual belief thus turns out not to be safe and so, the dogmatist does not know S. Eschew plasticity for S and no similar explanation is available.

[20] There may be other kinds of ignorance that do not fall into the two categories I have just described. Suppose that there are higher-order natural kinds and fundamental but inscrutable principles about how they depend on the groundfloor. (Suppose, for example, that phenomenal properties are like that.) Our ignorance about whether bats have a certain quale might not then depend either on groundfloor ignorance or ignorance about how semantical laws work. It would then depend on ignorance of some principles of psycho-physics that hold of necessity. (Thanks to Hartry Field here.)

[21] I am grateful for conversations with Timothy Williamson here.

Someone who dogmatically accepted S would, it seems, express a truth at close worlds and so, by a 'safety'-theoretic test, count as knowing that S is true.

Is this a real problem for the current brand of epistemicism? I don't think so. To use the preceeding line of thought against that account is to presuppose an all-too-crude safety-theoretic account of knowledge (one that advocates of safety-based account—including Williamson—will be at pains to distance themselves from). We all know that if someone dogmatically cleaves to Goldbach's conjecture, that will not in itself secure knowledge. But, given that there seems to be no semantic plasticity in the relevant mathematical language, such a dogmatist would not be in error at close worlds. In that case, we are hardly inclined to use a crude safety based account as grounds for admitting that the dogmatist knows Goldbach's conjecture after all (assuming that it is true). We instead refine our conception of what knowledge comes to. Similar remarks apply to semantico-nomic ignorance, *mutatis mutandis*.

15

It is not clear that the semantic plasticity gloss on ignorance due to vagueness has to be jettisoned altogether. Return to (1), namely:

(1) Tokens of 'big number' as used by community C are true of any number greater than 154.

Consider an instance of (1), S, that is not semantically plastic. S is plausibly *about* a term that is semantically plastic. When it comes to evaluating sentences in our own language, semantical claims like S, made about ourselves, will be evaluated by way of sentences that do not contain semantical vocabulary. Thus,

(2) Utterances of '54 is a big number' in my community are true

in my language, will be evaluated by me (on the simplifying assumption that there is no context dependence) by way of

(3) 154 is a big number.

Suppose, as I have been suggesting, (3) is semantically plastic but (2) isn't (or, at any rate, it isn't once 'my community' is made precise). If (3) is vague, then so is (2) on the grounds that indefiniteness transmits across known equivalences.[22] We cannot, then, quite say that indefinite sentences are semantically plastic. But there is a thesis that is still arguably defensible—call it the *Modified Plasticity Thesis*—according to which, when a sentence in our own language is vague, the canonical means for evaluating it will be via a plastic sentence.

Note, though, that if we adopt strategy B above for handling personal identity issues, then it is not clear that even the Modified Plasticity Thesis is correct. And that is because, on that view, 'person' is vague without being semantically plastic. On that

---

[22] Assuming that definiteness satisfies the distribution principle of normal modal logic and that knowing P implies definitely P, then it just won't do to say (2) is definite but (3) is indefinite. For it is known by me that (2) implies (3). So it is definite that (2) implies (3). By distribution, definitely (2) implies definitely (3). By contraposition, indefinitely (3) implies indefinitely (2).

view, then, sentences such as 'Some person has Clean as a part' are not semantically plastic.[23] Someone who adopted that strategy can endorse the view that vagueness turns on semantico-nomic ignorance, but cannot endorse even the Modified Plasticity Thesis. (The thesis fares even worse when we face up to the proliferation of context-dependence in our language.)

16

Suppose I introduce a predicate 'is a dommal' by a pair of stipulations: let 'is a dommal' be true of dogs and false of non-animals.[24,25] My stipulations do not settle whether

(4) Cats are dommals.

Williamson accepts bivalence here. On his preferred picture, the truth value is determined by a default principle, the two candidates being, roughly,

> P1: A sentence is false unless one has done enough to secure its truth

and

> P2: A sentence is true unless one has done enough to secure its falsehood.

Williamson seems to think that he knows which default principle is the true one, but such an epistemic stance does not seem very plausible to me. Do we really have access, *a priori* or otherwise, to the relative merits of P1 and P2? I reckon it better to combine bivalence with an admission of principled ignorance: we do not know (4) owing to semantico-nomic ignorance.

Imagine a sorites sequence of cases in which, at one end,[26] a community is very firmly in favour of P1, and thus finds 'Cats are dommals', as introduced by a member of their community, obviously false; and at the other end, a community that is very firmly in favour of P2, and thus finds 'Cats are dommals', as introduced by a member of that community, very obviously true. Imagine that we are somewhere in the middle, accounting for the borderline status of 'Cats are dommals' in our mouths.

Do we at last have a case where it is plausible to think that the meaning of 'true' is intensionally shifty? Should we say that the community at one end means one thing by 'true' (governed by P1) and that the community at the other end means another thing by 'true' (governed by P2). Such a reaction would conflate intensional

---

[23] Thanks to Nicolas Silins here.

[24] The dommal example figures in both *Identity and Discrimination* (Oxford, 1990), p. 107 and *Vagueness*, p. 213, though Williamson's take on the example changed between books.

[25] Another interesting kind of case to consider is where symmetric constraints are at work. Suppose I stipulate that Fs are dommals and Gs are gommals, that everything is to be either a dommal or a gommal, and that nothing is to be both a dommal and a gommal. It is dangerous to say that in such cases the terms have no semantic value, since similar phenomena may be prevalent in subtler form in natural language. In the pure case, I would suppose that the epistemicist should say that one of the stipulations fails to hold (it being unknowable which). I shall not pursue the matter here.

[26] Thanks to Timothy Williamson and a member of an Oxford audience for bringing sorites series of this sort to my attention.

with extensional considerations. After all, it is reasonable here to think that each community ought to be deferential to the other. Suppose I am in a community that favours P1. Suppose I look at a community that is heavily in favour of P2. Should I, using 'false' in my mouth, say that 'Cats are dommals' is false, even as uttered by the community of P2 followers? This seems like the wrong reaction. It seems much more natural to suppose that when I say 'Cats are dommals', that is false, and expresses one proposition, but when the community of P2 lovers says 'Cats are dommals', they express a quite different proposition. And that is because the practices of my community determine 'dommal' in my mouth to have the same intension as 'dog', but the practices of that community determine 'dommal' in their mouths to have the same intension as 'animal'. Thus the P1 lovers should only endorse a principle such as P1 when it is suitably restricted to their linguistic locale. No one in the sorites sequence should think that P1, unrestricted, might be a necessary truth. On this conception, which I take to be the most plausible way of thinking about the case, the intension of 'true' is invariant along the sorites sequence. (It is interesting to notice the structural affinities between this case and the discussion of deference above.)

17

Let us turn to the phenomenon of semantico-nomic ignorance itself. The picture is one according to which semantic mechanisms transcend our grasp of them in a deep and principled way. Some will find this deeply intolerable. It is interesting, here, to note a contrast between our attitudes towards mathematics and semantics. In the realm of mathematics, the view that there are evidence-transcendent features of this or that mathematical structure, while hotly debated, is not regarded as extreme or bizarre. Yet analogous views about semantics are apt to strike readers as somewhat outrageous. This reaction is at least in part rooted in a reluctance to recognize semantical properties as natural kinds, joints in nature with distinctive real essences. This 'hyperinflationary' conception of semantical properties would not, of course, suffice to establish the current brand of epistemicism. But it would render the idea of semantico-nomic ignorance rather more palatable and thus help to make my favoured version of epistemicism a going concern.

Let me thus offer a few preliminary motivating remarks in support of hyperinflationism.

Consider first the following frequently voiced concern about epistemicism:

For any predicate, there are ever so many functions from use to extension that 'fit' the use of that predicate. What on earth could it be that makes one of those functions special in such a way that 'true of' should be specially associated with it? Shouldn't we instead make every attempt to do justice to the thought that each of the functions provides an equally good candidate extension?[27]

[27] The relevant notion of 'fit' deployed in such arguments is typically left unexplained, but I take it that talk of an interpretation 'fitting' use of some term is tantamount to a claim that some interpretation provides some reasonably charitable interpretation of our settled dispositions to use a term.

The concern needs refinement. Recalling Kripkenstein,[28] none of us (or hardly any of us) think that quus is an equally good candidate semantic value for 'plus' in the mouths of our earlier selves as plus (where plus and quus are functions that differ only with regard to pairs of natural numbers whose sum we are unable to entertain due to our finitude). But both candidates 'fit' use in some fairly obvious sense, since each interpretation is equally charitable with regard to our actual and counterfactual use of 'plus' (so long as suitable compensating adjustments are made in the interpretation of other pieces of arithmetical vocabulary in which generalization about addition are stated). The lesson generalizes to non-arithmetical vocabulary. Bizarre interpretations can be concocted to 'fit' use which none of us are very inclined to think are acceptable interpretations.

In response to all this, some will go the way of Kripkenstein's sceptical solution,[29] combining a suitably disquotationalist story about our truth predicate with a recognition that there are no deep objective constraints on the acceptability of a translation. The Quine-Field[30] development of this view would have us believe that an ascription of truth to some utterance made by my earlier self (or some interlocutor) has to be relativized to a translation scheme. Semantico-nomic ignorance will have no place in that framework. Indeed, the chasm between such theorists and the current brand of epistemicism is far too vast for me to hold out much hope of closing it here. (For many of us, it is cost enough for that view that it relinquishes all hope of salvaging straightforward truth for claims made by our earlier selves and our fellows.)

Of more interest to me here is the Lewisian reaction to Kripkenstein,[31] one which allows the distinction between natural and gerrymandered properties to do work in the foundations of semantics. Roughly speaking, the picture maintains there are two desiderata on interpretation, namely: (a) The Requirement of Charity: *ceteris paribus*, interpret us so that our claims come out true so interpreted; and (b) The Requirement of Eligibility: *ceteris paribus*, interpret us so that our predicates get assigned more rather than less natural properties as their semantic values.

On Lewis' picture, naturalness of reference is what explains there being a fact of the matter as to what something refers to: more specifically it is the comparative naturalness of one candidate over others that explains why a term determinately refers to that candidate. What makes a plus-interpretation more acceptable than a quus interpretation? Well, while both interpretations may do equally well on the score of charity, one interpretation scores far higher with regard to eligibility. Thus the quus interpretation can be discounted. Consider by contrast the case of 'bald'. Each 'candidate' semantic value is, intuitively, equally natural. So neither charity nor eligibility can break the tie.

There is a second role that naturalness plays in the Lewisian account, namely: naturalness begets semantic stability. If we refer to a highly natural property by some

---

[28] Saul Kripke, *Wittgenstein on Rules and Private Language* (Blackwell, 1982).

[29] See *Wittgenstein on Rules and Private Language*, chapter 3.

[30] See W. V. Quine, *Word and Object*, (MIT Press, 1960) and Hartry Field, *Truth and the Absence of Fact*, (Oxford University Press, 2001).

[31] See David Lewis, 'New Work for a Theory of Universals', and 'Putnam's Paradox', in *Papers in Metaphysics and Epistemology* (Cambridge University Press, 1999).

term *t*, a property which is more natural than properties in the vicinity, then the semantic value of *t* often remain stable despite quite significant shifts in use.

It seems as if the epistemicist has little to gain from a Lewisian distinction between natural and non-natural properties.[32] Such reaction would be far to hasty, I think. Let me explore a few themes in that connection, making vivid those ways in which a Lewisian distinction between natural and non-natural properties can serve as a springboard for hyperinflationism.

(i) Suppose one were to embrace the Requirement of Eligibility, along with an objective distinction between natural and unnatural properties. This is already to recognize the existence of deep principles about semantics that transcend the ken of ordinary folk. Perhaps one might think that we semantic theorists can appreciate the plausibility of such a requirement and even know that it is probably true. But it would be outrageous to suggest that ordinary linguistic competence brings with it knowledge of any such principle. To claim that such a principle is known 'implicitly' by ordinary folk is to court further confusion: to claim that those principles that describe how terms refer are automatically known implicitly by people simply on account of their ability to refer is, in truth, no more plausible than the claim that those principles that describe how we maintain our balance are automatically known implicitly by people simply on account of their ability to avoid falling over. The eligibility requirement does not govern the semantics of ordinary folk by being known implicitly by them. Rather, it governs the semantics of ordinary folk (if it does so at all) by virtue of being a correct (if partial) account of the nature of semantical relations. Accepting the eligibility requirement is, obviously, not yet to accede to epistemicism. But to accept it is to embrace the existence of fundamental semantic mechanisms that are beyond the ken of ordinary folk, a move that should provide real encouragement indeed to the epistemicist.

(ii) The version of epistemicism I am interested in is best served by a metaphysic according to which semantic properties—reference, truth, and so on—are themselves natural kinds, joints in nature. Where a property marks a natural kind, we are open to the thought that it has a 'real essence' that transcends our ordinary understanding of it, even one that in some respects transcends our cognitive capacities. The fundamental metaphysical task of my epistemicist, then, is to render plausible the picture of semantic properties as joints in nature. Does the Lewisian metaphysics help or hinder in this way?

First, some preliminaries. Lewis embraces a plentitude of properties, some of which are metaphysically 'haloed'—that is, natural. More precisely, there is a continuum from more to less natural properties, with perfectly natural properties at one end, and increasing 'gruesomeness' as one moves along the continuum. Which *are* the natural properties? Even supposing that we think that everything supervenes on physics, the issue is not settled. For if we accept a natural property framework, we must choose

---

[32] As noted, it does not, prima facie, help with predicates such as 'bald'. Moreover, Lewis would certainly have thought that there is no uniquely best way to weight charity versus eligibility when it comes to assigning semantic value. If one interpretation scores slightly better on charity, another slightly better on eligibility, then both will likely stand as acceptable interpretations that can be supervaluated over.

between an austere physicalism on the one hand and what might be called an 'emer-gentist' framework on the other. According to the austere physicalist, the perfectly natural properties will only be found at the microphysical groundfloor, relative nat-uralness being a matter of definitional distance from the perfectly natural properties: to calibrate the naturalness of a property, see how complicated the definition of that property would be in a 'canonical' language in which each predicate corresponded to a perfectly natural property.[33] From such a perspective, the property of, say, being a chair will likely turn out hopelessly unnatural, far less natural than, say, the dis-junctive property of being either a hydrogen atom or being fifteen feet from a quark. (Indeed, it wouldn't be surprising if the canonical definition of a chair was infinitary.) The 'emergentist' by contrast, believes that naturalness is not a matter of mere defini-tional distance from the microphysical groundfloor. (This kind of emergentist can of course allow that everything supervenes on the microphysical.) Perhaps being a cat is far more natural than certain properties far more easily definable in Lewis' canonical language. On the emergentist conception of things, there is no algorithm available for calibrating naturalness in terms of a perfect microphysical language.

Now Lewis's own development of the eligibility view certainly provides a hindrance to the picture of semantical joints—joints delineated by semantic predicates them-selves—since his physicalism is an austere one. Though lacking the space to develop the point here, I suspect that we find hereabouts a fundamental tension in his world-view. On the one hand he wishes the eligibility requirement to dispel the spectre of rampant indeterminacy presented by Kripkenstein and Quine. Yet on the other hand, he offers us an austere physicalist account of what eligibility comes to. It does not seem that the two perspectives can be reconciled. How can the eligibility requirement provide some reasonable measure of determinacy for 'gavagai' if the property of being a rabbit turns out to be hopelessly gruesome? Far better, it seems to me, to opt for an emergentist physicalism, in which semantical joints remain a live option.

We can go further. As we have noted, the eligibility framework offers a useful per-spective on the presence and absence of semantic plasticity. Suppose there is a highly natural property that distinguishes itself among the properties that 'fit' the use of a predicate reasonably well. The other 'candidates' are far less natural and so the highly natural property easily wins the semantic competition. Even if the use of the term had been slightly different, the highly natural property would win the competition, since even a slightly lower score *vis-à-vis* a gruesome property on the score of char-ity would be trumped by a far higher score in naturalness. Using language that has recently become popular: the highly natural property serves as a reference magnet. But we have seen above that semantical predicates are not semantically plastic. The reasonable conclusion seems to be that semantical properties are reference magnets and therefore highly natural themselves. Epistemicism is not yet forced upon us, but a suitable metaphysical underpinning for such a view—one replete with semantic mag-nets—is now in place.

In conclusion: I identified two themes in Lewis's own use of natural properties in semantic theory. First, we encountered the idea that a fact of the matter about

---

[33] See Lewis, 'Putnam's Paradox', p. 66.

reference typically requires there being a highly eligible referent. The epistemicist metaphysic I am envisaging denies this. There is a fact of the matter concerning the reference of 'bald', but it is not explained by the naturalness of the referent of 'bald'. (There is, of course, a way in which one might still be able to pay lip-service to the idea that reference to a particular property is begotten by naturalness. For there being a fact of the matter as to what 'bald' refers to is, on this picture, explained by the eminent naturalness of the reference relation itself.)

Second, we found the idea that eligibility begets semantic stability. This idea can be taken on board, pretty much as it stands, by the current brand of epistemicism. 'Bald' is plastic, on account of the non-eligibility of its referent. 'Refers' is stable, on account of the high eligibility of its referent.[34]

18

Do I suppose myself to have offered absolutely decisive arguments for the 'magnet' version of epistemicism over Williamson's? I do not.

Let me end by sketching what I think is the best strategy to pursue for one who repudiates semantic magnets and wishes to stick closely to Williamson's original vision. I will make a number of simplifying assumptions. Let us imagine that there is one community to a world, that sentences are worldbound, that each community speaks a language that is not context-dependent, and that languages contain their own truth predicate.[35]

Let us distinguish domestic ascriptions of a close variant of 'true', which are ascriptions of the predicate to sentences *in the language of that predicate*, from foreign ascriptions, which are ascriptions to sentences in a language that isn't the language of that predicate. Suppose communities C1 in alpha, and C2 in beta, are close variants of each other. Let the *home extension* of a variant of the truth predicate be defined thus:

Home extension: A sentence S is part of the home extension of a close variant v of the truth predicate iff S is in the language that v belongs to and v is true of S.

We can now state a thesis of *domestic stability* for 'true'.

Domestic Stability: 'True' (as we use it) is domestically stable just in case a sentence is part of the home extension of a close variant of 'true' iff 'true' is true of it.

---

[34] Suppose one says that 'true', as a predicate of utterances, is semantically stable. Here is a possible problem. I write down a string of marks. There is a question of the boundaries of the utterance. Suppose some bit of ink, call it Ink, is such that it is borderline whether or not it is part of the utterance. It seems that it may be that while 'true' in my mouth expresses a property that applies to a thing with Ink, a nearby community may go a different way. The problem is not obviously solved by shifting to a picture according to which the fundamental semantical relations concern mental representations, since their boundaries can be vague as well. The concern is not decisive. The earlier discussion is not irrelevant. For example, think back to strategy C above. That can be replayed here. Perhaps the vagueness in this case turns on the vagueness of 'part of'. In that case, there may be no vagueness concerning which object 'true' applies to, only vagueness concerning which are the parts of that object. I am grateful for discussions with Cian Dorr here.

[35] If these assumptions are relaxed, the relevant points can still be made, but are a little harder to both state and see.

Suppose, now that 'true' is domestically stable. At some close variant community C, if our predicate 'true' is true of a sentence S in the language of C, then the variant of 'true' in C will be true of S as well. But this is not yet semantic stability. For it is quite compatible with domestic plasticity that the variant of 'true' that is in C is false of some sentence of *our* language that 'true' is true of. Consider, for example, this scenario: there is a sentence of our language S1, and a sentence of their language S2, such that: (i) the intension of our term 'true' includes both S1 and S2, but (ii) the intension of their variant of 'true' includes S2 but not S1 (and indeed that the intension of their variant of 'false', while not including S2, does include S1). This scenario is quite compatible with domestic stability but not with semantic stability. Now, crucially, domestic stability is enough to ensure that close variants of instances of the T-schema are true. So it turns out that one can save the original Williamson approach from the argument given earlier by combining domestic stability with semantic plasticity.

Let 'true*' be the close variant of 'true', and assume the scenario just described. It is false that, for any variant of 'true*' something is part of the home extension of that variant iff 'true*' is true of it. After all 'true' is a close variant of 'true*' and while S1 is part of the home extension of 'true', 'true*' is not true of it.

Does this mean that while we would be quite correct in uttering the thesis of domestic stability, the nearby community would be making a mistake when uttering the counterpart of that thesis? And wouldn't that make us incredibly lucky? To think so is to miss out on the fact that 'true of' may not be semantically stable.

Let 'true', and 'true of' name our expressions, and 'true*' and 'true of*' be a pair of close variants. Let *being true of* * be the relation that is meant by 'true of*'. In the scenario described, 'true' is true of S1 and S2, 'true*' true of S2 but not S1. Supposing for simplicity that these are all the pertinent facts, we can say that 'true' is domestically stable but that a domestic stability thesis for 'true*' isn't true.

Suppose, however that 'true' is true of* S1 but not S2, and that 'true*' is true of* S1 and S2. Let some sentence S be part of the home extension* of a variant of 'true*' iff S is in the language of the variant and the variant is true* of it. Suppose the community of 'true*' users utters the sentence that we use to express domestic plasticity. We can allow that they would be saying something true (and not merely true*), since they would be saying that if something is a close variant of 'true*', then a sentence is part of the home extension* of that variant iff 'true*' is true* of it.[36] Each community gets to speak the truth by the variants of the domestic plasticity thesis owing to the fact that shifts in 'true' are accompanied by compensating shifts in 'true of'.

Similar considerations can be raised for a community with 'true' and 'says that' as their basic ideology. We certainly want close variants of the schema:

if 'S' says that S then 'S' is true iff S

---

[36] In the toy scenario described, something is a close variant of 'true*' iff it is a close variant of 'true'. In other cases, extra complications will arise via the fact that the close variant relation is not transitive.

to have only true instances. If we now allow that 'true' is not domestically stable, then we are in trouble. For we certainly want disquotational instances of ' 'S' says that S' to be true at close variant communities. Suppose, then, that S2 is true but that ' 'S2' is true*' is false, and that S2 belongs to the language of 'true*'. Then

If 'S2' says that S2 then ('S2' is true* iff S2)

will have a true antecedent and false consequent. Assuming, then, that we want disquotational instances of ' 'S' says that S' to come out true at close variant communities, we must think of 'true' as domestically stable.

But we do not have to think of 'true' as semantically stable. Let 'Talking donkeys are impossible' and 'Talking donkeys are impossible*' be S1 and S2 respectively. Suppose further:

'Talking donkeys are impossible*' says that talking donkeys are impossible.

Suppose 'Talking donkeys are impossible' and 'Talking donkeys are impossible*' are both true. Compatibly with all this I can allow that the variant community speaks the truth in saying:

'Talking donkeys are impossible' is false*,

and

'Talking donkeys are impossible*' is true*.

Suppose the following was true:

'Talking donkeys are impossible' says that* talking donkeys are impossible*.

Then there will be a false instance of the schema:

If a sentence S says that* P then S is true* iff P.

For, given that 'Talking donkeys is impossible*' is true, and ' 'Talking donkeys is impossible' is true*' is false, then

If 'Talking donkeys are impossible' says that* talking donkeys are impossible*, then ('Talking donkeys are impossible' is true* iff talking donkeys are impossible)',

would contain a true antecedent and a false consequent. But we can allow the schema in question to have all and only true instances by allowing for compensating adjustments in the meaning of 'says that'. In particular, we can allow that

' 'Talking donkeys are impossible' says that* talking donkeys are impossible*',

a sentence in the variant language, is false. Once again, we can perfectly well combine domestic stability with semantic plasticity.

19

I have, in effect, tried to develop two competing versions of epistemicism. It should be clear that I have a mild preference for the metaphysically inflationary version. But my main aim has been to map out the conceptual terrain, rather than to advance a view with any confidence.[37] At the very least, I hope that this discussion will serve as a useful springboard for future treatments of semantic plasticity and epistemicism.

[37] After all, the discussion will seem inevitably simple-minded once one takes stock of the literature on semantic paradox. It may turn out to be obligatory in that setting to complicate the picture of a few simple semantic magnets, especially if one wishes for a treatment that is compatible with a commitment (for any given truth predicate) to bivalence. Note, though, that this falls short of allowing some variant of a truth-predicate to be false of a sentence that the truth-predicate is true of. One might thus complicate the picture by (at a first pass) allowing for a range of 'truth' magnets of increasingly wider intensions, but none with competing intensions (in the sense that the intension of some variant of 'true' never includes a possible sentence that is also delivered by the intension of some variant of 'false').

10

Causal Structuralism[1]

How should we think as metaphysicians about the nature of properties? A promising place to begin, perhaps, is with the following observation: properties confer causal powers upon the things that have them. Being spherical confers a capacity to roll. Being hot confers a capacity to make ice melt. Being possessed with mass confers a capacity for gravitationally attracting other massy things. But what is the relationship between properties and the causal powers that they confer?

On one view, it is no part of the essence of a property that it confers the causal powers that it does. Properties have a causal role all right, but the role is utterly contingent. God could have bestowed a very different role upon, say, the property of being negatively charged. Such a view has been embraced, notably, by David Lewis. According to his conception of reality, the causal powers of a property are constituted by its patterned relations to other properties in the particular Humean mosaic that is the actual world.[2] In other worlds, that property will be embedded in different mosaics. In those worlds, then, the laws of nature governing it and thus the causal role it enjoys may be utterly different. In this regard, Lewis is largely following David Hume: Hume clearly thinks of the nature of simple impressions as given by how they are intrinsically and not by their patterned connection to other elements in reality: hence the denial of necessary connections between simple existences. What is missing in Hume is a robust realism about properties.[3] Simple impressions of a certain shade of red do not, literally, have some shade in common. Let us then call Lewis's view the 'neo-Humean view'.

On a second view, some or all of the causal powers of a property are essential to it. It does not go so far, though, as to insist that the causal powers of a thing exhaust its nature. Two possible properties may be distinct and yet the same causal powers be essential to each. Those powers do not, then, constitute an individual essence (where

This chapter has been published in *Philosophical Perspectives*, 15 (2001), 361–78. I am grateful for permission to republish it here.

[1] Thanks to Tamar Gendler, David Lewis, Ted Sider, Zoltan Szabo, Dean Zimmerman, and audiences at Cornell and Notre Dame for helpful discussion.

[2] See, for example, his introduction to *Philosophical Papers Volume II* (Oxford University Press, 1986).

[3] Lewis himself wavers on whether to endorse a full-blooded commitment to universals, conceived as more than set-theoretic entities. In this paper, I shall not be calling the existence of universals into question. I shall leave the reader to judge to what extent the issues are significantly affected by a shift to a set-theoretic conception of properties.

an 'individual essence' is a profile that is necessary and sufficient for some particular thing). Like the first view, this view holds that there is something more to the nature of a property than the causal powers that it confers—the intrinsic nature of the property, if you will—holding that two different internal natures might necessitate the same causal profile.[4] Call this the 'double aspect view'.

On a third view there is, for each fundamental property, a causal profile that constitutes the individual essence of a property. That is, the profile is both necessary and sufficient for each property. (The relevant profile, we should note, may include facts about how a property figures as an effect as well as how it figures as a cause.) Let us call this view 'causal structuralism'. The first two views but not the third holds that there is something to a property—call it its quiddity—over and above its causal profile.[5] Causal structuralism holds that quiddities are a will-o'the-wisp.[6]

Note that causal structuralism is not intended to be applied directly to properties that are neither vehicles of genuine change nor of serious causal explanation. As such, it does not offer a theory of mathematical and logical properties—such as the successor relation and the identity relation. (Also excluded, perhaps are such properties as *overlap* and *part of*, codified by the mereologist.) Nor does it, in the first instance, offer a theory of mere Cambridge properties, whose change does not intuitively amount to real change and which are not, intuitively, the conferrers of bona fide causal powers.[7] Call the candidate domain of properties for which causal structuralism is intended the 'natural properties'. I shall for the purposes of this paper assume that this category is reasonably well understood.

Note also that the causal structuralist needn't hold that all of a thing's causal profile is essential to it. She could consistently claim that some property A has the power to bring about both B and C, but that only the power to bring about B is part of its individual essence. But, *prima facie*, it would seem that to distinguish the essential from the accidental in this way would be to draw lines in an arbitrary way. For now, then, lets focus on a version of causal structuralism according to which the whole causal profile of a property is essential to it.

In what follows, I shall be looking at arguments for and against the following two key theses of causal structuralism: (i) that for any given natural property, there is some causal profile such that having that profile is sufficient for being that property, and

---

[4] Such a view was not uncommon, I believe, in scholastic philosophy. For example, while William of Ockham shows little willingness to think that a thing's nature is exhausted by some causal profile, he claims in Reportatio IV q2 that it is part of the very nature of an effect that it can be produced by one kind of efficient cause and not another.

[5] I am not requiring of the 'quidditist' that he be ontologically serious about quiddities, considered as something metaphysically distinct from the properties themselves.

[6] The causal structuralist will thus see something deeply misleading in Hilary Putnam's distinction between 'a causal description' and 'a canonical description' of a property, where a canonical description is of the form 'the property of being F' while the causal description picks out a property via its causal role. For the causal structuralist, it is the causal description that most deserves the label 'canonical'. See 'On Properties' in *Mathematics, Matter and Method: Philosophical Papers Volume 1* (Cambridge University Press, 1975), p. 316.

[7] Cf. Shoemaker 'Causality and Properties', in *Identity, Cause and Mind* (Cambridge University Press, 1984), p. 207.

(ii) that for any given natural property, there is some causal profile such that having that profile is necessary for being that property. I can't imagine anyone liking the first thesis but not the second.[8] Meanwhile, if one likes the second thesis but not the first, one will likely find the double aspect theory attractive. Finally, if one eschews both theses, one will likely find the neo-Humean position attractive.

Views on quiddities have rough analogues in debates about haecceities. The neo-Humean view on properties resembles a radical haecceitism according to which all the qualities of a particular are contingent to it: only its haecceity is essential. (I could have been a poached egg so long as my haecceity was present.) The double aspect view also has an analogue in the metaphysics of individuals: there are those who believe that certain kind-properties (and perhaps other origin-theoretic properties) are essential to individuals but that one cannot construct an individual essence out of such properties. Any such list would leave out the thisness or haecceity which distinguishes a particular individual from other possibilia of the same kind (and origin). Meanwhile, causal structuralism about properties is analogous to a view according to which some qualitative profile is both necessary and sufficient for being a particular individual and hence that haecceities are a fiction.[9] I shall be exploiting these analogies in due course.

In part one, I shall briefly explore various arguments for causal structuralism, considering semantic, metaphysical, epistemological and methodological considerations that offer *prima facie* support for one or both of its key theses.

In part two, I shall consider five kinds of considerations that apparently militate against causal structuralism, suggesting that none of them are decisive.

In part three, I shall consider an especially worrying kind of objection to causal structuralism, in response to which I shall offer a fresh way to think about that view.

PART ONE: ARGUMENTS FOR CAUSAL STRUCTURALISM

1 Semantic: Referring to Properties

One might think that if a pair of properties are alike in causal role, then one would be unable to single one of them out. And if that is right, then it will be incoherent to think of, say, 'redness' as singling out a property whose causal profile is exactly like some other actual property. In his 'Causal and Metaphysical Necessity' Sydney Shoemaker endorses something like this line of thought, viz: 'And what epistemological considerations show, in the first instance, is that if there are sets of properties whose members are identical with respect to their causal features, we necessarily lack the resources for referring to particular members of these sets.'[10]

---

[8] For one thing, if a number of profiles were sufficient, it would seem that the disjunction of them would be necessary. For another, I wouldn't know how to motivate the thesis that a pair of distinct possible properties could not share some profile once one has denied that the profile is necessary to either.

[9] Cf. Thomas Aquinas, who thought that form in the case of angels, and that form plus a certain originating quantity of matter in the case of corporal substances (where 'quantity of matter' was not conceived of haecceitistically) was sufficient for individuation. See his *On Being and Essence*.

[10] 'Causal and Metaphysical Necessity,' *Pacific Philosophical Quarterly* 79 (1998), p. 66.

This doesn't secure causal structuralism. But it is fair to say that it at least goes part of the way, by undermining the idea that, say, the property of being negatively charged might be distinct from some other property whose actual causal profile is just the same.

The argument's plausibility trades on an equivocation on 'causal feature'. Suppose A and B have the same causal powers. To simplify, lets suppose the following profile is exhaustive: 'A' and 'B' are both 50 per cent probable on C and both, if instantiated, bring about D. Suppose John has C. It is compatible with the profile of C that John has A and not B. Supposing John has A, can John uniquely refer to A? Surely he can. He can do this not by exploiting an asymmetry in the laws governing A and B but rather by an asymmetry in the pattern of instantiation. Thus he can say: 'Let 'Jones' pick out the property that C just caused to be instantiated in me.'

Response: but in the case described, A and B do differ in causal features, viz: A but not B caused the state of affairs 'John's being D'.

Reply: but this isn't the sense of 'causal feature' in question. The causal structuralist does not think it essential to A that it causes John to be D. What is essential to A, according to the causal structuralist, are the causal powers it confer upon whatever thing instantiates it. As the example shows, even if two properties have the same causal profile in the sense relevant to causal structuralism, we may have the capacity to single one of them out. The key point is that a pair of properties may have equivalent causal profiles and yet asymmetrical patterns of instantiation, the latter affording a perfectly good basis for unique reference to one of the pair. The line of thought we are considering is not all that much better than one which claims that if I have the same qualitative profile (relational and non-relational) as some other guy, then I can't single myself out.

2 Metaphysical: Intra-World and Inter-World Variation

It seems to me a general feature of our thought about possibility that how we think that something could have differed from how it in fact is [is] closely related to how we think that the way something is at one time could differ from the way that same thing is at a different time. In possible worlds jargon, the ways one and the same thing of a given sort can differ across worlds correspond to the ways one and the same thing of that sort can differ at different times in the same world. Could I have been a plumber or an accountant instead of a philosopher? The answer seems to be yes—and this goes with the fact that we acknowledge the possibility of a scenario in which something who was exactly as I was at some point in my life undergoes a series of changes resulting in his eventually being a plumber or accountant. Could I have been a poached egg? *Pace* Lewis, the answer seems to be no—and this goes with the fact that our principles of trans-temporal identity rule out the possibility of a scenario in which something starts off as a human being of a certain description and ends up a poached egg.[11]

This line of thought, taken from Shoemaker's 'Causal and Metaphysical Necessity' and aired earlier in his 'Causality and Properties' takes off from the idea that in the case of particulars, the possibility of something's being F is of a piece with the

----

[11] 'Causal and Metaphysical Necessity', pp. 69–70.

possibility of a world which branches from the actual world where that thing is F. It then generalizes that thought to all things. Combine this generalization with the thesis that a property cannot change its causal powers over the course of time and then it follows that there is no world where some property enjoys some power that it actually lacks—since there is no world branching from the actual world where that property enjoys that power.

Here's the motivating principle—call it the 'Branch Principle':

> For every possible world w, there is some time t such that at all times up to and including t, w is exactly like the actual world.[12]

Given that properties can't change their causal powers over the course of time, and assuming that every property has always been around, we can use the Branch Principle to secure at least one of the two key causal structuralist theses (that the causal powers of a property are essential to it).

Should we agree with Shoemaker that, at least in the case of particulars, the Branch Principle is right? If determinism is true, there is no branch world where I am a plumber. So, according to Shoemaker, if determinism is true, things could not have been such that I was a plumber. Even if one thinks that the laws of nature are metaphysically necessary, it does not seem that one wants to say that it is impossible that I be a plumber: for why not admit a world which is a bit different to ours all along where I am a plumber? To focus our intuitions, we might do well to consider a simple world, one where two particles have always existed (either since the beginning of time or for an eternity). Call them A and B. Intuitively, it seems that A could have existed alone. But there is no branch world where A exists alone. So Shoemaker is committed to the thesis that A could not have existed alone. At the very best, such modal commitments are extremely tendentious. It thus does not seem that a promising way to motivate causal essences for properties is by the Branch Principle.

3 Epistemological: An Argument from Recognition

Suppose a property is something over and above its causal profile. We then seem to have conceptual space for something like the following: there is negative charge 1 and negative charge 2 that have exactly the same causal powers. What we call an instance of negative charge is sometimes an instance of negative charge 1, sometimes an instance of negative charge 2. Since 1 and 2 have the same propensities to affect all possible detection mechanisms, there is no way of discriminating 1 and 2. We would now be unable to tell, it seems, whether two groups of particles that we call 'negatively charged' had the same property or else distinct but indistinguishable properties. But this is absurd: we *can* recognize property sharing. So we had better not allow properties to have an individual essence that transcends causal features. Here is Shoemaker:

---

[12] Cf. 'Causality and Properties', p. 218: 'the assertion that a certain particular might have had different properties than it does in the actual world ... implies that there is a possible history 'branching off' from the history of the actual world in which it acquires those properties ...'

.... if two property can have exactly the same potential for contributing to causal powers, then it is impossible for us even to know (or have any reason for believing) that two things resemble one another by sharing a single property.[13]

I myself am not much moved by arguments of this form. We are all familiar with arguments with the following structure: if metaphysics M is right, then there are unlucky worlds where our judgments are way off with respect to subject matter S. Further, there is a natural sense in which, if M is right, we can't tell whether we are in an unlucky world. But we are very knowledgeable about subject matter S. If we can't tell whether we are in an unlucky world, we are not knowledgeable about subject matter S. So metaphysics M is all wrong.

Examples: (i) If possible worlds are Humean mosaics then there are unlucky worlds where everything is just like this and then the world stops altogether at some point in the very near future. Supposing the world is a Humean mosaic, we can't tell whether we are in a world like that. But we know a whole lot about the future. So the world is not a Humean mosaic.

(ii) If metaphysical realism about physical objects is true, then there are unlucky worlds where we are brains in vats. Supposing realism is true, we can't tell whether we are in a brain in a vat world. But we know a whole lot about tables. So we should not be metaphysical realists about physical objects.

(iii) If qualia are superadded features of the world then there are unlucky worlds where everyone else but me is a zombie. . . .

Now its true that there is no stable consensus concerning how to react to these kinds of arguments. We haven't come as far as we'd like when it comes to epistemology. Some of us will go reliabilist and say that so long as we in fact don't live in an unlucky world and unlucky worlds are not nearby, our knowledge is not under threat. Applied to the case at hand, we will say that so long as there is not in fact any real risk of pairs of properties being presented to us that are role-indiscernible, then our knowledge that certain things share certain properties is safe. Some of us will go contextualist and say that once we start doing serious philosophy then we should all be sceptics when it comes to the deployment of 'know' but that the standards are far lower in ordinary contexts—when truth plus moderate credentials are sufficient for the proper applicability of 'know'. Applied to the case at hand, we will say that so long as scientists are lucky enough to be right when they say that the same feature is being presented over and over again and so long as they rule out alternatives that are relevant to *them*, they can say 'I know that is the same feature as that', but that we philosophers, having gotten all worried about duplication of role by different quiddities, should hesitate to claim to 'know'.[14] Some of us will go abductionist and say the simpler and more elegant hypothesis is evidence enough for knowledge, so long as there is belief and truth. Applied to the case at hand, we will say that it is reasonable

---

[13] 'Causality and Properties', p. 215.
[14] Cf. Lewis, 'Elusive Knowledge', *Australian Journal of Philosophy* 74 (1996), 549–567.

to believe in the simpler hypothesis—that there is only one quiddity there, not several—when presented with the negative charge role.

I don't know what to say of these various epistemological reactions. But I do admire a common thread—namely, 'Don't throw out a metaphysical hypothesis on the basis of unlucky world arguments'.[15]

There is one further thing to be said. Once one takes unlucky world arguments seriously then one sees soon enough that causal structuralism doesn't help all that much. Consider the following sceptical scenario. There is negative charge 1 and negative charge 2 that are exactly alike except that were property P which is in fact uninstantiated to be instantiated, charge 1 would interact with it in a different way than charge 2.[16] Such an unlucky world is perfectly possible even if causal structuralism is true. By hypothesis, charge 1 and charge 2 would engage with our sensory mechanisms and other detection devices in the same way. How then can we *know* that there is one property, negative charge, rather than a pair of properties whose causal differences are inscrutable? Insofar as causal structuralism is designed to offer respite against traditional scepticism, its comforts may be largely illusory.

4 Epistemological: Getting to Know a Property[17]

We distinguish, intuitively, between being able to refer to a property and knowing what that property is. Only in the latter case is the nature of the property genuinely revealed to us. One way to try to flesh out this intuitive contrast is via George Bealer's distinction between semantically stable and semantically unstable expressions:

An expression is semantically stable iff, necessarily, in any language group in an epistemic situation qualitatively identical to ours, the expression would mean the same thing. An expression is semantically unstable iff it is possible for it to mean something different in some language group whose epistemic situation is qualitatively identical to ours. . . .

Semantic instability has to do with the effects of the external environment. An expression is semantically unstable iff the external environment makes some contribution to its meaning. Natural kind terms are paradigmatic—'water', 'gold', 'heat', 'beech,' 'elm', etc. Logical, mathematical, and a great many philosophical terms, by contrast, are semantically stable: the external environment makes no such contribution. For example, 'some', 'all', 'and', 'if', 'is identical to', 'is' 'necessarily', 'possibly', 'true', 'valid'; '0', '1' '+' '÷', '∋'; 'property', 'quality', 'quantity', 'relation', 'proposition', 'state of affairs', 'object', 'category', etc. It seems clear that

---

[15] Similar considerations apply to the spectre that there are lots of inert properties that bear heavily on what really resembles what, falsifying most of our overall resemblance judgments as between particulars. See p. 215 of 'Causality and Properties'.

[16] Alternatively: negative charge 1 and negative charge 2 are exactly alike except that negative charge 1 causes epiphenomenon 1 (which is itself causally inert *viz-á-viz* our detection devices) and negative charge 2 causes epiphenomenon 2 (which is similarly inert).

[17] I am grateful to David Lewis here, who proposed something like the argument that follows in discussion at Notre Dame, 1999.

all these are semantically stable: any language group in an epistemic situation qualitatively identical to ours would mean what we mean by these 'formal' expressions.'[18]

The following seems rather natural as a necessary condition on knowing what a property is:

> K1: One knows what a property is only if one has a semantically stable way of referring to it.

On this gloss, users of the term 'water' that are altogether ignorant of chemistry succeed in referring to the property of being H_2O, but, lacking a semantically stable way of referring to that property, do not know what property it is that they are referring to. It is tempting, meanwhile, to suppose that many of us are now in a position to know what property it is that 'water' refers to—thanks to modern chemistry. Indeed, it is tempting in general to suppose that the advance of science has enabled us in many cases not merely to refer to causally efficacious properties but to know what they are. Thus:

> K2: For a large range of causally efficacious properties we are in a position to know what those properties are.

Accept K1 and K2 and we are in a good position to argue against quidditism. For suppose, as the quidditist admits, that a different quiddity could have played the hydrogen role. Then there would seem to be a community whose epistemic situation is qualitatively identical to ours but who refer to a different property by 'hydrogen'. Moreover, there seems to be no imaginable way of achieving a semantically stable way of referring to the property of being hydrogen, given quidditism. Any sort of role-description (whether rigidified or not)[19] will, in a qualitatively identical situation, be used by a counterpart community to pick out a different property. Does this spell real trouble for quidditism? I doubt it. Notice that we do not appear to have a semantically stable way of referring to any given person, such as Saul Kripke. I can't take a cognitive photograph of his haecceity. My ability to refer to him will exploit either intrinsic features that he happens to possess, or else relations that he stand to myself and others, or both. Whatever the means I have of referring to him, it seems clear that there will be a counterpart community that uses the same reference-fixing devices to refer to a different individual. So 'Saul Kripke' is not semantically stable in the relevant sense. Nor is a semantically stable way of referring to Saul Kripke available, even in principle. Does this mean that in the ordinary sense, people do not know Saul Kripke? Surely not. By analogy, the preceeding reflections should not be taken to show that, in the ordinary sense, people do not know which property is picked out by 'hydrogen'. It remains very unclear why it should count as a cost of a

---

[18] 'On The Possibility of Philosophical Knowledge', *Philosophical Perspectives 10: Metaphysics* (1996), p. 23.

[19] In the lingo made popular by David Chalmers's *The Conscious Mind* (Oxford University Press, 1996), the issue is whether there is a primary intension that always delivers the same property for any world, considered as actual, not whether there is a secondary intension that delivers the same property for any world considered as counterfactual.

theory that it reckons most or all causally efficacious properties to fail the demanding standards of knowability set by K1.[20]

5 Methodological: Don't Invoke What You Don't Need

The best case for thinking that the causal profile of a property exhausts its nature proceeds not via the thought 'Well otherwise we wouldn't know a whole lot of what we do know' but rather via the thought 'We don't need quidditative extras in order to make sense of the world.' Let us return to negative charge. All scientific knowledge about negative charge is knowledge about the causal role it plays. Science seems to offer no conception of negative charge as something over and above 'the thing that plays the charge role'. If there were a quiddity that were, so to speak, the role filler, it would not be something that science had any direct cognitive access to, except via the reference fixer 'the quiddity that actually plays the charge role'. Why invoke what you don't need? Unless certain logical considerations forced one to suppose that properties are individuated by something over and above their causal role, then why posit mysterious quiddities?

Bertrand Russell was certainly onto the idea that science reveals nothing beyond causal structure when it comes to fundamental properties when he tells us that while introspection reveals the intrinsic quality of percepts, '. . . we know nothing of the intrinsic quality of the physical world', adding that 'We know the laws of the physical world, in so far as these are mathematical, pretty well, but we know nothing else about it.'[21] Supposing we are unpersuaded by Russell's idea that role transcendent qualities are required to accommodate the facts of introspection, we can easily generate an argument for causal structuralism: why posit from the armchair distinctions that are never needed by science?

I recommend the current line of thought as the most promising for the causal structuralist to pursue. But one should be aware of a trade off: perhaps science doesn't need a robust conception of causation and can get by with thinking of causal laws in a Humean way, as the simplest generalizations over the mosaic. If so, it seems that one needs an independent characterization of the mosaic's pixels. It hardly seems plausible to be a deflationary Humean about causation and yet a causal structuralist about properties. To eschew quiddities on the basis of considerations of scientific economy may serve to saddle us with a view of causality that is far from economical.

PART TWO: ARGUMENTS AGAINST CAUSAL STRUCTURALISM

1 The Circularity Argument

Suppose we define A in terms of its capacity to bring about B and then go on to define B in terms of its capacity to be brought about by A. Isn't the definition circular? Perhaps Bertrand Russell was moved by something like this concern when he wrote:

---

[20] Though it may make trouble for the philosophical idea, in circulation since antiquity, that forms are more fully knowable than particulars, at least where the forms concerned are the causally efficacious properties that are found in the natural world.

[21] *The Analysis of Matter* (Kegan Paul, 1927), p. 264.

There are many possible ways of turning some things hitherto regarded as 'real' into mere laws concerning the other things. Obviously there must be a limit to this process, or else all the things in the world will merely be each other's washing.[22]

Its not so clear that the problem is very serious. We avoided circularities in the functional analysis of belief and desire in the philosophy of mind by defining belief and desire together. Perhaps we can do the same in the functional analysis of properties. Suppose with David Armstrong that causal laws are relations between universals.[23] Assume, then, that a causal necessitation relation N holds between certain universals. At the risk of oversimplification, let us look a simple world where the lawbook for properties instantiated in that world is very small. There are five properties A, B, C, D, E. Here are the laws in the lawbook: ANB, ANC, BND and DNE. Just as functionalism in the philosophy of mind was helped by aid of the Ramsey-Lewis technique for functional analysis, so the same is true of causal structuralism about properties. Take the laws of the lawbook and conjoin them. Replace each property name by a distinct variable ($F^1 \ldots F''$) and prefix each variable by a quantifier. So we have $\exists F^1 \exists F^2 \exists F^3 \exists F^4 \exists F^5 (F^1 N F^2 \wedge F^1 N F^3 \ F^3 N F^4 \wedge F^4 N F^5)$. The lawbook was supposed to be exhaustive. To capture this, we can add such clauses as $\forall F^6 (F^4 N F^6 \supset F^6 = F^5)$. Call this the Ramsified lawbook. We can now articulate causal structuralism very easily, and whatever its merits, we cannot be accused of vicious circularity. Since the variable 'F^1' replaced A, we can give a theory of the individual essence of A by the open sentence you get by dropping the existential quantifer prefixing 'F^1'. According to causal structuralism, it is a necessary truth that anything that satisfies that open sentence is identical to A. Generalizing, the causal structuralist will say that any natural property can be defined by a suitable open sentence delivered by the Ramsified lawbook for that property.

(Note that, according to the causal structuralist, one Ramsifies the lawbook and not the worldbook to get the essence of a property. If I am tall, that does not go into the definition of tallness. What goes into the definition are the laws concerning how tallness relates causally—as cause and effect—to other properties. Note also that the approach assumes what the Humean abhors—that the causal relation is fundamental. But that is to be expected of causal structuralism in any case. Note finally that the laws in the lawbook may be considerably more complicated that the simple single property to single property laws discussed above; but this makes little difference to the viability of the Ramsification strategy.)

2 Combinatorialism

On one attractive picture of modality, you get possible worlds by mixing and matching the intrinsic parts of worlds. Call this Humean combinatorialism. Here is David Lewis's version of that view: 'To express the plenitude of possible worlds, I require

---

[22] Russell's concern, taken from *The Analysis of Matter*, p. 325, is voiced by Simon Blackburn ('Filling in Space' in *Essays in Quasi-Realism* (Oxford University Press, 1993), 255–258), who adds that the point is particularly pressing if one uses a possible worlds account of powers).

[23] See his *What is a Law of Nature?* (Cambridge University Press, 1983).

a *principle of recombination* according to which patching together parts of different possible worlds yields another possible world.'[24]

Lewis goes on to deploy this principle against the thesis that is common to causal structuralism and double aspect theory:

Another use of my principle is to settle—or as opponents might say, to beg—the question whether laws of nature are strictly necessary. They are not; or at least laws that constrain what can coexist in different positions are not. Episodes of bread-eating are possible because actual; as are episodes of starvation. Juxtapose duplicates of the two, on the grounds that anything can follow anything; here is a possible word to violate the law that bread nourishes. So likewise against the necessity of more serious candidates for fundamental laws of nature.[25]

The principle of recombination offers a very elegant theory of possibility space. Pity to abandon it if there is nothing elegant to put in its place by way of expressing the plenitude of possibilities. But there is.

Let us replace Humean combinatorialism by Structural Combinatorialism. I sketched a simple lawbook above, containing five properties and four laws. Consider the Ramsified lawbook corresponding to that simple lawbook, the former sufficing to capture the content of the latter, according to the causal structuralist. That Ramsified lawbook expresses five possible properties. What other properties are possible? According to the Structural Combinatorialist, any logically consistent Ramsified lawbook expresses a possible set of properties. The structural combinatorialist can work with his own fundamental principle of plenitude—one that governs properties. It corresponds to the plenitude of consistent lawbooks. He can then build a theory of possible worlds upon that principle of plenitude. I see no reason for thinking that the result will be inelegant or unsatisfying.

3 Experience

One might instinctively react to causal structuralism by worrying that it fails to capture the colour of the world. Taken literally, the problem is not so pressing. After all, it is not so unreasonable to suppose that a property counts as redness so long as it has the appropriate capacity to cause sensations of the right sort. But how about the sensations themselves? One might think that, say, pain (or phenomenal red), is constituted by an intrinsic *thusness* and not simply by its causal role. On this way of thinking, something could duplicate the causal role of pain in its entirety and yet not *be* pain.

Clearly, part of what held Russell back from full blooded causal structuralism are considerations such as these, as is evidenced by his view that while 'we do not know their laws so well as we would wish,' we do know the intrinsic quality of percepts (which are in turn 'part of the physical world') by introspection.[26] One way to push this line of thought is via zombie thought experiments: there are, it seems, possible worlds with zombies that are structurally isomorphic to us. The zombies possess states with the right causal role but which lack any qualitative character. The difference

---

[24] *On The Plurality of Worlds* (Blackwell, 1986), pp. 87–88.
[25] Ibid, p. 91.
[26] *The Analysis of Matter*, p. 264.

between a zombie and us, on the current conception, is that the quiddities have been switched. Quiddity switching is what turns the light on and off, so to speak.[27] If that is right, only the neo-Humean and double aspect views remain as serious options.

It would be silly to try and engage at length with this objection in a survey such as this one. It is clear enough, though, what the causal structuralist should say in broad outline: how is one so sure that it is some intrinsic, role-transcendent quiddity that is responsible for consciousness? Consider me, and suppose I am in pain. Assume that I do have evidence-transcendent quiddities and that God were now to switch the quiddity that underlies my pain for another one—makes the quiddities dance, as it were. I would still believe that I am in pain, as the causal propensities with respect to my belief system would be unchanged. There are two perspectives here. On one perspective, the experiences dance with the quiddities—its just that we don't notice that pain has been replaced by ersatz pain. On another perspective, the experiences do not dance with the quiddities: we remain in pain and hence do not start making introspective mistakes when the quiddity switch occurs. Is it so clear that the first perspective is correct? I believe that the jury is still very much out on this issue.

(Note that even if one does believe in role-transcendent properties—as, say, Lewis does—this needn't be because one thinks that experience is role-transcendent. Lewis's perfectly natural properties are role-transcendent—but Lewis's reason for positing role transcendent properties has far more to do with his combinatorialism than with any deep intuition that introspection brings us into acquaintance with something role-transcendent. Analogy—there are plenty of people who believe in haecceities but who don't believe that self-consciousness brings us into special acquaintance with a peculiar sort of me-ness or you-ness that serves as the individual differentium.)

4 Categorical and Dispositional Properties

We've all learned that dispositional properties have a categorical basis. But isn't this violated by causal structuralism? Frank Jackson rejects the view that properties are defined by causal role for exactly this reason: 'This, to my way of thinking, is too close to holding that the nature of everything is relational cum causal, which makes a mystery of what it is that stands *in* the causal relations.'[28]

I find it hard to see how to make the worry compelling. Suppose, to parody Jackson, we worried about a necessity of origins thesis for substances in the following way: 'This to my way of thinking, is too close to holding that the nature of particulars is relational cum causal, which makes a mystery of what it is that stands *in* the causal relations.' That objection doesn't seem very compelling at all.

Its true enough that we wish to distinguish between the second order property of, say, being a property that causes headaches and those first order properties which

---

[27] Note that if one wishes to suppose that the quiddity of a property is always something like experiential character, then one will be driven to a sort of panpsychism and will not tolerate the possibility of zombies after all. Quiddity switching may make for spectrum inversion but cannot, on this view, turn the lights off.

[28] *From Metaphysics to Ethics* (Clarendon Press, 1998), p. 24.

instantiate that second order property. But the causal structuralist has no reason to deny distinctions like that. Consider, for example, the open sentence from a Ramsified lawbook that defines a property. There is a property that the open sentence expresses. And there is a different property that is the unique realizer of that open formula. No need for collapse.

Perhaps the worry is that categorical bases are supposed to be without any relational features essentially. It is true enough that if this is a requirement, then both the double aspect theorist and the causal structuralist are in trouble. But it seems that the requirement needs some sort of motivation rather than being put forward as an unargued axiom. Note also that the categorical basis would, *prima facie*, be a poor explanans for the disposition as explanandum, if the categorical basis did not drag any causal powers along with it.[29]

5 Hyperstructuralism

According to the hyperstructualist, one defines a property by taking a lawbook and Ramsifying through the whole thing entirely, so that every relational and non-relational predicate is replaced by a variable. This means that the relation of causal necessitation is itself replaced by a variable. The hyperstructuralist claims that the resulting Ramsified sentence (which, note, says nothing explicitly to the effect that its subject matter is causality) is sufficient to provide definitions of each predicate in the original vocabulary that figured in the lawbook, including the relation of causal necessitation.

I take it that none of us are hyperstructuralists.[30] None of us think that the truth conditions of the original lawbook is given by the purely formal sentence that the hyperstructuralist obtains by comprehensive Ramsification. So it looks like the content of the predicate 'causes' cannot be recovered by Ramsifying through the theory in which 'causes' figures. Why then believe—as the causal structuralist believes—that other predicates can be defined by the Ramsey–Lewis technique? What's so special about causality?

The question is fair enough. But it is not clear that the causal structuralist is devoid of an answer. After all, it is part of the metaphysical *picture* of causal structuralism that the structural properties of a system have a different status than the nodes of the structure. Causality is not the only property that turns out to be primitive and indefinable—probably the same goes for identity and for various mathematical and mereological properties. You may not like the picture. But it does not seem altogether arbitrary or *ad hoc* to treat the structure of the world (the 'form' of the world) in a different way to the nodes in the structure (the 'matter' of the world). It thus does not seem to me then to be altogether ad hoc or arbitrary to endorse causal structuralism but to resist hyperstructuralism.

---

[29] On this last point, see Blackburne's 'Filling in Space'. It is of course not decisive against the Humean—what the latter thinks as the appropriate explanation for some dispositional property is a combination of one or more perfectly natural properties *together with* some suitable set of laws.

[30] Especially if identity, mathematical relations (such as the successor relation) and mereological relations (such as being a part of) disappear into variables.

PART THREE: SYMMETRICAL ROLES–TWO VARIETIES OF CAUSAL STRUCTURALISM

The following seems to me to be a perfectly possible causal structure: there are four properties, call them A, B, C, D. Here are the laws governing them: AnC, BnC, (A and B)nD. It is *crucial* to this structure, note, that A and B are distinct. Their coinstantiation has different effects (the addition of D to the world) than is produced by either being instantiated alone. Not only are such causal structures intuitively possible; the structural combinatorialism that I sketched and which seems to me to be an elegant principle of plenitude for properties militates in favour of the their possibility.[31]

Suppose such a structure is possible. That spells trouble for causal structuralism. According to that view, the individual essence of a property can be given via the Ramsified lawbook. But that is no way for that to work here. Ramsify the lawbook and there is nothing to distinguish the pair of properties corresponding to 'A' and 'B' even though the structure does require that there *be* a pair and not just one. The situation is similar to that besetting the most straightforward version of anti-haecceitism, according to which some purely qualitative profile provides the individual essence of each individual substance. That view famously got into trouble when confronted with Max Black's symmetrical world[32] (and Scotus's duplicate angels),[33] which seemed to require that there be two substances whose qualitative profile is exactly the same. Anti-haecceitism of that sort is troubled by intra-world duplication of qualitative profiles. Causal structuralism of Shoemaker's sort is troubled by intra-world duplication of causal profiles. If causal structuralism is the view that each property has a unique individual essence consisting of a causal profile, then that view seems to be wrong.

David Lewis has provided an alternative way of thinking about anti-haecceitism than the one adumbrated above: Here is his favoured conception of haecceitism:

If two worlds differ in what they represent de re concerning some individual, but do not differ qualitatively in any way, I shall call that *a haecceitistic difference*. Haecceitism, as I propose

---

[31] Admittedly, what would be nicer still would be a sketch of how circumstances in the actual practice of science might compel the positing of a symmetrical structure such as the one above (embedded, presumably, in a more complex structure that preserves the symmetry between A and B). Mill's methods of agreement and difference certainly have no straightforward bite here, since the reidentification of circumstances is in this context epistemologically problematic. We normally discriminate properties by their differential impact on our sensory organs or on some detection instrument. But in the case described there is no straightforward basis for such discrimination. Where I posit a structure like the one above, you may posit a structure whereby there are four properties such that A N C and B N C and B N D. Nevertheless, the symmetrical structure does seem perfectly possible and well-motivated by proper principles of plenitude. It strikes me as *ad hoc* to deny its possibility

[32] 'The Identity of Indiscernibles,' in *Problems of Analysis*, (Routledge Kegan Paul, 1984), 80–92.

[33] See Ordinatio II d3 p1 q7.

to use the word, is the doctrine that there are at least some cases of haecceitistic difference between worlds.[34]

Lewis is clear that on this gloss, anti-haecceitism can allow intra-world duplication of things with the same qualitative profile. Max Black's world is perfectly possible according to this brand of anti-haecceitism. What is not possible is the existence of two qualitatively indiscernible worlds such that the *de re* truths concerning one are different from the *de re* truths concerning the other.

One might think that once the possibility of Black's world has been conceded, haecceitism quickly follows. For isn't there one world where one of the balls exists alone and a different world where the other ball exists alone in a qualitatively duplicate state? Here is Lewis:

I might have been one of a pair of twins. I might have been the first-born one, or the second-born one. These two possibilities involve no qualitative difference in the way the world is. Imagine them specified more fully: there is the possibility of being the first-born twin in a world of such-and-such maximally specific qualitative character. And there is the possibility of being the second-born twin in exactly such a world. The haecceitist says: two possibilities, two worlds. They *seem* just alike, but they must differ somehow. They differ in respect of 'cross-identification'. . . I say: two possibilities, sure enough. And they do indeed differ in representation *de re*: according to one, I am the first-born twin, according to the other I am the second-born. But they are not two worlds. They are two possibilities within a single world. The world contains twin counterparts of me, under a counterpart relation determined by intrinsic and extrinsic qualitative similarities (especially, match of origins). Each twin is a possible way for a person to be, and in fact is a possible way for me to be.[35]

Lesson: utilizing Lewisian counterpart theory we can resist multiplying worlds whenever we have multiple possibilities for a thing to be. In so resisting we can allow intra-world qualitative duplication without taking on haecceitism.

What is interesting is that there is a version of causal structuralism that exactly mimics Lewis's approach. Let a structural description of a world be a description which describes the world using certain structural primitives—like part/whole and causal necessitation—and which otherwise uses merely the resources of logic (if you want to be haecceitist about things but causal structrualist about properties, then throw in all the individual constants corresponding to each thisness). The causal structuralist can map out his position in the following way:

If two worlds differ in what they represent *de re* concerning some property, but do not differ structurally in any way (i.e. have the same structural description), I shall call that *a quidditistic difference*. Anti-structuralism is the doctrine that there are at least some cases of quidditistic difference between worlds. I say that there are no quidditistic differences between worlds.

Lewis' anti-haecceitist can allow that there is intra-world duplication of some qualitative profile. My causal structuralist can allow that there is intra-world duplication of a causal profile. One might think that one can generate quidditistic differences out

[34] *On The Plurality of Worlds*, p. 221.   [35] Ibid., p. 231.

of such duplication. Take the symmetric structure that I described earlier. Isn't there the possibility that there are two things that instantiate A and one thing instantiates B and another possibility where two things instantiate B and one thing instantiates A? The lesson learned earlier can be applied here: don't multiply possible worlds whenever one has a multiplication of possibilities.

Lewis' anti-haecceitism does not either require a deep answer to the question: 'Which elements of a thing's qualitative profile are essential to it?' His counterpart theory allows context-sensitive flexibility when responding to such questions. Neither does my causal structuralist need treat as deep the question 'Which element's of a property's causal profile are essential to it?' A counterpart theory can allow context-sensitive flexibility here too. What is crucial to this brand of causal structuralism is that it does not allow that worlds can be alike structurally and yet different concerning what is true *de re* of the properties in them.

Suppose one doesn't like counterpart theory and yet does believe in the possibility of Black's world of two numerically distinct but qualitatively duplicates balls. As I see it, there is then no resisting haecceitism. Suppose one doesn't like counterpart theory and yet does believe in the possibility of pairs of properties with symmetrical causal roles. As I see it, there is then no resisting anti-structuralism. But symmetric structures do seem eminently possible. So counterpart theory combined with a rejection of quidditistic differences between worlds is certainly the best way to pursue the causal structuralist's vision of reality. I leave it to the reader to judge whether that vision is worth pursuing.

APPENDIX: MODEST STRUCTURALISM

In replying to a version of this paper, Sydney Shoemaker noted the availability of a more modest version of causal structuralism than any discussed in the body of this paper (evincing some temptation to embrace it rather than any of the more radical versions of causal structuralism). Lest readers assume that his writings are unequivocally committed to full-blooded causal structuralism, let me sketch the modest view. Let the Shoemaker sentence for a target property P be obtained as follows: take the lawbook, conjoin it, and replace each occurrence of 'P' by a variable v (leaving the other property names as they are). The result is an open sentence. The modest structuralist claims that the open sentence produced by this procedure individuates the target property. Notice that the symmetric causal structure that I described is no problem at all for the modest structuralist. After all, the Shoemaker sentence for B (as it figures in that structure), will include some such clause as 'in combination with A, suffices for D', while the Shoemaker sentence for A will not say that. Thus we have a kind of 'anti-reductive' structuralism that is much more tolerant in that it can make room for symmetric structures. This modest version of causal structuralism will still put some constraints on possibility space: it will not allow the following pairs of lawbooks: (1) AⁿB, BⁿC (and that's all) (2) AⁿD, DⁿC (and that's all), since the Shoemaker sentence associated with B and D would be the same. Insist that these are different and genuinely possible lawbooks and the thesis of modest structuralism—that the Shoemaker sentence for a property individuates it—is violated. From the perspective of the causal structuralism examined in this paper, modest structuralism risks being far too permissive with regard to possible structures of properties. After all, modest structuralism can allow a distinction between the following pairs of lawbooks: FᴺG (and that's all), HᴺI (and that's all), since each of the properties F, G, H and I will have a different Shoemaker sentence associated with them. The radical structuralist will think that there is no such multiplicity of possibilities.

If one were to put an intuitive gloss on what modest structuralism amounts to, I would suggest it is this: there are quiddities, though one can get a necessary and sufficient condition for being a particular quiddity in terms of its causal relations to other quiddities. Whether this attempt to find a middle ground between the merits of causal structuralism and a metaphysic of quiddities has much going for it, I leave as a question for another time.

11

Quantity in Lewisian Metaphysics[1]

In the pages that follow, I present and discuss four ideas about fundamental quantities which appear in the work of David Lewis. Together they provide an overview of his thinking on the topic and a useful template for thinking about the metaphysics of fundamental quantities. I shall not be challenging any of the four ideas outright: some form of each may very well turn out to be defensible. But important caveats and qualifications are in order, lest the ideas be misapplied or their implications exaggerated. I shall begin with the most straightforward of the four ideas, and proceed in order of increasing complexity. I shall not speculate on the range of fundamental quantities. It will suffice for my current purposes to focus on a single example: the case of mass.

IDEA ONE: MASS IS INTRINSIC

The mass of an object is intrinsic to it: any possible duplicate of that object will share the same mass.

This view is not beyond dispute. Some have proposed to treat certain *relations* between objects as foundational to mass and other quantities. So, for example, Hartry Field contends that the relations of mass-congruence (4-place) and mass-betweenness (2-place) are basic, while mass is derivative.[2] On such a picture, certain representational constraints are assumed for the numerical scale (for example—that if xy is mass-congruent to wz, then the difference between the numbers assigned to x and y should match the difference between the numbers assigned to w and z) and then representation theorems, familiar from measurement theory, yield results concerning which sets of numerical assignments will be faithful to the relevant pattern of relations.[3] The assignment of numerical mass magnitudes to individual objects is then explained in terms of the pattern of such relations.

[1] Thanks to Frank Arntzenius, Jeremy Butterfield, Tamar Gendler, and Ted Sider for helpful comments and discussion.
[2] See Hartry Field, *Science Without Numbers* (Blackwell 1980) Chapter 7. Note that Field's use of 'intrinsic' in that chapter does not quite match Lewis's. Field uses 'intrinsic explanation' for explanations that proceed without making use of functions to causally irrelevant entities such as real numbers. An intrinsic explanation of a particle's behaviour, in this sense, might proceed by adverting to its relations to other particles.

[3] The particular numerical values chosen will, of course, reflect arbitrary choice in coordinate system: depending on the representational constraints certain transformations of those coordinates

Views that give relations between mass-bearing objects a foundational role—call these views *relationalist*—would appear to render extrinsic such facts as those expressed by statements of the form '*x* has mass of *n* kilograms'.[4] On such a picture, the mass of a point particle is explained in terms of relations between that particle and other things, relations that are not in turn grounded in intrinsic properties. (This is especially clear if one adopts a model—favoured by Lewis—according to which the intrinsic character of a thing is fixed by its perfectly natural monadic properties: on the relationalist picture, there are no such properties corresponding to mass-ascriptions.)[5]

The best-known objection to relationalism maintains that the posited relations can ground the assignment of numerical mass values only on the assumption that there are enough concrete relata.[6] Suppose only two particles existed: then the pattern of distribution of, say, mass-betweeness and mass-congruence could hardly ground a framework in which each object was assigned to some locus on the familiar scale. The worry is a serious one for most of us, though for those who endorse modal realism it is less pressing: in that case relations to otherworldly entities could play the required role.[7]

A second line of objection comes from considering a class of thought experiments familiar from disputes about space-time absolutism. It seems, for example. that there could be a pair of worlds w_1 and w_2, such that the same pattern of mass-betweeness and mass-congruence relations obtains between the objects in w_1 and their counterparts in w_2, yet the mass of each particle in w_1 is double that of its counterpart in w_2. From a relationalist point of view, it seems difficult to make sense

---

will preserve faithfulness. For example, the natural representational constraints for the Field framework tell us that if a set of numerical assignments is faithful, the set obtained by squaring each of those assignments will not be, but that the set obtained by multiplying each member of the original set by some number n will be. The central texts for the theory of measurement are R. Luce, D. Krantz, P. Suppes, and A. Tversky's three-volume *Theory of Measurement* (Academic Press, New York, 1971, 1989 and 1990). For technically informed treatments by philosophers, see Field, op. cit, and Brent Mundy, 'The Metaphysics of Quantity,' *Philosophical Studies* 51, 29–54 and 'Quantity, Representation and Geometry', in P. Humphreys (ed.), *Patrick Suppes: Scientific Philosopher* Vol 2 (Kluwer, 1994), 59–102.

[4] Of course the theory does not make *all* facts pertaining to mass extrinsic. In the case of a complex object, it may be intrinsic to that object that it has two proper parts which are mass congruent to some distinct pair of proper parts.

[5] See Lewis, 'New Work For a Theory of Universals', *Papers In Metaphysics and Epistemology* (Cambridge University Press, 1999), p. 27.

[6] See for example, Brent Mundy, 'The Metaphysics of Quantity', p. 32.

[7] Note that Lewis himself entertains fundamental external relations holding between entities from different worlds. See *On The Plurality of Worlds* (Blackwell, 1986), pp. 77–78 on like-chargedness. He offers this as one reason to stick to (at least analogically) spatio-temporal relations—rather than fundamental external relations in general—in his definition of what it is for objects to belong to the same world. Note that the like-chargedness hypothesis raises the spectre of a pair of worlds that are alike in how they are intrinsically, but for which different qualitative descriptions are true (consider a world with a lonely negatively charged simple and one with a lonely positively charged simple). This disrupts the standard picture of the relation between the intrinsic profile of a world and its qualitative representation. Thanks to Lewis Powell here.

of such possibilities. As above, modal realism offers a way out: if one is in a position to exploit cross-world facts about mass-betweeness and mass-congruence, then the relevant possibilities can easily be accommodated in a relationalist framework.

In Field's hands, relationalism is a step towards nominalism. By taking the basic congruence relations as holding not between mass properties but instead between objects, the door to nominalism is opened wider. But what of those philosophers for whom nominalism is anathema? Qua philosophers, we will have little to counteract the strong prima facie plausibility of the intrinsicality idea.[8] Of course, physics may have surprises in store. One recent popular text informs us that for the string theorist 'extradimensional geometry determinates fundamental physical attributes like particle masses and charges that we observe in the usual three large space dimensions of common experience.'[9] Such radical proposals may very well force conceptual reorientation on matters of intrinsicality. Putting nominalist programs aside, the only good arguments for mass being extrinsic are likely to be strongly empirical ones.

IDEA TWO: MASS IS LOCAL

Lewis has boldly conjectured that 'all there is to the world is a vast mosaic of matters of particular fact.'[10] As applied to mass, this tells us that the mass properties of objects are fixed by the spatio-temporal pattern of instantiation of intrinsic properties by point-sized bits of the world. Following Lewis, we might spell this out more carefully in terms of a supervenience thesis. In Lewis's favoured formulation—the doctrine he dubs 'Humean Supervenience'—every pair of worlds 'within the inner sphere of possibility' that are local duplicates are duplicates simpliciter.[11] As applied to mass, this gives us the thesis:

M1: Any pair of inner sphere worlds that are duplicates with respect to local matters of fact are duplicates with respect to mass-facts.

What is the inner sphere of possibility? On Lewis's initial formulation, it is the sphere embracing those worlds that do not contain fundamental—or 'natural'—properties and relations that are absent from the actual world: those worlds that contain no 'alien intrusions' relative to the actual world.[12]

There is reason to worry about M1. Consider a world where point-sized particles have zero mass and various continua of them have positive mass. (This would not, of course, violate the constraint of countable additivity on mass, since the objects with positive mass have continuum many point sized parts.) Call such a world a *continuum world*. At such a world the mass of the continua would not supervene on the local facts about mass—any more than the length of a line supervenes on the lengths of

---

[8] We may note in passing that the thesis of determinism—according to which the intrinsic state of the world at any time (plus the laws) fixes the future—will be a non-starter on the view just sketched, since the mass of a thing at a time turns on its relations to things at other times.

[9] Brian Greene, *The Elegant Universe* (Vintage 2000).

[10] Introduction to *Philosophical Papers Volume II* (Oxford University Press, 1986), ix.

[11] Ibid., x.   [12] Ibid., x.

the points that compose it.[13] So if continuum worlds fall within the inner sphere, M1 is false.[14]

Perhaps physics will tell us that continuum worlds cannot be built of the fundamental properties and relations that are instantiated in this world, and hence contain alien properties.[15] Or perhaps there are alternative construals of 'inner sphere' according to which continuum worlds would lie outside of it.[16] But as things stand, M1 seems shaky.

Given this, we might be tempted to move to a slightly weaker supervenience claim. Let us say that a world is a local and occupation duplicate of this world iff there is a one-to-one map from the objects in that world to the objects in this world that preserves facts of spatio-temporal relation, facts of mereology, facts of occupation and facts about the instantiation of intrinsic properties by point-sized bits of the world. We are then in a position to articulate the following locality thesis:

M2: Any local and occupation duplicate of this world is a duplicate with respect to mass facts.

Assuming that modern physics is right to reject continua, worlds containing them are irrelevant to M2, since none of them are local and occupation duplicates of this world (at least assuming that there are no worlds where continuous regions of space-time themselves have mass). Of course, theses like M2 are not adequate to the motivations of Humean Supervenience.[17] Nevertheless, pending some suitable refinement of the latter proposal my tentative verdict is that M2 is the locality thesis of choice for mass.

---

[13] Which is not to say any length-like relation must be primitive, of course. For instance, in line with mathematical physics of the last 75 years, we might opt for a path-dependent notion of spatiotemporal distance, according to which distance is fundamentally path-relative. Then distance along a path, intuitively speaking, amounts to the sum of the lengths of all the infinitesimal segments of that path—more formally, it equals the path integral of the metric tensor.

[14] One could try to rescue locality by claiming that at such a world there would be fundamental mass-density properties. But on the assumption that at this world the facts of mass are more natural than those of mass-density, the claim that mass-density is fundamental at all continua worlds is somewhat dubious. (It is also worth remembering that a world might contain a *mixture* of continua made of zero-mass pointy parts, and finite mass point particles.) Note in this connection that Lewis does not think that perfect naturalness is a contingent property of a property. (See *Plurality of Worlds*, p. 60, n. 44).

[15] Consider also worlds—if there are such—containing extended simples with mass. We might note in this connection that some versions of string theory replace point particles with very small but extended simples.

[16] Elsewhere, and for rather different reasons, Lewis has entertained imposing further restrictions on the inner sphere beyond the 'no alien intrusions' dictum. In that context, he offered no specific proposal as to how such a restriction might be articulated. I leave it to others to contrive some suitable restriction that is both non-gerrymandered and also true to the motivations of the original. See 'Humean Supervenience Debugged,' in *Papers in Metaphysics and Epistemology*, p. 226.

[17] Suppose that the actual distribution of local matters of fact guaranteed the actual distribution of pain, but that some other distribution of charge and mass was compatible with either the presence or absence of pain—even restricting our attention to worlds free of alien intrusions. Lewis would count such a scenario as a counterexample to Humean Supervenience (and not a reason to fiddle with its formulation). But it would not be a counterexample to any pain-locality thesis modelled after M2.

IDEA THREE: MASS HAS ITS CAUSAL POWERS
ACCIDENTALLY

Mass properties have a causal role that is encoded by various laws of nature. Lewis, following Hume, holds that the causal roles of the fundamental properties are not essential to them: a given mass property could have lacked any given feature of its causal role.

My goal here is not to challenge this idea, but to stress that its implications may not be all that they seem.[18] Not all relations between properties are causal, and not all properties of properties encode their causal role. Take some primitive monadic intrinsic mass property. Clearly, such a property has certain of its properties and relations necessarily: it is necessarily monadic, and it is necessarily not identical to the number 6. But there may be other somewhat more interesting properties and relations—ones that are broadly structural but not causal—that are essential to the property. Take the additivity properties concerning mass—say that the sum of 15 kgs and 5 kgs is 20 kgs. One might think that there is a basic additivity relation between the three associated monadic properties that holds necessarily (and that constrains our numerical assignments). Similarly for congruence relations mentioned above; and so on.

Suppose such structural relations did hold of necessity. Then, even given the accidentality of causal relations, we should be careful about making claims like 'The natural property associated with being 15 kgs could have played the role actually played by 120 watts'. Part of the role, broadly construed, of being 15 kgs is its additivity relations to other mass properties. We are in no position to think that these relational features of that mass property could have been enjoyed by 120 watts, even given a broadly Humean attitude to causal facts. Similarly, for example, one might think that the bifurcation of charge into positive and negative is not a causal feature at all, but rather a non-causal structural feature that, along with those just mentioned, makes for various necessities in the realm of charge. Once again, if this is right, then claims such as that mass and charge could 'switch' need to be handled with considerable caution.

The non-causal structural constraints on the magnitudes put constraints upon which causal roles are possible. The laws of nature, if contingent, make contingent selections from the available roles. The distinction between contingent features of causal role and those mandated by non-causal structure is not always luminous. There can be surprises. Consider the following toy example. It might seem possible that the acceleration that results from application of a force F could be proportional not to the mass of the object accelerated, but to the square of the mass. But suppose that, just as it is of the nature of mass that the mass of the fusion of two non-overlapping objects x and y is the sum of the mass of x and the mass of y, so it is in the nature of force that the force on the fusion of two non-overlapping objects x and y is the vector sum of the forces on x and y. If so, and if we suppose that the acceleration resulting from

---

[18] Some of the relevant issues are explored in 'Causal Structuralism', this volume.

a force F is proportional to the square of the mass, we would find ourselves presented with the rather unwelcome conclusion that when a force F is applied to each of two halves of an object, the fusion of two halves of an object will accelerate at a different rate to each of its halves.

In conclusion, while the causal role of mass may be contingent, the modal freedom that this bestows on mass may be significantly less than one might think.

IDEA FOUR: MASS IS ELITE

Lewis famously held that not all properties are metaphysically speaking on a par: a small subset of the properties—the perfectly natural ones—enjoy an elite status, marking out the fundamental joints of the world. The rest of the properties are (to varying degrees) less natural, more gerrymandered. On Lewis's picture, the contrast is not an artifact of our systems of representation and classification: it is part of the objective structure of reality.

The business of physics, according to Lewis, is to provide a list of the perfectly natural properties. In *On the Plurality of Worlds*, Lewis tells us that physics has its 'short list of "fundamental physical properties": the charges and masses of particles, also their so-called "spins" and "colors" and "flavor", and maybe a few more that have yet to be discovered.' Elsewhere, he writes in a similar vein: 'the most plausible inegalitarianism seems to be one that gives a special elite status to the "fundamental physical properties": mass, charge, quark color and flavor. . .'[19]

This elite list is then put to work on a variety of fronts. Here are three (there are others). First, the list helps to characterize the 'inner sphere' crucial to his statement of Humean Supervenience: while worlds within the inner sphere may instantiate certain sorts of properties that are absent from the actual world, they do not instantiate *elite* properties that are so absent. Second, the list is used to provide an account of duplication and, co-ordinately, of intrinsicality: objects are duplicates iff they (and their parts) are alike with respect to the elite properties (and the elite relations holding between their parts); a property is intrinsic iff for any pair of possible duplicates, both or neither have it.[20] Third, elite properties figure in Lewis's favoured account of laws of nature: the laws are the simplest and most informative generalizations, where simplicity is calibrated by ease of expression in a language in which 'the primitive vocabulary that appears in the axioms refer[s] only to perfectly natural properties'[21] (let us call this an 'elite language').

What of the properties which are not elite? It is important to Lewis that they not all be treated as on a par. Indeed, he provides guidelines for calibrating their degree of naturalness: characterize the property appealing to nothing but elite terms, and see how long the definition is:

---

[19] See *On The Plurality of Worlds*, p. 60, and 'Putnam's Paradox,' *Papers in Metaphysics and Epistemology*, p. 66.

[20] Lewis, for convenience, often omits these clauses about parts. On occasion, I allow myself the same convenience in this paper.

[21] See 'New Work For a Theory of Universals', p. 42.

The less elite are so because they are connected to the most elite by chains of definability. Long chains, by the time we reach the moderately elite classes of cats and pencils and puddles; but the chains required to reach the utterly ineligible would be far longer still.[22]

Or again: '[other properties] are somewhat natural in a derivative way, to the extent that they can be reached by not-too-complicated chains of definability from the perfectly natural properties.'[23]

While I think that something in the vicinity of the natural/non-natural contrast is plausible and important,[24] and while I think Lewis is right that some such metaphysical hypothesis can earn its keep by performing explanatory work, I am less sanguine about some of the fine points of his view. In elaborating on his inegalitarianism, Lewis ignores some important matters of detail, and proposes certain related theses that cannot reasonably be sustained.

Notice first that in the initial pair of quoted passages above, Lewis switches back and forth between determinate and determinable: we are given both 'mass' and 'the masses of particles' as examples of truly elite properties. On the face of it, at least, these are different proposals:[25] on one, the determinable *mass* belongs to the elite; on the other it is the *determinates* of that determinable—the masses of particles—that so belong. On the first proposal, one might still hope that the list of elite properties will be reasonably short; on the second, such a list would be very long indeed.[26]

This ambivalence may not seem significant, but I think it ramifies in important ways. The relative merits of determinable and determinate vary according to which roles the natural is supposed to play. Consider first its role in determining which worlds belong in the 'inner sphere' of worlds 'just like ours'. And suppose that there is some determinate mass value that is uninstantiated in the actual world: no fusion of objects has exactly mass n. Surely we should not conclude that a world where some fusion of objects has that value thereby falls outside the inner sphere. When thinking of alien intrusions, Lewis has determinables, not determinates in mind.

Meanwhile, when thinking about duplication, it is determinates, not determinables, that are suited to the task. Being alike with respect to all the relevant determinables is clearly not adequate for duplication—but sharing all the fundamental determinates may well be. (A special case of this idea is the actual world itself: a duplicate of this world is one which shares all the same fundamental determinates.)

---

[22] 'Putnam's Paradox', in *Papers in Metaphysics and Epistemology*, p. 66.

[23] *On the Plurality of Worlds*, p. 61.

[24] As Lewis notes in various places, the thesis that the naturalness scale has an endpoint of perfect naturalness goes beyond the hypothesis that there is such a scale. I shall not in these pages pursue the question of how and whether the existence of such an endpoint might be justified.

[25] Suppose there was just one unit mass property and that the mass of bodies was determinated by the number of distinct parts with the unit property. Then we could tolerate a single elite mass property whose distribution could accord for all the facts about mass. But (absent surprises from physics) such a proposal seems very unrealistic, since it will not generate the kind of scale of mass values we want (such that for each non-zero mass, there is a smaller mass, and where, for any given mass value m, there can be pairs of objects whose mass difference is less than m).

[26] It is one thing to provide a short list of non-elite determinables under which elite properties fall, but it may be quite another to provide a list of the elite properties themselves.

What of the more informal but intuitive idea that the elite properties are the ones that makes for objective similarity and difference?[27] Here determinable and determinate seem to share the spoils: being alike with respect to a mass determinate bestows more objective similarity than being alike with respect to the determinable mass; being divided by a mass determinate guarantees less objective difference than being divided by the determinable mass.

An additional complication for the view that puts determinates but not determinables among the elite arises when applying Lewis's chain of definability test. For if the elite language contains only simple predicates for each determinate, then the determinable will enjoy no finite definition. While one might live with the view that the determinable mass is a 'very natural' though not quite perfectly natural property, the view that it falls among the 'utterly ineligible' is totally unacceptable.

What of the role of natural properties *viz-à-viz* the laws? Here neither the determinates nor the determinables nor their combination seem well suited to play the relevant role. Consider the following simple challenge. Imagine actually writing down, say, the laws of Newtonian physics in an elite language that includes distinct primitive predicates for each determinate (with or without a simple predicate corresponding to the determinable of having mass). Note that such a language will not have in its primitive vocabulary the relational predicates to numbers that constitute the machinery of ordinary classical physics,[28] nor, crucially, will it have in its primitive vocabulary predicates like 'x is between y and z' or 'xy is congruent to wz', here understood (contra Field) as predicates of properties rather than of objects.[29] Indeed, such predicates could only be introduced via infinitely long definitions in the elite language and so would have to be treated as expressing wildly gerrymandered relations. So if we restrict the elite language to an uncountable number of lexical primitives for the determinates (plus or minus one for the determinable) then, by Lewis's own

---

[27] I note in passing that it is not likely that one can strictly build an account of naturalness out of this intuitive idea, at least not in any straightforward way. The conjunction of two determinates makes for more similarity than either of its conjuncts: but it does not seem plausible to reckon the conjuncts less elite on that account. Regardless, the contrast in the text strikes me as instructive.

[28] Lewis is quite right to exclude such relational predicates as 'x is the mass in kilograms of y' from an elite language, since such predicates encode an arbitrary choice of coordinate system.

[29] A theory of quantity that took such predicates of properties as basic, justifying numerical representation in their terms, would be what Brent Mundy calls a 'second order theory of quantity', as contrasted with the 'first order' theory of Field's. See Mundy's 'The Metaphysics of Quantity' for an extended defence of the second-order approach. As Mundy is well aware, the second-order version (especially when combined with a claim of necessary existence for the properties over which the relations are defined), has nothing to fear from the problems confronting relationalism that were alluded to earlier. For example, the second-order version has the resources to rigidify on one actual quantity and claim that some isolated individual 'could have had that quantity', where there is no similar device is available for the relationalist. The relationalist could, of course, rigidify on some actual object and then claim that some possible object 'could have been twice as big as that'. But this does not capture the intended idea, since the object rigidly designated will be of different sizes in different worlds. By contrast, one can reasonably insist that it makes no sense to suppose that some particular mass property—being 15 kgs, for example—counts as a greater mass in other worlds: the predicate 'is 15 kgs', like all predicates, does not express different properties relative to different worlds.

standards, any so-called dynamical laws taken seriously by physics will be very poor candidates indeed to be the laws of nature.

There are, it seems, only two options. First, one might enhance the elite stock with certain relations such as congruence. Then the above considerations would provide no obstacle to Lewis's account of the laws. Rather, it would encourage one to think that the true laws of nature are statable in terms of such predicates and thus do not crucially rely on a relational vocabulary that deploys numbers as relata.[30] This is essentially Field's idea, adapted now to a framework in which the crucial relations take properties as relata. Second, one might give up the chain of definability test on naturalness and make corresponding adjustments in the account of the laws of nature.[31] On such a picture, powerful generalizations using very natural predicates might make excellent candidates for laws, even if their expression in a strictly elite language is wildy complicated—for highly natural predicates may be linked to the elite language only by lengthy chains of definition.

So while the Lewisian contrast between the natural and the gerrymandered is intuitively very compelling, its implementation has been revealed to be somewhat problematic. Two potential trouble spots have been identified. First, it is not obvious that we should follow Lewis in testing for relative naturalness by length of definition in an elite language. Second, it appears that the roles Lewis wishes elite properties to play cannot all be filled by properties from a single domain. As a result, it is unclear which properties in the vicinity of mass should be counted among the elite.

How should we respond to these problems? Should we retain the test for relative naturalness but enrich the stock of elite predicates to include not just the 'base level' determinates but also determinables and certain basic relations between the determinates? Should we give up on a single scale of naturalness and make do with a variety of naturalness scales corresponding to the various roles that Lewis's concept of naturalness needs to play? Should we maintain a limited view of the elite properties but revise the account of relative naturalness? This is not the place to resolve these issues. For now, it is enough to notice that while the naturalness picture may have merit, there is much work to be done if we are to use it to build an adequate metaphysics of quantity.

---

[30] As far as Lewis' framework is concerned, it does not follow that generalizations stated in terms of numbers do not express laws of nature. For they may express the very same propositions—construed as functions from worlds to truth values—as the generalizations couched in the elite language.

[31] Of course, one should have realized that the simple version of the complexity-of-definition idea fails owing to the fact that disjoining hurts naturalness more than conjoining but does not introduce additional complexity. But one might have hoped that some idea in the vicinity of the simple version would work. The current suggestion is that this hope is misplaced. Naturalness is not a function of the Boolean structure of a definition couched in ground-floor microphysical vocabulary.

12

Determinism De Re[1]

Consider two descriptions of some segment of world history. The first—the *qualitative description*—says everything that can be said about the intrinsic character of that history with one exception: it cannot name individuals or otherwise encode haecceitistic information about which particular individuals are caught up in that segment of world history. The second—the *de re description*— includes the qualitative description and, in addition, all haecceitistic, singular information.

So, for example, a complete qualitative description may include:

$\exists x$ x is a queen at some time,

and

$\exists x$ x is a princess at some time t and a queen ten years after t.

But it won't include

Victoria is a queen at some time.

The de re description, by contrast, includes all three of these statements.

Drawing on this distinction, we can formulate two different versions of the thesis that the actual world is deterministic:[2]

> *Qualitative Determinism*: For all times t, there is no possible world which matches this world in its qualitative description up to t, and which has the same laws of nature as this world, but which doesn't match this world in its total qualitative description.

> *De Re Determinism*: For all times t, there is no possible which matches this world in its de re description up to t, and which has the same laws of nature as this world, but which doesn't match this world in its total de re description.

On first inspection, it may seem to be an open question whether either form of determinism holds. Against this, I shall argue that De Re Determinism is a priori rather implausible.

Here is a concern for De Re Determinism. Suppose that at this world an earring, Catherine, is made out of some gold at some time t. It seems clear enough that there

---

[1] Thanks to Tamar Gendler, Ted Sider, and Timothy Williamson for helpful comments and conversation.

[2] If we are interested in whether our *laws* are deterministic, as opposed to whether the actual world is deterministic, one will wish to consider a pair of stronger theses. Here is the qualitative version: for all times t and all worlds w with the same laws of nature as the actual world, there is no world y with the same laws that matches w in its qualitative description up to t but which has a different total qualitative description to w.

could have been earrings other than Catherine made out of the very same gold, even earrings of the same shape. (Suppose for example that Catherine is flattened and a new one is made out of the gold.) Even if the originating matter is essential to Catherine, it is not sufficient for the existence of Catherine. Prima, facie, then, Catherine's origins are nomically compatible with the creation of a numerically different earring. Why not then suppose that there is a world that matches this world in its de re description up to t, but where a numerically different earring is made?

Some philosophers have assumed that a richer construal of origins will answer this concern. Timothy Williamson, for example, proposes that 'for nearby worlds if not for all', some combination of circumstances that include material, craftsman, time and place (and other such details) suffice for the identity of artifacts.[3] How does this play out when we look at the details?

Begin with the following sufficiency condition on the identity of artifacts: if an artifact x is the product of a particular blueprint, quantity of matter and craftsman, then any possible artefact made from that blueprint, quantity of matter and craftsman will be identical to x. This will not do.[4] Suppose a ship, the Queen Elizabeth, is made by a craftsman c using a blueprint b and matter m. The wood planks (m) of the Queen Elizabeth are slowly replaced so that at $t+$, none of the original wood remains part of the ship. At $t+$, c makes a second ship, the Queen Mary, using b and the now-discarded wood m. It is clear that there are two distinct ships here—each made from the same material and the same blueprint by the same craftsman.[5]

What if we strengthen the conditions to include, say, time of creation? This blocks the Queen Elizabeth–Queen Mary case, but introduces problems of its own. If we allow that time of origin is not a necessary condition on artifact identity[6]—which seems plausible—then the new sufficiency principle faces troubles. For suppose the Queen Elizabeth was originally made at t_2 and the Queen Mary at t_3. If time is inessential, then the Queen Elizabeth could have been made at t_1 and the Queen Mary at t_2. In that case, the Queen Mary could have been created at the time that the Queen Elizabeth actually is, with the same originating blueprint, craftsman and originating matter as those that the Queen Elizabeth actually has. We now have a counterexample to the proposed sufficiency condition.

---

[3] *Identity and Discrimination* (Blackwell, 1990), pp. 128–9.

[4] For further relevant and in places overlapping discussion, see John Hawthorne and Tamar Szabo Gendler, 'Origin Essentialism: The Arguments Reconsidered', *Mind* (April 2000). For additional discussion, see: Graham Forbes, *The Metaphysics of Modality*, (Oxford University Press, 1985); 'The New Riddle of Existence', *Philosophical Perspectives* 8 (1994), 415–430; T. McKay, 'Against Constitutional Sufficiency Principles', *Midwest Studies in Philosophy*, X1 (1986), 295–304; N. Salmon, *Reference and Essence* (Princeton University Press, 1981); 'The Logic of What Might Have Been,' *Philosophical Review* 98 (1989), 3–34; T. Robertson 'Possibilities and the Argument for Origin Essentialism,' *Mind* 107 (1998), 729–749.

[5] See the work cited in n. 2. above.

[6] Even if it were, there are always Ship of Theseus stories involving time travelling matter to worry about(!), though that might not make any trouble for a *nomologically* sufficient condition, which is all we need.

Perhaps we can block the unwanted identification by adding order to our conditions.[7] On this proposal, if x is made of originating matter m, using blueprint b, by craftsman c, and there were exactly n things preceding it, made of m, using b, by c, then is not possible that there be some y that is not identical to x that is made of m using b by c such that there were also exactly n things before x made of m using b by c. But here again it is not particularly difficult to contrive counterexamples. Consider a world where a craftsman has been making Theseus-like ships from eternity, reusing the same wood over and over. Each ship is preceded by infinitely many ships made of the same wood by the same craftsman and the same blueprint. By the proposed sufficiency condition, there is just one ship in this possible world. But that is absurd.

Even if we restrict ourselves to finite cases, a problem arises if we allow that a given ship could have been made from a numerically distinct block of wood that contains much of the same matter and that it could have been constructed according to a numerically distinct but very similar blueprint[8]. Suppose the Queen Elizabeth is made out of blueprint b and wood w. Let b^* be a blueprint just enough different from b to count as a different blueprint and w^* a slightly different quantity of wood to w. Consider a world where the Queen Elizabeth is made of b and m^* and then a different ship is made from b and m, and a world where the Queen Elizabeth is made of b^* and m, and then a different ship is made from b and m. Our order principle, says, unacceptably, that in each case the *second* ship is the Queen Elizabeth.

This last problem is resistant to a natural fix. Consider a ship made of matter m using blueprint b which could have been made from slightly different hunks of matter and slightly different blueprints. Call such possible hunks and blueprints m-variants and b-variants respectively.[9] And now consider the following revised principle: if a thing is made by craftsman c from matter m using blueprint b and is preceded by n things made by craftsman c from m-variant matter using b-variant blueprints, then

---

[7] Cf. Forbes, 'New Riddle of Existence'.

[8] What of the objection that, since small changes add up to big changes, one will be left allowing that a statue could have been made of a totally different block of wood? (Consider a sequence of worlds $w_1 \ldots w_n$ each of what has a block that differs by a molecule.) Suppose that for every function from worlds to filled regions of spacetime, there exists an object whose modal occupation profile is given by that function (call this 'plenitude'). At this world, in the vicinity of the statue there are many objects, some more forgiving than others with regard to origin. Our conceptual scheme admits some but not others as candidate referents for 'that statue'. Objects that are completely origin indifferent are prohibited, as are objects that could not have been made from a slightly different block. Take a candidate C that can, we might suppose, be made of a block that is 5 per cent different from the actual one but no more. Consider a world where it is made of a block that is 5 per cent different. Won't people at that world make mistakes when judging what changes are possible with regard to the statue's origins? Not if they refer to something else (something less fragile as it were) by 'that statue'. Of course, assuming that statues are necessarily statues and that S4 is correct, it still turns out not to be necessarily true that if a statue s is made of some quantity of matter m, then, for any variant v of m, it could have been made of v. Yet interestingly, given plentitude (as true and a priori), it may yet be a priori (contingently a priori) that if a statue exists and is made of some quantity of matter m, then, for any variant v of m, it is possible that it be made of v. Such a package strikes me as quite attractive. Salmon has recommended a different approach (that I do not favor), one that turns on rejecting S4. (I am grateful for discussions with Timothy Williamson here.)

[9] Let a hunk or blueprint be a variant of itself.

it is not possible that there be something else made by craftsman c from matter m using blueprint b preceded by n things made by c using m-variants and b-variants. The proposal does not work. Suppose the Queen Mary is made from m^*, and the Queen Elizabeth is made from m. Some possible variants of m^* will not be variants of m (something which is not too different from m^* may be too different from m). Consider now a world in which the Queen Mary is made of a variant of m^* which is not a variant of m, and then the Queen Elizabeth is made of m, and a third ship, the Lusitania, is made of m (in each case the craftsman and the blueprint is the same). Our principle says, unacceptably, that the Lusitania is the Queen Elizabeth.

In sum, it does not seem that there is a plausible sufficiency condition for the identity of artefacts that can rule out troublesome de re branching. And absent such a condition, De Re Determinism is in trouble.

What other strategies are available? One might try invoking a global supervenience thesis: the de re facts about macrophysical objects at a world supervene on the qualitative description of that world plus the de re facts about the microphysical particles at that world. But the very sorts of cases we have been considering raise analogous problems for any such supervenience thesis. Consider a world where infinitely many earrings are made of the same gold by the same craftsman for all eternity, and suppose that he regularly destroys the earring he has recently made and then makes another one. Suppose Jane is made at t_2 and Anne at t_3. Suppose, from a qualitative point of view, that world is an eternal return world, duplicating itself qualitatively at regular intervals, and that t_1, t_2, and t_3 are qualitative duplicates. Since (as we have been assuming throughout) the time of construction is inessential to a thing, it seems that there is a world w where Anne is made at t_1 and Jane at t_2, such that w both qualitatively duplicates the original world and matches the original world with regard to the de re facts concerning the microparticles. If so, we have a counterexample to the global supervenience thesis.[10] The idea of using it to rescue de re determinism is a failure.

Supposing that no metaphysical sufficiency condition on the identity of artefacts is correct, might we not still hope (recalling Williamson's appeal to 'nearby worlds') that there is some *nomologically* sufficient condition? Such a hope seems misplaced. For it is implausible to suppose that the actual laws of nature make special mention of individuals such as Catherine and the Queen Elizabeth. And if the laws do not make special mention of individuals, and the de re history up to t does not metaphysically require one earring rather than another, then on what basis are we to suppose that the *metaphysically* possible worlds that share our world's qualitative history but that branch de re are not *nomologically* possible?

---

[10] Those who balk at the required haecceitistic facts about times might wish instead to consider worlds where the pattern of recreation is the same but where some particular earring in the sequence—say Anne—is never made. Another case to consider in this connection in a world where a craftsman makes infinitely many earrings and then stops. Suppose the last pair made are Catherine and Anne. Consider now a world in which he stops with Catherine.

The following conclusion suggests itself. Supposing that the general apparatus of singular propositions and haecceistic distinctions is not challenged (here is not the place to discuss counterpart theoretic approaches to de re modality), we are forced to conclude—on more or less a priori grounds—that de re determinism is radically implausible. Should we care about this result? Perhaps qualitative determinism was the only determinism worth caring about in the first place.[11] Speaking for myself, it seems at least somewhat interesting to learn that the past and the laws of nature did not determine that I exist. Moreover, consider a symmetrical world where there is a pair of qualitatively identical ships, one in each symmetrical half. Suppose the laws dictated that exactly one of the ships would sink, but left it undetermined which. Qualitative determinism might still hold of such a world, since the qualitative description of a world in which one ship sank need not depart in any way from the qualitative description of a world in which the other did.[12] But would that give us all the determinism worth caring about?[13]

---

[11] On certain assumptions, de re indeterminism will spill over into qualitative indeterminism. Suppose that when the earring is destroyed, that does not, so to speak, destroy that earrings's potentiality for existing in the future. Suppose, then, that while there is no guarantee that that very earring will pop back into existence when the gold is suitably crafted in the future, there is no modal prohibition on such gappy existence either. Suppose as a matter of fact that two duplicate but non-identical earrings are made at different times of the same gold, the one created ten years after the other is destroyed. Qualitative indeterminism now threatens. For there would seems to be a world where the very same earring pops back into existence. In this situation, the proposition '$\exists x$ x is an earring at some time t and x exists ten years after t but x does not exist five years after t' will be true at one world but not the other.

[12] Note that I am not assuming relationalism about space here. Even if spacetimes points exist, they cannot be named in a qualitative description of the world.

[13] One might concede that qualitative determinism is not all that is worth caring about, but claim instead that centered qualitative determinism is what matters: given any object, the complete qualitative relational description of its past, plus the laws, entails its complete relational description. This is not determinism enough, though; consider a world with three objects, x, y, and z, and an asymmetric relation R where none of the objects bear R to each other until a time t, after which either xRy, yRz, and zRx; or zRy, yRx, and xRz—but the history of the world until t does not settle which. This world satisfies centered qualitative determinism, but is intuitively not deterministic. A generalization of the centered approach to ordered n-tuples will handle this. (Thanks here to Ted Sider and Timothy Williamson.)

13

Why Humeans Are Out of Their Minds

According to Humeanism, the causal facts pertaining to any subregion of the world are extrinsic to that region,[1] supervening on the global distribution of freely recombinable fundamental properties.[2] For example, according to the Humean, a spatio-temporal region in which a certain intrusion of a bullet into a body is followed by death is only extrinsically a region in which the intrusion causes the death. The latter causal fact will, if it obtains, be underwritten by certain global regularities (most obviously, those connecting death to certain bodily disturbances) that are extrinsic to the region in question. Embed an intrinsic duplicate of that region in a global setting where very different regularities are in play and it may be false of that duplicate region that its intrusion and its death are causally connected. Similarly a spatio-temporal region that contains a substance that has a certain causal power—say of poisoning human beings—is only extrinsically a region where that causal power is present. Embed an intrinsic duplicate of a region in very different global settings and the relevant power may be absent. Humeanism thus delivers the thesis that the causal facts pertaining to a region are extrinsic to it. But that thesis, no matter how it is embellished, is incompatible with a pair of very obvious facts about my own nature. Accordingly, Humeanism is untenable. That many philosophers subscribe to it ought not to convince us to the contrary. History provides reminders aplenty of philosophers' willingness to believe strange doctrines

This paper is an expanded and revised version of that which appeared in *Noûs* 38 (June 2004) pp. 351–358. I am grateful for permission to publish it here.

[1] This paper relies throughout on a contrast between the extrinsic and intrinsic facts pertaining to a region. Cf. David Lewis, Postscript to 'Survival and Identity,' *Philosophical Papers Volume I* (Oxford: Oxford University Press, 1983), 76–7. Here is not the place to engage those who are sceptical about that very distinction. Note that, following Lewis's usage in that paper, I count it as, say, an intrinsic fact about a spatio-temporal, region that it is wholly occupied by a spherical object even though in some yet more austere sense that fact might count as extrinsic (it has to do with how the region is related to something distinct to it by the occupation relation). Note also that I include intrinsic relations between occupants of a relation as part of the intrinsic profile of that region. (For more on intrinsic relations see David Lewis and Rae Langton, 'Defining Intrinsic', *Papers in Metaphysics and Epistemology*, Cambridge: Cambridge University Press, p. 129.)

[2] The best-known Humean in recent times is David Lewis. See, for example, his introduction to *Philosophical Papers Volume II*, (Oxford: Oxford University Press, 1986); 'Humean Supervenience Debugged', *Mind* 103 (1994), 473–90; *On The Plurality of Worlds*, (Blackwell, 1986), pp. 14–16 and pp. 87–92.

THE ARGUMENT

(1) An intrinsic duplicate of any region wholly containing me will contain a being with my conscious life.[3]

(2) There are causal requirements on my conscious life.

Therefore, Humeanism is false.[4]

COMMENTARY

Premise One

A spatiotemporal region wholly contains a being if and only if every spatiotemporal point that the being occupies in its lifetime belongs to that region. A spatiotemporal region contains a being if and only if some spatiotemporal point in that region is occupied by that being. If a spatiotemporal region wholly contains me and I am conscious and some other spatiotemporal region does not contain a conscious being, then the two regions are not duplicates. Deny this connection between consciousness and intrinsicality and our very handle on the notion of intrinsicality (and the coordinate notion of duplication) may be thrown into doubt. At the very least, this connection is highly intuitive. While one might try to argue for the premise—say, by maintaining that we have privileged access to our conscious life and that such privileged access would not be possible unless Premise One were true[5]—any such argument seems doomed to rely on assumptions more controversial than the conclusion it seeks to

---

[3] Some dualists will worry that, strictly speaking, I don't occupy space. Those with such concerns ought to consider a version of the argument that replaces premise one with 'Any intrinsic duplicate of me will be a part of a being with my conscious life' (Note that Humeanism also has the consequence that the causal facts pertaining to any given object are extrinsic to it.)

[4] Don't react, as some have done, by saying that this argument 'begs the question' against the Humean. This would be to lapse into that confused use of 'begging the question' whereby one complains of any valid argument against a view that it begs the question by forcing one who accepts the premises to accept the falsity of the theory at issue. It is clear, of course, that the argument will not be dialectically effective against Humeans (and fence-sitters) who do not find the premises intuitively compelling. But I predict that they will be few in number. The Humean, of course, is free to deny one of the premises despite its intuitive force. If the argument points to a cost of Humeanism, even by the lights of most Humeans, it will have served its purpose well enough.

[5] A more sophisticated (or at least trendy) version of the argument (using the language of David Chalmers's *The Conscious Mind*, Oxford: Oxford University Press, 1996) goes as follows: The primary and secondary intentions of phenomenal concepts are identical, and yet this would not be possible unless premise one were true. The underlying thought is that there is a way in which phenomenal properties are revealed to us (in some especially powerful sense of 'revelation'), and that this could only be so if they were intrinsic to our mental life. Such arguments are certainly worth exploring. But I doubt that any will be more dialectically effective than a raw appeal to the intuitive force of the intrinsicality premise.

establish.[6] So I will rest content with the fact that premise one is highly intuitive in its own right.[7] Every argument has its intuitive bedrock.[8]

It is not merely true that intrinsic duplicates of a region wholly containing me will contain a conscious being; they will contain a being that possesses the particular qualitative properties that characterize my phenomenal life.[9] Let L stand for my phenomenal profile: it is the complex property that characterizes my conscious life. (Let L be understood so that a being that had all my phenomenal life and more—say, by outliving me—would still count as having L.) Premise One tells us that any duplicate of a spatiotemporal region that wholly contains me will contain a being with L. For example: if I am in pain, then any region that is not occupied by someone who is in pain will fail to duplicate any region wholly containing me.[10,11]

Two disclaimers

I say that a duplicate of a region wholly containing me will contain a being with L, but I am not insisting that any such duplicate will wholly contain a being with L. Consider a brain in a vat. The boundary of the subject of consciousness plausibly coincides

---

[6] Relevant here is Tyler Burge's 'Individuation and Self-Knowledge', *The Journal of Philosophy* (November 1988), 649–663 and Donald Davidson's 'First Person Authority', *Dialectica* 2–3 (1984), 441–458.

[7] It has been my experience that anyone who calls forth the concept of phenomenal consciousness finds Premise One extremely compelling once it is grasped. Note that one who allowed that consciousness was extrinsic would need to make room for true speeches along the following lines: 'Region *y* wholly contains a conscious being and had *x* occurred, then the internal goings on in region *y* would have been unaffected. Nevertheless had *x* occurred, then region *y* would not have been occupied by a conscious being.' Such a speech strikes us as very odd. (As Tim Maudlin noted in conversation, this would make for some very curious types of anesthetic!)

[8] Are there other mental state types that are intrinsic in the relevant sense? Ernest Sosa has suggested (in conversation) that an argument similar to that given in the text could be run for the property of performing an inference (where Twin Earth considerations are arguably irrelevant). I shall not investigate the matter further here (though I suspect that the relevant style of argument has most dialectical force when applied to phenomenal consciousness).

[9] Readers may also wish to consider a version of the argument built upon the simple fact of my being conscious: (1′) Any intrinsic duplicate of any region wholly containing me will contain a being that is conscious. (2′) There are causal requirements on being conscious. Therefore Humeanism is false. (1′) is even more obvious than (1), though premise (2′) is perhaps a little harder to justify than (2).

[10] Granted, there are on occasion surprising discoveries of extrinsicality. (Consider special relativity and shape.) Yet it seems especially difficult to imagine becoming convinced that consciousness is extrinsic. (Consider, for example, how very difficult it is for most of us to imagine becoming convinced that swampman—an intrinsic duplicate of one of us forged by fortuitous happenings in a swamp—lacks phenomenal states.)

[11] Admittedly, there are philosophers of mind who explicitly defend the extrinsicality of phenomenal pain: in his *Naturalizing the Mind*, (MIT 1995) Fred Dretske maintains that phenomenal character is constituted by evolutionary history (so that an intrinsic duplicate of me with a suitably deviant history would lack my phenomenal states). Meanwhile, in 'Mad Pain and Martian Pain' (*Philosophical Papers Volume 1*, Oxford University Press, 1983, 122–132) David Lewis suggests that intrinsic duplicates can differ with respect to whether they are in pain on account of differences in the population each belongs to. Such views are apt to evoke incredulous stares precisely because of the claimed extrinsicality of phenomenal character.

with the boundary of the brain.[12] Embed a duplicate of that brain in a human body and the boundary of that subject of consciousness plausibly coincides with the boundary of the human body. Suppose I am a brain in a vat. We can now see that perhaps there is a duplicate of a region wholly containing me that does not *wholly* contain a being with L. But the duplicate region will still contain a being with L.[13,14]

Second, note that Premise One is neutral concerning the thesis that consciousness will be contained in a region that duplicates all the intrinsic physical characteristics of a region wholly containing me. Perhaps there might be a world exactly like this one in all physical respects where there is a zombie who is physically just like me but who lacks consciousness. If so, then there is more to duplicating a region wholly containing me than mere physical duplication. Perhaps, on the other hand, consciousness is identical to a physical property. If so, then the imagined zombie scenario is not possible. I need not take a stand.[15]

One final point of clarification: It might seem that we have an intrinsicality intuition about causality itself. If a hammer has a causal power, don't we think of that as intrinsic to the hammer? And if a hammer causes a window to break, don't we think of that causal transaction as intrinsic to the region in which the breaking occurs? Why not attack the Humean by wielding the intuition that causation is intrinsic rather than taking a detour through consciousness as this essay does? In response,

[12] I remain neutral here as to whether the brain is identical to the subject of consciousness or merely constitutes it (an issue that turns in part on the plausibility of a counterpart-theoretic approach to de re modality). See Lewis's 'Counterparts of Persons and Their Bodies,' *Philosophical Papers Volume I* 47–54.

[13] There are less drastic ways of illustrating the same point. Supposing that I am a four-dimensional object, there are duplicates of me that are arguably not conscious beings on account of the fact that they are proper temporal parts of persons. (My life could have been part of a longer life even though it isn't.) Such considerations suggest that I cannot say with any great confidence that the property of being a conscious being is an intrinsic property of me. For a duplicate of me might not be a being that instantiates that property—owing to the fact that the duplicate is not maximal in the relevant respects. (This theme is explored in detail in Theodore Sider, 'Maximality and Microphysical Supervenience', *Philosophy and Phenomenological Research* 66 (2003), 139–149. See also Trenton Merricks's 'Against the Doctrine of Microphysical Supervenience', *Mind* 107 (1998), 59–71.) Premise One is thus a preferable way of articulating the intrinsicality of consciousness intuition that we all share.

[14] But doesn't the intuitiveness of Premise One derive from the prima facie intuitiveness of the stronger claim that consciousness is an intrinsic property? And since the latter claim is thrown into question by the preceding paragraph, shouldn't we then be led to have grave doubts about premise one? I submit that this is the wrong way of looking at the matter. Quite often, when we find a claim prima facie intuitive, it turns out that further a priori reflection reveals that the claim is not in fact correct but that a subtle variant in the neighborhood stands up very well to a priori scrutiny. That is the situation here.

[15] Similarly (though somewhat implausibly), suppose the modal connection between mental and physical is such that my intrinsic physical makeup in combination with certain surroundings necessitates some phenomenal property F, but that certain intrinsic physical duplicates embedded in other environments would not have phenomenal property F. Even if this picture were correct, it would merely show that an intrinsic physical duplicate may not be an intrinsic duplicate simpliciter. (Note also that the necessary connections invoked by any such picture would hardly be acceptable to the Humean.)

it is important to recognize that the intrinsicality-of-causality intuition is not nearly so immediate or rationally compelling as the idea that consciousness is intrinsic (or more precisely, as the idea that it is intrinsic to any region wholly containing me that it contains a conscious being). Consider some causal power that belongs to a hammer. Here are two competing views: (a) That causal power is fixed by the intrinsic properties of the hammer, so that any duplicate in any possible world will share that causal power. (b) That causal power is fixed not by the intrinsic properties of the hammer alone but by those intrinsic properties plus the laws of nature.[16] (So while each duplicate of the hammer in a world which shares our laws possesses the relevant causal power, certain duplicates of the hammer in worlds where the laws of nature are different lack that causal power.) Is it immediately obvious which of (a) and (b) is correct? It seems not: deciding between them requires argumentation. Matters are different with consciousness. It is perfectly obvious that a region that does not contain a conscious being could not be a perfect duplicate of a region wholly containing me. It is just not intelligible to suppose that there be a perfect duplicate of a region wholly containing me which, owing to a difference in the laws of nature, does not contain a conscious being.[17] Our hesitancy to affirm the intrinsicality of a causal power has no analogue here.

Premise Two

There are true propositions that tell us about what causes what. There are also true propositions that tell us about what causal powers a thing has. Let both types of true proposition count as 'causal facts'. For any set of causal facts, S, there is a property q, such that necessarily, an object has q iff all the members of S hold. (Think of q as the property of being such that all the members of S are true.) Call any such property a *causal profile*. What (2) asserts is that there is some causal profile such that no being could instantiate L without instantiating it. That profile provides a necessary causal condition for a being's having a phenomenal life just like mine.

To say this is not to subscribe to some tendentious version of functionalism about phenomenal states (which I take to be the thesis that such states can be individuated by causal role). Rather, premise two asserts the altogether reasonable thesis that my conscious life requires certain causal facts to be in place. It seems plausible, for example, that the essence of certain particular types of phenomenal state is constituted in part by certain causal powers. Consider the trio: phenomenal red, phenomenal orange, phenomenal blue. It is certainly true that when an attentive subject enjoys

[16] Perhaps there are some causal powers that satisfy neither (a) nor (b). I shall not pursue this matter here.

[17] This is not to deny that there are useful notions of narrowness that fall short of intrinsicality and in particular, one according to which a property is narrow iff it is shared by all intrinsic duplicates within nomologically possible worlds. (See, for example, Lewis 'Reduction of Mind', p. 315, in *Papers in Metaphysics and Epistemology*, and also David Braddon Mitchell and Frank Jackson, *Philosophy of Mind and Cognition* (Blackwell, 1996), pp. 214–216.) Perhaps some mental state types are narrow but not intrinsic. The point remains that it is overwhelmingly intuitive that phenomenal consciousness is intrinsic in the sense stated.

all three phenomenal states simultaneously and is invited to judge which pair is most similar, she will judge that phenomenal red and orange are most similar. Phenomenal colors are thus disposed to produce certain similarity verdicts. These dispositions are causal powers of the phenomenal colors. And they seem to be causal powers that the phenomenal colors possess essentially. A possible world where a trio of phenomenal states R, O, and B are not disposed to evoke the judgment that R and O are most similar could not be a world where the R, O, and B are identical to phenomenal red, orange, and blue, respectively.[18,19]

To return to Premise Two: it is obvious that any possible phenomenal duplicate of me will be a subject that (a) is aware of certain of its experiences, (b) attends to certain of its experiences, (c) persists through a stream of conscious experience and (d) has synchronically unified conscious experience. And there is reason to doubt whether these phenomena—for short, awareness, attention, persistence, unity—could exist without certain causal facts of connection and/or power.

Let us explore the second and third of these considerations in a little more detail. Begin with attention. I am currently attending to a mild headache. Clearly, any intrinsic duplicate of a region wholly containing me will contain a being that is attending to a mild headache. The idea that a being might duplicate my phenomenal life and yet, unlike me, fail to attend to any of it, is dubiously intelligible. The facts of attention cannot be factorized out in this way. Now a causal theory of attention is a priori compulsory when it comes to, say, an episode of attending to a firework display. To attend to a firework display requires some causal relation between a worldly episode and an attentional act. (It is no accident that the causal theory of perception has been almost universally acknowledged as capturing at least a necessary condition of perception.) When the fireworks are phenomenal rather than incendiary, it hardly seems like the causal model should be dispensed with. In the particular case in question, it thus seems clear that there must be a causal relation between phenomenal state and attentional act.

Turn now to persistence. It is dubious that an instantaneous being—a being that lasted for a mere instant—would enjoy consciousness. The events that constitute consciousness plausibly take time—the flame of consciousness cannot flicker for only an instant. Arguably, then, it is a mistake to suppose that an instantaneous being that

---

[18] This is even more obvious for the trio phenomenal red, phenomenal orange and phenomenal sour.

[19] Of course, various familiar puzzles attending to ascriptions of dispositions arise here too: we say that a certain poison is disposed to kill you when ingested even though it will not do so when ingested with an accompanying antidote. (This example is drawn from Lewis's 'Finkish Dispositions', *Papers in Metaphysics and Epistemology*, p. 145.) I say that phenomenal colours dispose certain similarity verdicts even though, doubtless, there are some situations in which the characteristic manifestation of the disposition will not be forthcoming. That all our ordinary disposition claims may be false approximations to the truth is not a matter I need worry about here. What is crucial is that there are causal powers essential to phenomenal colors, not that I have succeeded in characterizing one of them with full exactitude. This is not to require, of course that some functionalist reduction of phenomenal colour be possible.

intrinsically duplicated me for a single instant would instantiate any of the ingredients of L. If I have a headache, that phenomenal state is intrinsic to my life—but it is not intrinsic to any single instant in my life. Similarly, a series of instantaneous beings, one for each moment of my existence, each of which intrinsically duplicates that moment of my existence, might be a series in which no consciousness occurs. The fusion of those instantaneous beings—a being which perdures[20] throughout the period—might not be a conscious being.

What is missing? Part of the answer is clear enough. At a minimum, consciousness requires there to be causal connectedness among the instantaneous beings.[21] Absent any such connectedness, even if there were a composite being composed of precisely those time-slices,[22] it would not be a conscious being.

I now turn to a final (and I think rather powerful) cluster of considerations that exploit persistence and unity. In discussing this issue, I shall speak separately to two different metaphysical pictures of consciousness, both of which concede Premise One. On one picture, my conscious history is metaphysically necessitated by my intrinsic physical history—call this the *supervenience picture*. On a second—quite different—picture, the facts of my conscious history constitute a set of intrinsic facts that are not metaphysically necessitated by my physical make-up. Call this the *emergence picture*.

Turning first to the supervenience picture, consider the spatiotemporal region that I occupy and divide it into four quarters, each having the same temporal length as my own life (hopefully 80 or so years). Consider a world where there are four separated regions, each distant from each of the others, each of which intrinsically duplicates one of the four actual quarters. Assume that the quarters are not only far apart, but that there is no causal commerce between them. No one would think that the fusion of the quarters in that world would share my conscious life.

What would be missing? One might suggest that the relevant difference is that my quarters are close together at this world but far apart at the other. How plausible is this diagnosis? Not very, I think. Consider a series of worlds where the quarters are closer and closer together, culminating in my world. (Even in my world, of course, the particles in each quarter are presumably separated from each other, since particles do not touch.) It seems unlikely that there is some magical set of distances such that when the quarters are less than that distance apart, my conscious life pops into being, but at distances that are greater, it does not.

But if distance does not make the difference, what does? By far the most plausible answer is that it is the causal relations between the quarters. In support of this, note that if we imaged the distance between the quarters large, but the causal commerce between them to somehow proceed just as it actually does, then our confidence that

---

[20] I borrow the term 'perdures' from Lewis. See, for example, *On The Plurality of Worlds*, p. 202.

[21] Note, by analogy, the standard requirement of causal connectedness put forward in discussions of personal identity.

[22] If the standard axioms of mereology are correct, then there will be a being composed of those short-lived beings whether or not there is causal connectedness.

they do not jointly constitute a conscious life is shaken. This renders it radically unstable for the proponent of the supervenience picture to hold that my conscious life is intrinsic to any region that I wholly occupy but that all of its causal fabric is extrinsic.

Consider now an emergence picture according to which the facts of phenomenal consciousness are constituted by how some set of *sui generis* phenomenal properties are instantiated, ones that do not supervene on my physical state. And imagine within this context a world where two physically duplicate human beings, Bill and Ben, have qualitatively duplicate phenomenal lives L. Consider the fusion of the right half of Bill and the left half of Ben. Presumably we do not wish to say that this being is conscious. But is it a primitive and inexplicable fact that this gerrymandered fusion is not conscious? And is there another world which physically duplicates this but where a different set of primitive and inexplicable facts obtain: Bill and Ben do not have L, but the fusion of Bill's right half and Ben's left half do (along with the fusion of Bill's left half and Ben's right half)? It strikes me that even supposing that consciousness is not reducible to the physical, such a position should be a sort of metaphysical last resort. Surely it is far more natural to say that we can explain why Bill but not one of the gerrymandered fusions enjoy consciousness: this is because Bill's body has the causal power of producing and sustaining consciousness, whereas the fusion does not. (Perhaps a world where the gerrymandered fusion has consciousness is possible, though that would have to be a world where the causal powers of things are rather different.) Such a metaphysical vision seems by far the most natural version of the non-reductive view. But assuming that consciousness is intrinsic, we will then be embarrassed by any view that reckons the relevant elements of causal profile extrinsic.

Granted, there may be those who are sufficiently primitivist to allow that the fact of Bill's being conscious in this world and the gerrymandered fusion being conscious in another is an absolutely primitive fact about the instantiation of phenomenal properties—about which nothing further can be said. (Presumably there is also then a pair of worlds, in one of which Bill has L, in another of which some atom that is within Bill has L and Bill does not.) If a Humean is willing to be primitivist in this way (note that he should presumably be at least somewhat open to the idea that some point particle that permanently resides in his left toe is in fact that bearer of his conscious life) then his position will be stable but unenviable.

THE INFERENCE

Humeanism, as we noted at the outset, entails that any causal profile pertaining to a subregion of the world is extrinsic to it. Call that thesis *Extrinsicality*.[23] Consider a subregion of the world that wholly contains me. Call it REGION. From premise one, we know that any intrinsic duplicate of REGION will have the property of containing a being that instantiates L. Call that property L*. Suppose for reductio that

---

[23] Note that to deny extrinsicality is not to insist that all the causal facts pertaining to a region are extrinsic to it, only that at least some of them are.

Extrinsicality were true. Then for any causal profile c, there is a possible world that contains an intrinsic duplicate of REGION but which lacks c.[24] But premise two tells us that there is a causal profile—call it PROFILE—whose instantiation is entailed by the instantiation of L^*. Extrinsicality tells us it is possible that there be an intrinsic duplicate of REGION where PROFILE is absent. Premises one and two tell us that it is not possible that there be an intrinsic duplicate of REGION where PROFILE is absent. We have a contradiction. Extrinsicality must be rejected, and its parent doctrine, Humeanism, along with it.[25,26]

[24] I assume the altogether plausible principle—one that is arguably analytic to our notion of extrinsicality—that if a property p is extrinsic to x, then it is possible that there be an intrinsic duplicate of x that lacks p. (Cf. Lewis, 'Extrinsic Properties,' in *Papers in Metaphysics and Epistemology*.) It is hard to imagine a Humean resisting the argument by challenging this principle.

[25] Perhaps Hume saw the trouble coming. Having eschewed causation as a source of real connection, he offers the following despairing remark in his Appendix to the Treatise: 'The present philosophy ... has so far a promising aspect. But all my hopes vanish, when I come to explain the principles, that unite our successive perceptions in our thought or consciousness' *A Treatise of Human Nature*, Selby-Bigge edition (Oxford University Press, 1968 reprint), p. 636.

[26] I am grateful to Jose Benardete, David Chalmers, Troy Cross, Tamar Gendler, Hud Hudson, Mark Johnston, Tim Maudlin, Brian McLaughlin, Daniel Nolan, Mark Scala, Ted Sider, Ernest Sosa, Brian Weatherson, Dean Zimmerman, and an anonymous reviewer for helpful comments and conversation.

14

Chance and Counterfactuals[1]

On those interpretations of quantum mechanics according to which the wave function for a system delivers probabilities of location, it seems that in any mundane situation, there is always a small chance of some extremely bizarre course of events unfolding. Suppose I drop a plate. The wave function that describes the plate will reckon there to be a tiny chance of the particles comprising that plate flying off sideways.

Suppose we embrace some such scientific theory. What then should we make of counterfactuals? We shall certainly be tempted to think that most ordinary counterfactuals are false. After all, having assimilated the theory, we shall be led to accept:

(1) If I had dropped the plate, it might have flown off sideways.

This in turn will induce us to think that (2) is incorrect:

(2) If I had dropped the plate, it would have fallen to the floor.

It would seem that we should instead embrace:

(3) If I had dropped the plate, it would very likely have fallen to the floor.

We then conclude that those propositions expressed by ordinary counterfactuals like (2) are false.

The threat can be recast in terms of the standard semantics for counterfactuals,[2] which tells us that

(4) 'P > Q' is true iff all closest P worlds are Q worlds.

Don't we learn from our chancy science that while at *most* of the closest worlds where I drop the plate, it falls to the floor, there are a few worlds just as close where the plate flies off sideways? It thus seems that we should conclude that the ordinary counterfactual is false.

This article first appeared in *Philosophy and Phenomenological Research* 70(2) (2003), pp. 396–405. I am grateful for permission to reprint it here.

[1] I am grateful here for discussions with and comments from Frank Artzenius, Adam Elga, Tamar Gendler, David Manley, Ted Sider, Ryan Wasserman, and Timothy Williamson.

[2] See David Lewis, *Counterfactuals* (Blackwell, 1973). On Robert Stalnaker's alternative supervaluationist approach (see notably Robert Stalnaker, 'A Defense of Conditional Excluded Middle,' in W. Harper, R. Stalnaker and G. Pearce (eds.) *Ifs* (1980) 87–104. the threat is one of untruth rather than falsehood. Many of the considerations that follow can be adapted to the Stalnaker framework.

How do we resist this pressure towards an error theory of ordinary counterfactual judgements while retaining the relevant type of scientific theory? I know of two strategies: one replaces 'all' in (4) with 'most'; the other suggests a particular understanding of 'closest' according to which the possibility expressed in (1) can be discounted. After a few remarks about the first strategy, I will devote the bulk of this paper to discussing the second.

FIRST STRATEGY

The first strategy maintains that the truth of (3) is in fact sufficient for the truth of the English sentence (2). In effect the first strategy suggests replacing the standard semantics by

'P > Q' is true iff most of the closest P worlds are Q worlds.

(We need not worry here about exactly what threshold corresponds to 'most'. Presumably it is vague. Most likely it will also be reckoned context-dependent.) There is a striking intuitive cost of the first strategy, one which flows from the fact that it is perfectly possible that most of the closest P worlds are Q worlds and that most of the closest P worlds are R worlds without it being the case that most of the closest P worlds are Q and R worlds. (This is just an instance of the more general fact that for any n less than 100, it is perfectly possible that $n\%$ or more of a given class is F and that $n\%$ or more of that class is G, while less than $n\%$ is F and G.) The cost is that we have to deny the following inference rule.

Agglomeration

(6) P > Q, P > R ⊢ P > (Q and R)

Agglomeration is overwhelmingly intuitive.[3] A speech of the form 'If I had dropped the cup, thus-and-so would have happened and if I had dropped the cup, such-and-such would have happened, but it is not the case that if I had dropped the cup, thus-and-so and such-and-such would have happened' strikes us as profoundly odd.

SECOND STRATEGY

The aim of this paper is to examine in some detail a second strategy, one which offers the hope of saving Agglomeration. It is inspired by some remarks of David Lewis,[4] and is based on the simple idea that worlds with bizarrely low probability outcomes are, ceteris paribus, more distant than worlds without such outcomes. Thus even if the bizarre outcomes do not violate laws of nature, they will be reckoned too distant to undermine ordinary counterfactual judgements. Lewis introduces the notion of a

---

[3] The standard semantics for counterfactuals reckons Agglomeration valid. That is one intuitive virtue of that semantics. Jonathan Bennett, in *A Philosophical Guide to Conditionals* (Oxford University Press, 2003), p. 249 ff., is somewhat sympathetic to the first strategy, though does not address the Agglomeration problem. A further difficulty for the first strategy is indicated in n. 6 below.

[4] See his 'Counterfactual Dependence and Time's Arrow', in *Philosophical Papers Volume II* (Oxford: Oxford University Press, 1986), 32–66.

'quasi-miracle', an event which is both of low probability and which has a pattern which is, by our lights, *remarkable*. Mere low probability does not by itself make an event a quasi-miracle. A good thing too. Any high probability outcome will divide into a set of low probability subcases. The notion of quasi-miracle will not help if *any* sequence of events counts as a quasi-miracle on account of it being of low probability that that very sequence, in all its detail, would occur. Rather, quasi-miraculousness consists of low probability *in combination with* remarkableness. Here is one of Lewis's examples:

If the monkey at the typewriter produces a 950-page dissertation on the varieties of anti-realism, that is at least somewhat quasi-miraculous. . . . If the monkey instead types 950 pages of jumbled letters, that is not at all quasi-miraculous. But, given suitable assumptions about what sort of chance device the monkey is, the one text is exactly as improbable as the other.[5]

Lewis's thesis is that if a world contains a quasi-miracle, that detracts from its similarity to this world.

We now have a recipe for salvaging mundane counterfactuals like (2). Worlds in which a bizarre chance event unfolds are quasi-miraculous worlds and as such are, ceteris paribus, further from the actual world than worlds in which such events do not occur. The worlds in which the plate flies off sideways are thus, by virtue of containing a quasi-miracle, more distant from the actual world than worlds in which the plate falls to the floor. Thus (2) is not undermined by the facts postulated by our scientific theory. What of (1)? Lewis is happy to concede that if I had dropped the plate, there would have been a small chance of it flying off sideways. Suppose we read (1) as:

(7) If I had dropped the plate, it would have been the case that its flying off sideways was (nomically) possible.

On the semantic proposal at hand, this is perfectly compatible with (2). Lewis points out that there is another reading of claims like (1), where 'might' is equivalent to 'not would not'. On that reading, (1) is false. But on that reading (1) is not secured by the scientific theory and in particular is not secured by (7).

Some will reckon the notion of 'remarkableness' too woolly to serve as the basis for an account of the truth value of counterfactuals. Others will have a principled objection to any semantics that appears to tie the truth value of counterfactuals to the contingent make-up of human psychology—which will inevitably be the basis of any articulate distinction between remarkableness and unremarkableness that can do the job here. I shall not pursue these general methodological concerns. Rather I wish to point to four (related) problems that any development of Lewis's view will run into. For my purposes, then, I shall treat 'remarkableness' as something of a primitive, assuming a rough and ready sense on the part of readers as to what Lewis had in mind.

Problem 1

Recall that neither remarkableness nor low probability is alone sufficient to render an event a quasi-miracle. Consider then a remarkable event of reasonably high probability. Suppose, as it happens some monkey at a typewriter is currently so configured

---

[5] 'Counterfactual Dependence and Time's Arrow', p. 60.

that, if left alone, there would be a 20 per cent chance of it typing something that looks much like a novel. You take away the typewriter. Nothing remarkable actually happens. Clearly, the counterfactual

(8) If you hadn't taken away the typewriter, the monkey wouldn't have typed something that looks much like a novel,

is false. So far, no problem. A monkey's writing something much like a novel is remarkable but in the situation described does not seem to count as a quasi-miracle, since it is not of low probability. But there is a problem lurking. Recall that high probability outcomes invariably divide into low probability subcases. The same will be true of *remarkable* high probability outcomes. So consider each particular nomically possible sequence of events ($e^1 \ldots e^n$) in which the monkey types something that looks much like a novel. The disjunction of $e^1 \ldots e^n$ is of reasonably high probability. But each of e^1 to e^n is of very low probability. Moreover each of e^1 to e^n is remarkable. After all, each of e^1 to e^n is a sequence of events in which the monkey writes something very much like a novel. Let us compare those closest worlds w in which the typewriter is not taken way and the monkey types something much like a novel to those closest worlds w^* in which the typewriter isn't taken away and nothing looking much like a novel is produced. Each world w will contain some particular one of the sequence $e^1 \ldots e^n$. Thus each world w will contain a quasi-miracle. Apply Lewis' similarity metric and we will reckon various w^* worlds as closer than any w world on account of the occurrence of a quasi-miracle in each w world. But now (8) comes out true. An intolerable result. General lesson: whenever remarkable non-low probability outcomes divide into remarkable low-probability subcases, Lewis's account, as it stands, will deliver unacceptable results.

(Proposals for a fix should be tested against the following simple counterexample recipe: properties that make for remarkableness in a long sequence of coin flips include: all heads; all tails; being all of the same orientation. For any sequence of fair coin tosses, having the latter property will be twice as likely as having either of the former pair. Suppose being a quasi-miracle requires remarkableness plus being below threshold n. Then one can easily describe a case in which a counterfactual sequence of coin flips is just low enough that the chance of that sequence being all of the same orientation is higher than n but where each subcase—all heads, all tails—is lower than n and hence quasi-miraculous. . . .)

Problem 2

Lewis tells a story according to which (7) is perfectly compatible with (2). But it also predicts other compatibilities that are, intuitively, far more jarring. Consider the following case. A coin flipper is poised to flip a fair coin a million times. You steal the coin. Consider the counterfactual:

(9) If you hadn't stolen the coin, the coin flipper wouldn't have tossed all heads.

A natural enough claim to make in the midst of ordinary thought and talk.[6] And Lewis tells us that it is true. (Granted, there is no nomic prohibition on a world containing a sequence of coin flips which comes up heads each time. But that is a world where a paradigmatically remarkable low probability event occurs, and that world thus contains a quasi-miracle.) Digest Lewis's similarity metric and we can happily assert (9) while also being willing to assert

(10) If you hadn't stolen the coin, there would have been a small chance of the coin flipper's tossing all heads.

There are, obviously, many possible heads/tails sequences that the coin flipper might have produced ($2^{1,000,000}$, in fact). The sequence all heads is a remarkable sequence. But there are plenty of other particular sequences that are unremarkable. Call one such sequence S.[7] (All heads is to S as the monkey's 950 page dissertation is to the 950 page jumble in Lewis's original example.) Even if the combination of (9) and (10) does not immediately strike one as strange, the same cannot be said for various combinations of counterfactuals involving relative likelihood claims in their consequents. Consider:

(11) If you hadn't stolen the coin, the coin flipper's tossing all heads would have been exactly as likely as his tossing S.

(12) If you hadn't stolen the coin, the coin flipper's tossing either all heads or all tails would have been twice as likely as his tossing S.

Both (11) and (12) are incontrovertibly true.[8] Further, Lewis's account tells us that

(13) It is not the case that: if you hadn't stolen the coin, the coin flipper wouldn't have tossed S.

---

[6] Though even here, of course, it is not so hard to induce retraction by, e.g. telling a story in which we build a fair lottery around our coin flipper, such that for each particular sequence S of coin flips, there would be a lottery ticket which wins iff S occurs. Suppose we decide not to build a uniform lottery around the coin flipper. We steal the coin instead. Still, we could have built a fair lottery around the coin flipper in which, say, ticket number 1 corresponds to All Heads. And it seems very bad to outright assert that had we run such a lottery, ticket number 1 would have lost. (Thanks to Adam Elga here.) Moreover, it is also quite easy to get into a frame of mind according to which one thinks that, in effect, a wave function is a fair lottery, and thus a frame of mind in which an assertion of mundane counterfactuals like (2) is tantamount to an assertion that if a certain fair lottery had been run, certain tickets would have lost. The puzzles that arise are similar to those that I have written about at length elsewhere (*Knowledge and Lotteries* (Oxford: Oxford University Press, 2004)).

[7] While it is not my purpose here to unpack the notion of remarkableness, it is obvious enough that our comparative sense of remarkableness is connected to the fact that our conditional probability that a series of coin flips is the outcome of a chance process is much lower on it being all heads than it is on it being S.

[8] Notwithstanding the fact that ordinary people are notoriously bad at comparative likelihood judgements when one sequence seems more 'representative' of the randomness of the process than another to which it is being compared. See Kahneman, Daniel and Tversky, Amos. 1982. 'Subjective probability: A judgement of representativeness', in *Judgment under uncertainty: Heuristics and biases*. Kahneman, Slovic, and Tversky (eds.), 32–47.

(since S does not constitute a quasi-miracle). And we have already accepted

(9) If you hadn't stolen the coin, the coin flipper wouldn't have tossed all heads,

(since tossing all heads *does* constitute a quasi-miracle). Further, assuming Agglomeration (whose consistency with the second strategy is to my mind the main positive virtue of Lewis's proposal), we have:

(14) If you hadn't stolen the coin, the coin flipper wouldn't have tossed either all heads or all tails.

Lewis's theory fails to provide an adequate intuitive basis for asserting the trio (11), (9), and (13). That failure is made even more vivid by considering the trio of (12), (13) and (14). Having claimed that one outcome of a non-actual process would have been twice as likely as another, it seems absurd to use comparative remarkableness as a basis for outright asserting that the more likely outcome would not have occurred while denying that the less likely outcome would not have occurred. General lesson: once the relative likelihoods of remarkable events, as compared with other (less or equally likely) unremarkable events, are fully in view, Lewis's proposal, as it stands, delivers unacceptable results.

Problem 3

Sometimes we realize that it would be pretty surprising if an unremarkable thing never happened. Our scientific theory might say that it is very unlikely indeed that an atom perform a certain patterned motion of geometrical significance at a particular time but that it was pretty likely that sooner or later some atom would perform that patterned motion. Suppose, to illustrate, there are $2^{10,000,000}$ coin flippers $f^1 \ldots f^n$. Each is poised to flip a coin a million times. I arrange for their coins to be stolen. It is quite clearly false that

(15) If I hadn't stolen the coins, none of the coin flippers would have flipped all heads.

It would, after all, have been quite surprising if none of them had flipped all heads. However, bearing in mind (9), Lewis's account would have it true that

(16) If I hadn't stolen the coins, f^1 wouldn't have flipped all heads.

(After all when (9) is asserted, one needn't worry, it would seem, about whether there are other similar coin flipper elsewhere, in distant lands or times.)
    Similarly,

(17) If I hadn't stolen the coins, f^2 wouldn't have flipped all heads.

And so on, for each individual coin flipper.
    By Agglomeration we get

(18) If I hadn't stolen the coins, none of f^1 to f^n would have flipped all heads.

But this contradicts what we noticed earlier, namely that (15) is obviously false. General lesson: there are remarkable event types such that it would be surprising if that event type never occurred in some suitably long patch of history. Combine this observation with Agglomeration and Lewis's theory, as its stands, delivers unacceptable results.

Problem 4

A related worry. In passing, Lewis tells us that we needn't concern ourselves very much with the possibility that the actual world contains lots of quasi-miracles:

> What if, contrary to what we believe, our own world is full of quasi-miracles? Then otherworldly quasi-miracles would not make other worlds dissimilar to ours. But if so, we would be very badly wrong about our own world, so why should we not turn out to be wrong also about which counterfactuals it makes true? I say that the case needn't worry us.[9]

But isn't it obvious that the world it is full of quasi-miracles, construed as low probability events that we would find remarkable once pointed out? Consider, for example, the fact that the apparent size of the sun is that of the moon, the often discussed coincidences between the life of Kennedy and Lincoln,[10] the fact that the acceleration of gravity at the surface of the earth multiplied by one period of the earth's orbit is equal to the speed of light, Bode's Law concerning the relationship of the mean distances of the planets from the sun (misnamed because it describes a coincidence, not a law), facts describing a particular person's getting thirteen cards of the same suit in bridge hand (at odds of 4 in 635,013,559,600), that such and such drew in a single breath one or more molecules from each of the last gasps of the twelve disciples ... and so on.[11] It is hard to see why facts such as these should not count as quasi-miracles. But if they do, then the world contains lots and lots of them. General Lesson: if low probability remarkable events make for dissimilarity, that had better not be because one supposes that the actual world does not itself contain plenty of them.

CONCLUSION

Can Lewis's account be fixed? I hope that the problems make clear that any satisfactory development of Lewis's approach will require selective appeal to contextualism concerning remarkableness, perhaps even in combination with a denial of Agglomeration.[12] We can well anticipate progress being made on our problems by suitable appeal to a context-dependent grain of description that determines which quasi-miracles are relevant, or to some rule of attention according to which the

---

[9] 'Counterfactual Dependence and Time's Arrow', p. 61

[10] See, for example, the Skeptical Inquirer, Sept/Oct 1998.

[11] A rich source of examples like these can be found on the Dartmouth College 'Chance' website at http://www.dartmouth.edu/~chance.

[12] Though the later concession would lead one to wonder whether there was any issue of substance between the first and second strategies.

salience of some low probability event enhances its closeness.[13] One is reminded here of discussions of knowledge where selective appeal to contextualism, sometimes in combination with a denial of epistemic closure, is used to ward off the threat of scepticism. I hesitate to claim that no such package can be made more palatable than the error-theoretic alternative.

In closing I might mention that my own preference is to opt for a picture according to which, for any possibility that P, and any world w, there is a unique closest world to w where P.[14] I realize, of course, that this is to give up altogether on the Lewisian idea of analysing counterfactual closeness in terms of similarity, and to give up on the Lewisian thesis of Humean Supervenience (since it becomes hard to resist allowing for pairs of worlds which are intrinsic duplicates but not counterfactual duplicates). It is also to give up on all neo-verficationist analyses of counterfactual discourse, since the closeness relation between worlds and the counterfactual operator on propositions form a family into which there is no entering reductive wedge.[15] From this perspective, matters are obviously very different when it comes to the problems at hand. Suppose I do not drop a plate at t and the world is chancy. There is a closest world where I drop the plate at t. If it goes off sideways at that world the counterfactual is false. Otherwise it is true. One might protest that there is a residual epistemological problem: how then can we know the truth of the counterfactual that if I had dropped the plate it would have fallen to the floor? Doesn't this require an utterly mysterious kind of modal insight? Consider a happy case in which I make a counterfactual judgement of this sort and the closest world where the antecedent is true is one where the plate I am speaking of falls to the floor. Consider an unhappy case in which the plate I am speaking of flies of sideways at the closest world at which the plate is dropped (at the time I am speaking of). Suppose that there are many more happy cases than unhappy cases, but that there are unhappy cases. The sceptical challenge, when articulated, will

---

[13] Cf. the 'Rule of Attention' in Lewis's 'Elusive Knowledge,' *Papers in Metaphysics and Epistemology*, (Cambridge: Cambridge University Press, 1999), 418–445. Note, though, that adding a dose of contextualism along these lines might very well indict various of the claims made in 'Counterfactual Dependence and Time's Arrow', such as 'If Nixon had pressed the button, there would not have been a quasi-miracle,' where the nomic possibility of a quasi-miracle is obviously very salient and yet discounted.

[14] This is not the place to engage with worries arising from putative cases in which, for every P-world, there is a closer P-world. (See Lewis, *Counterfactuals*, on 'The Limit Assumption' and Stalnaker, 'A Defense of Conditional Excluded Middle,' p. 96ff). Note also that the picture I am tentatively endorsing is rather different from Stalnaker's supervaluationist approach, according to which each precisification of a counterfactual involves a selection function (from a proposition and a possible world to a possible world), but where there are different selection functions on different precisifications. The picture here (leaving aside complications connected to the Limit Assumption) is that there is a single correct selection function that (like metaphysical necessity) is part of the fundamental structure of reality.

[15] What of the worry that 'it is unrealistic to assume that our conceptual resources are capable of well ordering the possible worlds' (Stalnaker, 'A Defense of Conditional Excluded Middle')? The whole point of the view (for better or worse) is that it is a mistake to think that the relevant closeness orderings are fixed by our intuitive constraints on counterfactuals. (Compare: many of us think it is a mistake to think that the line between what is metaphysically possible and what isn't is fixed by our conceptual resources.)

have a familiar shape: 'We cannot discriminate the happy case from the unhappy one. Since we are making a mistake in the unhappy case, we do not know in the happy one.'[16] It remains to be explained why, if we are not sceptics in general, we should nevertheless succumb to scepticism in this particular domain.

I trust that this paper has provided at least some motivation for my preferred orientation. For those intent on pursuing other strategies, I hope at least to have illustrated some of the myriad pitfalls than any such strategy must try to avoid.

---

[16] For a helpful discussion, see Timothy Williamson, *Knowledge and Its Limits* (Oxford: Oxford University Press, 2000) chapter 8. Note that just as scepticism about the future becomes particularly powerful when we, in thought, divide the future into many low probability subcases, so scepticism about counterfactuals becomes particularly powerful when we bring an epistemic space of that kind to bear on it. Can we, despite these pressures, ward off scepticism? I shall not pursue the matter further here.

15

What Would Teleological Causation Be?[1]

with *Daniel Nolan*

As is well known, Aristotelian natural philosophy, and many other systems of natural philosophy since, have relied heavily on teleology and teleological causation. Somehow, the purpose or end of an object can be used to predict and explain what that object does: once you know that the end of an acorn is to become an oak, and a few things about what sorts of circumstances are conducive to the attainment of this end, you can predict a lot about the sprouting of the acorn and the subsequent behaviour of the piece of vegetation that results. Once you know that a rock seeks to move towards the centre of the Earth, you gain some insight into why it falls when released, and why it deforms the carpet or foot that it lands on. Once you know that the rabbit seeks to preserve itself, you can predict it will run from the fox. And so on.

There are at least three features of Aristotle's teleology, and more generally of an Aristotelian frame of mind about teleology, that may induce suspicion. One is that an end can serve as a 'cause': as well as the sort of causation we all recognize, efficient causation, there are other forms, one of which is teleological causation.[2] However, this can look less odd if we think of causes as things that figure in 'because' answers to 'why' questions. Whether or not self-preservation, or the rabbit's continued existence, or something similar, causes the rabbit to run, the reply 'because it seeks to continue in existence' certainly makes sense as an answer, or part of an answer, to a question about why it ran from the fox. (At present we are only claiming that it makes sense—we postpone the question of whether it is strictly speaking correct or particularly informative.)

Another is the suggestion that things other than agents are influenced by teleology, and that objects can have these ends or purposes non-derivatively from the ends or

[1] Thanks, to Frank Arntzenius, Cian Dorr, Hilary Greaves, Hud Hudson, and Carrie Jenkins for helpful discussion, and to a reader for valuable and detailed comments. Thanks to John Carroll, Stuart Brock, and the audience at the 2005 Bellingham Summer Philosophy Conference for comments and critique. Thanks to the Ammonius Institute for research funding that helped John write this paper. Finally, thanks to Dean Zimmerman for providing the party that helped spark this paper.

[2] We do not wish to enter the debate about whether Aristotle's 'four causes' are properly thought of as *causes*, or whether the four somethings-or-other are best understood as something else. That teleological 'causation' was thought of as a kind of cause seems true of parts of the Aristotelian tradition, at least, whether or not it is a misunderstanding of Aristotle.

purposes of agents.[3] That human beings or gods might have purposes that are not explained by the workings of efficient causation is not so mysterious—the idea that some of the things we do are not produced by any antecedent cause but are predictable or explained by purposes and ends we have is not unfamiliar. Nor is it an unfamiliar idea that artefacts can have ends or purposes derivatively.[4] A pen is for writing, because we make pens to have things to write with. A chair is for sitting on, rather than being for, e.g., burning or throwing, in part because its maker made it with the intention that people might sit on it. (And if we were theistically inclined, we might conjecture that some object or project has an end or purpose derivatively from the intentions of God. Some natural disaster was for the purpose of bringing people to their senses, for example.) But that a rock could be *for* moving towards the centre of the Earth, or that we could come across a piece of nature that, independently of any human or divine actions, was *for* providing food to humans, is far from how we typically think of things today.

Of course, the attribution of natural ends, ungiven by human or divine agency, is not entirely absent from our ordinary habits of thought. A tree's roots are partly to draw moisture and nutrients from the soil, and partly to anchor the tree, and maybe there are other ends they serve as well. But we need not think that the tree is some sort of proto-agent, sending its roots out intentionally, and most of us at least understand the thought that trees might be around without the deliberate creation by a natural or supernatural agent. One's heart is for pumping blood, and even though it's around as a result of action by agents (e.g. parents), we don't think that they designed it or gave it its purpose.

There are various stories we can tell about this 'natural teleology'—we might think histories of selection explain why it is correct to attribute purposes to tree-roots, or we might think the hypothesis of deliberate divine creation explains why everything that has a 'natural' purpose or end has that end. Of course, we need not keep these explanations in the back of our minds when we agree that tree roots are to draw up moisture and not to spy on rabbits. But when contemporary philosophers and biologists tell stories about this natural teleology they tend to proceed as if there is a different underlying explanation: superficial teleology gives way to an underlying reality that is not fundamentally teleological at all. This is so even in the case of mental activity. Teleology gives way to mental representations that play efficient causal roles (which in turn may enjoy yet deeper explanations that proceed via categories that are not mentalistic at all).

---

[3] See also Hegel: 'One ought not to conceive the end under the form it assumes in consciousness,—that is to say, under the form of a representation' (*Logic*, Section 104) quoted in Paul Janet, (*Final Causes*, Scribner's, 1892, p. 346.)

[4] Though Bayle thought there to be something deeply misleading about this way of thinking: 'But if a faculty without consciousness and reason merely because it is created by an intelligent being, becomes fit to accomplish works that require intelligence, is it not as if it were said that, of two men equally blind, the one does not know his way, the other knows it because he has been created by a father with eyes? If you are blind, it matters little whether you were born of a blind or seeing father, for in both cases you always need to be guided by the advice and the hand of another.' (Quoted by Janet, p. 359.)

This brings us to a third, and perhaps most noteworthy, feature of the Aristotelian framework, one that is the most troubling of those that we will consider. Teleological explanation can be fundamental: it need not itself be true in virtue of some underlying efficient causal facts.[5] We are happy enough with stories about purposes and ends when there is some deeper efficient causal story to be told in the background. When we agree that a heat seeking missile flew north because it was seeking heat (e.g. a plane's engine or exhaust), we assume that an explanation of the inner workings of the missile in terms of infra-red radiation hitting detectors prompting electrons to flow around and electric motors moving internal workings around is also available to explain why the missile shifted direction and headed north. If we were told that no such explanation was available, and that Boeing had cracked the secret of how to make missiles just plain seek heat without such workings, we would be bewildered.

Contemporary orthodoxy does not, then, take the idea of fundamental teleology very seriously. What we would like to do in this paper is to explore some questions about what it would be to take some cases of teleological causation to be fundamental: that is, to take some cases of teleological causation to not require explanation in some other terms (e.g. in terms of an underlying network of efficient causal laws). Despite the importance of the Aristotelian tradition for teleological thinking, we are not particularly concerned with Aristotle exegesis. We think the concept of final causation answers to something in our pre-theoretic conception of the world (or at least is a natural development from that conception of the world), and also to ideas deployed in many theories besides Aristotle's own. In asking questions about what best sense could be made of this concept, we take ourselves to be asking a somewhat different question to the question of how Aristotle deployed it, or even what Aristotle's theories would look like after a little cleaning up. We should emphasize, in particular, that we have no intention of clarifying teleology by recourse to the kind of matter/substantial form metaphysic within which teleology was historically framed—where, roughly speaking, the end of a thing is determined by a substantial form, that in turn does not supervene on the material properties of a thing.[6] It is no accident that fundamental teleology was abandoned at the same time that matter/form metaphysics gave way to the 'catholick affections of matter'.[7] But it remains far from clear that fundamental teleology needs the kind of metaphysical underpinnings from which Boyle, Descartes, Gassendi, and others recoiled.

WHY CARE ABOUT FUNDAMENTAL TELEOLOGY?

Some of our readers will be asking why they should care. Isn't fundamental teleology part of a superseded, pre-scientific muddle about how the world works? Indeed,

---

[5] We shall clarify the relevant notion of 'fundamental teleology' in due course.

[6] And thus the substantial form serves as the formal cause of the final cause. It is one thing to attribute an end to a thing, quite another to say that it is fixed by a substantial form that does not supervene on the ordinary physical properties of a thing.

[7] See Robert Boyle, 'About the Excellency and Grounds of the Mechanical Hypothesis (1674), reprinted in Thomas Birch (ed.), *The Works of the Honorable Robert Boyle*, Volume IV (1772).

haven't reflective minds known this for quite a long time? Centuries ago, Francis Bacon remarked: 'Inquiry into final causes is sterile, and, like a virgin consecrated to God, produces nothing.'[8] Perhaps there are some whose intellectual interests invite or compel an interest in fundamental teleology. For example, those who feel obliged to think that Thomas Aquinas is basically right about philosophy seem to face an especial burden to make sense of fundamental teleology. But as for the rest of us, aren't questions about final causation about as interesting as questions about phlogiston or angels dancing on the heads of pins?

We think there are some good reasons to be interested.[9] The first reason that one might be interested is that many people think that it was a matter for *a posteriori* discovery that there was no fundamental teleology. This was something that science revealed to us about the world, not something to be settled by *a priori* cogitation. If it is an *a posteriori* question, and one that we settled in the negative through scientific investigation, then what part of our evidence, exactly, bore on that question? If it is an eminently *a posteriori* matter, shouldn't we think that some possible courses of experience would count in its favour? If so, what would they be? If fundamental teleology is not to be dismissed *a priori*, then what is our good reason for dismissing it? Those interested in how general scientific questions are born upon by our empirical evidence should be interested in how our evidence impacted on such a high-level issue as whether there was primitive teleology.

On the other hand, the issue of whether there is fundamental teleology is interesting if it is not, after all, an *a posteriori* matter to be settled by general scientific inquiry. For the question of whether there is fundamental teleology looks like a general hypothesis about the nature of the world that is not obviously inconsistent (and perhaps not inconsistent at all)—and if general hypotheses of this sort are to be settled, if at all, by *a priori* means, then *a priori* cogitation has more of a role in the sciences than many are at first inclined to think. It would be interesting in understanding the history of science, at least, if the biologists of ancient Alexandria were being held up by having made an important *a priori* mistake, rather than the sort of mistake to be discovered and corrected only by *a posteriori* methods.

There are more subtle alternatives here that might be considered. Perhaps someone might think that whether there is fundamental teleology is not an *a priori* matter, but that while *a posteriori* evidence could count against it, no *a posteriori* evidence could count in its favour. Perhaps one could even think that it is discoverable *a priori* that no course of evidence could favour fundamental teleology. If one of these subtle options is true, that might cast some interesting light on the relation of theories to evidence or the role of *a priori* epistemology. One way or another, final causation seems unlike more ordinary cases of commitments discarded in the light of scientific investigation. The kinds of problems we have in working out what is evidence for or against the existence of phlogiston or Vulcan or smallpox-causing demons seem different, in that

---

[8] *De Augmentis Scientiarum* Bk iii Ch. 5, quoted in Woodfield, *Teleology* (Cambridge University Press, 1976), p. 3.

[9] We are interested in phlogiston and angels on the heads of pins, too, but we recognize some of our readers will have less broad interests.

it is relatively straightforward to gesture at what sort of evidence could have counted for or against these hypotheses, but the relation of the hypothesis of final causation to evidence is much more of a philosophical puzzle.

So those prepared to dismiss fundamental teleology as having been ground under the wheels of advancing science may be interested, given their position, in the articulation of how advancing science gave us reason to reject it, or alternatively to explain the *a priori* faculty that would have allowed us to dismiss it in advance of the *a posteriori* evidence. Others may be interested in the question of final causation because they are less sure that it ought to be consigned to the flames. This may be particularly plausible if one is a non-reductionist about scientific inquiry, and one thinks that very different sorts of investigations have their own fundamental theoretical commitments: even if fundamental teleology has no place in contemporary physics and chemistry, it is much less obvious, if one is a non-reductionist, that it has no place in contemporary zoology or ecology or psychology or sociology. The question of fundamental teleology is arguably to be settled on an inquiry by inquiry basis: and we may want illumination about what final causation amounts to in order to decide whether there is any in areas where it might be thought to be a live option.

We have been talking as if fundamental teleology is a dead option in physics and chemistry, but even this might be challenged.[10] There was certainly a revolt against it and other scholastic commitments at the beginning of the modern period, but we are not entirely sure how late live teleological alternatives existed even in physics. Consider anti-atomistic construals of the laws of thermodynamics, which remained respectable into the twentieth century. Suppose we construed closed thermodynamic systems as aiming at thermodynamic equilibria, and that the equilibria that the theory postulates are the ends towards which the system is tending, in a way that is not to be further explained in other physical terms. *Prima facie*, that theory looks rather teleological.

Perhaps some contemporary trends in physics are as well served by teleological interpretations as any other. Systems of laws dominated by 'principles of least action', for example, seem to lend themselves to descriptions of systems primarily in terms of what they tend towards, or what they 'aim at', everything else being equal (or ideally taking everything else into account).[11] Some would want to gloss this talk as being at best metaphorical, but in advance of some reason to reject the postulation of fundamental teleology, it is not clear why we should have to.[12]

Finally, some of our readers may be motivated to explore fundamental teleology for more esoteric reasons. They may still be attracted to Aristotelian or Thomist

---

[10] See, for example, von Weizsacker, The *World View of Physics* (London: Routledge Kegan Paul, 1952).

[11] This continues a thread that began at least as early as Leibniz (see, for example, his contributions to *Acta Eruditorum* in 1691 and 1697 on the catenary curve and the brachistochrone problem), who provides a fascinating case study for those interested in teleological thinking. See especially Jeffrey K. McDonough, 'Leibniz on Internal Teleology and the Laws of Optics", ms.

[12] A perhaps more interesting argument for certain least-action principles being non-teleological would be that they are time reversible.

conceptions of the natural world. Or they may want to consider teleology an option in theology: however a simple divine psychology operates, it is presumably not in virtue of a host of discrete underlying efficient causal mechanisms, so maybe purpose and end-seeking are brute in divine psychology. Or perhaps they are attracted to certain idealist or post-idealist metaphysical pictures: perhaps they believe that there is a *Weltanschung* that has its evolution explained and predicted teleologically; or they take the parts of our world to always and already be infused with the purposes for which humans use them, and that this 'ready-to-handedness' is not to be further explained in terms of the interaction of human psychology and a non-teleological world, perhaps because the latter are abstractions from the former which is taken as fundamental. One of us at least feels no need for these hypotheses, but we invite our readers who do have these commitments in joining with us in thinking about what primitive teleology would be.

WHY SUPPOSE OUR QUESTION HAS AN ANSWER?

Those readers who have persisted might have been convinced that our question is interesting. But there seem to be some reasons to think that it will not have an answer. Perhaps final causation is metaphysically impossible. Perhaps 'final causation' is a natural kind expression that fails to correspond to an actual natural kind, so even if it is conceptually coherent it still lacks enough meaning to be employed usefully. Perhaps, then, questions about final causation are, after all, and perhaps even *a posteriori*, semantically defective in a way that precludes answers to our question from being anything but indeterminate. Or perhaps final causation is possible, but there is no fact of the matter about what it would be like, were there to be some. At the extreme, one might even think that facts about final causation have no necessary connections with any other facts (or very few), so anything could be teleologically produced by any end whatever.

The discussion that follows is designed, in part, to answer these abstract challenges. What we hope to do is to describe nomic structures that first, are readily intelligible, and are thus immune to a charge of obscurantism; that second, are (plausibly) metaphysically possible; and that third, are good enough deservers of the name 'teleological laws'. That is to say that, all things considered, if a world was to enjoy fundamental nomic structures of the sort that we are about to describe then it would enjoy enough of the structure implicated by teleological thinking as to make true an ascription of fundamental teleology to it. There may yet be better possible candidates for primitive teleology than the ones we will describe: but we have done enough for this paper if we show that the notion is coherent and improve our understanding of how it could be applied. We are not going to say that our model is the only way that a world can have teleological laws—quite the opposite—but only that it is one good enough way.

SOME GROUND CLEARING

To begin it is worth noting that some standard philosophical decision points about efficient causation carry over to teleological causation. In the efficient case, there are those who see their task as that of providing an account of efficient causal laws, reckoning particular instances of causation to be manifestations of some governing law or other. And there are those who are singularist in orientation, allowing for the intelligibility of efficient causal connections between events that do not proceed via any overarching laws. So in the case of teleological causation, we might on the one hand take our task to be one of understanding the nature of teleological laws, assuming that any particular instance of teleological causation will implement some such law; and on the other, we might allow that something might do some activity for some end without this having anything to do with some covering law. At the extreme, one might even allow for duplicate worlds—qualitatively and nomically, one of which contains an object that does A for end E, another of which contains a duplicate object that does A for a different end. The topic of fundamental teleology is difficult enough without attempting to accommodate rampant singularism at the fundamental level. We shall thus set ourselves the task of getting a handle on what would reasonably count as a fundamental teleological law.

Another standard contrast within the space of positions on efficient causation is between reductionism and non-reductionism. There are those who believe that the causal facts supervene on a ground floor that can be perspicuously described without recourse to causal and nomic concepts. A paradigm case in point here is David Lewis, who believed that the facts about which causal laws obtain at a world and what causes what at a world supervene on facts about the spatiotemporal distribution of qualities at that world.[13] Since our focus is nomic, it is especially useful to recall his view about what makes it true that a set of laws is fundamental, namely, that it is the set of generalizations that best combines simplicity and informativeness. At a rough first pass, to gauge simplicity and informativeness, we examine a formulation of the laws in a language in which the most natural properties correspond to lexically simple predicates, and less natural properties are expressed by complexes. Simplicity is then gauged by the length of the total expression of the laws, and informativeness is gauged by some natural measure on how much is ruled out by the law. We are by no means committed to this sort of reductionism about laws of nature. But it would certainly aid the cause of fundamental teleological laws were they presented in such a way as to be compatible with reductionism—thus requiring no strange causal-telic primitive relations at the metaphysical ground floor. We will thus present a conception of teleological laws that is *compatible* with reductionism. Better still, we will present an

---

[13] See especially *Philosophical Papers Volume II* (Oxford University Press, 1986) and *Papers in Metaphysics and Epistemology* (Cambridge: Cambridge University Press, 1999), where this picture plays a frequent and systematic role.

account of fundamental teleological laws that is compatible with Lewis's gloss on fundamental laws: there are possible worlds for which fundamental teleology provides the best combination of simplicity and informativeness. Teleological causation and laws could be perfectly coherent, and perhaps even possibilities, even if they were irreducible. The advantage of providing a description compatible with reductionism about laws is that we can appeal to a broader audience.[14]

TELEOLOGY AND BACKWARD CAUSATION

There are some initial thoughts we want to dispose of about what counts as fundamental teleology. One initial thought is that we have teleology exactly when current states are systematically nomically correlated with future states. Aristotle's acorn, which seeks to become an oak tree, has its behaviour predicted and explained, it seems, with reference to its future state: specify what a mature oak tree is like, and tell me that the acorn will change so as to move closer to that state, and you're on the way to enabling me to predict what the acorn and young oak will do in a variety of situations—the roots will sprout down and the leaves will sprout up, the sapling will get taller and wider each year, and so on. When we treat a heat-seeking missile teleologically, we keep in mind that its 'aim' is to impact a strong heat source in its vicinity—the twists and turns of a heat-seeking missile following a fighter-jet engaged in evasive action can be predicted when we think of the missile as 'trying' to hit the plane's engines.

There are several reasons why we should not just take teleology to be a matter of nomological correlation with a future state. One is that if the laws are suitably deterministic (so that the state of the world at a time determines both a unique future and a unique past), a specification of the future state of a system together with the laws will determine the past state of a system—and we would not want Newtonian mechanics to count as teleological simply because it is deterministic.

There is another kind of conceivable prediction and explanation which relies on specifications of a future state to predict and explain past states, and which we think is worthwhile to not confuse with teleology. Many people think that it is at least conceptually possible that there be backwards causation (backwards efficient causation, that is). Perhaps the best-known thought experiments about backwards causation are time travel ones: my packing a sandwich now before stepping into my time machine explains the presence of a sandwich covered in plastic wrap in the twelfth century, and if you know how the insides of my time machine are now, you can better predict and

---

[14] Even having provided an account of teleological laws, there remain tricky issues about how to deal with the causal relation between particular events. One might think that an earlier event causes a later event only if that sequence is 'covered' by the efficient causal laws. But such a thought risks relying on the currently unfashionable deductive-nomological account of event causation. Nor is it true to the teleological tradition: many teleologists had the idea that an earlier event couldn't cause a later event without there being final causation, since what makes an event suited to cause what it does is something final. Thus Thomas Aquinas says in *De Principiis Naturae*, 4.22 'Whence the end is the cause of the causality of the efficient cause'. On that view, then, teleology explains efficient causation between events. We shall not pursue these issues further here.

explain the goings-on inside my time machine when it arrives in the twelfth century. Despite this, in these sorts of cases we are not inclined to think that the way the sandwich is in medieval times is explained by some fundamental purpose it has to then be a certain way in the early twenty-first century.

Consider a sequence of events like the following: we have a black box travelling at a constant velocity through space, surrounded by a miscellany of objects. At some point, some objects behind the box have particles that leave them on a trajectory that will impact with the box (so they are emitted at angles that will strike where the box will be, not where it is at the time of emission). Shortly afterwards, more objects have particles that leave them behind the box, together with some objects well ahead of the box's path. All of these particles are moving with velocities and trajectories so that they will 'impact' the box at the same time. As the time of intersection of the various paths gets closer, objects nearer and nearer the box have particles leave them. Finally, all the particles touch the surface of the box at the same time and disappear, and it turns out that their momentums all cancel out (and let us suppose the box's mass-energy changes at that point to become the sum of its previous mass-energy plus those of the particles). If that is what we knew of the behaviour of this system, what sorts of laws might we conjecture governed the movements and causal reactions of those particles, the objects they came from, and the box?

We should give some credence to this being a massive coincidence. We could give some credence to the hypothesis that this was all a massive set-up, and that some past causal process 'primed' the situation to produce a coincidence in the future, of many particles striking the box at once from all directions. We could, if we thought it made sense, ascribe primitive 'purposes' to these particles, or perhaps the objects they came from, to seek the box at the time of intersection. Or, finally, we could describe it as a case of backwards causation—the 'intersection' event was actually an emission event, when the box released many particles travelling backwards in time, and as a causal result of this, the particles were absorbed by the objects in the box's environment some time before the emission. In both of the latter cases, the state of the box at 'intersection time' would in an important way explain and predict (or retrodict) the movements of the particles. But the style of understanding this sequence of events as involving emission of time-travelling particles seems very different from attributing primitive teleology.

We think we have some grasp on when it would make sense to interpret these events as being a result of backwards causation (though to make the choice might require more information than we are given just by the description above). For example, if we found particles like that in our world, and they conformed to the equations of relativity theory, given our confidence that those laws are near-enough right in describing the velocities and mass-energies of particles, we would have reason to believe that they were moving backwards in time rather than forwards at faster than the speed of light. If we further had a reasonable conjecture about how such particles were produced, and we found the box was set up as predicted while the objects that the particles were first observed next to were a physical miscellany which were not plausible emitters of these exotic particles, then the case for backwards causation of the particles by the box would be very strong.

This example suggests that when we have a course of events where past states seem to be nomologically dependent on future states and not vice versa, we should not rush to a teleological explanation of the future states. If we discover that the behaviour of acorns now is predicted and explained by the flourishing of mature oaks later, one possibility we need to rule out is that those oak-states-of-affairs are causing the acorn-sprouting states of affairs through backwards efficient causation. When the missile flies towards the heat-source, one option to discount (though normally we discount it without a second thought) is that exploding jet engines spit out heat-repelled backwards-in-time-travelling missiles, which explains why there are missiles in missile cradles some time before the relevant sorts of engine explodings.

It is worth pausing to characterize the difference between backward causation and final causation. One point of divergence has to do with the stepwise character of backward causation. In the standard cases, when some future state s_1 backward causes some past state s_2, there is some chain running from s_1 to s_2 such that proximate members of the chain standard in backward causal relations to each other. The Aristotelian picture of final causation is not like this. The development of a tree at a given time is explained by the mature state, but not by the state right after that time.

Of course one might not insist that backwards causation absolutely must proceed in the stepwise fashion just alluded to. In the case of past to future efficient causation, some of us wish to allow for action at a temporal distance, so that some event at t causes some event an hour after t without there be a connecting causal chain. Similarly, then, one might wish to allow backwards causation at a temporal distance. Why not treat final causation in this way?

This last suggestion still overlooks one absolutely crucial feature of teleology, namely that final causation is supposed to be compatible with the end not actually being reached, so there need not be any later state for the earlier state to be nomologically correlated with at all.[15] The acorn sprouts and turns into a sapling even if it gets cut down before it becomes a mature oak. The rock tumbles to the bottom of the hill, even if it never reaches the centre of the Earth. The agent saves money to buy a house, even if a bank crash bankrupts him before he has enough. An object can act because of its aim, or its function, even when it never reaches its aim or its function cannot be successfully carried out. Whatever final causation would be, it does not seem that it could be a matter of something being brought about by a future event, unless non-existent future events were as able to bring things about as well as existent ones. To the extent that we find causation by non-existents absurd, we should hunt for another way of getting a grip on final causation.[16]

(A further reason to distinguish final causation from nomological dependence on future states of affairs is the coherence of the notion of backwards final causation,

---

[15] Of course some may allow efficient causal laws to connect properties F and G in worlds where F is instantiated and G is not. But the point is that in the efficient causal case, the law explains by way of connecting two events (the cause and the effect), whereas in the final case, application of the law will not require a pair of existing events as relata.

[16] One way to keep the idea that the final states always do causing in cases of final causation would be to employ Aristotle's distinction between existence in actuality and existence in potentiality. If we said that there was already a mature oak existing in potentiality as soon as the acorn came into

where the transitions of a system are explained in terms of an aim or function concerning its state in the past. Backwards final causation has never been discussed, so far as we know. We shall focus, with orthodoxy, on forwards final causation, though it will be obvious how to extend the discussion to backwards final causation.)

ARISTOTELIAN ROCKS AND TELIC PYRAMIDS

The Aristotelian tells us that rocks fall in order to be at the centre of the Earth. Even in this simple case, there are a number of implicit assumptions that are worth bringing out, ones that will help us a great deal in articulating a serviceable version of final causal laws.

First, as we try to adopt an Aristotelian perspective on the case, we naturally suppose there to be a number of jointly indeterministic non-final constraints upon the rock. We suppose that it is not possible for the rock to move discontinuously. The final causal law doesn't explain that. Nor is it clear that the final causal component of nomic space will explain the limitations of speed on the rock's descent. And so on. On the other hand, the non-final constraints on the rock cannot themselves determine a unique path. Otherwise there would be no work for final causal laws to do! In general, when final causation explains the path of a system, there will be non-final constraints upon the path.

Second—and this is crucial—there are possible cases in which we wish to say that a rock acts in order to reach the earth despite the fact that its actual motion was far from the best way to reach the earth. Indeed, its motion may have made it radically less likely to reach the earth. Suppose the rock begins by being dropped just above the lip of a suspended open bucket. Suppose the 'constraints', whatever they are, do not determine whether the rock will go down or sideways. Now if the rock first went sideways and then went down it would do a far better job at reaching the earth than if it headed straight into the bucket. How, then, is one entitled to say that the rock went down in order to reach the earth? If the law says 'Do what it takes to get to the earth', then the rock will violate the law. Meanwhile, if the constraints require the rock to fall, then it will be the constraints and not the teleology that explains its falling.

It is of no use at this point for the Aristotelian to tell us that the rock 'thought' that going down was the best way of reaching the earth—and that the laws say that rocks will do what they think is the best way of reaching the earth. This response would confirm the already significant suspicion that Aristotelian teleology is bound up with an illicit projection of mental states on to unthinking things.

The challenge can be answered. Doing so brings to the fore the kind of ideological structure that will be appropriate to rigorous development of the final causal picture. First, given a system, there will be a state that is thought of as the end state. Second, one will deploy a natural metric for calibrating the system's distance from the end state. (Let us be clear, distance is not being thought of as something that in general

existence (or a mature-oak-state-of-affairs existing in potentiality) that mature oak (or oak-state-of-affairs) could be the final cause we need. To the extent one wishes to reject a kinds-of-existence doctrine, one will find final causation so described as unappealing.

correlates with physical distance from some object or place. For this reason, the rock example can be somewhat distracting.) Now once such a distance metric is in place, we can define an abstract notion of end-velocity in terms of (abstract) distance and time. Whatever the relevant notion of distance the coordinate notion of end-velocity will be such that end-velocity (which can be positive or negative) over an interval is a matter of the change in distance from the end point divided by duration of the interval, and the end-velocity at a time is the derivative of distance over time.[17]

Return to the rock hovering over the bucket that is released. We could imagine a law saying:

L1: If a rock has one or more paths to the end state compatible with the constraints, it will take a path (that is compatible with the constraints and) which gets it to the end state at least as quickly (in time) as any other path compatible with the constraints.

But note that this gloss on the law—one that makes no reference to the notion of end-velocity and hence doesn't depend on any suitable notion of distance—does not accord at all with the Aristotelian picture of the teleological behaviour of rocks (or, relatedly, with the actual behaviour of rocks). The rock goes down and not sideways, but the law recommends otherwise. Moreover, in a situation where the constraints preclude the rock reaching the ground (suppose it to be in surrounded on all sides by a suspended sphere), it will still be a fit subject for teleological explanation.[18] But L1 will be silent in a case where there is no available path to the end state that is compatible with the constraints.

Imagine, instead, the following law:

L2: At any time t, a rock will follow a continuation c_1 of its path in such a way that, for every other continuation c_2 compatible with the constraints, there is a period after t such that the rock has greater end velocity on c_1 than on c_2 during that period.[19]

If one is looking for metaphors, L2 invites the image that rocks act blindly towards their ends, while L1 suggests a picture according to which rocks act with foresight. As the Aristotelian thinks about it, teleological explanation as applied to unthinking matter is apt to be of the blind sort and so naturally regimented by L2.

We in no way mean to suggest, of course, that the most suitable system of fundamental laws for actual rocks will take the form of L2. But might there not be a world for which certain of the fundamental laws take the form of L2? Imagine a world of the

[17] Note that since there is a privileged end state, there are only two directions relevant to the vectorial component of end-velocity: towards and away from.

[18] Note that, similarly, Jonathan Bennett's account of teleological laws in *Linguistic Behaviour* (Cambridge University Press, 1976) does not make room for this kind of explanation. His 'basic theory' of teleological laws says 'any R thing will do whatever is required for and sufficient for its becoming or remaining G' (p. 39). A law of this sort cannot explain the rock's behaviour in this case. Meanwhile, his refined theory of teleology involves a kind of proto-belief—'registration'—which will be out of place for rocks. Of course, since Bennett is not trying to provide an account that could underwrite, say, fundamental teleology for rocks, these considerations may not spell trouble for his own project.

[19] Note that we do not mean to be arguing here that the only laws that deserve being called 'teleological' are ones that take the shape of L1 or L2.

following sort.[20] Now and then energy spawns clusters of distinctive particles—call them p-particles—that are distributed in all sorts of wild and wonderful patterns at the time of inception. The particles share a simple intrinsic structure. In general, we notice that the clusters of particles move in such a way that they form pyramidal structures, a fact that obviously cannot be explained in terms of the intrinsic features of the individual particles. Barring some violent external influence, clusters of particles form pyramids. And barring some violent external disruption, such structures stay in place once formed.

We investigate closer. We notice a fairly natural way of calibrating how close a cluster of particles is from being organized pyramidally, and that a correlative notion of end-velocity can be defined. We then notice that relative to such a calibration (and a plausible account of the other constraints on the system of particles), something very precise can be said about the behaviour of the system of particles: at any given time, the system acts so as to maximize end-velocity. We thus hypothesize that the following law obtains:

L2*: For any system s of p-particles at a time t, s will follow a continuation c_1 of its path in such a way that, for every other continuation c_2 compatible with the constraints, there is a period after t such that s has greater end velocity on c_1 than on c_2 during that period.

A few obvious points can be made in connection with the example. First, it is clear enough as an epistemological point that it would be very natural for the people in our imagined world to regard L2* as both fundamental and teleological. Second, if we accept the Lewisian story about what makes a fundamental law true of a world, we can very well imagine that some such law would figure—from a God's eye point of view—as the best combination of simplicity and informativeness and thus count as a fundamental law. Third, even leaving to one side the Lewisian story, there seems to be no good *a priori* reason why such a law could not be fundamental. Of course it may be that as a matter of deep *a posteriori* (or inscrutable) necessity, a law of this sort is impossible. But if this is so, it is a modal discovery that has not yet been made.

One final observation: L2*, as it applies to individual particles, is non-local, but this should not be confused with its teleological character. The non-local character consists in the fact that the behaviour of a particle at a time is not determined by its local environment but rather by the configuration of the other particles in the system. The teleological character of the law, meanwhile, consists in the fact that the behaviour of the system is to be explained in terms of getting closer to a privileged state (that may or may not be actualized). Non-locality certainly does not require teleology. And teleology does not require non-locality. (Imagine that point particles at some possible world had a very complicated set of intrinsic properties, and that the evolution of the internal life of a point particle was explained in terms of an L2 style law that depended upon some calibration of distance between possible intrinsic states of a point particle and some privileged state . . .)

---

[20] One interesting kind of case to consider, suggested by Frank Arntzenius, is a time-reversed version of this world, where everything ultimately collapses to a singularity.

A MORE FORMAL PRESENTATION[21]

Rigorous presentations of physical theories often proceed in terms of a state space
for physical systems, whereby the possible states of a system are given as points in an
n-dimensional space. Possible trajectories for the system (let us assume for now a classical notion of time) can be given as functions from times to points in the state space.
The ideas presented above can be formulated quite naturally in terms of some such
formalism.[22]

> Let Ω be the configuration space of the system.
> Let T be the set of times.
> Let a path be a function f from T to Ω
> Let F_{ant} be the set of paths f that are compatible with the constraints.
> Let C be a designated point in the configuration space. (Of course, it may be
> more natural in some cases to treat C as a region and not as a point. Think back
> to the pyramids—there is more than one point in the state space where a given
> cluster of particles forms a perfect pyramid. We shall ignore this complication in
> what follows.)
> Let $Vtt'(f)$ be the average end-velocity of path f between t and t'.
> Let $m(x)$ be a function from configurations $x \in \Omega$ to the real numbers $\mathbb{R}$, where
> $m(x)$ gives the distance of configuration x from configuration C.
> An L1 type teleological law can now be represented as follows:

$$F_{Tel\ 1} = \{f \in F_{ant} : (\forall t \in T)(\sim\exists f' \in F_{ant})(\forall t')(t \geq t')f(t')$$
$$= f'(t') \wedge (\exists t' > t)(f'(t') = C) \wedge (\sim\exists t'')((t' \geq t'') \wedge (f(t'') = C))\}^{23}$$

(Hereafter we shall call laws of this type 'quickest path laws'.)
  Laws of an L2 type can be expressed by the following type of constraint on paths:

$$F_{Tel\ 2} = \{f \in F_{ant} : (\sim\exists f' \in F_{ant})(\exists t \in T)\forall t'(t \geq t')f(t')$$
$$= f'(t') \wedge (\exists t'' > t)(\forall t''')((t'' > t''' > t) \supset Vtt'''(f') \geq Vtt'''(f))\}$$

(Hereafter we shall call these 'end-velocity laws'.)
  We are prepared to consider both sorts of laws as teleological laws, though our
primary interest is in the L2 type of law.[24]

---

[21] Thanks to Frank Arntzenius and Hilary Greaves here.

[22] This formalism is naturally applicable in a case where the relevant fundamental teleological
law says that the world-system has an end, as opposed to teleological laws that posit ends for certain
subsystems (i.e. where the development of a subsystem turns on how the entire system most quickly
approaches its end, rather than one accords each subsystem its own end.) It nevertheless serves a
nice illustration of how certain kinds of teleological laws could be articulated in a rigorous way.

[23] Here and in what follows further qualifications would be in order if one were to allow that in
certain cases, there is, for every path, a quicker path compatible with the constraints. (One may, for
example, write the law in such a way that it dictates nothing were this situation to arise.)

[24] For what it's worth our subjective probability of a fundamental law at the actual world being
an end-velocity law is also somewhat higher than it is for a quickest path law.

OBJECTIONS AND REPLIES

Objection One: Even if quickest path laws or end velocity laws obtained and were fundamental, that wouldn't make it true to say that there was final causation or fundamental teleology in the world in question, because the laws do not *say* that things act 'for' the sake of getting to C (the point relative to which the relevant notion of velocity is defined) or that have C as their end, or that they act with the purpose of getting to C. One can't simply *stipulate* that in such a case C is the end and that things act for the sake of C.

Reply: Quite often, when there is a disputed term or concept, the cogency of which is in question, one who wishes to defend the coherence of the relevant concept proceeds by describing situations using concepts that are not under dispute and then argues that the situation so described captures enough of the semantic intentions underlying the original concept as to make it reasonable to claim that were such a scenario to obtain, the concept in question would apply. Abstractly conceived, the strategy is an altogether familiar one. The defender of the cogency of the concepts of say, human choice or external colours, describes the world in terms that are acceptable to all parties and then argues that such a world would fit the relevant facts about use well enough to render correct various predications of freedom and colour. Such an advocate might, of course, concede various idiosyncrasies or natural tendencies in our conceptions of colour or freedom that could not be made good upon. Perhaps we habitually think that if a surface is yellow, then so is every part of the surface (which runs into conflict with the fact that atoms aren't yellow). Perhaps we habitually think that if one has a choice about x and y necessitates x then one has a choice about y. But a failure to fit every such twist and turn in our conceptions of colour and freedom is not yet to render such predications false. Such a move space ought to be absolutely familiar to philosophical readers.

Suppose one thought that specifying a fundamental end-velocity law, for example, was not sufficient for teleological causation. The challenge would be to say what more was needed. Such a law would at least be evidence that there is teleology, and we maintain that the law by itself would be enough, though presumably our opponent would think more is needed. One kind of opponent we might face is a teleological mystic who takes the view that teleological facts and laws were such that they could not be capturable in any other terms: unless a possible scenario is specifically described in teleological language, one has not done enough to ensure that there is anything teleological about it. By such lights, to deprive oneself of the concept of 'acting for' is *ipso facto* to become blind to teleological facts altogether. Such a primitivist might insist that there are two possible worlds governed by the same end-velocity laws, one containing teleology and one lacking it. She would not be sympathetic to our claim to have described a situation with teleology.

While it is difficult to say anything decisive against this form of primitivism, we are not sympathetic to it: it is one thing to allow that teleology be fundamental, quite another to insist that a teleological understanding of the world is so foundational and primitive that the facts about the world that make it correct cannot be described in any other terms. One puzzle for this sort of primitivism, for example, is to explain why lawlike behaviour of possible objects like our 'telic pyramids' suggests teleology so strongly if it has no conceptual connection with it. We are more open-minded about the challenge that allows a teleological set-up can be captured in other terms, but that it requires more than we have proposed. Of course, while we are open-minded, we are yet to be convinced that anything more is needed.

Objection Two: If one is sneaky about one's choice of metric, can't one always reformulate a law in terms of a teleological law that explains the world in terms of some abstract velocity-law? For example, can't one select an arbitrary point in a Newtonian state space and then cook up a gerrymandered distance function N and a coordinate end-velocity law L, such that things satisfy L iff they satisfy the laws of Newtonian mechanics?

Reply: Minor point: there will be some principled challenges to translating some sets of laws into teleological form. In particular, if a set of laws is time reversible (so that if a history is permitted by the laws, then so is the time-reversed version of the history), then there will be a problem in principle in coming up with a translation scheme, since teleological laws of the sort that we have been describing are not time reversible. Major point: The problem is essentially no different from Nelson Goodman's riddle of induction.[25] We know that, in general, a generalization that is framed in terms of 'projectible' predicates will be analytically equivalent to a generalization that is framed in terms of gruesome, gerrymanded predicates. But we do not standardly conclude that the both generalizations are equally good candidates for expressing a law of nature.[26]

Even those of us that do not approve of David Lewis's reductionism think that there is something right about the idea that the laws will be expressed in terms of predicates that express very natural properties. A similar lesson applies here. Not all distance metrics relating arbitrary points to a selected point in a state space will be equally natural: some will be deeply gruesome, others not. Generalizations that take the form of quickest path or end-velocity laws but which deploy highly unnatural distance metrics will not be very good candidates for expressing laws of nature. Meanwhile, it will certainly not be true that any system of efficient causal laws can be translated into a set of teleological laws that deploys fairly natural distance relations.

Of course, we are aware that some readers will be altogether wary of the Lewisian hierarchy of naturalness, and will urge that while not all properties and relations attract our attention equally, none are objectively more real, or natural, or haloed than others. It is clear what such readers ought to conclude: the question of whether

---

[25] See *Fact, Fiction and Forecast* (Harvard University Press, 1955).

[26] For those people that individuate propositions in a coarse way, so that sentences true at the same set of worlds automatically express the same proposition, the point will have to be put differently: a gruesome generalization will express a law of nature only if there is way of expressing the same generalization using projectable/natural predicates.

the world is teleological is theory dependent. From this neo-positivist perspective, it makes no sense to ask whether the world is teleological or not, only whether some notation for expressing the world's regularities is teleological or not. We are not inclined to such a view. Those that are will be forced to concede that the choice not to describe the world using laws couched in the teleological forms we have described is a choice that is not forced upon us by the world but by some suitable mixture of biology, fashion, and convention.

Objection Three: This account of teleological laws does not capture Aristotelian teleology because it makes no mention of the good. After all, Aristotle tells us that we explain what happens in terms of what is for what, he imagines that such explanations will take the form 'because better thus—better not simply, but in relation to the reality of the thing concerned'.[27] For Aristotle then, reality is governed by the overarching principle that each thing tends towards that which is good for it. The present account makes no mention of this.

Reply: It is obviously right that the good plays an important role in Aristotelian teleological theory. Nevertheless, we think clarity is best served by proceeding in the way we have. For we think it is useful to separate the question whether any fundamental laws are end-velocity or quickest path laws from the question of whether such laws are instantiated by normative target points and distance metrics that correspond to some normative better/worse ranking. Let us agree, for example, that in order to come reasonably close to the Aristotelian vision in respect of teleology, it would not be enough that some end-velocity laws obtain. For the Aristotelian would no doubt hope that each relevant C would be the state that is best for the system, what constitutes flourishing for the system. Furthermore, the Aristotelian would hope that for any system (or at least any system that deserves the name 'substance'—let us not dwell on this subtlety here), there is a law that tells us that, when other things are equal, the system heads towards its flourishing point. Moreover, in such a situation, the maximal blend of simplicity and informativeness would be achieved by a general law that said that any system will tend towards its flourishing point (where each flourishing point bears a natural similarity to any other with respect to the abstract—but far from gruesome—property for being what is good for the system that is at that point).

One reason that clarity is best served by the proposed separation of issues is that while some people will object to the idea that end-velocity or quickest path laws might be fundamental, others will confine their concerns to the hypothesis that flourishing points and normative better/worse relations might figure in such laws.

As we see it, it is eminently natural to regard at least end-velocity laws as teleological even if they are detached from notions of flourishing and even if, on that score, they do not vindicate certain important aspects of the Aristotelian tradition. In particular,

---

[27] Physics Book II, Chapter 7 in Ackrill, *A New Aristotle Reader* (Princeton University Press, 1987), p. 106. See also the way that Aristotle ties the good to 'that for the sake of which things are done' in the Nichomachean Ethics and elsewhere.

it is natural to do so on account of deep structural analogies between explanations that proceed via end-velocity laws and paradigmatically Aristotelian explanations.

Let us say that a world is Robustly Aristotelian iff a very large range of its inhabitants are governed by end-velocity laws in which the designated end state for a thing corresponds to what is best for the thing in question and where the relevant distance metric corresponds to what is better or worse for the system. We have indicated that we see no objection in principle to the possibility of worlds governed by end-velocity laws. What though of the suggestion that a world might be Robustly Aristotelian? There are two obvious kinds of obstacles to such a suggestion. The first is scepticism about the very possibility of the normative properties required for such laws—being good for a system and so forth. It will hardly be obvious to everyone that Aristotelian flourishing properties—which apply to non-biological systems and that hold of systems independently of the intentions of minded users and creators—are even possible. Second, even if such properties do exist, one might think them insufficiently natural to count as suitable bases for generalizations that deserve the name 'natural law'. These, indeed, seem to be the fundamental objections. Once the relevant domain of natural properties is conceded, it will at least be rather difficult to see why a Robustly Aristotelian world is impossible (at least on *a priori* grounds). Once again we can take the Lewisian conception as an initial springboard. At least by Lewisian standards, it will be very hard to argue that Robustly Aristotelian worlds are impossible (once the above concession is made), and this is because it will be extremely difficult to argue for the metaphysical impossibility of a world in which suitably normative end-velocity laws are the best compromise of informativeness and simplicity.

WHY IS THERE SOMETHING RATHER THAN NOTHING?

We end on a lighter (some will think heavier) note. Turning to one of the 'big', time-honoured, questions in metaphysics, one might reasonably wonder whether teleological laws could explain why there is something rather than nothing. We incline towards an affirmative answer. Consider a world in which the following obtain: (i) The 'constraints' in that world do not prevent something following nothing. (ii) The teleological laws entail that if a world is such that there is nothing at any time, then reality gets closer to C (the end given by the laws) by having not nothing after that time than if reality stays at nothing. (Note that this requires an end-velocity law that applies to reality itself rather than to some subsystem within it.) With this in place it is quite clear that it is nomologically impossible that reality always contain nothing. Since we are inclined to think (i) and (ii) are possible, we are inclined to think that at least at some worlds, there is a teleological reason why there is something rather than nothing. Moreover, if (a) time stretches back infinitely, (b) the constraints never require something becoming nothing, and (c) a move from a situation *s* that is not nothing to nothing is always a move further from C than a move from *s* to a situation that is not nothing, then it will be nomologically impossible that there is ever nothing.

Such explanations have obvious limitations. If the laws are contingent, then the explanation will not tell one that there *has to be* something rather than nothing. And if one wishes to liberalize 'something' to include time itself, the explanation will no longer be satisfying. In that case, if a teleological explanation can proceed at all, it will have to be embedded in an abstract state space in which not every point is one in which time even exists, but to which the by now familiar machinery of constraints and teleological laws can apply. We postpone such flirtations with the limits of understanding to another occasion.

16

Before-Effect and Zeno Causality[1]

In his 1964 monograph *Infinity: An Essay in Metaphysics*, Jose Benardete presents the following intriguing puzzle:

Let the peal of a gong be heard in the last half of a minute, a second peal in the preceding 1/4 minute, a third peal in the 1/8 minute before that, etc. *ad infinitum*. . . . Of particular interest is the following puzzling case. Let us assume that each peal is so very loud that, upon hearing it, anyone is struck deaf—totally and permanently. At the end of the minute we shall be completely deaf (any one peal being sufficient), but we shall not have heard a single peal! For at most we could have heard only *one* of the peals (any single peal striking one deaf *instantly*), and which peal could we have heard? There simply was no first peal. We are all familiar with various physical processes that are followed by what are called after-effects. We are now tempted to coin the barbarous neologism of a *before-effect*.[2]

He goes on to offer some more examples:

A man is shot through the heart during the last half of a minute by A. B shoots him through the heart during the preceding 1/4 minute, C during the 1/8 minute before that, &c. *ad infinitum*. Assuming that each shot kills instantly (if the man were alive), the man must be already dead before each shot. Thus he cannot be said to have died of a bullet wound. Here, again, the infinite sequence logically entails a before-effect. Consider now the following even more radical version of this paradox. A man decides to walk one mile from A to B. A god waits in readiness to throw up a wall blocking the man's further advance when the man has travelled 1/2 mile. A second god (unknown to the first) waits in readiness to throw up a wall of his own blocking the man's further advance when the man has travelled 1/4 mile. A third god . . . &c. *ad infinitum*. It is clear that this infinite sequence of mere intentions (assuming the contrary-to-fact conditional that each god would succeed in executing his intention if given the opportunity) logically entails the consequence that the man will be arrested at point A; he will not be able to pass beyond it, even though not a single wall will in fact be thrown down in his path. The before-effect here will be described by the man as a strange field of force blocking his passage forward.[3]

What, if anything, can be learned from these cases? Section one explores a case that is structurally similar to the above puzzle cases, though rather easier to think about. Having unpacked that puzzle case, we shall be in a position to defuse a number of the

This article appeared in *Noûs*, December 2000, 622–33.
 [1] I am grateful to Jose Benardete, David Chalmers, Tamar Gendler, Trenton Merricks, Jeff McDonough, Ted Sider, Peter Van Inwagen, Dean Zimmerman and audiences at Rutgers University and the Mighty Midwestern Metaphysics conference, 1998, for helpful discussion.
 [2] *Infinity: An Essay in Metaphysics* (Oxford: Clarendon Press, 1964), 255–9.
 [3] Ibid. pp. 259–60.

before-effect cases presented above. Section two explores the 'more radical version of the paradox'.

SECTION ONE

Consider a world where a series of walls are laid out on a two mile stretch of road in the following way. The road has two endpoints, A and B. At B, which is two miles from A, there is the surface of a wall which is a foot thick, the other surface being two miles plus one foot from A.[4] At the point between A and B that is one and a half miles from A, there is the surface of a wall which is half a foot thick, the other surface being one and a half miles plus half a foot from A. At the one and a quarter mile point, there is a wall that is quarter of a foot thick . . . and so on. There are thus infinitely many walls, such that for each wall there are infinitely many walls closer to A than that wall. For convenience, let us suppose that each wall has a number tag such that the wall at B is numbered '1', the wall next furthest from A is numbered '2' and so on.

A sphere made of material y is rolled from A. There are no objects standing between the sphere and the walls and hence the first mile stretch is empty. Let us stipulate that the stretch is on a slight incline, inviting the sphere to naturally roll towards B. It is not causally possible for it to burrow into the earth, nor for it to leave the ground. The motion of y-objects is continuous: if a y object is at p_1 at t_1 and p_2 at t_2 then it has travelled some continuous path connecting p_1 and p_2 between t_1 and t_2.[5] We stipulate further that each wall is impenetrable by y-constituted objects. In addition, each wall is rigid with respect to y objects: that is, upon contact with a y object, each wall will remain immobile with respect to the ground.[6] Let us also stipulate that there is nothing else in the vicinity—stampeding elephants, sphere interceptors, and so on—and nothing else by way of causal powers belonging to individual walls—extra repulsive forces and so on—that is importantly relevant to the behaviour of the sphere or the walls.

Some may complain that the world is too distant to be worth being interested in. Actual walls do have extra repulsive forces, don't get to be rigid and impenetrable at any thickness and so on. Such a reaction is far too hasty. Distant worlds can often be either revealing or therapeutic with regard to our actual conceptual scheme. So let us press on. What happens?

The mixture of circumstances and causal powers—and in particular the impenetrability and rigidity of the walls—make true the following set of material conditionals:

> C1: If the sphere hits wall 1, it does not proceed beyond the boundary of wall 1.
>
> C2: If the sphere hits wall 2, it does not proceed beyond the boundary of wall 2.
>
> . . . and so on.

---

[4] It does not matter whether the walls have open or closed surfaces. See later discussion for an explanation of the open/closed distinction.

[5] Of course, in a world where things are sometimes brought to a halt by contact with a body that does not in turn move at all upon contact, velocity will not be continuous.

[6] To be precise, we should add 'Also, for each wall: upon contact of a thing of which the wall is a part with a y object, the wall will remain immobile with respect to the ground.' See n. 8.

Further, we have been told that in order to reach wall 1 the ball has to proceed beyond wall 2 and so on. Such facts make true the following set of material conditionals:

D1: If the sphere hits wall 1, it makes contact with wall 2 and proceeds beyond the boundary of wall 2.

D2: If the sphere hits wall 2, it makes contact with wall 3 and proceeds beyond the boundary of wall 3.

. . . and so on.

From these sets of material conditionals, we can deduce that

E1: The sphere does not hit wall 1.

E2: The sphere does not hit wall 2.

. . . and so on.

For, assume that it hits wall 1. We can then deduce a contradiction from C2 and D1. And so on.

Each wall has a natural number assigned to it and to no other wall. So it is true to say in the scenario that

P1: If the sphere hits a wall, then for some natural number N, the ball hits wall N.

If we claim further that

P2: The sphere hits a wall.

we will arrive at an inconsistency, since P2, P1 and E1, E2 . . . are inconsistent. Sure enough, this is only an omega inconsistency, since P2, P1 and E1, E2 and so on do not comprise a finite list and no finite subset of that list is inconsistent. But omega inconsistency is bad enough, since an omega inconsistent set of statements can't all be true at the same time. (Moreover, quantified versions of the premises would condense the inconsistency into a finite set.) Since P1, E1, E2 and so on are in effect built into the description of the world, we should reject P2. We should thus conclude that in worlds that satisfy the original description, the sphere does not make contact with a wall.

It also follows from the description of the world that

P3: If the ball proceeds beyond one mile, it makes contact with a wall.

(Note in this connection the importance of the continuity of motion requirement as well as the 'no stampeding elephants' clause.)

So, by *modus tollens* we can conclude that the ball does not proceed beyond one mile.

(What if we stipulate in addition that the laws of nature in the world are such that the ball will proceed unless it makes contact with a wall? We will then have an inconsistent description which at once entails that the ball will not hit a wall and which also entails that the ball will hit a wall. There is no possible world satisfying that description and so the question as to what happens in such a world is illegitimate.)

We can thus deduce what happens: the ball does not proceed beyond a mile and it does not hit a wall. Does it stop dead at the mile mark or rebound? The description of the case offers no determinate answer to the question. For each world that satisfies the description, one of the two following scenarios will obtain:

> A: There are laws of nature which determine what the sphere will do upon reaching the mile mark, in which case the sphere obeys those laws.

> B: There are no laws of nature which determine what the sphere will do upon reaching the mile mark, in which case the behaviour of the sphere upon hitting the wall is causally undetermined.

The logic of the wall case is pretty straightforward. What can be learned from it? There is a real danger of thinking one has learned too much. For it is tempting to suppose that one has learned from this case that one can conjure up action at a distance out of very mundane objects that do not, when finitely combined, ever act at a distance. It seems that we have taken a bunch of walls that act by contact and conjured up a scenario where a sphere is brought to a stop without contacting anything.

In discussing a similar case (one where a man undertakes to crash into a series of boards ordered rather as the walls are ordered), Benardete seems to offer just this diagnosis: 'The infinite series of boards logically entails what we may describe as a field of force which shuts us out from further advance.'[7] However, if we think carefully about contact, we shall see that no such conclusion can be reached.

Suppose space to be continuous. Suppose each thing to enjoy determinate location so that it determinately occupies a particular region which is in turn constituted by a particular set of points. There are two kinds of surfaces a thing can enjoy: a thing may have an open surface, enjoyed insofar as that surface occupies an open region (which is such that there is no outmost layer of points). Alternatively, a thing may have a closed surface, enjoyed insofar as that surface occupies a closed region (which is such that there is an outmost layer of points).[8] What is contact? There are three cases to consider. I offer what I take to be the most intuitive gloss on 'contact' in each case:

A closed surface contacts an open surface insofar as there is no unoccupied space in between the two surfaces. Call this *open-closed contact*.

An open surface contacts an open surface insofar as there is no more than a line's breadth of unoccupied space between them (the line can then be called the boundary of the two surfaces). Call this *open-open contact*.

A closed surface contacts a closed surface insofar as the outer skin of each overlaps. Call this *closed-closed contact*.

Consider the fusion of walls.[9] Call it Gordon. On reflection it is clear that the sphere contacts Gordon. Gordon has an open surface. When the ball stops proceeding at the one mile mark, there is no unoccupied space between the sphere and

---

[7] *Op. cit.*, p. 258.

[8] Of course an object may have an open surface on one side and a closed surface on another.

[9] I have discovered that Peter van Inwagen reached a similar conclusion to what follows in some informal correspondence with Allen Hazen.

Gordon.[10] Contact occurs (which may be open-open or open-closed depending on the nature of the sphere's surface). So the ball is stopped by contact: the ball hits something, though the thing that it hits is not one of the walls.[11]

(The case we have been describing thus provides no metaphysically exciting locus of action at a distance. If you want a surprising source of action at a distance, then impenetrability—even as between finite things—is the place to look. If closed surfaces are impenetrable to the extent of prohibiting even minimal overlap, then the causal power of impenetrability associated with closed surfaces is a power of acting at a distance. The limiting case of impenetrable point particles illustrates this nicely: by virtue of being impenetrable, point particles will constrain each other's trajectory whenever they are headed towards each other, even though those point particles will never come into contact.)

Insofar as we were originally puzzled by the case of the walls, I believe it is because we are not clear about how to relate fusions to contact. The following principles hold in full generality:

If y is the fusion of xs and the xs are impenetrable, then y is impenetrable.

If y is the fusion of xs and the xs are immovable, then y is immovable.

Consider though what we may call 'The Contact Principle':

If y is the fusion of xs and z contacts y, then z contacts one of the xs.

That principle holds for the finite case. But it is false if the xs are infinite in number. Once we are clear about this, there is no residual puzzle, nor anything further to learn about the wall case. It is clear what happens in worlds that satisfy the original description: at a mile, the ball makes contact with the fusion of walls, which is rigid and impenetrable. As a result, it does not proceed further. The ball does not, however, make contact with any wall.

SECTION TWO

We are now in a position to defuse some of the before-effect cases. Consider the bullets penetrating the heart. The assumption was 'each shot kills instantly'. What does that mean? Does it mean that each bullet kills upon contact with the heart? That seems very strange. Let us say that the laws of nature are such that if a metal object penetrates 1/4 inch into the heart, then the person dies at that very moment. We need some such stipulation in order for the case to admit of rigorous reasoning. By parity of reasoning with the above, we can now say that in such a case, the fusion of the bullets will, upon penetrating the heart to 1/4 inch, kill the person. At the point at which the fusion penetrates 1/4 inch, no bullet will have so penetrated. So we should say that the fusion of the bullets kills the person without any bullet doing so. Any puzzlement will be removed once we recall the falsity of the contact principle.

---

[10] The relevance of n. 6 should be apparent: without that extra clause, it is strictly speaking consistent to say that Gordon moves when contacted.

[11] Of course it also hits Gordon minus, where Gordon minus is the fusion of all the walls minus wall 1. And so on. Causal overdetermination in abundance!

Similar remarks apply to the gongs. Assume that each gong creates a sound wave—a sort of wall of sound. Then the sequence of peals will generate, it seems, an open-ended series of walls of sound. Assume that contact of a sound wave is sufficient for deafening and we can happily say that the fusion of the walls of sound cause deafening upon contact with the ear. (If one insists that only contact with a sound wave and not with a fusion of sound waves can cause deafening, then the description will pertain to no possible world. That is like building into the wall case the requirement that only a wall can stop the sphere proceeding.)

What remains troubling is the 'yet more radical version' of the paradox, one that cannot, it seems, be unpacked simply by thinking hard about contact. After all, in that case there is not a wall thrown down and so there is no fusion of walls with which to come into contact. To avoid distraction that might be caused by talk about Gods, let me rewrite the problem a bit:

There is an infinite series of assassins, each tagged with a natural number, no pair tagged with the same number, no number that isn't tagged to some assassin. Assassin 1 is disposed to attack Bob with a machete if Bob is still around at 2 pm. If he attacks, he will take half an hour to kill Bob. It is causally impossible for assassin 1 to attack Bob and fail to kill him within half an hour. Assassin 2 is disposed to attack Bob with a machete if Bob is still around at 1:30 and will take quarter of an hour to do it. It is causally impossible for assassin 2 to attack Bob and fail to kill him within quarter of an hour, and so on. Each assassin is unsurvivable as far as Bob is concerned. (Notice that the unsurvivability of a particular assassin attack corresponds to the impenetrability of a particular wall, while the fixed time threshold for an assassin's success corresponds to the rigidity of a wall.) For each time which is such that an assassin is disposed to begin attacking Bob at that time, there are infinitely many assassins which are disposed to attack Bob earlier.

To avoid the distractions of thinking of conscious beings, we can do yet more rewriting (those who prefer thinking about assassins to thinking about point particles might prefer to reckon with the above case rather than the one that follows). Make the assassins A-type point particles. Make Bob a B-type point particle. The A particles are laid out on a two mile line to the right of Bob. No. 1 particle is two miles away. No. 2 particle is one and a half miles away. No. 3 particle is one and a quarter miles away. And so on. Assassination is the transformation of a B particle into an A particle. This occurs by an A particle interpenetrating a B particle at t and at that time irradiating x radiation—this being what constitutes 'attack'. 'Survival' here and in what follows is 'remaining as a B-particle'. The causal laws and state of the world are such as to make the following three claims true:

> Particle 1 will not move with respect to the point occupied by Bob before 2 pm.
>
> If at 2 pm Bob still exists as a B particle, then by 2:30 p.m. Bob will have been assassinated by particle 1.
>
> If at 2 pm Bob doesn't exist as a B particle, particle 1 will not move with respect to the point occupied by Bob between 2 pm and 2:30 pm.

and also to make the following three claims true;

Particle 2 will not move with respect to the point occupied by Bob before 1:30 pm.

If at 1:30 pm Bob still exists as a B particle, then by 1:45 Bob will have been assassinated by particle 2.

If at 1:30 pm Bob doesn't still exist as a B particle, particle 2 will not move with respect to the point occupied by Bob between 1:30 and 1:45.

and so on.

Let us also assume that the causal laws are such as to make true the following conditional:

If Bob changes into a B-particle he will never change back into an A particle.

(The case as I have described does rely on the possibility of superluminous signals. As the number of N gets higher, assassin N will have to move quicker and quicker. Given that none are closer than a mile, and that the time required for assassination approaches 0 as N gets higher, infinitely many assassins would have to be able to move faster than the speed of light. Assuming with orthodoxy that the laws of nature are contingent, I don't see this as undermining the possibility of the scenario I have described. In any case, we can change things so as to not require superluminous signals by letting shorter distance compensate in the right way for speed of kill—so that the assassins are laid out in the mile immediately to the right of Bob so their fusion occupies an open line whose external boundary point is the point occupied by Bob.)

What happens? Once again, the logic of the case is pretty straightforward. It is part of the case that Bob can't survive any of the relevant attacks. We can thus generate the following material conditionals:

C1*: If Bob is attacked by assassin 1, he does not survive the attack.

C2*: If Bob is attacked by assassin 2, he does not survive the attack.

. . . and so on.

The case also requires that in order to be attacked by assassin 1, Bob has first to survive the attacks of each of assassin 2, 3 and so on. It thus requires the truth of the following material conditionals:

D1*: If Bob is attacked by assassin 1, he is attacked by assassin 2 and survives the attack.

D2*: If Bob is attacked by assassin 2, he is attacked by assassin 3 and survives the attack.

. . . and so on.

We can deduce:

E1*: Bob is not attacked by assassin 1.

E2*: Bob is not attacked by assassin 2.

. . . and so on.

Each natural number is assigned to one assassin. So it is true to say in the scenario that

P*: If Bob is attacked, then for some natural number N, assassin N attacks Bob.

If we claim further that

P2*: Bob is attacked by an assassin.

we will arrived at an inconsistency, since P2*, P* and E1*, E2* . . . are omega inconsistent. We should thus conclude that Bob is not attacked by an assassin.

It is also part of the description of the world that

P3: If Bob survives past 1 pm, he is attacked by an assassin.

So by modus tollens we can conclude that Bob does not survive past 1 pm.

(What if we stipulate in addition that the laws of nature in the world are such that Bob will survive unless he is attacked by an assassin? There is no possible world satisfying that description and so the question as to what happens in such a world is illegitimate.)

Is there anything we have learned from this case? I suggested that the puzzlement associated with the case described in section one can be traced to a faulty principle that is all too readily relied on in our thinking, namely, that if z touches the fusion of the xs it touches one of the xs. By parity of reasoning with the wall case, we can say that the fusion of the assassins cause the assassination of Bob, even though no individual assassin causes the assassination of Bob. But the question remains: 'HOW does the fusion cause Bob to be assassinated?' The puzzlement resides in the fact that we think of the assassins as individually having to do something—whether it be swinging a machete or irradiating x radiation or . . . in order to produce a certain effect c. Yet the assassin fusion seems to accomplish effect c without doing anything at all. (*That* puzzle didn't arise in the wall case because the walls weren't required individually to be able to do anything in order to individually produce the relevant effect, namely stopping the motion of the sphere.) Its not as if there is a super-machete (or its radiatory correlate) that is used to assassinate. If x is the fusion of ys and the ys don't move with respect to z, x doesn't move with respect to z. So it follows that the fusion causally secures the assassination of Bob without even moving! Nor does the fusion need to undergo any other type of change at all in order to assassinate Bob. Our puzzlement thus relies, I suggest, on our tacit endorsement of the following principle relating fusions to their parts, which we can call the 'Change Principle':

If x is the fusion of ys and ys are individually capable only of producing effect e by undergoing change, then x cannot, (without the addition of some non-supervening causal power), produce effect c without undergoing change.[12]

This principle is mistaken, which I suggest is a big metaphysical surprise. By suitably combining things that need to change in order to produce a result, we can generate a fusion that can produce that result without undergoing change. Things that operate

---

[12] By a 'non-supervening causal power', I mean a causal power that doesn't supervene on facts about the causal powers of the x's together with facts about the number and distribution of x's. Clearly we can allow that big things could act changelessly even though little things didn't thanks to some extra law that said that big things generate, say, a magnetic field.

in relatively mundane ways can be combined to generate things that act in almost magical ways. If there were special laws of magic in operation for big things in force at a world, this would not be surprising. What is surprising is that getting together enough of the mundane things and suitably arranging them is all by itself logically sufficient to entail changeless causation. Just as the contact principle broke down in certain cases where *y* is a fusion of infinitely many *x*s, I suspect that the above principle breaks down in some such cases.[13]

The Contact Principle, in full generality, could be given up fairly readily on reflection. The Change Principle has a rather deeper hold on us. It seems to us scarcely thinkable that mundane causal powers—say that of killing with a machete—could combine so as to logically entail the causal power of producing some effect without the agent of the effect undergoing change. Nevertheless, surprising as this may be, the Change Principle should be rejected. The diagnosis is complete. The logic of each case is very much in order. And our puzzlement has been traced in each case to some faulty principle relating fusions to parts. Once we discard those principles, we will have no problem in accepting the required conclusions about what happens in each case. What we have exposed along the way are some natural mistakes about the related topics of contact and causality that beset our thinking.

APPENDIX

The reader may sense some family resemblance between the cases I have described and the famous lamp introduced by J. F. Thompson.[14]

There are certain reading-lamps that have a button in the base. If the lamp is off and you press the button the lamp goes on, and if the lamp is on and you press the button the lamp goes off. So if the lamp was originally off, and you pressed the button an odd number of times, the lamp is on, and if you pressed the button an even number of times the lamp is off. Suppose now that the lamp is off, and I succeed in pressing the button an infinite number of times, perhaps making one jab in one minute, another jab in the next half-minute, and so on. . . . After I have completed the whole infinite sequence of jabs, i.e. at the end of the two minutes, is the lamp on or off? It seems impossible to answer this question. It cannot be on, because I did not even turn it on without at once turning it off. It cannot be off, because I did in the first place turn it on, and thereafter I never turned it off without at once turning it on. But the lamp must be either on or off. This is a contradiction.[15]

The case of Thompson's Lamp has a straightforward solution, noticed by Paul Benacerraf:

. . . Thompson's instructions do not cover the state of the lamp at t1, although they *do* tell us what will be its state at every instant *between* t0 and t1 (including t0). Certainly, the lamp must

---

[13] A hybrid between the wall and the assassin cases also serves as a counterexample to the change principle. Make it a law that walls with a closed surface will turn red upon contact with a *y* object. Make it a law that a blue wall with a closed surface will stay blue if not contacted by a blue object. Assume each wall is blue and has a closed surface. Each wall's individually stopping a *y* object will thus involve its changing to red. The fusion has an open surface and, thanks to its blue parts is blue. It will not change colour when it stops a *y* object.

[14] 'Tasks and Super-Tasks,' *Analysis* 15 (October 1954), 1–13.

[15] Ibid. p. 5.

be on or off (provided that it hasn't gone up in a metaphysical puff of smoke in the interval), but nothing we are told implies which it is to be. The arguments to the effect that it can't be either have no bearing on the case. To suppose that they *do* is to suppose that a description of the physical state of the lamp at t1 (with respect to its being on or off) is a logical consequence of its state (with respect to the same property) at times prior to t1.[16]

The answer in short is that the description underdetermines which state the lamp will be in. If the description captures all that is casually relevant in the world, the lamp will be in one of the states: on, off, though it is causally underdetermined which it will be. If the description does not capture all that is causally relevant, we need the extra information in order to figure out the state of the lamp at t1.

The Thompson's lamp case figures an open ended series of events whose limit is a point later than each event. The assassin's case figured an open ended series of hypothetical events (grounded in actual causal powers) whose limit is a point earlier than each hypothetical event. The hypothetical nature of the events and the orientation of the open ended series separate the two cases. But why does that make any significant difference?

It is important to notice that in the Thompson lamp case, the description does NOT entail anything about the state of the lamp at t1. By contrast, in the assassin case, the description DOES entail something interesting about the state of Bob at 1 pm: in particular, that he will be assassinated. Similarly, the case in section one (which we can think of usefully as an open ended series of hypothetical wall-hittings whose limit is a time earlier than the hittings) DOES entail something interesting about the state of the sphere at 1 pm — namely that it stops proceeding.

(Of course, there may be other kinds of indeterminacy. Suppose the walls have closed surfaces that alternate between positively and negatively charged surfaces. Suppose that it is a law that balls rebound quickly from positively charged surfaces, slowly from negatively charged surfaces. How will it rebound when it hits the fusion? The laws as described underdetermine how the sphere will behave when it hits an open surface where neither positive nor negative layers dominate.)[17]

The puzzlement that arose in sections one and two had everything to do with the fact that the sequence described, and the causal powers ascribed to it, *did* entail something interesting about the state of the target object at the limit point. In the Thompson's lamp case, the observation that there is no state entailed by the description of the case (nor any prohibited) was pretty much therapy enough. By contrast, the therapy in sections one and two required an account of why we were even inclined to reject the limit description that *is* logically required by the description of the case.

---

[16] 'Tasks, Super-Tasks and the Modern Eleatics,' *The Journal of Philosophy*, 59 (24), p. 708.

[17] See also my discussion in section one concerning whether the ball will rebound or stop.

Index

Made in the USA
Lexington, KY
05 December 2012